The Brave New World of European Labor

THE BRAVE NEW WORLD OF EUROPEAN LABOR

European Trade Unions at the Millennium

Andrew Martin & George Ross

with

Lucio Baccaro, Anthony Daley, Lydia Fraile, Chris Howell,
Richard M. Locke, Rianne Mahon, Stephen J. Silvia

Berghahn Books
NEW YORK • OXFORD

First published in 1999 by
Berghahn Books

Library of Congress Cataloging-in-Publication Data

The brave new world of European labor : European trade unions at the millennium / Andrew Martin and George Ross, et. al.
p. cm.
Includes bibliographical references and index.
ISBN 1-57181-167-2 (hc. : alk. paper).
ISBN 1-57181-168-0 (pbk. : alk. paper)
1. Trade-unions—Europe. 2. Collective bargaining—Europe. 3. Trade-unions—Europe—Forecasting. 4. Collective bargaining—Europe—Forecasting. 5. Employment forecasting—Europe. 6. Twenty-first century—Forecasts. I. Martin, Andrew, 1929- . II. Ross, George, 1940- .
HD6657.B73 1999 98-42943
331.88'094—dc21 CIP

British Library Cataloguing in Publication Data
A catalogue record for this book is available from the British Library.

Printed in the United States on acid-free paper.

CONTENTS

LIST OF TABLES

PREFACE

Over the past century trade unions have played central roles in European society. As they move into the Third Millennium European unions are being profoundly challenged, however. The national political economies in which they are embedded are being eroded by simultaneous economic internationalization and a decentralization of employer strategies, rapid European integration, and a neo-liberal reassertion of the primacy of markets. Unionism in Europe is nonetheless no relic from the past. Despite their problems European unions remain by far the largest single "associational" component in their societies and are crucial to the governance of European economies. What they do continues to matter. This is why we have written this book.

Using a common framework developed by a collaborative research team, *The Brave New World of European Labor* surveys and analyzes the strategic responses of six national unions plus unionism at a transnational European level. The team worked at Brandeis University and the Minda de Gunzburg Center for European Studies (CES) at Harvard University. It follows directions set out nearly two decades ago by Harvard CES researchers who examined European unions after the two oil shocks of the 1970s.[1]

The research team was composed of coordinators Andrew Martin of the Minda de Gunzburg Center for European Studies, Harvard University and George Ross, Hillquit Professor, Brandeis University, Senior Associate and Acting Director, Minda de Gunzburg Center. Team members were: Lucio Baccaro, Assistant Professor of Labor and Human Resource Policy, Weatherhead School of Management, Case Western Reserve University; Anthony Daley, Acting Assistant Professor, Connecticut College; Lydia Fraile, Ph.D. candidate in Political Science, Massachusetts Institute of Technology; Richard Locke, Associate Professor, Sloan School of Management and Department of Political Science, MIT; Rianne Mahon, Professor of Public Administration and Associate Dean, Graduate Studies, Carleton University (Canada); and Stephen J. Silvia, Associate Professor, the School of International Studies, American University.

Comparative research demands lots of scholarly, financial and administrative help. Our group received an initial grant for collaborative research from the National Endowment for the Humanities. Matching funding came from the Program for the Study of Germany and Europe at Harvard CES, the Canadian Social Science and Humanities Research Council, the Hans Böckler Stiftung, Oberlin College and Brandeis University. Roberta Nary at Brandeis was indispensable in guiding us through the incomprehensible accounting universe which came to exist. At CES Abby Collins, Guido Goldman and Charles Maier facilitated our job.

The research team met periodically to focus the project and review results. The book's virtues and faults are the products of this collaboration. All translations, except where noted, are those of the chapter authors. Tony Daley thanks Bob Hancké, and Jacques Rojot. Lydia Fraile thanks José Botella and Robert Fishman for insightful comments, plus Isidor Boix, Raimundo Fisac, Manuel Garnacho, Agustín Moreno, María Jesus Paredes, José María Zufiaur and many other Spanish union leaders for their help. Chris Howell wishes to thank Rachel Bailey, David Cameron, John Kelly, David Metcalf, Jeremy Waddington, Lord Wedderburn, and acknowledges the help of the many trade unionists who gave their time and opened their archives, in particular Garfield Davies, John Edmonds, Sir Gavin Laird, David Lea, Lief Mills, Jon Robinson, David Souter, Rosemary Stone, and Owen Tudor. Richard Locke and Lucio Baccaro thank Aris Accornero, Mario Agostinelli, Arnaldo Camuffo, Mimmo Carrieri, Horst Kern, Marino Regini, Ida Regalia, Bruno Trentin, Tiziano Treu, and Jonathan Zeitlin. Rianne Mahon has benefitted from the assistance of Ann Britt Hellmark, Jennifer King, Rob Ryan, the Swedish Institute for Working Life Research in Stockholm (and Bengt Åkermalm, its librarian). Mahon also thanks Kristina Ahlen, Greg Albo, Wallace Clement, Lars Ekdahl, Alan Hunt, Anders Kjellberg, Rob Ryan, Donald Swartz and Rosemary Warskett for comments. Steve Silvia thanks Jane Cremer, Reiner Hoffmann, Karl Fedengut of the DGB, Michael Fichter of the Freie Universität Berlin, Hartmut Küchle, Andrei Markovits, Jennifer Paxton, Matthias von Randow, Wolfgang Shröder of IG Metall and Mikolas Simon, David Soskice, Wolfgang Streeck and the Hans Böckler Foundation. Andrew Martin and George Ross have huge debts to friends at the European Trade Union Confederation (ETUC) and the European Commission in Brussels, including Franco Bisegna, Jeff Bridgford, Peter Coldrick, Jan Cremers, David Foden, Emilio Gabaglio,

Reiner Hoffmann, Jean Lapeyre, Marc Sapir, Peter Seideneck, Bernadette Tesch-Segol, and Patrick Venturini. Thanks also to their good comrades Mateo Alaluf, Jon-Erik Dølvik, Jane Jenson and Philippe Pochet.

Notes

1. See Peter Lange, George Ross, and Maurizio Vannicelli, *Unions, Change and Crisis: French and Italian Union Strategy and the Political Economy, 1945-1980* (London: George Allen and Unwin, 1982). Peter Gourevitch, Andrew Martin, George Ross et *al. Unions and Economic Crisis: Britain, West Germany and Sweden* (London: George Allen and Unwin, 1984). Martin and Ross are the coordinators of the present study.

LIST OF ABBREVIATIONS

ABM	Employment creation measures (*Arbeitsbeschaffungsmassnahmen*)
ABS Gesellschaft	Employment promotion, and structural development corps (*Arbeitsförderung, Beschäftigung und Strukturentwicklung Gesellschaft*)
ACAS	Advisory, Conciliation and Arbitration Service
ACSH	Advisory Committee on Health and Safety at Work
AEEU	Amalgamated Engineering and Electrical Union
AEU	Amalgamated Engineering Union
APEX	Association of Professional, Executive, Clerical and Computer Staff
ASTMS	Association of Scientific, Technical and Managerial Staffs
ASU	Working Group of Independent Entrepreneurs (*Arbeitsgemeinschaft Selbständiger Unternehmer*)
AVE	Declaration of universal applicability (*allgemeine Verbindlichkeitserklärung*)
BDA	Federal Organization of German Employers' Associations (*Bundesvereinigung der Deutschen Arbeitgeberverbände*)
BIFU	Banking, Insurance and Finance Union
CBI	Confederation of British Industry
CCOO	Workers' Commissions
CDA	Christian Democratic Employees' Group (*Christlich Demokratische Arbeitnehmerschaft*)
CDU	Christian Democratic Union (*Christlich Demokratische Union*)
CEEP	European Confederation of Public Enterprises
CEN	Comité Européen de Normalisation

CENELEC	Comité Européen de Normalisation Electrotechnique
CEOE	Spanish Confederation of Employers' Associations
CEPYME	Spanish Confederation of Small-and Medium-Sized Firms
CF	Sveriges Civilingenjörsförbund Sweden's Association of Civil Engineers
CFDT	*Confédération Française Démocratique du Travail* (French Democratic Confederation of Labor)
CFTC	*Confédération Française des Travailleurs Chrétiens* (French Confederation of Catholic Workers)
CGC	*Confédération Générale des Cadres* (General Confederation of Technical and Supervisory Employees)
CGM	Christian Metal Employees' Union (*Christliche Gewerkschaft Metall*)
CGT	*Confédération Générale du Travail* (General Confederation of Labor)
CIG	Galician Interunion Confederation Clerical, Professional and Technical Employees.
CNPF	*Confédération Nationale du Patronat Français* (National Council of French Employers)
CNT	National Labor Confederation
COHSE	Confederation of Health Service Employees
CSU	Christian Social Union (*Christlich Soziale Union*)
CWU	Communication Workers Union
DAG	German White-Collar Employees' Union (*Deutsche-Angestellten Gewerkschaft*)
DGB	German Trade Union Federation (*Deutscher Gewerkschaftsbund*)
DPG	German Postal Employees' Union
ECB	European Central Bank
ECOFIN	Council of Economics and Finance Ministers
EETPU	Electrical, Electronic, Telecommunications and Plumbing Union
EFBWW	European Federation of Building and Woodworkers
EIF	European Industry Federation
ELA	Basque Workers' Solidarity
EMF	European Metalworkers Federation
EMU	Economic and Monetary Union
ERDF	European Regional Development Fund
ESCB	European System of Central Banks
ETUC	European Trade Union Confederation
ETUCO	European Trade Union College
ETUI	European Trade Union Institute
EU	European Union

EURO-FIET	European Regional Organization of the International Federation of Commercial Employees
EWC	European Works Council
FDI	Foreign Direct Investment
FDP	Free Democratic Party (*Freie Demokratische Partei*)
FEN	*Fédération de l'Education Nationale* (National Federation of Teachers)
FIEC	European Federation of the Construction Industry (*Fédération Industrielle Européenne de la Construction*)
FNV	Federatie Nederlandse Vakbeweging
FO	*Force Ouvrière* (Workers' Force), Full title: *Confédération Générale du Travail – Force Ouvrière*
FSU	*Fédération Syndicale Unitaire* (Unified Workers' Federation)
GdED	German Railroad Employees' Union (*Gewerkschaft der Eisenbahner Deutschlands*)
GdP	Police Officers' Union (*Gewerkschaft der Polizei*)
GDR	German Democratic Republic
Gesamtmetall	*Gesamtverband der metallindustriellen Arbeitgeberverbände* (General Association of Metal-Industry Employers' Associations)
GEW	Education and Scientific Employees' Union (*Gewerkschaft Erziehung und Wissenschaft*)
GGLF	Agricultural and Forestry Employees' Union (*Gewerkschaft Gartenbau, Land- und Forstwirtschaft*)
GHK	Wood and Plastic Workers' Union (*Gewerkschaft Holz und Kunststoff*)
GL	Leatherworkers' Union (*Gewerkschaft Leder*)
GMB	This is the registered name of the union rather than an acronym
GMB	General, Municipal and Boilermakers' Union
GPMU	Graphical, Paper and Media Union
GTB	Textile and Apparel Employees' Union (*Gewerkschaft Textil-Bekleidung*)
Handels	Svenska Handelsanställdas förbundet (Union of Swedish Commercial Workers)
HBV	Retail, Banking and Insurance Employees' Union (*Gewerkschaft Handel, Banken, Versicherungen*)
HTF	Handelstjänstemannaförbundet (Union of Commercial Employees)
ICFTU	International Confederation of Free Trade Unions
IG BAU	Construction Agriculture and Environmental Employees' Industrial Union (*Industriegewerkschaft Bauen-Agrar-Umwelt*)

IG BCE	Mining, Chemical and Energy Employees' Industrial Union (*Industriegewerkschaft Bergbau, Chemie, Energie*)
IG BSE	Construction Employees' Industrial Union (*Industriegewerkschaft Bau- Steine-Erden*)
IG Chemie	Chemical Employees' Industrial Union (*Industriegewerkschaft Chemie- Papier-Keramik*)
IG Medien	Media Employees' Industrial Union (*Industriegewerkschaft Medien*)
IG Metall	Metalworking Employees' Industrial Union (*Industriegewerkschaft Metall*)
IGBE	Mining and Energy Employees' Industrial Union(*Industriegewerkschaft Bergbau und Energie*)
INI	National Industry Institute
ITS	International Trade Secretariat
KFS	koncernfackligt samarbete (cooperation among union locals organising workers employed by the same firm)
Kommunal	Svenska Komunalabetareförbundet (Swedish Union of Municipal Workers)
KTK	Kommunaltjänstemannakartellen (bargaining cartel of municipal employees)
LAB	Nationalist Workers' Commissions
LO	Landsorganisation i Sverige (Confederation of Swedish Trade Unions)
LSR	Legitimerade Sjukgymnasters riksförbund (union of physiotherapists)
Metall	Svenska Metallindustriarbetareförbundet (Swedish union of metal workers)
MSF	Manufacturing Science Finance
NALGO	National and Local Government Officers' Association
NCU	National Communications Union
NGA	National Graphical Association
NGG	Food, Restaurant, Hotel Employees' Union (*Gewerkschaft Nahrung- Genuss-Gaststätten*)
NUM	National Union of Mineworkers
NUPE	National Union of Public Employees
NUR	National Union of Railwaymen
NUS	National Union of Seamen
OECD	Organization for Economic Cooperation and Development
ÖTV	Public Service, Transportation and Transit Employees' Union (*Gewerkschaft Öffentliche Dienste, Transport und Verkehr*)
PCE	Communist Party of Spain
PCF	*Parti Communiste Français* (French Communist Party)
PDS	Party of Democratic Socialism

PP	People's Party
PS	*Parti Socialiste* (Socialist Party)
PSOE	Spanish Socialist Workers' Party
PTK	Privattjänstemannakartellen (Federation of Salaried Employees in Industry and Services bargaining cartel)
QMV	Qualified Majority Vote
RCN	Royal College of Nursing
RMT	National Union of Rail, Maritime and Transport Workers
SACO	Sveriges Akademikers Centralorganisation (Central organisation of Professional Employees
SACO-K	Bargaining cartel for SACO members employed by municipalities
SAF	Sveriges Arbetsgivareföreningen (Swedish Employers Association)
SALF	Svenska Arbetsledareförbundet (Union of Foremen and Supervisors)
SAP	Socialdemokratiska Arbetareparti (Social Democratic Party)
SED	German Socialist Unity Party (*Sozialistische Einheitspartei Deutschlands*)
SEKO	Service and Communication Workers Union
SF	Statsanställdasförbund (union of national government workers)
SFIO	*Section Française* de l'Internationale Ouvrière (French Socialist Party), pre-1969
SHSTF	Svenska hälso- och sjukvårdens tjänstemannaförbund (Swedish Federation of Salaried Employees in Hospitals and Public Health Services)
SIF	Svenksa Industritjänstemannaförbundet (Swedish Union of Clerical and Service Workers
SIPTU	Services, Industrial, Professional, and Technical Union
SKAF / SKTF	Sveriges Kommunaltjänstemannaförbundet (Swedish Union of Municipal and Salaried Employees
SNCF	Société Nationale des Chemins de Fer (French national railway)
SOGAT	Society of Graphical and Allied Trades
SPD	German Social Democratic Party (*Sozialdemokratische Partei Deutschlands*)
SSE	*section syndicale d'entreprise* (union section at the workplace)
SSR	Sveriges Socionomers riksförbund (Swedish Union of Social Workers)
ST	Statens Tjänstemannaförbundet (Federation of Civil Servants)

TASS	Technical, Administrative and Supervisory Staffs
TCO	Tjänstemännens Centralorganisation (Central Organisation of Salaried Workers)
TCO-S	TCOS Stattjänstemannasektion (Bargaining Section for State Employees) Technical Employees)
TGWU	Transport and General Workers' Union
THA	*Treuhandanstalt* (Trust Holding Agency)
TUC	Trades Union Congress
TUTB	Trade Union Technical Bureau
TVG	Collective Bargaining Act (*Tarifvertragsgesetz*)
UCATT	Union of Construction, Allied Trades and Technicians
UCW	Union of Communication Workers, The
UD	*union départementale* (departmental union)
UGT	General Workers' Union
UL	*union locale* (local union)
UNICE	Union of Industrial and Employers' Confederations of Europe
UNISON	This is the registered name of the union rather than an acronym.
UNSA	*Union Nationale des Syndicats Autonomes* (National Association of Autonomous Unions)
USDAW	Union of Shop, Distributive and Allied Workers
USO	Workers' Labor Union
VI	Verkstadsindustri (formerly VF Sveriges Verkstadföreningen: Swedish Engineering Industry Employers Association
WEM	Western European Metal Trade Employers Organization
WFTU	World Federation of Trade Unions
WS	Worker Statute

Chapter 1

EUROPEAN UNIONS FACE THE MILLENNIUM

George Ross and Andrew Martin

Trade unions helped build modern European democracy. From their beginnings they struggled for collective representation and mass participatory democracy. They insisted on the decency of bargained compromise instead of chronic conflict. They worked to expand citizenship into economic, social, and workplace rights. In the culmination of these quests, during the "Golden Age" following World War Two, unions helped generate a "European model of society" with broad democratic political participation, collective negotiation between large social forces, protection against risks of illness, accident, aging, and the capriciousness of markets, and a commitment to provide employment for all.[1]

In recent years this model and the unions that contributed to it have confronted menacing new conditions. Monetary instability, oil shocks, and "stagflation" undercut the Golden Age pattern of growth. Then, in the 1980s, full employment was sacrificed in the interests of price stability, financial globalization, employer pressures for "flexibility," and elite neo-liberalism. A new era of low growth, high unemployment, accelerated European integration, and general economic internationalization has followed.[2]

In this book, we examine how these changes have affected European unions and how they have responded. We have deeper questions as

Notes for this section begin on page 22.

well. If the European model depended on strong unions, do weaker unions augur a different future? To answer, we will analyze union responses to change in six countries and at the European Union (EU) level.[3] While unions have faced common challenges to their broadly common roles, there is considerable national variation. We capture this by concentrating on the EU's five largest countries, Britain, France, Germany, Italy, and Spain. To them we add Sweden, so long seen as the most successful variant of the European model of society, and EU level transnational unionism.

Unions as Social Movement Organizations

To paraphrase an earlier authority, unions "make their own history, but they do not make it just as they please … but under circumstances directly encountered, given and transmitted from the past."[4] To understand the challenges faced by European unions we conceptualize them as organized strategic actors speaking for a large and historically important social movement. As such, they must constantly make choices about their identities, their goals, and who their opponents and allies are. European unions are "social movement organizations." The term social movement refers to "rebel" mobilizations of the under-represented seeking to oblige those in power to recognize their causes and redress their grievances. Most social movements generate "relatively stable patterns of relationships within the movement," organizations to further their goals.[5] These organizations, which begin as animators in searches for a new order of life, can continue at the center of multifaceted, long-lasting mobilizations. Moreover, when social movements succeed, their organizations may become institutionalized as legitimate actors.

For decades labor was *the* major social movement in industrialized societies and until quite recently the ideal-typical model for all social movements.[6] Unions are the organizations of the labor movement. Union history dates from the early stages of industrialization. Union struggles to create organizational forms, win recognition, and defend their supporters continued over more than a century. As they achieved certain of their goals, they acquired respectability, their causes became laws and rules, they took on the trappings of formal, bureaucratic institutions, and in some countries even entered national establishments.[7] Even after European unions reached this point, however, their identities, practices, and power remained profoundly marked by their origins. Built from grassroots mobilization, unions have always had to mobilize supporters using techniques like strikes and demonstrations. They still parade people up and down public avenues, turn out their "bases" in support of friendly political groups, and use strong ideological language.

Unions, first of all, must manage exchanges between supporters and their labor market situations to generate "market/ bargaining" resources.[8] They then must find space to act in broader economic and political "opportunity structures."[9] As they thus acquire market/bargaining resources they acquire a voice, in terms of "identity resources," discourses which justify union goals, place them in broader "idea" contexts, and encourage solidarity. To function effectively they also need "organizational resources." In addition, since labor markets are structured by law and policy unions need "political resources."[10] Finally, all such resources are interdependent, such that significant change in one realm will affect others.

Market/bargaining resources come from concessions unions get from employers through the strategic use of mass support. These concessions – higher wages, job security, decent working conditions, limitations on employer authority etc. – are the heart of what unions promise to supporters. If unions deliver, they earn enthusiasm, willingness to mobilize, financial support, and loyalty. Loyalty is more than a matter of providing "selective incentives," however. The sense of belonging to something larger, of participating to win collective goals "in solidarity" are very real, evident in shorthand phrases like the "working class" and "working people." Unions thus also need "identity resources," shared notions of unionists' "selves" which help define the identities of "others" and are deeply engaged in struggle over the meanings that people give to their lives.

Unions also need organizational resources – legitimated leadership and procedures, disciplined mobilizing habits, and, most important, funding. Funding comes primarily from supporters and its supply must be predictable and institutionalized (often involving obligatory contributions, dues check-offs, for example, that may need legal sanction). Unions usually have additional sources of funding, particularly from politics. They need staff to create continuity and ordered communication, perform routine tasks, do research, lobbying, and other functions. They also must institutionalize ways to consult with their base and methods for making decisions. Finally, they depend upon rank-and-file mobilization. The ability to "call out the troops," or to threaten it credibly, is vital.

Unions depend on help from states and need political resources to get it. Parties and governments need to know that unions can support or sanction them in serious ways. Unions have many tools for this, like campaign financing, expertise, support by prominent leaders, etc. But the most significant union political resources in democracies are the votes of unionists. Generating political resources is not automatic: it is easy for union supporters to dissociate market from political concerns. Strong unionist identity may help to make the association. Conversely, the need for political help may lead parties and politicians to incorporate dimensions of unionist identity into their programs. Policies that favor union goals, once converted to rules and regulations, may then become the legal contexts which frame union activities. Such legal contexts will themselves be resources, especially if unions can invoke the law to obtain "payoffs" for their members.

The world of unions is not easily reducible to parsimonious analytical models.[11] At any given moment a union faces multidimensional problems with a toolbox of varied, somewhat fungible, resources. It must make many choices simultaneously with each one presenting roughly equivalent options. In addition, unions are complex organizations composed of complex organizations, locations of chronic internal conflicts where multiple stakeholders – groups and individuals – connected to a sometimes mercurial and fractious broader social movement compete for power.[12] Finally, they are "path dependent," constrained organizationally by their pasts.[13] They tend to move in directions which will not threaten shared ideas, values, and habits and their organizational learning will be skewed towards what is already known.[14] Union organizations thus navigate with an undisciplined, sometimes mutinous, crew, an unwieldy chain of command and inherited, often inaccurate, maps about the unpredictable waters around them. Unions are thus likely to be "conservative," often discounting longer term threats in favor of short run "satisficing," in part to avoid costly and organizationally difficult changes. They may even take head-in-the sand positions undervaluing fundamental challenges. In short, unions' choices may be "rational" in the sense that they are explainable – indeed, this is why we write. But they are unlikely to approximate the ideal type of a unitary, self-interested, actor maximizing utility.

On a subject as important as the fate of European unions there is bound to be much scholarly debate.[15] Perhaps the most important contributions come from an "industrial relations" school, predominantly Anglo-American, which views the "industrial relations system" as a changing matrix of negotiated interactions between employers and unions at the firm and industry level.[16] Unions as intermediaries between employers and workers, help develop and administer rules to keep the peace, regulate disputes, and generate predictability.[17] The perspective assumes that there are a limited number of activities that always need to be carried on to coordinate work in modern industrial societies, and they take on roughly similar forms in societies at similar stages of development.

"Industrial relations" research provides rich data. From our point of view, however, the approach oversimplifies by looking at actors in bounded workplace environments in a system standing more or less on its own. What is lost is the presence and valence of actors and processes central in shaping and perpetuating the system itself.

Multiple schools of "political economy" all conceptualize unions as intermediaries between employers and workers in structuring methods of production which, in their turn, have their place in larger models of capitalist economies, but there diversity begins. Some "historical institutionalists" understand unions as elements of macro level "production regimes" or as parts of micro level "workplace regimes."[18] Others perceive them as organizations whose preferences are determined by their sectoral situations.[19] Marxists see unions as organized intermediaries between the "working class" and capitalists whose performance is measured by the degree to which they promote "class interests."[20] To the neo-Marxist "regulation school" capitalism involves relationships among class actors, including labor, the state, social and industrial institutions which together "regulate" patterns of economic development.[21] Capitalist history then becomes a succession of "modes of regulation" of relatively stable patterns, punctuated by crises in which old patterns dissolve and new ones eventually emerge. Methodological individualists, finally, see unions as "special interests" engaged in a quest to shield parts of the workforce from the market.[22] Given the overwhelming likelihood of free riding, unions need to provide "selective incentives" for their members which are appropriated out of society's larger pool of available welfare.[23]

We have problems with the quest of most political economy for ideal-typical understandings of the "capitalist economy." This is primarily because we intend to work at a lower level of abstraction to study the choices of a limited number of actors at a specific time. Marxists are thus troublesome because they tend to be reductionist, looking not at what unions do but at how closely they approximate the pursuit of "class interests" assumed a priori. The "regulationist approach," while more appealing because it is more actor-centric, suffers from a fundamental epistemological flaw. In any present there are multiple forces at work and we cannot know the systemic role each one may be playing at the time. The outlines of a "mode of regulation" exist clearly only when it begins to dissolve in crisis. In short, regulationism can only look backwards. Methodological individualists, finally, are correct to argue that collective action is more difficult to explain than most sociological traditions have realized. But assuming that groups like unions exist through siphoning off goods from the general pool of social welfare (i.e. "rent seeking") is problematic. The range of non-economic as well as economic benefits that unions provide can be broad. They may help keep peace, endow supporters with "social capital," legitimate economic and political authority and enhance productivity and efficiency.[24]

There are two assessments of the current predicament of European unions. The first is that unions have exhibited staying power and a continued capacity to influence outcomes.[25] Our view, the second, is that trade unions are experiencing a deep and prolonged crisis which is transforming their positions. To a certain extent this disagreement is an artifact of chronology. Earlier data made it easier to advance arguments anticipating union recovery because the deeper logics of economic change were still clouded. How one selects cases is important as well, since some union movements, as we will see, have survived better than others. But the terms of the debate go deeper, resting in large part upon how one measures union strength and whether measures used in the past are appropriate to what is emerging. The "optimist" argument rests upon a broad set of measures of union strength – union membership, union centralization, levels of collective bargaining and wage setting. Organizational resiliency is not always an adequate measure of union strength, however. Organizations may carry on as relatively empty structures, persisting in accustomed places while profoundly weakened.

From Golden Age to Millennium: The New Challenges

New challenges to unions stand out against the political economy of the postwar "Golden Age." During this period European unions advocated reformist discourses informed by class-analytical understandings in which workers, as the largest, most progressive group in society, had common interests in humanizing their world. The fundamental problem was that European capitalism had theretofore insisted upon minimalist definitions of citizenship, confined narrowly to the political realm. Unions saw themselves as the labor movement's agents for extending workers' rights and citizenship in general into economic areas. What characterized the period was their unusual success at doing this.

This success was inextricably linked to postwar economies. In the decades after 1945 national political economies thrived in a virtuous circle of growth and change, at whose core were large corporations engaged in "Fordist" mass production of goods, primarily for sale to a national market. This was the heyday of assembly line work, when little training beyond basic literacy skills and physical endurance was demanded of workers. It was also the heyday of the "affluent worker," at least in Northern Europe.[26] Successful firms were often willing to pay higher wages and grant greater job security to obtain cooperation in work and deepen the market for expensive consumer goods to those who actually produced them.

The Golden Age model tied production and macroeconomic policy into a national system. Widespread elite acceptance of Keynesianism, facilitated by the optimism created by high growth, led the state to acquire new roles.[27] Full employment, a union dream, briefly became a reasonable goal. The state redistributed part of the system's profitability in new or expanded social programs. In this "full employment Keynesian welfare state" – in many places more goal than achievement – strengthened unions became central to the regime itself.[28] Strong unions could prevent downward pressure on wages and prices, help keep wage levels in line with productivity growth, and prod the demand needed for full employment.

Unions knew that bargained limitations on employers' power and legal regulation could make wage work, particularly the dismal Fordist kind, less insecure, better paid and less subject to arbitrary employer authority. Success began with organizing wage earners, but also involved soliciting solidarity from others. This need for broader solidarity, perhaps more than anything else, underlay the universalism of union discourses and ideas. Unions advocated redistributing income, wealth and authority, aims that brought them into the political arena. Rules to define and actualize labor citizenship in the workplace were in part the result of legislation. Governments developed macroeconomic policies favorable to full employment and growth. Unions advocated including workers as partners in major public decisions and demanded that they themselves be recognized as the organized manifestations of larger labor movements.

The resulting positions endowed most unions with increases in resources. Full employment made large corporations concede higher wages and greater job security, while governments promoted favorable new legal positions. This, in turn, increased unions' rank-and-file support. Organizational resources, particularly dues and governmental subsidies, increased, strengthening union structures. Political resources grew with the importance of class politics.

The national focus of postwar growth meant that there was tremendous diversity in union positions across Europe. In Sweden, a full employment policy regime, Fordism, consumerism, "neo-corporatist" cooperation plus a large welfare state converged in growth and international competitiveness – the much vaunted Swedish "third way."[29] West Germany pursued a low wage reconstruction strategy until the end of the

1950s and then shifted to mild Keynesianism promoting full employment plus an industrial policy (private arrangements between banks and large companies) around a strong monetarist central bank. One secret of German success was cooperation between powerful employers associations and sectoral unions. "Modell Deutschland" was the product. In Great Britain many of the elements for a "Swedish deal" seemed present in the 1940s, but inept policies, bad judgments about European integration, employer conservatism, and overenthusiastic commitment to sterling nourished serious problems. "Latin" Europe had its own particularities. *Dirigiste* France achieved full employment and radical economic change by substituting technocratic statism for negotiations among "social partners" and, to an extent, private entrepreneurialism.[30] In Italy, where Cold War politics initially promoted "labor exclusion," new prospects had opened for unions by the later 1960s.[31] Spain, an outlier because of Francoist authoritarianism with little tolerance for trade unionism, grew behind protectionism.[32]

The Maelstrom: The 1980s and After

The first lesson drawn by European unions from the postwar period was that the national level was the key to success, given the relative isolation of national political economies. The second was that the ideal-typical model for such success was what scholars later labeled "neo-corporatism."[33] Unions should become "big citizens," alongside large corporations and the state, shape the priorities of their societies, promote redistribution (to the less fortunate, to be sure, but mainly to their own supporters), constrain employers' choices and influence political decisions. In exchange they could offer dedicated consumers, controllable labor forces, wage growth tied to productivity gains, price stability and, in general, a more predictable socioeconomic world.

The disintegration of Golden Age growth models that began in the late 1970s threatened unions by a "double shift." Simultaneously, decisions most important to unions moved away from national arenas "upward" toward transnational arenas and "downward" toward subnational ones, transferring matters from arenas where unions could be effective toward those where they were weaker. Decisions on macroeconomic conditions were increasingly made, not in national policy arenas where neo-corporatist deals could be struck, but in intergovernmental negotiations and global markets beyond most union control. Decisions about wages and working conditions were increasingly made not in multi-employer collective agreements but at a company level where unions' influence could be diluted. Other trends accompanying the "double shift" included demographic and structural changes in the labor force (such as feminization and tertiarization). Growth in part-time, temporary, and "atypical" jobs increased the proportion of the labor force that unions had not organized well. The abandonment of full employment as an economic policy goal may have been most damaging, however. By the end of the 1980s, a shift to policy that put top priority on price stability had been completed. European governments then tied themselves to it in the Maastricht Treaty's provisions for European Monetary Union (EMU). The resulting unemployment at Great Depression levels was a catastrophe for unions.

Internationalization

Intensified internationalization – freer and greater international trade, transnational investment and financial globalization – was bound to increase the vulnerability of unions, if only because it ended the relative isolation of postwar national political economies. Transnationalization lowers the exit costs of capital and reduces corporate loyalty to the nation state. Spillovers from increasing trade, globalized financial markets, and corporate "regime shopping" reduce the effectiveness of national policies. Other national regulatory capacities decline while the costs of national policies running counter to international market logics rise.

Evidence about internationalization is clear. Trade grew faster than output between 1960 and 1989, with exports of the twenty-four OECD countries increasing at an average annual rate close to twice that of GDP (6.3 compared with 3.7 percent). The share of imports and exports in those countries' GDP correspondingly increased over the same period (from 37.6 to 56.3 percent).[34] Foreign direct investment (FDI) grew faster than trade: world FDI outflows grew 3 times faster than output and 2.5 times faster than exports and domestic investment between 1986 and 1990.[35] The annual rate of FDI more than quadrupled from the late 1970s to 1992, and the world's stock nearly quadrupled between 1980 and 1991. By 1990, total sales (domestic and export) of transnational corporations (TNCs) reached $5.5 trillion, 2.5 times the $2.2 trillion total value of exports of goods and services (excluding trade within TNCs), making TNCs central players in the world economy.[36] Financial integration increased even more rapidly than trade, FDI and TNC sales. Portfolio outflows rose fourteen times from 1980 to 1991, from $15.0 billion to $205.3 billion.[37] Rapid as this seemed, it was dwarfed by the growth of transactions in foreign exchange markets, from a negligible daily trading volume in the late 1950s to about a $1 trillion in the early 1990s – fifty times the daily value of international trade.[38]

There is good reason to be skeptical of hyperbolic claims about "globalization" as the "independent variable" of our time.[39] For one thing, the transnational flows described are unevenly distributed around the globe, concentrated heavily in the OECD countries, and within them, regionally.[40] Although the trade : GDP ratio is higher in European countries than in North America, most of the trade is within the EU – 92 percent of consumption is based on EU production. The share of extra-EU trade has remained rather stable, while intra-EU trade has doubled over the last few decades.[41] More important, much transnationalization is the result of political decisions of OECD governments to eliminate trade barriers and liberalize finances. This is especially the case in the EU. Whatever was happening globally, the renewal of European integration after 1985, in the form of completing the Single Market, meant that relatively closed national markets gave way to an open EU market. EU members often invoked "globalization" as a reason for their decisions, but what really counted was their deliberate choice to "marketize" significant economic policy prerogatives and capacities and delegate others to European-level actors like the EU Council of Ministers, the European Commission, and the European Court of Justice.

Decentralization

In countries where neo-corporatist bargaining was established during the Golden Age, unions participated in setting parameters for wages and employment conditions through national-level exchanges with governments and organized employers. Even where such arrangements did not exist, the effectiveness of unions in setting national standards was contingent on their ability to engage in multi-employer collective bargaining by providing both positive and negative incentives (e.g., protection against competitive wage bidding and strikes embracing whole sectors). For some time, however, many European employers (and economists) have argued that such bargaining obstructs flexible adaptation to new technologies and rapidly changing international market opportunities. Bargaining therefore should be limited to the company level and permit diversification of matters like work scheduling, the structure of the workweek and year, skill requirements, pay systems, and employment contracts (to allow more "atypical" jobs).

How much real economic requirements call for decentralization is uncertain. Flagging interest in cooperative national and sectoral relationships with unions and a tendency to see unions as obstacles rather than associates may also represent a return to old-fashioned employer anti-unionism. Moreover, other changes weakening unions can be seen as opening up opportunities to employers to weaken them further. Whatever the reasons for the drive to decentralize, conspicuous instances of the dismantling of neo-corporatist arrangements and multi-employer bargaining have occurred.[42] Where it has happened unions have lost important resources while employers' ability to promote firm loyalty among workers and threaten earlier conquests has grown. In the process, decentralization makes levels of union organization above the firm – national sectoral and confederal – harder to sustain.

There are limits on employers' ability to establish exclusive local control over bargaining. The dismantling of national labor market institutions in Europe is constrained by custom, public opinion, national legislation, and the danger of conflict. Moreover, threats to unions from decentralization and flexibilization vary, greatest for centralized union movements with poor organizational links to the workplace and least for those with a vital decentralized organizational life. But possibilities for adapting bargaining agendas to demands for greater flexibility while preserving a cross-company union role in the regulation of employment relations depend on much else, including the extent to which government policies uphold or destroy such a union role. In short, there is reason to expect national stories to be diverse. These national stories do not exhaust the potential for decentralization, however. Within the larger European Single Market and EMU, even those collective bargaining structures which remain most centralized are likely to become components of a decentralized EU bargaining structure.

Changing Structures of Employment

Challenges posed to unions by the "double shift" are amplified by longer run changes in the labor force. Tertiarization, feminization, and "precarization" are bound to diminish resources on which unions depend, particularly the strength in numbers and identity given them by blue-collar workers of the "old working class." The shift from industry to services is a long-term structural trend. Whether such "deindustrialization" is accelerated by competition from new entrants to the industrialized world or by intensified competition, as in the Single Market, is debatable.[43] That the reduction in manufacturing jobs has been especially great in Europe is evident, however.[44] In our six countries, the decline in the percentage of the labor force in industry between 1975 and 1994 ranged from 6.4 (in Italy) to 12.6 (in the United Kingdom) while the rise in the percentage in services over the same period ranged from 11.9 (in Germany) to 20.3 (in Spain). Service sector jobs have risen to 60-70 percent of total employment.

The "old working class" was largely male. Growing female labor force participation, important in Europe in most of the postwar period, continues. In the EU, the number of men employed declined by 4 percent between 1975 and 1985, largely because of the decline in industrial employment, while the number of women, mainly in the services, grew by 10 percent. The change slowed in the later 1980s and resumed in the 1990s, possibly because employers find it easier to fit women into their strategies of numerical flexibility. Women work fewer hours than men, and even when they work longer hours, they do so for shorter periods over their working life. Women have been filling a larger portion of growing "atypical" employment – part-time, fixed-term and temporary agency jobs – than men.[45] Part-time and temporary jobs are also disproportionately held by young people, while women and young people under twenty-five are found more than men in low-paying work.[46]

There is variation in changing employment patterns within Europe depending upon definitions and rules governing employment in national labor markets. Atypical employment need not be precarious, for example. Job security can be lower in a country with lower levels of nonstandard jobs because law and collective bargaining provides less protection for those with standard jobs. Nonetheless, male industrial workers in full-time permanent jobs, the core of Golden Age union membership, have been declining as a proportion of the labor force. Unions are challenged to recruit newer and growing components of the labor force to offset the change. Some service workers are employed in large commercial and financial firms and may already be unionized. But many are employed in smaller firms, often in "atypical" conditions, however, and this makes the task of expanding service sector union membership difficult.

Conflicts of interest between the declining traditional working class and growing labor force components make it difficult to redefine union identities in terms that could encompass both. Insider-outsider conflict is likely when lines between them coincide with lines between declining and growing segments of the workforce, and where, as in Germany, unions have been especially successful in protecting insiders' positions. Conflicts of a different kind may arise where the dividing lines are between insiders – different groups of unionized workers, as in Sweden. While women's union membership there is as high as men's, showing that unions need not be hurt by very high female labor force participation, there is a growing division between unionized women, who are highly concentrated in public and private services and sheltered from international competition, and unionized males who dominate the exposed manufacturing sector.

The effects of such changes will be mediated by the unions' inherited structures and government policies. The absence of legal guarantees of equal treatment between women and men and between workers in standard and nonstandard employment may tempt employers to use women's employment and atypical jobs as ways of escaping existing labor standards and seeking flexibility on their own terms. If, on the other hand, such guarantees are extended to workers differentiated by gender and forms of employment, it could encourage a flexibility that meets the needs of workers with more diverse life situations. This should in turn open opportunities for unions to appeal to such workers by securing such flexibility through collective bargaining.[47]

The challenges facing unions from these changes may depend most of all on the macroeconomic policies governments pursue. In the full employment of the Golden Age, such challenges might have been manageable, but unemployment now makes them harder to confront. Unemployment in the entire OECD area averaged under 10 million between 1950 and 1972. It tripled over the next decade, spanning the two oil shocks. After slightly declining in the later 1980s, it rose to 8.5 percent of the OECD labor force by 1995.[48] European numbers are even more striking. Europe's unemployment rate was lower than North America's in the earlier postwar decades, persistently higher since the early 1980s, and nearly twice as high in 1995.[49]

Unemployment reflects a profound shift in Europe's macroeconomic policy regime. A quest for price stability has replaced full employment as the primary goal.[50] The rationale behind this is that the source of inflation lay in a change in the ways which labor market institutions – collective bargaining plus social benefits – had come to relate wage growth to productivity growth. In the Golden Age such institutions were credited with keeping wages abreast of productivity, assuring sufficient demand to induce investment and continued growth while leaving enough profit to finance investment. However, the argument goes, this "virtuous circle" broke down when labor market institutions could not adjust real wage growth downward when productivity growth slowed and real national income was abruptly cut by oil price hikes. The results of this "real wage rigidity" were inflation, squeezed profits, lower investment, and even slower productivity growth. Having been part of the solution, in this view, unions had become part of the problem.[51] The ultimate remedy was to make the labor market more "flexible" by changing its institutions. Pending this, however, there was nothing to do but bring inflation down and hold it there with a tight monetary policy. This required tough action by central banks insulated from political pressures, regardless of the unemployment that resulted.[52]

Whatever its causes, unemployment at Great Depression levels seriously threatens union resources. That unemployment undermines union bargaining power is axiomatic. As labor markets slacken and employment insecurity spreads, unions will have greater difficulty producing market/bargaining resources. With workers thrown into competition with each other for scarce jobs, it becomes much harder for unions to reconcile the interests of old working class members to whom unions bring some, if dwindling, job security and those of the new groups to whom they must appeal. The sectoral concentration of unemployment, with manufacturing jobs disappearing twice as fast as in North America, is eating away rapidly at the unions' traditional core. Its age distribution hurts in different ways. Latin Europe (France, Spain, Italy) has suffered a plague of youth unemployment. Since young people entering the labor market constitute a fertile source for recruitment, high youth unemployment aggravates the problem of generational renewal. High rates of long-term unemployment are yet another drain, since the long-term unemployed are disproportionately union supporters. Low growth plus the strictures it places on deficit spending also threaten unions in the public sector by slowing or even reversing the expansion of public sector employment. Resultant fiscal exiguity reinforces pressures to reduce social benefits that cushion the impact of unemployment, further shifting the balance of bargaining power against unions. Together these impacts limit the scope for reducing unemployment by using public spending to stimulate demand.

Political Decline

Political exchange was essential for unions in the Golden Age. They all needed rights to organize, be recognized, and raise money, instruments for protecting memberships in the workplace and enforcing labor standards and rules guaranteeing employer good faith in bargaining. They also needed the ears of economic policy makers. In return, unions could offer electoral support. The breakdown of this exchange is now manifest. "Class voting" has diminished. Governments are markedly less friendly. In some cases there have also been threatening modifications in unions' legal rights. The growing deafness of political and administrative classes to union claims is most evident in the realm of economic policy. Whatever the validity of arguments for price stability, they also call into question the legitimacy of unions and their policy demands amidst claims that the "European model of society" is too costly and impairs the adaptiveness of the economy. Frontal attacks have been blunted by the continued political force of Christian and Social Democratic ideas, on the continent if not in the U.K. In Europe more generally, voters still support the welfare state.

The renewal of European integration after 1985 is the most important political change for European unions. The Single Market Program and EMU have enshrined market liberalization, price stability and austerity in international treaties. Formal sovereignty over industrial relations and social policy is retained by member states but the determination of the economic conditions on which they depend has either been marketized or conferred on EU institutions. This renders unions and welfare states vulnerable regardless of the domestic political support they have. It also provides member state governments with new arguments justifying unpleasant policy courses plus tools for "exogenizing" responsibility for domestic economic restructuring. Elites can claim that "Europe makes us do it," obscuring the fact that these same elites have themselves been responsible for Europe's choices.

Another widespread political change has been divorce, or at least separation, between left parties and trade unions. In many countries social democratic governments took the lead in implementing liberalizing policy shifts. Left parties have privatized, deregulated, restructured, deindexed wage growth, cut back the public sector, flexibilized the labor market and encouraged entrepreneurs with zeal. Indeed, lefts have become umbrellas for new technocratic elites, whose ideas come more from the mantras of the Ecole Nationale d'Administration, the *Economist* and the *Financial Times* than from socialism. Finally, the science and art of politics has changed around unions. With fewer and fewer "traditional" workers, old *ouvriériste* notions lost their legitimacy and working class votes lost some of their clout. Left parties have always needed to forge coalitions among groups which held different world views. Earlier, unions and workers were the central building blocks. They no longer are.

Comparing Unions as Strategic Actors

There remain striking differences between European political economies. The effects of internationalization and Europeanization are more or less significant depending upon the position of particular national economies. Unemployment may be more or less severe and localized in different parts of the labor force, depending upon the country. The timing of new challenges varies: some unions faced severe problems early on while others have just discovered the gravity of the situation. There is also important variation in the structures and organizational patterns of union movements. Some movements are nationally centralized, others decentralized, while still others focus primarily on economic sectors. Some national union movements are unified umbrella organizations, while others are divided. Some depend heavily upon the state, others very little. Some are hyper-politicized, others relatively indifferent to formal political activity. Certain organizations are rich, others poor, some heavily bureaucratized, others organizationally light. The thicket of differences is dense and each one is likely to predispose a union movement to particular strategic perceptions and responses.

Recognizing diversity is therefore essential. Local positions and resource bases make each union movement distinctive. Our unions will all have been touched, to differing degrees, by destabilizing economic and political changes, but they will respond strategically in the context of specific "paths" built from national systems of exchange, regulatory contexts and organizational legacies. The national chapters which follow will thus detail the particularities of each movement while submitting each to the same general questions. Each will portray specific Golden Age arrangements, review changes in the national political economy, consider employer strategies, and then discuss unions' strategic responses. This focus on the impact of common trends on different contexts should enable us to make informed observations about emerging union responses to common challenges.

Why do we think that all this is important? The answer takes us from the world of industrial conflicts, union organizations, employer desires and economic flows back to our starting point. Unions in Europe have been central actors – although not the only ones – in securing a more democratized and humanized capitalism. Their achievements, if they fell far short of what many desired, nonetheless stand as the high water mark of social citizenship, the foundation stone of a "European model of society." This European model institutionalized notions of solidarity between different social groups in ways unique in the history of capitalism. The challenges that contemporary European unionism has faced since the early 1980s threaten to undermine the central actors in this virtuous correlation.

It may well be that many of the patterns, processes and structures established and perpetuated with union help need serious reexamination in the new era. Reexamination is not the same as dismantling, however. There is considerable danger that those toward whom the new balance of power is leaning will do the latter while claiming to do the former. To the degree to which unions regroup – something that will necessitate self-examination and new thinking – they will survive as significant collective actors into the new millennium. We think that this is important not only because unions, social citizenship, and democracy are great achievements. Those who advocate the marketization of all public goods and the dissolution of all negotiated settlements in the economy in the interests of flexibility are arguing that democracy and social citizenship have gone too far and should be rolled back. They are also making the claim, which history demonstrates to be dangerous indeed, that the closer societies are to pure markets, the more efficient they will be. The closer societies are to pure markets, we suspect, the more fragmented and harsh they will be. This is why our subject is important!

Appendix: By The Numbers

Table 1.1 Trade Union Density (percent)

	1985	1985	1995	1995	Change	1985-95
Country	Non-farm	Salaried	Non-farm	Salaried	Non-farm	Salaried
France	11.6	14.5	6.1	9.1	–47.5	–37.2
Germany	30.7 (1991)	35.0 (1991)	29.6	28.1	–3.5	–17.6
Ex-GDR	41.1 (1991)	46.2 (1991)	34.1 (1993)	42.4 (1993)	–17.2	–8.3
Ex-BRD	29.5	35.3	24.5	29.1	–16.8	–17.4
Italy	32.9	47.6	30.6 (1994)	44.1	7.0	–7.4
Spain	7.3	11.5	11.4	18.6 (1994)	+56.2	+62.1
Sweden	79.3	83.8	77.2	91.1 (1994)	–2.7	8.7
UK	36.0	45.5	26.2	32.9	–7.2	–27.7

Source: 1985-1995, International Labour Office, *World Labour Report 1998* (Geneva : 1998).

Table 1.2 Workdays Lost from Strikes and Lockouts (thousands)

Country	1980	1985	1990	1991	1992	1993	1994	1995
France	1523	727	528	497	359	511	521	
Germany	128*	355*	364*	154*	1545*	593	229	247
Italy	16457	3831	5181	2985	2737	3411	3374	909
Spain	6178	3224	2613	4537	6333	2141	6277	1457
Sweden	4429	504	770	22	28	190	52	627
UK	11964	6402	1903	761	528	649	278	415

Source: ILO, *World Labour Report, 1998*, table 4.3 *Former Federal Republic

Table 1.3 Key Employment Indicators by Country (Percent)

FRANCE	1975	1985	1990	1996
Unemployment	3.9	10.1	9.0	12.4
Youth unemployment (percent of 15-24 age cohort)	na	25.4	24.4	28.9
Employed in Industry	38.6	32.4	30.4	26.5
Employed in Services	51.1	59.4	63.2	68.6
Part-time female employment (% total female work)	na	21.8	23.6	29.5
Part-time male employment (% total male work)	na	3.2	3.3	5.2
Female employment in services (% total female work)	na	73.6	77.0	82.0

GERMANY	1975	1985	1990	1996*
Unemployment	3.5	7.2	4.8	8.9
Youth unemployment (percent of 15-24 age cohort)	0.4	9.5	6.7	10.3
Employed in Industry	54.7	50.8	50.1	47.1
Employed in Services	40.1	44.7	46.4	49.7
Part-time female employment (% total female work)	na	29.6	33.8	33.6
Part-time male employment (% total male work)	na	2.0	2.6	3.8
Female employment in services (% total female work)	60.2	68.1	70.7	77.9

*includes new *Länder*

ITALY	1975	1985	1990	1996
Unemployment	4.8	8.4	9.1	12.0
Youth unemployment (percent of 15-24 age cohort)	na	29.4	30.0	33.5
Employed in Industry	38.5	33.5	32.4	32.2
Employed in Services	45.7	55.5	58.6	61.1
Part-time female employment (% total female work)	na	10.1	9.6	12.7
Part-time male employment (% total male work)	na	3.0	2.4	3.1
Female employment in services (% total female work)	53.3	64.0	67.4	72.0

SPAIN	1975	1985	1990	1996
Unemployment	4.4	21.7	16.2	22.1
Youth unemployment (percent of 15-24 age cohort)	na	47.8	46.3	41.9
Employed in Industry	38.3	31.8	33.5	29.4
Employed in Services	39.7	52.0	54.6	62.0
Part-time female employment (% total female work)*	na	13.9	12.1	17.0
Part-time male employment (% total male work) **	na	2.4	1.6	3.1
Female employment in services (% total female work)	52.7	69.4	72.2	79.9

* Spain has a particularly high level of women on short-term fixed contracts (36.7 percent, 1996) rather than part-time.

** Likewise there is a high level of men on similar contracts (31.9 percent, 1996).

SWEDEN	1975	1985	1990	1996
Unemployment	1.8	3.0	1.8	10.0
Youth unemployment (percent of 15-24 age cohort)	na	7.1	6.7	21.1
Employed in Industry	36.5	29.6	29.0	25.9
Employed in Services	57.1	66.3	67.5	56.5
Part-time female employment (% total female work)	na	45.6	40.9	41.8
Part-time male employment (% total male work)	na	6.8	7.4	8.9
Female employment in services (% total female work)	77.1	83.4	84.3	86.2

UK	1975	1980	1985	1996
Unemployment	3.2	11.8	7.4	9.9
Youth unemployment (percent of 15-24 age cohort)	na	18.5	18.3	15.5
Employed in Industry	40.4	34.7	32.3	31.2
Employed in Services	56.8	63.0	65.5	70.6
Part-time female employment (% total female work)	na	44.8	43.2	44.8
Part-time male employment (% total total male work)	na	4.4	5.3	8.1
Female employment in services (% total female work)	73.1	79.2	81.5	85.0

Source: EC Commission, *Employment in Europe, 1997* (Luxembourg: EC, 1998), pp 117-132

Table 1.4 Macroeconomic Indicators

	Britain	France	Germany	Italy	Spain	Sweden	EU
GDP: ave. annual percent change, 1970-80	1.9	3.3	2.7	3.6	3.5	2.0	—
1980-83	0.5	1.5	0.5	1.6	1.2	1.1	1.0
1984-90	3.3	2.8	3.1	2.9	3.8	2.5	3.0
1991-96	1.5	1.2	2.0	1.0	1.5	0.6	1.5
Monetary policy:[a] annual ave. 1974-79	2.9	-0.7	2.6	0.1	—	2.3	—
1980-89	-1.3	0.8	0.3	-0.7	-1.1	0.0	—
1990-93	-3.3	-3.2	-3.2	-2.4	-3.4	-3.5	—
Inflation: ave. annual rate, 1970-80	14	9.8	5.2	15.0	15.1	9.8	10.8
1980-83	10.9	11.0	4.2	18.0	12.9	10.2	11.1
1984-90	6.4	5.1	2.3	7.9	8.0	7.0	5.3
1991-96	3.6	2.4	2.3	5.1	5.0	3.1	3.6
Unemployment:[b] annual ave., 1974-79	5.0	4.5	3.2	6.6	5.2	1.9	—
1980-83	9.5	7.2	4.8	6.6	14.5	3.0	—
1984-90	9.7	9.8	6.2	9.2	19.5	2.4	—
1991-96	9.3	11.3	7.0	10.6	21.1	8.0	—

Sources: GDP, inflation (GDP deflator), and unemployment, OECD *Economic Outlook* 56, December 1994 and 62, December 1997, annex tables 1, 14, 22; monetary policy, calculated from real interest rates, OECD *Historical Statistics* 1996, tables 10.8, 10.10.

a. The yield spread (the difference between long-and short-term real interest rates) is a measure of monetary policy restrictiveness, which increases as real short term interest rates approach and exceed real long term rates. The index indicates the restrictiveness of a country's policy relative to policy in the U.S. in terms of the difference between the yield spread in that country and in the U.S., so that a positive sign indicates a less restrictive and negative sign a more restrictive policy than in the U.S.

b. Standardized rates

Table 1.5 Internationalization

	France	Germany	Italy	Spain	Sweden	UK	EU*
Exports percent GDP, 1990-94 ave.	22.5	24.3	21.8	18.7	31.0	24.7	8.0
Foreign Direct Investment							
Inflows: $billion, 1980-85 ave.	2.2	0.6	1.0	1.7	0.3	3.8	14.2
1986-96 ave.	14.0	2.9	3.8	8.5	4.0	20.2	50.5**
Inflows: % outflows, 1980-85 ave.	78	20	65	565	23	40	67
1986-96 ave.	67	15	73	332	77	71	74**

Sources: National exports, OECD, *Historical Statistics 1996*; EU exports, EU Commission, "Europe as an Economic Entity," 4 December 1996. Foreign direct investment, OECD, *The OECD Jobs Study: Evidence and Explanations*, part 1, tables 3.B1 and 2; and OECD *International Direct Investments Statistics Yearbook 1997*, tables 2 and 3.

* EU member state exports are mainly to other EU member states.

** 1986-92

Notes

1. We borrow here from Stephen Marglin and Juliet Schor, eds., *The Golden Age of Capitalism* (Oxford: Clarendon, 1990).
2. The appendix to this chapter provides general indicators.
3. The present European Union (EU) has been called successively the European Economic Community (EEC), European Community (EC), and the EU. We use EU throughout.
4. Karl Marx, *The 18th Brumaire of Louis Napoleon Bonaparte*, in Marx and Engels, *Selected Works* Vol. I (Moscow: Foreign Languages Publishing House, 1962), 247.
5. The relationships between support base (those susceptible to participation), movement itself (a selection from the support base), and "movement organizations" is a complicated one that has to be examined carefully in specific cases." Roberta Garner, *Contemporary Movements and Ideologies* (New York: McGraw-Hill Inc., 1996), 25. For "state of the art" discussions, see Doug McAdam, John D. McCarthy and Mayer Zald, eds., *Comparative Perspectives on Social Movements: Political Opportunities, Mobilizing Structures and Cultural Framings* (Cambridge: Cambridge University Press, 1996).
6. Charles Tilly, *Movement to Revolution* (Reading, Mass: Addison-Wesley, 1978) struggles with this "model" problem.
7. See Sidney Tarrow, *Power in Movement: Social Movements, Collective Action and Politics* (New York: Cambridge University Press, 1995).
8. Early statements of exchange theory are in Chapter 3 in Lange, Ross, and Vannicelli Unions, Change and Crisis; Alessandro Pizzorno, "Political Exchange and Collective Identity in Industrial Conflict," in Colin Crouch and Alessandro Pizzorno, *The Resurgence of Class Conflict in Western Europe Since 1968* (London: Macmillian, 1978), Vol.2.
9. This notion of "opportunity structure," now used quite widely in the social sciences, was originally formulated by specialists in social movements. See Hanspieter Kriesi, "The Political Opportunity Structure of New Social movements: Its Impact on Their Mobilization," in *The Politics of Social Protest*, ed. J. Craig Jenkins and Bert Klandermans (Minneapolis: University of Minnesota Press, 1996).
10. On "constructivist" outlooks see Richard Locke and Kathleen Thelen in "Apples and Oranges revisited: Contextualized Comparisons and the Study of Comparative Labor Politics," *Politics and Society* (September 1995). Also Locke and Kathleen Thelen, eds., *The Shifting Boundaries of Labor Politics: New Directions for Comparative Research and Theory* (Cambridge: MIT Press, 1997).
11. Here we are close to the notion of organizational "satisficing" presented by James March and Herbert Simon in *Organizations* (New York: Wiley, 1958).
12. Organization theory has taught us not to expect one-to-one correspondence between challenges and organizational perceptions of, and responses to, them. See James G. March and Johan P. Olsen, *Rediscovering Institutions* (New York: Free Press, 1989); chaps. 1-4. Also Walter W. Powell and Paul J. DiMaggio, eds., *The New Institutionalism in Organizational Analysis* (Chicago: University of Chicago Press, 1991).
13. As economists note, there exist processes of "increasing returns" in technology, location and organizational pattern which can bias firms toward choices which confirm a specific path rather than abstractly free choices that might be more efficient (or "rational"). There are good reasons to think that the further one moves away from organizations subject to strict market constraints the more path dependency is likely to play a central role. Unions live in a less than well-defined environment with large "sunk costs" in their processes, perceptions, behaviors and choices. See Paul Pierson,

"Increasing Returns, Path Dependence and the Study of Politics," Jean Monnet Lecture, European University Institute, April 1997.

14. This is because, "in contexts of complex social interdependence, new institutions and policies will often generate high fixed costs, learning effects, coordination effects and adaptive expectations." Pierson, "Increasing Returns," 17.
15. Among general works see Anthony Ferner and Richard Hyman *Industrial Relations in the New Europe* (Oxford: Basil Blackwell, 1992) and *European Industrial Relations* (Oxford: Basil Blackwell, 1994).
16. The model for such work is Clark Kerr, John T. Dunlop, Frederick Harbison and Charles A. Myers, *Industrialism and Industrial Man* (Cambridge: Harvard University Press, 1960). For recent overviews see, for North America, Thomas Kochan, Harry Katz and Robert McKersie, *The Transformation of American Industrial Relations* (New York: Basic Books, 1986); for Europe, see Colin Crouch, Industrial Relations and European State Traditions (Oxford: Clarendon Press, 1993). See also Richard Locke, Thomas Kochan, and Michael Piore, eds., *Employment Relations in a Changing World Economy* (Cambridge: MIT Press, 1995).
17. Politics enters the picture, only peripherally, as an exogenous supplier of legal rules which frame the bargaining arena.
18. For a particularly good example of an historical institutionalist micro-approach see Wolfgang Streeck, *Social Institutions and Economic Performance: Studies of Industrial Relations in Advanced Capitalist Economies* (London: Sage, 1992). Michel Albert's *Capitalism vs. Capitalism* (New York: Four Walls Eight Windows, 1993) presents an historical institutionalist macro-analysis.
19. For "sector determines preference" arguments see Ronald Rogowski, *Commerce and Coalitions: How Trade Affects Domestic Political Alignments* (Princeton: Princeton University Press, 1989) and Jeffry A. Frieden and Ronald Rogowski "The Impact of the International Economy on National Politics: An Analytical Overview" in *Internationalization and Domestic Politics*, eds. Robert Keohane and Helen Milner (Cambridge: Cambridge University Press 1996).
20. Paradoxically, Marxists have not been very good at theorizing or writing about trade unions, and traditional Marxist interpretations of trade unions have not been prominent in recent years.
21. See Robert Boyer, *La Théorie de la régulation: une analyse critique* (Paris: La Découverte, 1986); Robert Boyer and Yves Saillard, eds., *Théorie de la régulation, l'état des savoirs* (Paris: La Découverte, 1995); "The Rise and Fall of the Golden Age," by Andrew Glyn, Alan Hughes, Alan Lipietz and Ajit Singh, in Marglin and Schor *The Golden Age*. Chris Howell's *Regulating Labor: The State and Industrial Relations Reform in Postwar France* (Princeton: Princeton University Press, 1992) uses regulationism apparatus to discuss the French union movement.
22. Mancur Olson, *The Logic of Collective Action* (Cambridge: Harvard University Press, 1965) and *The Rise and Decline of Nations* (New Haven: Yale University Press, 1982).
23. Olson thinks that when unions are all-encompassing – i.e. made up of virtually everyone, the appropriation of resources for selective incentives from other groups becomes difficult and they can act in the interests of all.
24. The renewed interest in Karl Polanyi's social constructivist economic history reflects this concern. Karl Polanyi, *The Great Transformation* (Boston: Beacon Press, 1944).
25. Miriam Golden and Michael Wallerstein, *Reinterpreting Postwar Industrial Relations: Comparative Data on Advanced Industrial Societies* (forthcoming) promises to adjudicate between the two positions using comparative time-series data for unions across a

wide range of capitalist countries. It concludes that most national union movements have shown resilience with weakening in but a handful of cases. See also Colin Crouch and Franz Traxler, eds. *Organized Industrial Relations in Europe: What Future?* (Aldershot: Avebury, 1995).

26. John Goldthorpe and David Lockwood, *The Affluent Worker: Industrial Attitudes* (Cambridge: Cambridge University Press, 1968); *The Affluent Worker: Political Attitudes and Behaviour* (Cambridge: Cambridge University Press, 1968); *The Affluent Worker in the Class Structure* (Cambridge: Cambridge University Press, 1969).
27. Peter A. Hall, ed., *The Political Power of Economic Ideas* (Princeton: Princeton University Press, 1989).
28. Among our cases France, Germany, and Sweden achieved full employment. The British lagged somewhat while the Italians had higher unemployment. Figures for Spain under Franco would not be pertinent.
29. See Andrew Martin, "Trade Unions in Sweden," in Peter Gourevitch, Andrew Martin, George Ross et al., *Unions and Economic Crisis: Britain, West Germany and Sweden.*
30. Andrew Shonfield, in *Modern Capitalism* (Oxford: Oxford University Press, 1964) paints a glowing portrait of the alleged virtues of this French model.
31. In both Italy and France during most of the period the largest parts of the union movement were excluded from direct participation in policy deliberations It was no coincidence that in both countries the major unions were Communist dominated.
32. See Robert Fishman, *Working-Class Organization and the Return to Democracy in Spain* (Ithaca: Cornell University Press, 1990).
33. Philippe Schmitter's "Still the Century of Corporatism" is the foundation of this literature. See also Philippe Schmitter and Gerhard Lehmbruch, *Trends Towards Corporatist Intermediation* (London: Sage, 1979).
34. Organization for Economic Co-operation and Development (OECD), *Historical Statistics 1960-1989* (Paris: OECD, 1991), tables 3.1 and 4.8.
35. *World Investment Directory*, vol. 3 (New York: United Nations, 1992), v.
36. Ibid, v.
37. Bank for International Settlements, *Sixty-Third Annual Report* (1993), 90-91.This figure refers to transactions on the nine major national markets in April 1992. Eichengreen estimates the daily volume at the slightly lower amount of $880 billion. Barry Eichengreen, *International Monetary Arrangements for the 21st Century* (Washington, D.C.: The Brookings Institution, 1994), p. 60.
38. Ibid, 61.
39. The list of works in the hyperbolic genre is very long. See, among others, Lester Thurow, *Head to Head: The Coming Economic Battle Among Japan, Europe, and America* (New York: Morrow, 1992); Edward N. Luttwak, *The Endangered Dream: How to Stop the United States from Becoming a Third World Country and How to Win the Geo-economic Struggle for Industrial Supremacy* (New York: Simon and Schuster, 1993); Kenichi Ohmae, ed., *The Evolving Global Economy, Making Sense of the New World Order* (Cambridge: Harvard Business School Press, 1995);and Richard Barnet and John Cavanaugh, *Global Dreams* (New York: Simon and Schuster, 1994).
40. As two critics put it, "The Triad of the EU, Japan and NAFTA ... is likely to account for a majority share of the world manufacturing output, world trade, and FDI for a long time to come." Paul Hirst and Grahame Thompson, *Globalization in Question* (Cambridge: Polity, 1996), 152.
41. Padraig Flynn, paper prepared for Conference on Social Policy and Economic Performance, Amsterdam, 23-25 January 1997, 10.

42. See Harry Katz, "The Decentralization of Collective Bargaining: A Literature Review and Comparative Analysis," *Industrial and Labor Relations Review* 47 (October 1993). The data presented by Miriam Golden and Michael Wallerstein in "Unions, Employers and Collective Bargaining: A report on Data for Sixteen Countries from 1950 to 1990" (unpublished paper dated 30 March 1995) makes it clear that the tendencies Katz projected have not been anywhere near as strong as he had anticipated.
43. Dani Rodrik's *Has Globalization Gone Too Far?* (Washington: Institute for International Economics, 1997) provides a lucid discussion of this issue.
44. OECD *Jobs Study* (Paris: OECD, 1994), part 1, 2. See also the accompanying tabular material.
45. See European Commission, "Flexibility in working time and security for workers" background paper for first-stage consultations with the social partners, 1995, annex 1, table 2.
46. See OECD, *Employment Outlook*, July 1996 (OECD: Paris, 1996), 72-74, table 3.2. Women are particularly penalized in Germany and the United Kingdom.
47. They may not necessarily make the most of the opportunities. It is often very difficult for European unions to negotiate flexibility (in hours, work rules, employment security) because the "rigid" rules they won over the years have become a major reason for the basis of support they still get. Moreover, many of the roles which active unionists hold (shop stewards, works committee members, etc.) are based on functions derived from these same rules.
48. *The OECD Jobs Study: Evidence and Explanations*, part I (Paris: OECD, 1994), 1-2.
49. Ibid, 35.
50. On policy regimes see Peter Temin, *Lessons from the Great Depression* (Cambridge: MIT Press, 1989) and Ton Notermans, *Money, Markets and the State* (New York: Cambridge University Press, 1999).
51. For adjustments in unemployment compensation see OECD *Employment Outlook*, July 1996 (Paris: OECD, 1996), 30. Health care and pension cutbacks have almost everywhere as well. The French strikes of December 1995 over pension changes and German unrest over health care reimbursement in 1996 are emblematic of the social tension that such changes can provoke.
52. In the strongest version of this line, unemployment cannot be reduced by macroeconomic policy at all. Only supply-side changes making it possible for labor markets to "clear" fully can do the job. This translates into the decentralization of wage determination (down to the unorganized individual if possible) and minimization of the "reservation wage" set by social benefits. The mainstream view, if the OECD is representative, acknowledges that deficient demand, resulting from overly restrictive implementation of the price stability regime itself, accounts for some unemployment, even if labor market institutions account for much of the rest See *The OECD Jobs Study: Evidence and Explanations*, Part I: 66. How much of unemployment that demand deficiency accounts for is much debated, however. Some European Commission documents, for example, give demand-side factors less weight than supply-side factors, while others do the reverse.

Chapter 2

UNFORGIVEN

British Trade Unionism in Crisis

Chris Howell

British trade unions are in crisis. While they have had to deal with the same broad forms of economic restructuring as their counterparts in the rest of the advanced capitalist world, they have also faced exceptional hostility from the state, and an accelerating aversion to collective bargaining on the part of capital. At precisely the time when unions needed to call upon all their collective and political resources to confront deindustrialization, international economic integration, and the range of practices that go under the label of "flexibility," they have seen those resources undermined and devalued by a state that denied any political access to trade unions and sought to severely restrict their industrial role, and devalued by an employer class that has shown a growing preference for individual, rather than collective, relations with employees. As a result, trade unions have lost 40 percent of their members, and have seen their political, social, and economic influence dwindle to a level unknown since the interwar period.

The Conservative assault upon trade unions since 1979 marks the third great state project of industrial relations restructuring in a century. Between 1890 and 1920, faced with cutthroat competition among large numbers of small producers in declining industries, and the growing strike power of national unions, successive British governments attempted to create an industrial relations system organized around industry level bar-

Notes for this section begin on page 70.

gaining and a raft of conciliation and arbitration procedures. That particular organization of class relations began to break down in the 1950s as older patterns of economic growth gave way to the particular flawed physiognomy of British Fordism. In the 1960s and 1970s, faced with the dual threat of a new set of functional needs on the part of British capital, and a resurgence of workplace militancy, Labour and Conservative governments sought to effect a simultaneous decentralization of industrial relations while strengthening the authority of both the state and trade union leaderships over rank-and-file class power on the shopfloor. This project clearly failed, and its failure paved the way for the much more radical Thatcherite project. Once again, a combination of the strike power of workers and unions, and a new set of economic conditions, provided the impetus for the attempt to, in essence, construct an industrial relations system without unions. Early indications from the Labour government elected in 1997 suggest a broad continuation of Conservative industrial relations policies, with changes only at the margins, suggesting a new consensus in this area.

This essay traces the challenges to British trade unions, and the consequences of those political, economic, and social challenges for unions and industrial relations. The impact of the Thatcherite class project has been more significant than simply to weaken unions. It has also led to a process of fundamental strategic reconceptualization on the part of the British labor movement. Indeed, this period of crisis and decline has also been one of unprecedented innovation on the part of trade unions. While unions denied the scale of the crisis and hence the need for change for as long as they could, in the period since the mid-1980s they have adopted a wide range of new strategies, practices, organizational forms, and discourses. There are, however, serious questions about the direction of strategic change, and the kind of labor movement that is resulting. Despite, or perhaps because of, the recent innovations, union decline has continued and the erosion of collective bargaining has accelerated. The reconstruction of British trade unionism, along quite different strategic lines from the past, is thus a central legacy of Thatcherism, in both its original and Blairite forms.

From Power to Crisis

When the Labour government was defeated by Margaret Thatcher's Conservative Party in the 1979 election, British unions had experienced a decade of very rapid growth and were at the height of their power. The dramatic growth in union strength from the mid-1960s to the end of the 1970s followed from a number of factors. First, workplace strength based on full employment combined with employers' need for greater productivity to foster the growth of workplace union institutions. Second, the state played a more important role in promoting union strength. The period from 1965 onwards saw an increase in the role of the state in British industrial relations, as government and as employer, as trade unions received a formal recognition procedure, new rights in the workplace, encouragement in the public sector and pressure on employers in the private sector. Third, economic crisis in this period both encouraged workers to join unions for economic protection, and gave unions an enhanced political role as successive governments sought wage restraint as a cure for Britain's persistent inflationary bias and balance of payments problems.

By 1979 trade union strength – numerical, institutional, political, and economic – was at its peak. 13.3 million people belonged to trade unions, and of these, over 90 percent belonged to unions affiliated to the Trades Union Congress. Between 1968 and 1979 union membership increased by more than 3 million, and union density increased from 44 percent to 55.4 percent, making this one of the great periods of union growth in British history.[1] Unionization became more entrenched in its traditional strongholds in engineering, transport, and the core mass production industries as the old industrial and general unions expanded their memberships. But the real source of growth was among white-collar and service sector workers, particularly in the public sector. The 1970s was also exceptional in the degree of industrial conflict with annual averages of 2631 stoppages, almost 13 million work days lost.[2] A plausible case can be made that strikes brought down two governments in the 1970s.

By any measure, British trade unions were powerful industrial and political actors by the end of the 1970s. Yet, the fragility of that strength, and its reliance upon the particular economic and political conjuncture of the 1970s must be recognized to understand the crisis of British trade unionism since then. Unions in the 1980s were captives of weaknesses inherited from past choices, with the result that, for all their numbers and influence, they remained deeply vulnerable to attack from employers and the state. This remarkable period of union growth rested first upon an economic context of full employment and the interest of employers in large Fordist firms in developing stable workplace bargaining relationships, and second upon a political context of state support for trade unionism. Even the brief, failed, legislative attempts to restrict union action, embodied in "In Place of Strife" and the Industrial Relations Act, were designed more to extend the authority of union officials over industrial action and to integrate the two systems of industrial relations identified by the Donovan Report, than to attack trade unionism and collective bargaining. Nor did the growth in union numbers overcome the fragmentation of British trade unionism, and the combination of the decentralization of bargaining and incomes policies meant that the influence of union leaderships over their members declined rather than increased. This was to make the implementation of new strategies in the late 1980s extremely difficult.

Finally, trade unions did not seek to institutionalize their conjunctural strength by acquiring comprehensive legislative protection from the state. For all these reasons, the way in which unions grew after World War II, the conditions under which growth took place, and the choices that they made during a period of strength, formed a legacy which made British trade unionism singularly ill-equipped to face the economic conditions of post-Fordism and the political conditions of a hostile state. Furthermore, trade unions failed to respond to the economic crisis of the 1970s with any strategic reassessment, relying instead upon a schizophrenic oscillation between strike action and political incorporation. The "Winter of Discontent" strike wave in 1978-79 only made clear what should have been obvious, that the expansion of unionism in the 1960s and 1970s was a response to a particular economic and political conjuncture rather than a secular growth of union organizational power or a radicalization of union members.

When Margaret Thatcher swept to power in May 1979, a central part of her agenda for change was a frontal attack on union power. While it was possible, until the mid-1980s, to argue that British trade unions had weathered the hostile economic and political environment remarkably successfully, such an argument is no longer tenable. British trade unions are now visibly in a state of crisis. Union membership is lower than at any time since World War II, strike levels are at their lowest since records began being kept in 1891, and the industrial relations system has undergone the greatest institutional shift since the 1910s, when the system of industry level bargaining was first put in place.

Total union membership is now 7.9 million (a fall of 5.4 million, or 40 percent, since 1979), and union density is 30 percent.[3] Of this total, 6.75 million belong to unions affiliated to the TUC, which has lost 44 percent of its members.[4] Union membership has fallen for eighteen straight years since 1979, in recession as well as in periods of economic growth. If one looks instead at individual trade unions, it is very difficult to identify success stories. To be sure, some unions have suffered more than others, but it is striking that there is no clear, recognized "model" trade union which has managed to buck the general decline, with the exception of the specialist Royal College of Nursing (RCN).

As for collective bargaining, there has been a quite dramatic decline in the proportion of employees covered by collective bargaining.

Figure 2.1 Trade Union Membership

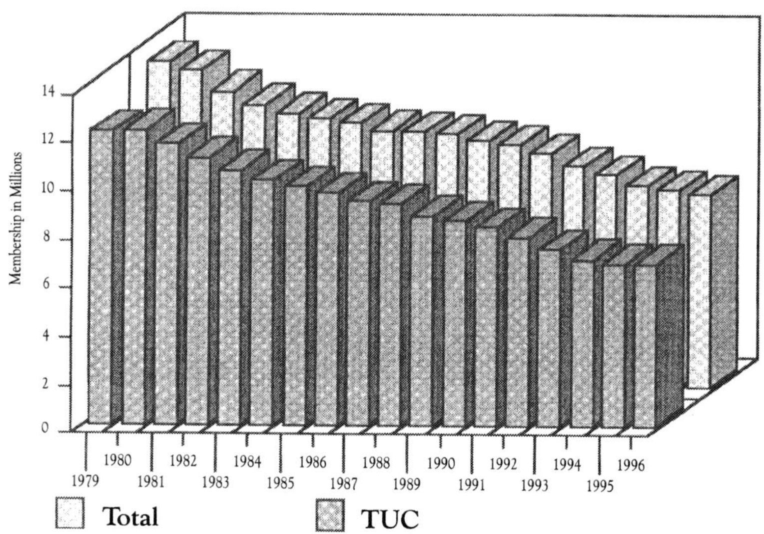

Source: Figures for total membership come from Mark Cully and Stephen Woodland, "Trade Union Membership and Recognition 1996-97: An Analysis of Data From the Certification Officer and the LFS," *Labour Markets Trends* 106, no. 7 (July 1998). Figures for TUC membership come from the annual reports of the TUC.

The third Workplace Industrial Relations Survey (WIRS3) estimated that only 38 percent of employees are covered by collective bargaining, and more than half of those are in the public sector.[5] WIRS3 also failed to capture more recent change, particularly the bulk of the restructuring of the health service and local authorities since 1990, which has undoubtedly had an impact on union recognition and collective bargaining.

The simultaneous decline in union membership, union recognition, and collective bargaining means that collective bargaining between unions and employers is no longer the dominant system of industrial relations. In its place, we see the growing dominance of workplaces where management sets the terms and conditions of employment unilaterally, in some cases after consultation with employees, but with only minimal constraint from trade unions, national or industry level agreements, or legislation protecting individual workers. The issue is not simply the relative size of the collective bargaining and noncollective bargaining systems of industrial relations, but the trajectory, which is clearly away from trade unions and collective bargaining. Evidence of newer firms, particularly on "greenfield" sites, suggests that such firms are much less likely to recognize trade unions than older, more established firms.[6]

Strike levels have also declined dramatically: the 1990s have seen fewer stoppages and days lost to strikes than at any time since records began being kept in the last century. In 1994 the strike level was 1 percent of that in 1979. If one eliminates large individual strikes the downward trend is clear: the average annual days lost to strikes in the 1980s was one-third that of the 1970s, and the figures thus far for the 1990s are one seventh that of the 1970s.[7] And while strike rates have declined in most industrialized countries, they have fallen faster in Britain than in the rest of the OECD.[8]

New Conjunctures

The Conservative assault upon trade unionism did not come out of the blue. It was one element of a particular form of capitalist restructuring in response to the crisis of British Fordism. The effect of the changed economic circumstances was to change the interests of an important block of employers leading them to reconsider established industrial relations practices, and enable the state to aggressively relocate the British economy within the international division of labor.

This process of restructuring can be captured by the notion of a "double shift," which describes a reduction in the economic capacity of the state and of national forms of economic regulation through a simultaneous shift in the locus of economic power downward to the firm and outward to the international economy. Neither element of the double shift was new to Britain in the 1980s. Nevertheless, the internationalization and decentralization of the British economy has continued, and even accelerated since 1979. Both elements were encouraged by employers seeking greater autonomy and flexibility in the management of their firms, and by the state. Government policy under the Conservatives actively *promoted* the loss of state economic capacity. From the removal of exchange controls in July 1979 to Britain's refusal to accept the social chapter of the Maastricht Treaty in December 1991, Conservative policy was to deregulate economic activity so as to encourage domestic entrepreneurs and lure foreign investment.

The British government clearly attempted to position Britain as a relatively low wage, deregulated economy which could attract foreign investment, by both European firms shopping for a liberal regulatory environment, and non-European firms seeking access to the European Community but without the costs of other European countries. The Department of Trade and Industry's pitch to inward investors marketed Britain's "quality people at low cost" and argued:

> Unlike most continental countries, employment regulations are largely on a voluntary basis with no requirements for works councils and mandatory union agreements, while single-union agreements are relatively easy to negotiate. There are also fewer restrictions on both recruitment and dismissal.[9]

As the *Economist* put it, "Britain comfortably comes bottom in surveys of EU employers' perceptions of the stringency of employment protection regulations."[10]

Britain's economy became increasingly internationalized after 1979. The numbers employed in the manufacturing industry by British subsidiaries of foreign companies, after remaining constant at 12-13 percent for most of the 1980s, rose to 16 percent in 1990,[11] and Britain became the second most popular location of foreign direct investment after the United States.[12] An additional incentive for foreign firms has been government regional development policies which provided incentives for investment in areas with relatively high unemployment.[13]

There have also been important shifts in industrial structure and labor force composition, though these, too, largely continued long-term trends. The combination of the recession of 1980-83, a high interest rate policy, and the high value of sterling because of North Sea oil receipts, had a particularly devastating impact on domestic manufacturing. Between June 1979 and June 1992, employment in manufacturing fell by more than a third. By 1990 manufacturing employment as a proportion of the total workforce was 21.9 percent. Meanwhile the service sector saw a big increase in employment, accounting for over 70 percent of jobs in 1991, the largest increases coming in banking, finance and insurance, hotels and catering, and health.[14] Parallel, and related to deindustrialization, has been the rise of small firms. Growth in employment by small firms accompanied a big decline in employment by very large firms, so that between 1979 and 1986 the share of total employment in firms employing less than fifty people rose from 33.6 percent to 42.5 percent, while the share of firms employing over 1000 people halved, falling to 18.2 percent.[15]

The feminization of the labor force has been a marked feature of the changes in the labor force in this period. Between 1979 and 1991, female labor force participation increased from 63 percent to 71 percent while male participation decreased from 91 percent to 88 percent, so that by 1991 there were 1.7 million, or 19 percent, more women working than in 1979.[16] More dramatic than the feminization of the labor force has been the collapse of secure, full-time jobs and their replacement by various forms of atypical work. In 1993, 23 percent of those in employment worked part-time, and the 1980s saw self-employment increase by over 50 percent to 3.1 million in 1993. Overall, then, 38 percent of those in employment are self-employed, or work on part-time or temporary contracts.[17]

The importance of these economic and demographic shifts is that they create a different, more hostile, environment for British trade unions. They are more exposed to international competition and to firms which seek flexibility and compete on the basis of wage costs than before. Internationalization has also meant having to deal with firms with different industrial relations practices. Many of the industrial relations innovations of the 1980s were popularized by inward investors, and have since been diffused into British-owned companies. Changes in industrial structure and workforce composition have shifted the British economy away from precisely those firms, sectors, and workers – full-time, male workers in large manufacturing firms – where unions have traditionally been strongest.

State Strategy

The 1980s and 1990s have been marked by the unremitting hostility of the British state to trade unions. This period has seen the most sustained assault on trade unionism among advanced capitalist countries in the postwar period. The Conservative Party arrived in power in 1979 with the recent memory both of the defeat of Edward Heath's 1970-74 government at the hands of the National Union of Mineworkers (NUM), and the collapse of the Social Contract in the 1978-79 strike wave. Those concrete experiences reinforced a diagnosis of Britain's economic problems that ascribed them largely to the combination of union industrial and political power. This was the basic rationale of Conservative industrial relations legislation.

Ideological in its content, direction, and coherence, the legislation was pragmatic in its timing and the manner in which it sought to achieve its aims. Its primary goals were to abandon corporatist practices, reduce industrial action, and most importantly, to allow employers more freedom in the management of their firms and their relationship with their workforces. While Conservative hostility toward trade unions has been clear, the main aim of government policy has been not to prescribe a particular model of industrial relations, but to remove any state restriction upon the right of employers to choose the industrial relations arrangements that they feel most appropriate. If trade unionism and collective bargaining have weakened over the past decade and a half it is because employers have used the opportunity afforded them by Conservative governments to change their relationship with their labor force. With the big exception of the public sector, the role of the state has been primarily *facilitative* rather than prescriptive.

That said, by the end of the 1980s, Conservative policy had become increasingly concerned with encouraging an individualization of industrial relations in which trade unions and collective bargaining have a limited role. Conservative ministers urged unions to get out of the business of collective bargaining and instead offer individual services to their members and government White Papers called upon employers to reconsider their industrial relations practices and stressed the merits of individual contracts, promising to support "the aspirations of individual employees to deal directly with their employer, rather than through the medium of trade union representation or collective bargaining."[18] Thus decollectivization has been a state strategy under the Conservatives, though it has been facilitated by legislation rather than imposed upon employers.

It is important to stress that the role of the state has been expressed not only in the explicit industrial relations legislation of the Conservative governments, but also, and perhaps more importantly, through the withdrawal of support for collective bargaining, union recognition, and full employment, all of which were crucial props to union strength in the postwar period. The dominant thrust of macroeconomic policy since 1979 has been to privilege fighting inflation over fighting unemployment. As a result unemployment was much higher in the 1980s than at any time in the postwar era. Similarly, labor market policy has encouraged various forms of flexibility. The deregulation of the labor market made hiring and firing easier and encouraged the use of atypical labor and the Conservatives abolished the Wage Councils in 1993, leaving Britain without any form of statutory minimum wage.

The Thatcherite industrial relations legislation itself ranged so widely, and touched so many areas of trade union activity, that only its main provisions can be discussed here.[19] There were six major packages of union legislation: the 1980, 1982, 1988 and 1990 Employment Acts, the 1984 Trade Union Act, and the 1993 Trade Union Reform and Employment Rights Act. Their main concerns were to restrict the freedom to organize industrial action, end the closed shop, provide union members with new rights against their unions, remove legislative support for union recognition, and regulate internal union government, particularly political action. Each piece of legislation had a number of elements, and successive Acts frequently returned to the same subject. The 1993 legislation was potentially the most far reaching. Indeed as the hapless government of John Major appeared increasingly bereft of new economic and social ideas, union policy was one of the few areas of continued vitality. The net result of this avalanche of legislation is that secondary industrial action is practically outlawed; all strikes are now much more difficult to organize (and unions place themselves at great risk when they call strikes); the closed shop is illegal; and union governance is tightly bound up by statutory regulation.

At least as important as legislation has been the more indirect role of the state in withdrawing support and encouragement for collective bargaining and union recognition. The goal of Conservative policy was profoundly radical in the context of British industrial relations, in that it sought to end the presumption, embedded in more than eighty years of legislation and government policy, that collective bargaining between employers and representative trade unions was a more favored or more legitimate form of industrial relations than any other. Some of these developments were substantive – the 1980 abolition of the statutory recognition procedure, the derecognition of the staff union and then the security guards at the Government Communications Headquarters (GCHQ), the recision in 1983 of the Fair Wages Resolution, the phasing out of government funding for trade union education and training courses, and trade union ballots; and some primarily symbolic – revoking the 1972 Industrial Relations Code of Practice, ending ACAS's statutory duty to encourage collective bargaining. But taken together they served to demonstrate to employers the acceptability of doing without trade unions. Thus the 1993 provision permitting employers to bribe their employees to give up collective bargaining rights through higher pay settlements was a logical culmination of government policy.

Government policy to deal with the corporatist bias of British policy-making has been straightforward to implement and clear-cut in its effects. High level contacts between the TUC and Conservative governments were practically nonexistent. When Major met TUC leaders in 1992, it was the first prime ministerial meeting since 1984. The destruction of tripartite bodies was particularly serious for the trade unions, as the tripartite bodies of greatest importance to the trade unions – the Manpower Services Commission and the National Economic Development Council, probably the most potent symbol of the postwar "British Consensus" – were first weakened and then abolished. Furthermore, the emasculation of local government has drastically reduced the ability of trade unions to find safe havens from the impact of central government industrial relations policy. It has also eliminated most of the political resources of the trade unions that had not already disappeared with the Labour defeat in 1979.

Conservative governments also shaped industrial relations through their role as employer in the public sector. In the early 1980s government policy toward the nationalized industries centered upon the appointment of tough "macho managers" – Michael Edwards at British Leyland, Ian MacGregor at British Steel and the British Coal Board – prepared to break with what the Conservatives saw as a somewhat cozy relationship with the trade unions and undertake the restructuring necessary to bring nationalized industries closer to profitability. This imperative became more important as certain industries were targeted for privatization and therefore had to be made attractive to investors. The government was an important actor in several public sector disputes, despite protestations that managers had autonomy, encouraging management to resist concessions. This was certainly the case in the most important strike of the decade, the mineworkers' strike in 1984-85: the Conservative Party, stung by defeat at the hands of the miners in 1972 and 1974, prepared extensively for the likelihood of a strike.[20] The police were used much more aggressively to counter picketing than in previous disputes, and the government prevented any compromise settlement.

Most important for public sector industrial relations has been privatization and the restructuring of the public sector. There has been very little explicit derecognition of trade unions in privatized firms, not least because unions tend to be well entrenched with large memberships, though there have been exceptions, such as some of the regional water companies, the electricity supply companies, and British Telecom, primarily through the replacement of collective bargaining by personal contracts among managers. In practically every case – British Steel, British Telecom, and the water companies being particularly good examples – privatization has ended national bargaining, decentralizing it to either regional centers or different business groups.[21] Additionally, privatization has almost always been followed by broad-ranging flexibility agreements, including multitasking and performance-related pay.

Restructuring of the public sector itself has gathered pace since the late 1980s, emphasizing greater autonomy for local units of the public sector – hospitals, schools – while also injecting some form of competition. This process began in local government with contracting out and then compulsory tendering. It forced public sector employees to compete with private contractors for the provision of certain services. The most important forms of restructuring came in the National Health Service where since 1991 its constituent parts have been encouraged to become self-governing "trusts." Again, outright union derecognition has been rare, but the trusts have used their autonomy from local government control to "rationalize" their bargaining arrangements.

A distinctive feature of privatization and public sector restructuring is that they have emerged as *anti-strike strategies*. Faced with strikes in the rail industry in 1995, and in the Royal Mail in 1996, the Conservative response was to accelerate the former's privatization, and lift the latter's monopoly on small letter-carrying. The decentralization of collective bargaining now taking place in the NHS and railways will make *national* strikes in these industries extremely difficult. Instead, strikes are more likely to be local and confined to one hospital trust or one railway company. Thus, changes in the ownership and organization of the public sector have industrial relations goals as well as broader economic ones.

The section below on trade unions and the political sphere will examine the industrial relations agenda of the new Labour government, and suggest a basic continuity with Thatcherism. But, at least until the change of government in 1997, the impact of the British state upon industrial relations in the period since 1979 has been wide ranging and dramatic, seeking a fundamental change in the balance of power between labor and capital. Legislative obstacles which limited the freedom of employers to establish the industrial relations that they wished have been removed. How employers have chosen to use this greater freedom is the subject of the next section.

Employer Strategy

For a number of reasons, employer attitudes toward trade unions changed in the 1980s. Changing economic pressures forced employers to change their relations with their labor force, and to increase flexibility in pay, labor, and working practices. The presence of a Conservative government created the opportunity for employers to confront trade unions with a greater chance of success, and to have greater autonomy from both legislation and union pressure in how industrial relations were organized in the workplace. And the 1980s saw the development of new, more confident, and more combative, managerial practices. Some have talked of a "managerial renaissance" in this period, capturing both the confidence and the experimentation of the period.[22] Some new practices were imported from abroad, particularly Japan, and some were the product of fashion, but there is no doubt that employers, in a more competitive economic environment, and afforded greater opportunity by the state, sought new forms of industrial relations.

There have been a number of common themes to employer strategy. The first is a preference for decentralizing collective bargaining. The 1980s have seen the breakdown of industry-level agreements in the private sector, so that two-tier bargaining has given way, in a number of industries, to single-employer bargaining. While more than half of full-time employees were covered by a national sectoral agreement in the 1970s, by 1992 that figure had fallen to 34 percent. At least fourteen major industry agreements have collapsed since 1986, covering 1.2 million workers, including buses, banking, food trades, and, most spectacularly, engineering.[23] One should also note the overwhelming preference of new firms, particularly foreign-owned firms for single-employer bargaining.[24] Only very rarely would a newly created firm opt to join an industry agreement.

The second theme is a greater preference for various forms of flexibility. There is evidence of very significant changes in working practices in the course of the 1980s. During the decade, three-quarters of collective bargaining groups introduced changes in working practices, and there was an acceleration in the signing of these flexibility agreements as the decade progressed.[25] The great bulk of flexibility agreements concerned changes in working practices. Employers have also sought greater use of part-time workers, and pay flexibility.[26]

The third theme is a changed relationship with trade unions. There has been some outright derecognition, as employers chose not to recognize one or more unions for collective bargaining purposes. Research indicates something over 400 cases of successful derecognition in the past decade, covering an estimated 150,000 workers. The number has been clearly accelerating over time with five times as many cases in 1988-94 as in 1984-88. Derecognition tends to be concentrated among nonmanual, managerial, and professional grades, and a small number of industries with particularly poor industrial relations, like printing, the oil industry, ports, and shipping.[27] Still, this kind of outright withdrawal of union recognition remains limited. The great bulk of the decline in union recognition has come from the disappearance of firms which recognized trade unions and the overwhelming preference of new employers to either dispense with union representation altogether or to rationalize their relations with unions, by reducing the number of unions recognized for collective bargaining purposes. ACAS argued that most new cases of union recognition since the mid-1980s have involved "single unionism," where one union receives exclusive recognition. Single unionism allows an employer to play one union against another as they compete for recognition, which probably explains why single union agreements are often associated with wide-ranging flexibility agreements. Moreover, single unionism is a weak form of unionism; it is much more likely to be associated with partial, rather than full, recognition and with lower levels of membership than traditional unionism.[28]

A fourth theme might be labeled a preference for the individualization of industrial relations. The term "Human Resource Management" (HRM) is often used in this context, though it may obscure more than it clarifies. The radicalism of the broad goals outlined by employer associations is remarkable.[29] The Institute of Directors has called for the almost complete individualization of industrial relations, meaning individual pay contracts and merit pay in place of national agreements and collective bargaining; employee shareholding; individualized training; and either the elimination of any role for trade unions, or, a minimalist role in which trade unions provide services for their members but do not engage in collective bargaining and have a limited right to strike.[30] The Confederation of British Industry (CBI) is scarcely less radical with its call for an "individualization of workplace relations."[31] The CBI sees a continued role for shop stewards, but again a very limited role for trade unions external to the firm.[32] This implies, where unions continue to exist, something akin to enterprise unions, though employers do not use the term.

What is most striking about the industrial relations practices of employers is their hostility toward the panoply of new forms of worker participation, works councils, quality circles, and other forms of consultation, indeed toward *collective* representation of any kind. Employers have consistently objected to EU proposals for statutory worker participation, arguing that employee consultation must be voluntary and flexible.[33] WIRS3 found that the various forms of employee involvement are deeply underdeveloped in Britain, with less collective representation of any kind than in the past, and the emphasis instead being upon one-way communication between managers and the workforce. The conclusion was that:

> Britain is approaching the position where few employees have any mechanism through which they can contribute to the operation of their workplace in a broader context than their own job. There is no sign that the shrinkage in the extent of trade union representation is being offset by a growth in other methods of representing non-managerial employee interests and views. There has been no spontaneous emergence of an alternative model of employee representation that could channel and attenuate conflicts between employers and employees.[34]

Thus, with the erosion of collective bargaining and trade unionism, employers are not, for the most part, seeking alternative *collective* forms of representation, but rather informal and *individual* forms of consultation. This has been possible because Conservative legislation allowed employers to choose the type of industrial relations they wanted rather than encouraging any particular alternative.

Differences between industrial relations practice in foreign-owned and British-owned firms have been much commented upon since 1979, though, in fact, foreign-owned firms have always taken the lead in the import and diffusion of techniques and practices in Britain. In the 1980s Japanese firms have been seen as the industrial relations innovators. Their importance lies less in their numbers than in their distinctive style of industrial relations. Beginning with the 1981 agreement between Toshiba and the EETPU, Japanese firms have been associated with a package deal known as a "single union agreement" (SUA). The real innovation of SUAs, no one element of which is entirely new, lies in the package as a whole, which ties together most of the themes of new management practice in the 1980s. SUAs typically involve recognition of a single union; an agreement to exhaust all avenues of negotiation, mediation, and arbitration before recourse to a strike (often involving "pendulum arbitration"); a company council in which employees are directly represented alongside union officials; single status for all employees; and a comprehensive package of flexibility in which workers agree to a high level of functional flexibility. SUAs remain rare; nevertheless, this type of agreement has been tremendously influential in its linkage of representation to flexibility, and it caused the biggest conflict within the trade union movement in the past eighteen years.

Though studies have demonstrated some differences in the practices of British and foreign-owned firms,[35] it is questionable whether there are clear differences based on ownership. Just as there has been a convergence in industrial relations practice between public, recently privatized, and private sectors, so has there been a convergence within the private sector. A better indicator of the adoption of new industrial relations practice is the age of a firm and whether it exists on a "greenfield" site.

Overall, then, the environment facing trade unions has changed dramatically in the period since 1979. On every side – the international economy, labor force composition, the state, and employers – that environment has become more hostile for unions. These changes posed a long list of problems for British trade unions. The rest of this essay examines the ways in which they have responded.

Trade Union Strategies

The last decade has seen a wide-ranging process of strategic reevaluation on the part of the labor movement. Trade unions were slow to recognize their vulnerability and the scale of the crisis facing them after the Labour Party was defeated in the 1979 general election. Nevertheless by the end of the 1990s, trade union strategy had undergone a metamorphosis along almost every dimension. The changes were linked. Unions came to believe that they could not depend upon their own industrial strength and the resources that they had traditionally relied upon. Instead, all aspects of their activity – recruitment, collective bargaining, industrial action – required much stronger legal support. The labor movement now sees a wide range of legal rights, both for individual workers and for trade unions, as central to its basic function of protecting people at work. This strategic shift has entailed a series of other changes – in attitude toward the European Union, in recruitment activity, in collective bargaining, and so on.

Trade Unions and the Political Sphere

Trade unions in the 1980s and 1990s have faced an attack from the state upon both their political role and their market power. At the same time, their ability to deploy political resources in opposition to this attack has been removed by the electoral dominance of the Conservative Party and the absence of any alternative point of access to the political system. Trade unions responded in this period with an almost complete reformulation of their relationship with the political sphere. The response was twofold and contradictory. On the one hand unions moved away from political activity as their ties with the Labour Party weakened, and corporatist-style bargaining with the state collapsed. This shift was not simply a temporary response to the presence of a hostile government, but a strategic choice to focus more upon market activity and less upon attempting to influence policymaking. On the other hand, the *market* vulnerability of trade unions which was exposed in this period, forced a shift away from voluntarism to support for a wide range of legislative props for union action. Thus by the early 1990s voluntarism was, for all intents and purposes, dead, as the trade union movement committed itself to a remarkable juridification of both individual and collective relations at work.

Faced with Conservative hostility, the policy of the TUC toward the government was initially equally hostile. In 1982, at the Wembley Conference, the TUC declared a policy of noncooperation with the government and its legislation, the second major package of which had just been passed. Noncooperation with legislation had served the TUC well after the 1971 Industrial Relations Act, but Conservative legislation in the 1980s did not require unions to register as the earlier legislation had done, and this was utilized by individual employers (who were cautious in using the legislation in the first few years) rather than by the government. As a result, TUC noncooperation in practice came down to refusing to accept government funding for the balloting requirements contained in the legislation. This was not only symbolic; it was expensive, and it provoked a series of rows within the TUC.

Within a very short time hostility gave way to an attempt to reach an accommodation. At the TUC conference in 1983 a doctrine known as the "New Realism" was introduced. This referred both to a more compromising attitude vis-à-vis employers, and to a willingness to talk to the government and to other opposition parties. However, the New Realism was stillborn with respect to more harmonious relations with the Thatcher government. Thatcher did not display the slightest interest in opening up discussions with the TUC. This was most clearly demonstrated when the government declared a staff union illegal at GCHQ. Here the TUC, in the spirit of the New Realism, offered a compromise which would have allowed the union to remain, but only with a no-strike pledge. The government rejected the compromise and the brief flicker of an alternative relationship between the Conservative government and the trade union movement was extinguished.

A decade later, however, when Thatcher was replaced by John Major and the Labour Party was defeated for the fourth time, there was a cautious return to the New Realism on the part of the TUC. In mid-1993 the new secretary-general of the TUC, John Monks, called for talks with the government, and this culminated in March 1994 in a full-blown declaration by the TUC, as part of its "re-launch," that it would no longer privilege its ties with the Labour Party but would seek to be a campaigning body, attempting to talk to and influence any party and any government. The aim of the TUC is:

> to refocus its links with Whitehall and Parliament in order to maximise its influence on public policy. It [the TUC] needs to build understanding of trade union work and objectives right across the political spectrum. While maintaining close links with the Labour Party and the broader labour Movement, the TUC is, therefore, actively seeking to extend its influence across the other major political parties.[36]

The character and form of the relationship between the trade union movement and the Labour Party has been at the center of their respective political identities. The Conservative Party came to power in 1979 claiming that the closeness of the unions to the Labour Party made the latter unfit to govern, and was a large part of the explanation for British economic decline. For both the Labour Party and the unions, the memory of the collapsed Social Contract and the Winter of Discontent had a crucial part in shaping behavior in the 1980s and 1990s. Union leaders took as its lesson that wage restraint was inevitably a one-sided bargain that could only weaken them inside their own unions, and the Labour leadership saw themselves cast as a sectional party, in hock to the unions, and unfit to govern. In addition, the material base of the party-union relationship has been undermined by the shifting social bases of unions and party, and the terms of political exchange have been changed by the economic problems associated with incomes policies, which had been the centerpiece of the relationship between the unions and the Labour Party.[37]

From 1983 onwards, after Neil Kinnock became party leader, the unions and the party grew steadily apart as the party's leadership came to see ties to the unions as an electoral liability. While earlier efforts to shed its "cloth cap" image largely failed, "New Labour" has replaced the language of class with the language of citizenship and consumption, and replaced a collectivist discourse with an individualist one. In a very basic sense the centerpiece of the party's attempt to "modernize" its image has been its distancing from the unions. After the 1992 election defeat the issue of union institutional power within the party erupted as a major crisis. The new party leader, John Smith, won a reduction in union influence at the 1993 party conference by the narrowest of margins. The change was crucial in retrospect because the new voting system enabled Tony Blair to be elected party leader in July 1994, after Smith died unexpectedly.

It is still early in the Blair government, but not too early to judge its likely impact on trade union power and influence. Blair is unquestionably more hostile toward trade union influence, in the Labour Party and in the economy, than any previous postwar leader, and there appears to be a cultural chasm between union officials and those close to the Labour leader.[38] "New Labour" simply does not like unions, and does not appear to recognize their value. Blair has recruited prominent employers from British Petroleum, Barclays, the Prudential, and British Airways – some of them recently embroiled in strikes – to run key government task forces, but no significant trade unionist has entered the government.

The Labour government has genuinely embraced the macroeconomic prescriptions of neo-liberalism, particularly price stability, as evidenced by the grant of independence to the Bank of England. Labour's commitment to controlling inflation by monetary policy and, eventually, Economic and Monetary Union, also obviates the need for the quid pro quo that was at the heart of the postwar relationship between the unions and the Labour Party: wage restraint for a voice in public policy. Since 1979, unions have consistently rejected any notion of an incomes policy with a future Labour government. A combination of the more decentralized unions (which would have the greatest difficulty in encouraging wage restraint), those representing more skilled and hence better paid workers (who tend to lose most from wage restraint), and public sector unions (which bear the brunt of incomes policies), was more than enough to defeat any such proposals. This reflects the huge structural obstacles to the unions delivering an incomes policy. Trade unions themselves are highly decentralized, added to which, collective bargaining has become (as Ron Todd of the Transport and General Workers Union put it) "too decentralized, too close to the point of production, too democratic in the broadest sense of the term, to be amenable to the sort of simple wage restraint arithmetic which has been the traditional basis of incomes policies."[39] New Labour has also repeatedly stressed the importance it attaches to labor market flexibility, to the point of using the EU as a forum to preach its virtues to other European leaders, and it has made clear that it has no intention of reversing privatization.

This is not the place for a comprehensive account of Labour industrial relations policy, but its trajectory is now clear, particularly since the publication of the White Paper, *Fairness at Work*, in May 1998.[40] Broadly, Labour Party policy has moved toward the provision of positive rights at work, though even here action is limited because of the commitment to labor market flexibility. Blair reneged on Smith's pledge of full employment rights from the first day of employment, opting instead for a reduction in the qualifying period necessary to claim unfair dismissal to one year, and a smattering of other minor individual rights at work. A low pay commission was created to investigate the level for a minimum wage. The hourly rate set by the government is a full pound (1.67 dollars) lower than unions had been hoping for, with a still lower rate for young workers. The government has signed Britain up for the Social Chapter, while pledging not to extend European social rights in such way that they limit flexibility, and promising to block further consultation rights. For the most part, the new government's gestures have been welcome but symbolic, the restoration of union rights at GCHQ, for example.

A statutory right to union recognition, which is the cornerstone of trade union legislative demands (see below) was initially delayed as the government encouraged the TUC and CBI to reach agreement before legislating. That dialogue failed, and a furious debate erupted inside the Cabinet over whether the Labour election manifesto pledge to recognize a union where "a majority of the relevant workforce" wanted it, should be interpreted to mean a majority of those voting, or a majority of the bargaining unit (with abstentions therefore counting as "no" votes). The White Paper opted for a high threshold of participation in any recognition ballot (to win, unions will need a majority of those voting and at least 40 percent of those eligible to vote), and excluded small firms (employing less than 20 workers) from the legislation. The battle over this piece of legislation has set the tone for government-union relations for the first term of this Labour government. Despite the limited gains for workers and unions from Labour legislation thus far, Blair has made it clear that no further industrial relations legislation is planned until after the next election.

Labour is mirroring the shift in its industrial relations policy with an institutional shift away from direct union participation in the party. Since Blair's election to the party leadership, union sponsorship of Labour MPs has been abolished, the union vote at party conferences has been reduced, and a series of well-orchestrated leaks in the second half of 1996 have suggested that the Labour Party plans to further reduce the institutional role of the unions inside the party. The 1997 party conference passed the document *Partnership into Power*, which proposed a radical restructuring of policymaking within the party; this would shift power to a new Joint Policy Committee in which unions would be marginalized.[41] It is also worth noting that union donations made up only 45 percent of Labour Party funds in 1996, down from 76 percent in 1986 (with the balance coming from a huge increase in fundraising from nonmembers), suggesting that even the financial dependency of the party on the unions is being reduced.[42]

The relationship between the unions and the Labour Party has fundamentally changed both in form and content. Arthur Scargill's creation of a Socialist Labour Party, to challenge the Labour Party, has little appeal to the bulk of the trade union movement, but there is a deep-seated sense that unions cannot and should not rely upon a privileged relationship with the Labour Party in the future. The TUC announcement, in March 1994, of its intention to broaden political contacts beyond the Labour Party (an announcement which the Labour Party welcomed) was thus the culmination of twenty years of disappointment with the party-union relationship, and a decade in which the trade unions and the Labour Party have drifted apart.

So, for reasons beyond the control of organized labor, the period since 1979 has seen the near collapse of the dominant trade union political strategy of the postwar period, which is to say, the attempt to develop access to a friendly government and use political exchange, or simply political negotiation, to achieve policies that were in the interests of unions. Corporatism, in short, died after 1979. Instead, trade union political strategy has undergone a shift which entails a fundamental change in the way in which trade unions view the role of law in industrial relations.

Rights at Work

British trade unions have traditionally, and famously, opposed the intervention of law into the sphere of industrial relations, preferring to rely upon union strength and collective bargaining to achieve their ends. The ideology which opposed state intervention and the juridification of industrial relations has been called "voluntarism." There has always been a certain mythology about voluntarism. It has tended to be an anti-court rather than anti-state doctrine, reflecting the deep hostility of British courts toward trade unions, and it has on occasion drawn a distinction between protective and punitive legislation. Nevertheless, voluntarism did indicate deep misgivings about the ability of legislation to influence the conduct of industrial relations.

Voluntarism is now effectively dead, as the TUC has endorsed embedding a wide range of individual and collective rights at work in legislation. In part this was driven by external political events. Conservative hostility and Labour coolness forced unions to recognize that they need a protective legal environment that is independent of whichever party is in power.[43] But there is more to this shift than simply a reaction to the end of corporatist bargaining and the deregulation of the labor market. It is also, and more importantly, the result of a strategic reevaluation of the sources of union strength in the workplace. The 1980s demonstrated the vulnerability of British unions to employer hostility. This vulnerability is not new, but in the 1970s it was masked by government support and a reluctance on the part of employers to disrupt peaceful industrial relations. By the end of the 1980s, however, it was clear that unions simply could not force employers to recognize them, that recruitment policies were yielding limited new members, and that bargaining agendas were now dominated by the concerns of employers.

In this context a new strategy emerged in which industrial relations legislation came to play a role in redefining the role of trade unions, and in aiding in the recruitment of new members. The strategy involves using the establishment of new individual rights at work to undergird collective bargaining. As John Edmonds of the GMB puts it:

> We must accept that within the next decade trade unions are not going to be in a position to force contract cleaners, for example, to pay reasonable pay and conditions through traditional trade union organization ... That means you have got to rely on the law to create minimum rights for the people who work in those industries ... and this will help us organizationally in these industries very substantially indeed. Because we can then go to the workers in a particular establishment and say, 'look, these are your legal rights. Are you getting them?' And if the answer is 'no,' we

> can say, 'join us, we can make bloody sure that your employer does what he has to.'[44]

Thus, unions will serve as enforcers of these new rights. This strategy recognizes that unions have been largely unsuccessful in organizing the low-paid and female workers, and that they therefore will have no protection unless it is provided by legislation. The provision of basic minimum rights enshrined in legislation then provides a wedge for unions to build upon.

A final factor in explaining this strategic shift lies in the changing balance of power within the TUC. It has traditionally been the industrial craft unions which have opposed the juridification of industrial relations, in the belief that minimum rights at work are of little interest to their members, while white-collar and public-sector unions, which organize a disproportionate amount of the low-paid, women and black workers, have wanted the establishment of legislative protection. The weight of the trade union movement has shifted toward public-sector and white-collar unions. Furthermore, a 1982 reform of the manner in which the TUC General Council is chosen led to greater representation for white-collar and public-sector unions, and hence their greater influence in policymaking.[45]

In any case, the result has been that after a lengthy process of consultation at various points in the 1980s and 1990s, the TUC is now committed to a new framework of labor law, including a statutory national minimum wage, equal rights to full-time and part-time workers, restrictions on the length of the workweek, a right to union recognition, new rights to organize in the workplace, and, most importantly of all, the right of all workers to some kind of collective representation. These are all policies which the TUC rejected in the past, and taken together, they amount to a tremendous shift in the political strategy of British unions.

While there is now widespread agreement on a minimum wage and rights for atypical workers, the issue of collective labor rights remains a divisive element of any new framework of labor law. Statutory union recognition and the possibility of nonunion employee representation – and by implication, the creation for the first time in Britain of statutory works councils of some kind – divides British trade unions because it raises the thorny question of who represents whom.[46] Unions have a long history of suspicion to alternative or dual institutions of representation in the firm. They have painfully constructed mechanisms – disputes procedures in the TUC, workplace joint consultative committees, joint shop steward committees – to manage multi-unionism during the twentieth century, and in this context, alternative forms of representation are likely to be seen as a threat which will certainly disrupt existing forms of union coexistence, and possibly threaten union representation altogether.

The 1980s saw unions forced to confront the issue of alternative employee representation. In large part this was driven by the industrial relations practices of inward investors – Japanese firms usually wanted company or works councils alongside unions – and the threat, or opportunity, of European Union directives concerning employee representation and access to information in the firm. A strong undercurrent of opposition to alternative forms of worker representation remains within the trade union movement. Nevertheless, the pressure of external events, and enthusiasm from within the TUC bureaucracy, has led to increasing momentum on the issue. The 1995 TUC Congress supported a TUC policy document, *Your Voice at Work*, proposing three statutory levels of employee representation: an individual right for all workers to be represented by a trade union, with accompanying organizational rights for trade unions in the workplace; the collective right of a firm's workforce to consultation; and union recognition and collective bargaining rights for unions after a majority vote in a ballot.[47] The intermediate level of consultation rights can be exercised either through union representation or the creation of a workplace consultative body, akin to a works council.

For the first time in their history, then, British unions are committed to a very significant juridification of industrial relations – including both individual and collective rights. The obvious problem, prior to the arrival of a Labour government, was how to put this new political strategy into place. In response, the unions looked for an alternative political arena in which to seek the legislative protection that they could not win from the British government. This led British unions to embrace the EU, marking the second shift in union political strategy.

Hostility toward European integration has run deep in the British labor movement. After the 1975 referendum, during which the TUC campaigned for a "No" vote, the TUC supported integration; but support was only skin deep, and hostility resurfaced after Labour lost power in 1979. This view of Europe derived for the most part from a commitment to a national Keynesian model of economic management, and a hostility to the language of free trade and free markets which underpin the Treaty of Rome.[48]

The conversion of the bulk of British unions to support of European integration had a number of sources. There were economic reasons for becoming more involved in Europe, particularly for unions like BIFU, concerned about financial deregulation, and public-sector unions like NUPE, concerned about public procurement.[49] More generally, many unions felt by the end of the 1980s that British capitalism was in such a state of crisis that there was much to learn from the rest of Europe, whether on issues of training policy, the coordination of wage bargaining, or even a more cooperative form of industrial relations. Comparisons with Europe became much more widespread in this period. However, the main reason for the sudden enthusiasm in trade union circles for European integration was clearly political. Europe was "the only game in town" at a time when the Thatcher government was impermeable to union interests. Thus it provided the potential to do an end-run around the nation-state, and win legislative protection which could not be won at the national level.

The unions' main interest in European integration was to gain European legislation providing new forms of protection to British workers in the firm. Hence their interest in the Social Charter and then the Social Chapter. However, the British opt-out limited the utility of this strategy. In fact, the most promising aspect of European integration for British unions has been its judicial impact. The 1993 Trade Union Reform and Employment Rights Act was not simply a government initiative. A whole range of its provisions were, in effect, forced on the government to bring it into line with European law.[50] Two recent decisions in the House of Lords have used the 1972 directive on equal treatment as the basis for wide-ranging challenges to government attempts to reduce employment protection, partially reversing government deregulation of the labor market.

The way in which British trade unions view the political sphere has changed markedly. Within a year of becoming secretary general of the TUC, John Monks "re-launched" the TUC in March 1994 with much fanfare. The TUC was to become more political but less partisan. Its goal was to establish legitimacy across the political spectrum as a lobbyist on behalf of the trade union movement. Trade unions have come to recognize their vulnerability in the labor market and to seek a wide range of legislative supports for industrial activity. That British trade unions should now contemplate a framework of labor law which includes a range of individual rights at work, where previously they favored the collective negotiation of substantive outcomes; and a set of collective rights including statutory union recognition and works councils, where previously they rejected any challenge to their monopoly on employee representation, is nothing short of remarkable.

This set of strategic developments suggests a partial shift in the focus of union activity away from collective bargaining toward a role as legal experts, enforcers of legal rights which represent their members in court rather than in collective bargaining. The priority unions have given to the use of EU directives demonstrate that unions are now seeking to win in the courts what they cannot win through bargaining. Unions had limited success protecting their members during privatization, or incorporating equality issues into collective bargaining; but now they are hoping to use European legislation to achieve the same ends. The TUC sees legislation as "supporting and underpinning, and not replacing and undermining, structured collective bargaining,"[51] but the obvious question is what role workers will see for trade unions once their rights are enshrined in legislation instead of resulting from the collective bargaining activities of their unions, particularly if legislation brings entirely new forms of worker representation.

Organizational Restructuring

Economic restructuring, and the increased state and employer hostility toward unions that accompanied it, posed a series of organizational problems for the established structures of trade unionism. The decentralization of collective bargaining, government legislation on the internal workings of trade unions, European integration and the necessity of supranational action, and the preference of employers for different relationships with their employees, especially single unionism, all forced trade unions into organizational change. Furthermore, British unions tended to respond organizationally to problems which were not necessarily organizational in origin. For example, union mergers and single unionism emerged as central strategic responses to the difficulty encountered in increasing union recruitment. Trade unions often preferred organizational change to more fundamental change in union goals and practices.

There have been important and contradictory changes in trade union structures, toward both decentralization (and the development of new union competencies at the local level), and a concentration and centralization of trade unionism. Overall, however, decentralizing tendencies have been fairly limited. While the decentralization of collective bargaining has continued and extended during the 1980s and 1990s, this has not posed serious problems for British trade unions because private-sector trade unions in Britain are used to bargaining locally and have been doing so since the 1950s and 1960s; and because many unions had already engaged in a parallel decentralization of their own organizations in order to take advantage of the change in bargaining levels. British unions underwent a "radical democratization" in the period since the 1960s, as lay participation in bargaining expanded and deepened.[52] The union structures inherited from the past were already remarkably decentralized.

Vertical authority was weak both within the TUC itself and within most individual unions, and trade unions tended to have relatively small administrative structures and to have limited financial resources, making them reliant upon shop stewards and small numbers of officers.

It is true that unlike in the earlier period, unions have been much more critical of decentralization. However, this reflects the concerns of public-sector unions far more than private-sector unions, and it reflects fears not of decentralization per se, but of decentralization in the context of higher levels of employer hostility to trade unions, and the absence of state supports for trade unionism. Firm-level bargaining now takes place under conditions of persistent high unemployment, severe legal restrictions on industrial action, and employer and state ambivalence or outright opposition to dealing with unions. In fact, the main fear of trade unions is not so much that decentralization will lead to lower wage settlements or flexibility agreements, as that it will encourage union derecognition. Once an employer withdraws from an industry negotiating body, there is the risk that he or she might choose not to recognize one or all of the unions that were represented in the industry body. This is a fine opportunity for an employer to "rationalize" collective bargaining by moving to single unionism. Again, this is most acute in the public sector, or former public sector, where the negotiating structure was immensely complicated and entirely new employers have been created (the hospital trusts, regional water authorities, etc.). The big advantage of multi-employer bargaining for unions has always been that it simplifies the task of trade unions seeking recognition. The primary response of public-sector unions to the decentralization of bargaining has been organizational, in the form of the merger of the three largest public-sector unions to create UNISON. The effect will be to make derecognition very difficult.

Decentralization has been offset by other organizational changes. Faced with a hemorrhage of union members, British trade unions have sought to limit interunion competition and rationalize their organizations. In this respect, probably the most dramatic organizational change of the period since 1979 has been the pace of merger and amalgamation activity. In 1979 there were 441 unions, of which 109 were affiliated with the TUC. The largest five unions had 47 percent of TUC membership. There are now 254 unions, 68 of them affiliated to the TUC, and the largest five unions have 63 percent of TUC membership.[53] The real organizational importance of mergers in the 1980s and 1990s has been the mergers between two or more large and influential unions, with the subsequent creation of what have been called "super unions." Major union mergers created a general public sector union (UNISON), a general technical union (MSF), a joint engineering and electricians' union (AEEU), a joint transportation union (RMT), a combined communications union (CWU), and a combined print union (GMPU).

The reasons for this remarkable recourse to mergers by trade unions are various, though the most important impulse is defensive. That is to say, mergers are being driven by membership loss and the attempt to respond to employer and state offensives against unions. In a period of membership loss, the potential financial savings from merging union structures and reducing the duplication of union servicing seems attractive. Mergers can also reduce destructive competition from other unions. BIFU, which pursued a strategy of amalgamations of staff associations in banking and finance, rather than merger with other sizeable unions, was motivated primarily by the fierce competition in those industries and the traditional use that employers made of staff associations to bypass or undermine BIFU. In the public sector the most important factor in the UNISON merger was government restructuring and the consequent threat to union recognition from the breakup of national public services and the resultant decentralization of bargaining. There are also strategic reasons for merger. The GMB has adopted the closest one can find to a strategic approach to mergers. It sought merger partners in areas where it was hoping to increase recruitment, for example, the white-collar union APEX.

It is extremely difficult to evaluate the success of merger as a trade union strategy. Trade union organizations that merged survived, but it is unclear if any further benefits accrued. The main mergers of the period under discussion experienced a series of problems which hampered the ability of unions to take advantage of the organizational change. Mergers involve attempting to make a single structure out of two unions with different structures, histories, and cultures. This proved to be so difficult that the AEU and EETPU, after several failed attempts at merger, were only finally successful because they agreed to merge first and agree upon the merged structure later. In a number of mergers, traditionally decentralized unions merged with more centralized unions, creating worries about the degree of lay participation in the new union.[54]

One result of the wave of merger activity has been the further weakening of the TUC and the increased concentration of union members in a handful of unions. The fragmentation of British trade unionism is, as a result, being partially overcome. But the new structure of trade unionism is not along industrial lines, for the most part, but along general lines. It is possible, as the TUC and ACAS have argued, that the impact of new technology and multiskilling makes general unions the most appropriate form of unionism for a post-Fordist economy,[55] but if so, that end is being achieved by accident rather than design. One last question mark hangs over the long-term impact of mergers. It remains to be seen whether workers will feel comfortable and be able to develop a sense of identity and solidarity inside superunions shared with workers from numerous occupations and industries. Smaller unions which can encourage a professional identity may be more successful in retaining members than larger unions.

An alternative to limiting competition from other unions by merger is to seek exclusive union recognition agreements with employers. These single union agreements (SUAs) assumed increasing prominence as the 1980s progressed, though there is some evidence of a slackening pace in recent years. One can question whether this is correctly labeled a trade union or an employer strategy. Employers clearly preferred to deal with a single union if they were going to deal with unions at all. But it was also a conscious union strategy, aimed at capturing new membership. Unions which were associated with SUAs, the EETPU, and to a lesser extent, the AEU (which helps to explain why merger was possible between them) argued that these were the only kind of union recognition agreements that employers would sign – particularly inward investors – and so, pragmatically, it was better to have some union representation than none. This kind of agreement created a critical problem for British trade unionism. SUAs were not so much a labor management problem as an interunion problem. The overlapping structure of multi- unionism in Britain, and the absence of clear industrial spheres of union influence, ensured that this would be a deeply conflictual issue.

Union objections to these agreements were that unions engage in "beauty contests" before employers to win recognition, and hence that the decision of which union is to represent workers is made by the employer rather than the workers, resulting in a strong incentive to make "sweetheart" agreements in order to win exclusive recognition. Moreover such agreements negotiate away basic rights (the right to strike) of workers. A union can promise an employer such an agreement in order to poach members in firms or areas where other unions have traditionally been recognized.

The TUC was forced to step into the dispute over SUAs by unions which had lost members to the EETPU. The EETPU was expelled from the TUC in 1988 for a series of technical violations and because the general secretary of the EETPU, Eric Hammond, showed no interest in a compromise. The Special Review Body (SRB) was set up to look into the general issue of responses to membership loss. The first report of the SRB made a series of recommendations, including a code of practice aimed at encouraging unions to consult with other unions that might be affected by their recruitment activities.

The TUC also recommended "single table bargaining" as a solution to the problems of multi-unionism. This simply meant that in firms where multiple unions were recognized for collective bargaining purposes they would endeavor to all bargain at the same time, around a "single table." This strategy would only work, of course, if the primary motivation of employers for SUAs was to limit the complexity of collective bargaining with several unions. If, on the other hand, employers liked the kinds of substantive concessions which they were able to extract from exclusive recognition agreements, single table bargaining was unlikely to solve the problem.

The recourse to mergers and single union agreements indicates a preference on the part of British trade unions for what has been called "market share" unionism, meaning that unions have been inclined to increase or maintain union membership through mergers or single union agreements, which primarily redistribute union members from one union to another, rather than increasing the overall number of trade union members. Given the cost of recruitment, particularly in a period of heightened employer hostility, privileging an organizational response to membership decline in this way makes a certain amount of sense. But it is also a continuation of the long-standing reliance of trade unions upon employer recognition, and a reluctance to launch large-scale recruitment drives.

Mergers also helped to diminish the TUC's role. It had been greatly enhanced in the late 1960s and 1970s by virtue of its role as interlocutor with the government during a period of incomes policies. But this source of the TUC's influence disappeared when corporatism, however fragile it had been in the past, was effectively killed off in the 1980s. The increased pace of union mergers and the creation of superunions, which permitted much of the work of coordination and even dispute resolution to be done bilaterally, also reduced the influence of the TUC.

For these two reasons, the TUC's main roles have somewhat changed. Despite bilateralism, the main role played by the TUC, as we saw, has been mediating interunion disputes. The TUC also played an important role in developing union strategy, particularly with regard to member services and new recruitment. Finally, the conversion of the TUC and many British unions to support for European integration created a new role for the TUC because it was an obvious area of competence for a peak organization, which undoubtedly contributed to the TUC's enthusiasm for Europe. Those inside the TUC bureaucracy immediately saw a new role for the TUC in Europe, one that could compensate for its declining role elsewhere.

The TUC undertook a series of organizational changes including some internal restructuring of the research departments, the creation of a "Committee on European Strategy" to coordinate European policy within the TUC, and a "European Network," which brings together a representative of each union to discuss European issues. The TUC has also expanded its organizational resources devoted to Europe by creating a Brussels office with a full-time officer, and by starting a regular bulletin, "Network Europe Update." The overall effect of this reorganization has been to make the TUC much better able to gain information about European developments and respond to them; and it has provided, in a very short period of time, a high degree of expertise on European issues.

As the 1980s progressed, criticism of the TUC from the larger trade unions increased. The duplication of function, as large unions felt better able to perform many of the services and coordinating activities of the TUC, and the expense of affiliation fees played a part in this growing disenchantment. But more important was a sense that far too much of the TUC's time and energy was directed toward servicing its own bureaucracy. A series of union leaders became more outspoken in their criticisms, calling for a "slimmed-down" body, and for a focus upon a smaller number of tasks which individual unions could not carry out themselves. The March 1994 relaunch of the TUC saw a dramatic restructuring of the TUC. All policymaking and industry committees were suspended or abolished, and their powers transferred to the finance and general purposes committee, renamed the "Executive Committee."[56] These reforms imply a more streamlined, more focused peak organization, with much less emphasis upon general research activities. They also concentrate power in the hands of the general-secretary and the new Executive Committee, which is smaller than the General Council, represents fewer unions than the General Council, and has no reserved seats for women. This new role clearly conforms to the wishes of the larger trade unions, which see a limited role for the TUC. But it poses real problems for smaller trade unions, which, throughout the debate on TUC structure, have argued that many activities are more efficiently carried out by the TUC. This feeds into a fear that in an era of a weak TUC and a few super-unions, smaller unions will lose their autonomy and become "satellites" to those larger unions.

The period since 1979 has seen a major restructuring of the British trade union movement. This process of organizational reconfiguration has resulted in contradictory tendencies. If there is a common tendency it is toward an erosion of workplace organization as the core locus of union activity. This tendency is consistent with the argument that there has been a general shift from "participative" to "managerial" unionism, as union power and activity shift both upwards to the leadership and downwards to individual union members who exercise "voice" through postal ballots completed in the isolation of the home, separated from work and the workplace.[57]

Recruitment

Trade unions have faced a number of problems in the area of membership recruitment in the last eighteen years. To a certain extent these problems were not new. British unions have historically been relatively weak at recruiting new members, and the diffusion of the dues check-off mechanism and the early emergence of workplace bargaining tended to encourage union activists, and particularly stewards, to think of themselves as negotiators rather than recruiters. In addition, long-term structural economic change was expanding precisely those areas of employment – private services, industries traditionally dominated by female wage earners, atypical work – where unions were most weakly implanted, and where unions had employed the fewest resources for recruitment. In this period the only growth in union members came among women, and the only unions to either increase their membership or avoid catastrophic losses were those unions which recruited heavily in industries and occupations dominated by women.[58] Female union recruitment thus became necessary for survival.

The TUC played an important part in defining the recruitment problem facing unions, which was addressed by the second report of the SRB the TUC set up in 1987.[59] Reviewing labor market trends, it showed that unions were relatively weakly implanted among some of the fastest growing categories of worker, particularly women, young workers, part-time workers, and highly skilled managerial and professional workers. The TUC proceeded with two pilot projects, one in Manchester's Trafford Park and the other in London Docklands, combining detailed local labor market analysis with multi-union organizing campaigns. They are widely recognized to have been a failure, however, with enormous expenditure of resources for few new recruits. The TUC also took the lead in popularizing the notion of aggressive organizing drives as part of its "New Unionism" project. Speakers from the AFL-CIO have become frequent guests at TUC conferences, and in 1998 the TUC set up an "Organising Academy," explicitly modeled on the AFL-CIO's "Organizing Institute."

The TUC itself made a series of structural changes designed to accommodate new categories of workers better than in the past. The mode of election of the General Council was reformed twice. The first reform, in 1982, increased the representation of white-collar and public-sector unions. The second, in 1989, doubled the number of seats reserved for women from six to twelve, though it did this by increasing the total number of General Council seats by five. The TUC also set up an Equal Rights Department in 1988, and gave a higher profile to the annual TUC Women's Conference. Black trade unionists also received reserved seats on the TUC General Council in 1994. However, with the reorganization of the TUC in March 1994, which downgraded the importance of the General Council, it is unclear how valuable its reserved seats now are.

Individual trade unions responded to membership loss in a wide variety of ways, and recruitment became a major focus of union activity from the mid-1980s onwards, when it became clear that union losses were not going to be easily reversed. "Designer unionism," involving the use of public relations firms to design new logos and names (GMB, MSF, for example, and UNISON, which does not stand for anything at all, but is designed to give a warm, cuddly sense of solidarity), was one minor element of this overall strategy. Mainly, it involved two kinds of action. One was the development of a service model of trade unionism which focused union activity upon the provision of membership services. The other, by far the most important, though also the least successful, was new recruitment, particularly of specific underunionized categories of worker.

British unions have placed a great deal of emphasis upon the provision of membership services – the most important of which have been financial and legal – in response to the difficulty in attracting and retaining members. At its most straightforward this is simply an attempt to overcome the free rider problem by tying a wide range of services to membership, though there is limited evidence that workers consider such services an important reason for joining a union.[60] There is another more radical notion of service unionism. Membership services tend to refer to benefits which are entirely peripheral to unions' day-to-day activity. The notion of "service unionism," however envisages a change in the workplace role of trade unions. They would become less collective bargaining agents on behalf of groups of workers than outside experts, engaged by individual workers, to provide advice and help at work. So, for example, legal issues at work – unfair dismissal, discrimination of various kinds – are an obvious area where workers might seek advice from a union on their rights at work, and retain that union to prepare a case against the employer at an Industrial Tribunal. The connection between this conception of the role of trade unions and the greater interest that many unions now show in the juridification of individual rights at work is clear. The presence of such rights is a precondition for service unionism.

Service unionism, understood in this fashion, has two important implications. The first is that it can exist and thrive where unions are not recognized by employers and have no collective bargaining rights. When unions are primarily collective bargaining agents there is no incentive for workers to join a union unless that union is recognized or is likely to be recognized for collective bargaining purposes. However, workers might contemplate individual union membership if that membership brought with it a package of rights to legal advice and representation at work. Thus service unionism has the potential to provide unions with a role in new, expanding sectors where they have not been able to overcome employer opposition, or among categories of workers that have been resistant to unionization. The second implication is that this is an entirely different conception of trade unionism from the traditional one of union as collective bargainer and as representative of a collectivity of workers. Instead unions would be external to the firm, providing primarily legal services, and they would have an individual relationship with workers. It is important to stress that no one inside the labor movement is advocating service unionism as the exclusive function of trade unions. The hope of many unionists is that collective bargaining and service unionism can work in tandem, with service unionism giving unions a foothold inside the firm and encouraging union membership, so that trade unions can then gain union recognition and collective bargaining rights.

British unions most clearly took recruitment more seriously after 1979 with respect to women workers.[61] Broadly speaking this tended to involve three kinds of union response: reform of union internal structures, to make unions more hospitable to previously underunionized groups; a change in bargaining agendas; and a new articulation of collective bargaining and the law.

The most widespread internal reforms in the 1980s were the creation of equal opportunity structures for women. A number of unions have set up workplace, branch, or regional women's committees, organized women's conferences, or created reserved seats for women on various union policymaking bodies. USDAW, organizing in retail services, created national and divisional women's committees in 1986, with responsibility for monitoring bargaining agendas, developing policy on issues of particular concern to women, and encouraging the training and education of women inside the union. The GMB created a comprehensive equal rights structure from the branch to the national level, and also developed a "Women's Workplace Project" in order to train and encourage female union members to become more involved with union work. Perhaps the most comprehensive attempt to represent women more equally inside union structures is the organizational plan of UNISON, which organizes one-third of all women trade unionists in Britain. UNISON's structure promises proportionality (of female members to officers) at all levels of union organization by the year 2000, and it has a detailed equal opportunities structure.

For all this effort, however, women still remain underrepresented within union structures, particularly at the top. A 1994 study covering thirty eight trade unions, representing 96 percent of TUC-affiliated union members, found that while 66 percent of unions had a national women's committee or equality committee, only a small minority of unions (16 percent) had created reserved seats on the union executive for women, and only about half (47 percent) had a national women's officer or equality officer. Only a third of unions have women represented in the top policymaking body in the same proportion as membership, and there are actually fewer female union general secretaries now than five years ago.

The attempt to recruit new members, especially where recruitment was targeted at particular groups, also involved changes in union bargaining agendas. This aspect of union strategy is the hardest to assess because it is very difficult to see whether items which appear on a union bargaining agenda, and might be encouraged by the union leadership, actually form important parts of what negotiators press for. To a certain extent, the success of bargaining over equal opportunities depends upon the internal structural reforms discussed above, because there is evidence that female union representatives have somewhat different bargaining agendas than their male colleagues and are more likely to press issues of particular concern to women.[62]

Heery and Kelly, in a discussion of women full-time union officials, make the useful distinction between bargaining issues that directly affect women (for example, maternity leave, sexual harassment, cancer screening) and those that could affect any worker but disproportionately affect women by virtue of their concentration in certain occupations and industries, such as low pay, regrading, training, and new technology.[63] The GMB did make a comprehensive effort to move women's issues up the bargaining agenda in its "Winning a fair deal for women" campaign, begun in 1987. But by and large, unions seem much more comfortable negotiating over the indirect issues, that they can sell as gender-neutral to their male members and negotiators, than the direct issues.

Certain unions also focused attention upon part-time and temporary work, however, since women make up the overwhelming number of part-time workers, it is impossible to separate issues of gender from those of atypical work. The TGWU launched a major campaign, Link Up, aimed at temporary and part-time workers in 1987.[64] The campaign was nationally coordinated, involved more resources for recruitment, and attempted to link recruitment to changes in collective bargaining priorities. It also involved an attempt to project a different image for the TGWU – one which emphasized community and social justice more than in the past. The TGWU model agreement covering the use of atypical workers had the following as its main elements: a guarantee of a contract, union representation, an opportunity to become permanent employees, and equal *(pro rata)* pay and conditions as full-time permanent employees.

The central problem for this strategy, however, is that unions tend to be weakest in precisely those workplaces where women and atypical workers are employed, and hence, with the best will in the world, unions find it very difficult to bargain successfully on these issues. It is for this reason that unions increasingly look toward a new relationship between law and collective bargaining in order to permit gains to be made for traditionally underunionized, and economically precarious, groups in the workforce, despite union weakness. Union weakness in expanding areas of the workforce means that legislative protection is a precondition for union organization and collective bargaining.

The area where trade unions have been able to put this strategy into practice – given the absence of most of the minimum legislative rights that they want – is equal pay for work of equal value. This legislation, forced on the British government in 1983 by the European Community, has been a focus of union activity both because it enables unions to recruit women, and because it well illustrates the way in which a new relationship between law and collective bargaining would work. USDAW's relative success in recruiting new members at supermarkets is credited in part to its aggressive use of this legislation.[65]

In conclusion, a number of trade unions have made tremendous efforts to improve their ability to recruit. Those efforts were most serious in the area of recruiting women, and clearest in the prosecution of equal-pay cases and the reform of internal union structures in order to better represent women. In other words, where union leaders had control over strategy and where unions were not dependent upon sympathetic employers or the government for success, recruitment and representation had a much higher priority than in the past. However, the actual success of union recruitment strategies is much more difficult to identify. To a certain extent, the poor success of recruitment efforts can be explained by the difficulty which a union leadership can have in bringing about change when power is relatively decentralized within the trade union. One study of union officers suggests that officers feel greater accountability to members than their union superiors, creating a problem because members act as "insiders," seeking traditional trade union goals, while it is the leadership of unions who propose "a redirection of union policy and resources away from the existing membership towards groups of unorganized workers," and hence place a high priority upon recruitment and equal opportunities.[66] In other words, the decentralized and democratic nature of British trade unions poses an obstacle to new recruitment strategies.

But it would be a mistake to blame union resistance alone. The fortunes of USDAW illustrate the basic problem facing union recruitment efforts. Throughout the 1980s new members accounted for between one-fifth and one-third of USDAW's total membership every year. But its membership still fell by 20 percent over the decade because of the tremendously high turnover in the private service sector.[67] Similarly, the TGWU's Link Up campaign did not fail because of insufficient enthusiasm on the part of recruiters. It failed because recruiting part-time workers is extremely difficult, and, as with USDAW, there was high turnover. By 1990 the TGWU had come to believe that gaining employer recognition through changing its image was more likely to be effective than new recruitment. The problem for trade unions is the inhospitable nature of employers and the labor market in the areas into which they need to expand.

Social Partnership

Despite the increasing interest of British unions in providing member services, collective bargaining remains their primary activity, but it is one in which they faced a series of problems in the 1980s and 1990s. At the national level, as we saw, corporatist bargaining had never been well developed, and under the Conservatives it collapsed altogether. Collective bargaining decentralized further and for the first time affected the public sector. Much greater employer interest in human resources management (HRM), in the individualization of industrial relations, and in new ways of representing and organizing the workforce, all tended to bypass or marginalize collective bargaining. And where collective bargaining did continue to operate, persistent high unemployment weakened the bargaining power of unions and made workers reluctant to engage in strike action. This made resistance to a new agenda of employer concerns extremely difficult.

In this context trade unions were constantly on the defensive. Bargaining agendas were set primarily by employers while a range of union issues – training, equal opportunities, new technology, and environmental concerns – were difficult to get on the agenda, and even more difficult to win. The only exception was worktime reduction, where some successes were registered. By and large, union collective bargaining strategy during this period had two elements. First, where topics of interest to unions were concerned, strategy was premised on the attempt to extend collective bargaining into new areas through the use of model agreements. Second, where unions were faced with employer demands which potentially challenged their traditional role in the firm, union strategy aimed, at a minimum, to secure recognition. As one union official put it, the bottom line is that the union must retain its "place in the representational process ... all the rest we can live with."[68] Thus the goal was to minimize the individualizing features of HRM and the "new industrial relations."

Of increasing importance for trade unions in recent years has been the issue of how to respond to HRM. The term is imprecise, meaning different things to different people. Here it refers to the preference on the part of employers for creating direct channels of communication and representation, whether formal or informal, which bypass, or at least are not mediated by, unions. As argued earlier, British employers have shown little interest in the development of formal, collective institutions in the firm, but they have shown much greater interest in the management of their workforces and a reluctance to leave issues of personnel policy to collective bargaining. A 1992 survey of union officials found that there had been a wide, and increasing, experience of HRM initiatives.[69]

For the most part, the trade union response has been hostile.[70] Many unionists see HRM as having a high "degree of bullshit and fad."[71] The TUC commentary on quality circles as early as 1981 captures much of the skepticism and fear of trade unions, and the general response that unions tended to adopt.[72] Quality circles, it was argued, were not particularly new as an idea and did not amount to real representation or power for workers. They left managerial authority intact and created mechanisms for increasing the productivity of workers which bypass normal collective bargaining mechanisms. Unions were advised to accept quality circles only if their introduction was negotiated, if they did not challenge existing union machinery or practice, and if productivity gains were shared with workers.

So important is the issue of HRM that when the TUC was relaunched in early 1994, one of its three central tasks was to evaluate and formulate a response to HRM. The first report from the TUC used evidence from the 1990 Workplace Industrial Relations Survey to show that nonunion workplaces tended to have even fewer elements of HRM than union workplaces, and that union derecognition did not lead to alternative forms of employee consultation, let alone representation. As a result the TUC identified a "bad" and a "good" form of HRM. The bad form is a cover for avoiding unions and individualizing industrial relations, while the good form would "entail an extension of consultation with recognised trade unions, long term investment in training and a genuine attempt to develop social partnership."[73]

Nonetheless, for all the skepticism about HRM and the persistence of suspicion of alternative forms of worker representation, there has been a quite remarkable increase in support among trade unions for some kind of "social partnership" between unions and employers. In the most practical sense, the response of British trade unions to HRM has been to try to offer employers the cooperation that it is assumed they want, but without the baggage of "new industrial relations" which puts union representation at risk. The evidence for this conclusion is scattered, and still largely, though not exclusively, rhetorical, but this reflects a fear that unions and their leaders have of appearing too conciliatory and thereby losing credibility with their members and challengers within the union. Social partnership is still not a popular position within unions. It also reflects the fact that employers have shown very little interest in social partnership of the kind being offered by trade unions. However, driven by the TUC leadership, European developments, and growing pessimism about the competitiveness of the British economy, unions have shown much greater interest in more cooperative industrial relations.

For those union leaders, like John Edmonds and Bill Jordan, and for those within the TUC bureaucracy who favor more cooperative relations with employers, European integration plays an important role. Embracing Europe means supporting a more modern, more cooperative system of industrial relations, for which Germany is usually the model. For Edmonds "the present institutions actually *create* conflict – almost out of anything. The British industrial relations system is lousy, it's awful. It doesn't work."[74] Thus it is essentially the *failure* of British industrial relations which inspires an industrial relations premised upon partnership.

The somewhat idealized understanding of social partnership that has entered British trade union discourse operates at multiple levels. At one level it simply implies a broad cooperative relationship between employers and unions. At another, social partnership is a collective bargaining strategy.[75] The strategy is one in which minimum standards are enshrined in law and collective bargaining permits "negotiated flexibility."

The incentive to bargain comes from the threat of legislation should bargaining fail. The TUC proposes a "modern style of industrial relations" which attempts "to find a modern, middle way which brings together the best of the UK's tradition of collective voluntary agreements with the best European practices of rights spelt out in law."[76]

The argument made by unions seeking various forms of partnership was both pragmatic and more positive in that it stressed the requirement of teamwork, cooperation, participation, and motivation for the success of post-Fordist, flexible firms. This argument is made by the Involvement and Participation Society (IPA), which brings together progressive industrialists from the public and private sectors, and several union general secretaries. The founding document of the IPA called for a fresh approach to management-union relations, and argued that unions need to accept various forms of nontraditional employee involvement, representation for nonunionists (which implies a works council of some kind), and job flexibility in return for job security, a share of productivity gains, and rights of information, consultation and representation.[77]

Flexibility

This is not the place to tell the history of job-control trade unionism in Britain; however, two general points are worth making. First, hostility to change, to new technology, and to the flexibility with which it is associated has been exercised primarily by groups of workers rather than by union policy.[78] Unions have only very rarely opposed workplace change; they have instead sought to negotiate change, and share in its rewards.[79] Second, in Britain, there is a long history of negotiating over flexibility, which went by different names – productivity bargaining, new technology bargaining – and stretches back at least into the 1960s. All were about the freedom of managers to organize the workplace and the process of production as they pleased. Thus, while it is true that the language of flexibility became popularized from the early 1980s onwards, it would be wrong to conclude that bargaining over issues of flexibility was a new feature of this period.

Collective agreements which include provision for changes in working practices in order to achieve various forms of flexibility in the firm appeared with increasing frequency during this period. Union views of flexibility have been skeptical, but rarely overtly hostile. The general TUC advice to its members has been to negotiate on flexibility as long as it does not come "at the expense of collective workplace influence and control," or increase the number of insecure, atypical jobs.[80] Probably the most important reason that unions and workers were prepared to bargain over and accept flexibility was that, by and large, employers paid for it. A 1987 CBI study showed that higher pay settlements were associated with greater flexibility, particularly long-term pay agreements.[81] One of the remarkable features of this period is that despite union weakness, real wage levels remained relatively high. This does not appear to have been due to union strength because the union mark-up steadily declined in the 1980s.[82] Rather, wages remained high because employers were prepared to pay in order to achieve flexibility, or to attract and retain skilled workers.

Employers were able to achieve flexibility in another manner through compensating workers with reduced worktime. As far as trade unions were concerned, worktime reduction was one of the few success stories of the period since 1979. As early as 1981 the TUC called for a campaign to reduce hours, but there were important differences among unions over the issue of overtime limits and whether pay should be reduced along with worktime.[83] Male workers work more hours (including overtime) in Britain than in any other country in the EU, and the slow reduction in the length of the workweek that unions negotiated in the late 1970s and early 1980s has been offset by very high levels of overtime.

However, in the engineering industry, unions have pushed for successive stages of worktime reduction. A union campaign in 1979-81 led to the reduction from a 40-hour to a 39-hour week. By 1989 unions in engineering were contemplating calling for a further reduction in hours. There was some skepticism at the leadership level about whether workers had any interest in the issue, and so the AEU called for an additional levy on members to be used as a strike fund.[84] This was designed to test the commitment of members to worktime reduction; and, somewhat to the surprise of the unions, the call for a levy was strongly supported.[85] The AEU, in part because of its highly decentralized structure, and in part because it explicitly modeled its campaign on the *I.G. Metall* strike for a thirty five-hour week, chose to target firms on a case-by- case basis, starting with highly profitable firms. The result of the two-year campaign was that by 1991 1666 agreements had been reached covering 600,000 workers, and providing, for the most part, a thirty seven-hour week. In exchange, however, unions agreed to a whole series of changes in working practices – job flexibility, "bell-to-bell" working – which offset the reduction in hours with productivity gains.[86]

With the exception of the campaign to reduce worktime in the engineering sector, the period since 1979 has not been a good one for the collective bargaining strategies of trade unions. Employers and the state simply refused to bargain at the national level. At the firm level attempts on the part of unions to extend collective bargaining to cover issues of interest to unions and workers, such as new technology, training, and the environment, largely failed. Overall, trade unions have failed to shape the workplace or to put curbs on the ability of employers to do so. Employers have been able to implement flexibility, introduce new technology, and initiate new forms of personnel policy without significant obstacles. In return for the greater freedom of action in the workplace enjoyed by employers, workers in the private sector who kept their jobs received steadily rising real wages and, more rarely, worktime reduction. This outcome should not surprise us given the labor market conditions and the declining organizational and political resources of trade unions. Unions were simply not in a very strong position to bargain.

Conclusion

The British trade union movement has endured a period of hostility from the state and increasing numbers of employers over the past eighteen years without precedent in the postwar period. One has to go back to the 1926 General Strike to find a comparable assault upon unions. Successive Conservative governments enacted wide-ranging legislation restricting union activity, regulating their internal government, and undermining collective bargaining. In the public sector, privatization of state industries, combined with reforms of the public sector itself to implement decentralization, flexibility, and "best practice" both weakened unions and encouraged a convergence of public- and private-sector industrial relations. Employers, meanwhile, increasingly avoided unions or used their favorable bargaining position to restructure industrial relations within the firm and pursue new bargaining agendas. Unions have also had to deal with economic restructuring, which has created persistently high levels of unemployment and devastated traditional areas of union strength.

In this context, the response of British unions was initially cautious. But as the 1980s progressed, the TUC and increasing numbers of unions came to recognize the need for fundamental strategic change. The development of union strategy followed a political timetable with each successive Conservative victory, and consequent lack of relief for unions, encouraging further reevaluation and strategic innovation. After 1979, the initial trade union reaction was simultaneously defensive and aggressive, seeing any problems as conjunctural, resulting from a deep recession and a more-than-usually ideological government. The strategy was to hold on for a Labour government while engaging in a certain limited resistance to government policy, and to take strike action, which culminated in the massive miners' strike. But with each new Conservative election victory it became clearer to unions that their problems went much deeper than a cyclical recession, that they could not expect to be bailed out by a Labour government, and consequently that trade unions needed a new strategic repertoire.

Furthermore, it is now clear that the modernization of the Labour Party, begun in 1983, but vastly accelerated by the election of Blair as party leader in 1994, involves a substantial distancing of the party from the union movement, and a displacement of union priorities. A Labour election victory has simply meant that Conservative industrial relations legislation remains, and the priority of policies to promote low inflation and labor market flexibility has been confirmed. Workers have received a few limited rights at work, while unions have received only a flawed statutory recognition procedure. Unions can expect no further help from this Labour government. A final removal of the institutional link between the industrial and political wings of the labor movement is now almost inevitable. It is perhaps no surprise that, as the trajectory of "New Labour" has become clearer, the union movement has reduced its expectations of legislative support from a Labour government and instead increased its emphasis upon aggressive recruitment campaigns which do not depend upon a friendly government.

This realization has prompted the greatest degree of strategic innovation by British unions, certainly in the postwar period, and probably since the Triple Alliance strategy before the First World War. There have been major strategic shifts in a number of areas, and, while seemingly disparate, they have a coherence which was largely unanticipated and unintended. Union strategy has developed along three parallel, but related, tracks. The first track concerns the relationship between trade unions and the state, and involves a shift away from a political unionism toward a more neutral and apolitical unionism. It also involves a preference for a fixed institutional framework of labor law rather than a reliance upon a privileged relationship with the Labour Party and *ad hoc* attempts to influence whichever government is in power. The second track concerns the relationship between trade unions and employers, and it implies a less adversarial unionism, with a greater emphasis upon cooperation and partnership with managers in order to enhance economic performance. Unions have been prepared to construct new industrial relations institutions, and give up their monopoly upon employee representation, to this end. The third track affects the relationship between trade unions and their members, and it entails much greater emphasis upon recruitment and service unionism.

It is clear that the logic of these strategies has yet to be fully worked out. They are, instead, a series of strategic tendencies, some widely diffused within the union movement and some rarer and more isolated within a small number of unions. However, these are the dominant strategic tendencies, they have become much stronger and more entrenched in union thinking in the 1990s, and these are the strategies which the TUC and the larger, more influential trade unions are adopting. In this respect, the GMB and its general secretary, John Edmonds are paradigmatic of the new trade unionism of the 1990s. Edmonds has argued that trade union strategy should be to "go over the Government" and "under the Government," meaning a simultaneous search for an active European role to achieve the legislative agenda of the unions and a new relationship with employers in the firm.[87] Edmonds has championed the pivotal role that legislative rights at work can play in enabling unions to recruit among newly expanding segments of the labor force.

Despite the scale of the changes outlined above, what is striking is the failure of most union strategy in this period. Decline in union membership has been continuous, albeit exacerbated by the recessions at the start of each decade under consideration; and the decline has encompassed every sector and every type of union, including a modernizing vanguard like the GMB. The only exception has been the RCN, which has prospered on the model of a professional, apolitical, service-oriented unionism. However, very few unions could duplicate the strong sense of occupational identity that nurses have, nor would they want to limit membership to such a narrow group; there are clear limits to growth for such a union strategy. Union successes, where they have come, have been around relatively isolated campaigns, like the engineering campaign to reduce worktime, and the campaign to win political fund ballots. The wider implications of these successes for the union movement as a whole are difficult to identify.

What explains the inability of British unions to halt, or even to slow their decline? There is a strong temptation to blame the unions themselves for their predicament. Thus newspaper lead writers, politicians, industrialists, and even trade unionists routinely argue that the problem is that they have not changed enough. The unions are certainly not blameless, and union institutions and practices inherited from the past continue, as one would expect, to influence union action. The British labor movement's decentralized and democratic structure also make the imposition of new strategy from above difficult.

The period of peak union strength masked a series of weaknesses on the part of British unions.[88] Unions did not develop strong recruitment capacities – they relied upon shop steward organization, which was inexpensive but dependent upon employers, and they resisted the intrusion of the state into industrial relations at a time when they were strong enough to have gained important legal rights at work. After 1979 the chickens of voluntarism came home to roost. To a certain extent, then, unions are paying the price of their failure to institutionalize power or to develop a heightened solidarity and legitimacy in the 1960s and 1970s. In short, British trade unionism was far more vulnerable to a hostile political and economic environment than most commentators, and the unions themselves, thought.

Nonetheless, the problem with arguing that resistance to change and the traditionalism of the unions is the main obstacle to success, is not only that it is not easily falsified, but that it risks blaming the victim. It assumes that the fate of trade unions lies in their own hands, and that different policies, different strategies, and more innovation would have averted decline. The reality, though, is that union strategy has not mattered much during this period because, in the current economic context, neither the state nor increasing numbers of employers see unions as performing any useful function. The problem for British trade unions has not been a lack of ideas, but a lack of power, and this has meant the increasing irrelevance of trade union strategy.

Moreover, there are reasons for being pessimistic about the trajectory of strategic innovation on the part of the labor movement. For a start, the strategy largely depends upon the use of legislation, and hence rests upon courts and governments. There is little reason to believe that a comprehensive framework of labor law will prove any more resistant to politicization than in the past. It is chimerical to believe that class relations can be somehow rendered politically neutral. Second, the new strategy offers employers cooperation. But that cooperation is something that employers can now get without unions, whether by an individualization of industrial relations, by threat, or by new forms of workplace communication and control. In the Fordist period unions could, with varying degrees of plausibility, offer wage restraint, social peace, and to take labor costs out of competition. What is it that employers now need and only unions can offer?

Third, the emerging strategy also raises the question of what role workers will see for unions when the state provides a range of workplace rights and protections, and when insurance companies, law firms, and so on, compete to provide financial and legal services to workers. That problem is exacerbated if legal changes encourage the spread of firm-specific organizations of workers, like works councils. Comparative evidence suggests that whether works councils act to entrench unions or to marginalize them depends upon the attitude of employers. The deep hostility of the British employer class toward unions bodes ill for this development. Finally, and most importantly, this strategy risks losing the one genuinely independent asset of labor organizations, their collectivity, and hence a certain cultural or ideological sense of solidarity and shared interest. A trade union strategy which sees workers as customers and unions as service providers, and emphasizes the provision of noncollective services, amounts to responding to the individualization of industrial relations with a parallel individualization of the relationship between a union and its members. It is implausible that substituting individualism for collectivism will contribute to the long-term survival of trade unions. There is little prospect, therefore, that current union practice will ameliorate the deep crisis of British trade unionism.

Notes

1. George Sayers Bain and Robert Price, "Union Growth: Dimensions, Determinants, and Destiny," in *Industrial Relations in Britain*, ed. George Sayers Bain(Oxford, U.K.: Blackwell, 1983), 5 table 1.1.
2. Simon Milner and David Metcalf, "A Century of UK Strike Activity: An Alternative Perspective," Centre for Economic Performance, discussion paper, no. 22, March 1991, table A.1.
3. Mark Cully and Stephen Woodland, "Trade Union Membership and Recognition 1996-97: An Analysis of Data from the Certification Officer and the LFS," *Labour Market Trends* 106, no. 7 (July 1998): 353.
4. "Falling Membership Slows as Union Recruitment Offensive Gears Up," *TUC Press Release* (19 June 1996).
5. Neil Millward, Mark Stevens, David Smart, and W. R. Hawes, *Workplace Industrial Relations in Transition* (Aldershot, U.K.: Dartmouth, 1992), 91.
6. Neil Millward, *The New Industrial Relations?* (London: Policy Studies Institute, 1994), 27.
7. Derek Bird, "Labour Disputes in 1993," *Employment Gazette* 102, no. 6 (June 1994): 200.
8. Kate Sweeney and Jackie Davies, "International Comparisons of Labour Disputes in 1994," *Labour Market Trends* 104, no. 4 (April 1996): 153.
9. Labour Research Department (LRD) *Fact Service* 54, no. 6 (16 April 1992): 63.
10. "Pull Me Up, Weigh Me Down," *The Economist*, 24 July 1993.
11. LRD *Fact Service* 55, no. 10 (11 March 1993): 39-40.
12. "A Rentier Economy in Reverse," *The Economist*, 22 September 1990.
13. A good illustration of this development was the announcement in July 1996 that the South Korean LG Group was planning an investment that would create 6000 jobs in

South Wales, in part because local wages are *half* those in South Korea, and in part because of government subsidies estimated at $45,000 per job.

14. "Where Union Membership is Best," *Labour Research* 81, no. 3 (March 1992).
15. LRD *Fact Service* 52, no. 21 (24 May 1990): 81.
16. "Women and the Labour Market: Results from the 1991 Labour Force Survey," *Employment Gazette* 100, no. 9 (September 1992): 440.
17. Gary Watson, "The Flexible Workforce and Patterns of Working Hours in the UK," *Employment Gazette* 102, no. 7 (July 1994): 241.
18. See the Conservative White Paper *People Jobs Opportunity* (London: HMSO, 1992), 15.
19. For surveys of Conservative legislation see David Marsh, *The New Politics of British Trade Unionism* (London: Macmillan, 1992) and John McIlroy, *The Permanent Revolution? Conservative Law and the Trade Unions* (Nottingham: Spokesman Books, 1991).
20. For accounts of the miners' strike, see Seumas Milne, *The Enemy Within* (London: Verso, 1994); Martin Adeney and John Lloyd, *The Miners' Strike: Loss without Limit* (London: Routledge and Kegan Paul, 1986); and Tony Benn, *The End of an Era: Diaries 1980-90* (London: Arrow, 1994), chap. 6.
21. "Pay in the Privatized Utilities," *Bargaining Report* 136 (February 1994).
22. Robert Gilbert, director of Employment Affairs at the CBI, London, U.K., interview by author 22 June 1993.
23. Mark Beaton, "Trends in Pay Flexibility," *Employment Gazette* 101, no. 9 (September 1993): 406-407; and William Brown and Janet Walsh, "Pay Determination in Britain in the 1980s: The Anatomy of Decentralisation," *Oxford Review of Economic Policy* 7, no. 1 (Spring 1991): 49.
24. Millward et al., *Workplace Industrial Relations in Transition*, 227.
25. Peter Ingram, "Changes in Working Practices in British Manufacturing Industry in the 1980s," *British Journal of Industrial Relations* 29, no. 1 (March 1991).
26. "Labour Flexibility in Britain: The 1987 ACAS Survey," ACAS Occasional Paper Number 41 (London: ACAS 1987).
27. Gregor Gall and Sonia McKay, "Trade Union Derecognition in Britain, 1988-1994," *British Journal of Industrial Relations* 32, no. 3 (September 1994).
28. Millward, *The New Industrial Relations?* 47.
29. The evidence offered by employers to the House of Commons Employment Select Committee inquiry into the future of trade unions is a good source in this regard: Employment Committee Third Report, *The Future of Trade Unions: Volume II Minutes of Evidence* (London: HMSO, 1994).
30. See the Institute of Directors, A *New Agenda for Business* (London: IOD, 1987).
31. CBI, *People: The Cutting Edge* (London: CBI, 1988), 83.
32. Robert Gilbert, "Changing Industrial Relations in the UK," speech to the second FIDES International Symposium on the Future of Trade Unions, n.d., 17.
33. "CBI rejects 'back-door' worker participation," *CBI News* 18 (4-17 November 1988): 12.
34. Millward, *The New Industrial Relations?* 133.
35. See, for example, "The Employment Policies of Inward Investors: The Scottish Dimension," *IRS Employment Trends* 480 (January 1991); and Frank Peck and Ian Stone, "New Inward Investment and the Northern Region Labour Market: A Final Report," Employment Department Research Series Number 6, October 1992.
36. TUC, *Campaigning for Change: A New Era for the TUC* (London: TUC, 1994), 3.
37. For a more extended discussion, see Chris Howell, "Family or Just Good Friends? The Changing Labour Party-Trade Union Relationship in Britain Since 1979," *International Journal of Political Economy* 22, no. 4 (winter 1992-93).

38. Tony Blair, "No Favours," *New Statesman and Society* (18 November 1994).
39. Ron Todd, "Incomes and Incomes Policy," Fifth Hitachi Lecture at the University of Sussex, 18 November 1986, 22.
40. For a survey and analysis of Labour industrial relations policy, see Chris Howell, "From New Labour to No Labor? The Blair Government in Britain," paper presented at the 94th annual meeting of the American Political Science Association, Boston, 3-6 September 1998. Legislation based on the White Paper, *Fairness at Work* (London: Department of Trade and Industry, May 1998), will be sent to Parliament in the 1998-99 session.
41. *Partnership into Power* (London: Labour Party, 1997). See the analysis by Mike Marqusee, "New Labour and its Discontents," *New Left Review* (July-August 1997).
42. "Labour's Income Boost," *The Sunday Times*, 16 November 1997. Preliminary figures for 1998 suggest that the union share of Labour's income will fall to 30 percent. See "Union funding Falls to 30% of Labour's Income," *The Times*, 22 April 1998.
43. See John Monk's speech, "Renewing the Unions," at the *Unions* 95 conference, 18 November 1995.
44. "New Wave Unions," Beatrix Campbell interviews John Edmonds in *Marxism Today* 30, no. 9 (September 1986).
45. "TUC 1983: Decisions and the New General Council," *Labour Research* 72, no. 10 (October 1983): 257.
46. For example, statutory union recognition would use some threshold as a trigger for automatic recognition. Some unions, like BIFU, strongly favor such a mechanism because they have an extremely competitive relationship with staff associations in the banking sector. On the other hand, a white-collar union like MSF, which would be unlikely to win a majority of members in a firm is agnostic about how such a mechanism would work. There is some fear that the minimum threshold for the statutory procedure would become a minimum for any union recognition, and thus harm minority union recognition where it currently exists.
47. TUC, *Your Voice at Work* (London: TUC, 1995).
48. Paul Teague, "The British TUC and the European Community," *Millennium: Journal of International Studies* 18, no. 1 (1989).
49. Interestingly, NCU found itself sought out by trade unions in other European countries for advice on how to deal with a deregulated telecommunications industry.
50. K. D. Ewing, "Swimming with the Tide: Employment Protection and the Implementation of European Labour Law," *Industrial Law Journal* 22, no. 3 (September 1993).
51. TUC, *Collective Bargaining Strategy for the 1990s* (London: TUC, 1991), 16.
52. Edmund Heery and John Kelly, "Full-Time Officers and the Shop Steward Network: Patterns of Co-operation and Interdependence," in *Trade Unions and Their Members*, Patricia Fosh and Edmund Heery, ed. (Basingstoke, UK: Macmillan, 1990), 98.
53. The figures for 1979 are calculated from Marsh, *The New Politics of British Trade Unions*, 26-27. Current figures are calculated from the TUC *Directory* (London: TUC, 1995).
54. See also Bob Carter, "Politics and Process in the Making of Manufacturing, Science and Finance (MSF)," *Capital and Class* 45 (autumn 1991).
55. See, for example, the ACAS *1988 Annual Report* (London: ACAS, 1989), 12.
56. See the TUC discussion document (sent out with only two months to respond), *The Future of the TUC* (London: TUC, 1993).
57. Edmund Heery and John Kelly, "Professional, Participative and Managerial Unionism: Interpretations of Change in Trade Unions," *Work, Employment and Society* 8, no. 1 (March 1994).

58. See Chris Howell, "Women as the Paradigmatic Trade Unionists? New Work, New Workers, and New Trade Union Strategies in Conservative Britain," *Economic and Industrial Democracy* 17, no. 4 (November 1996).
59. TUC, *Organising for the 1990s: The SRB's Second Report* (London: TUC, 1989).
60. Colin Whitston and Jeremy Waddington, "Why Join a Union?" *New Statesman and Society* (18 November 1994).
61. One survey revealed that almost 80 percent of union respondents had initiated specific, targeted recruitment campaigns in the period 1985-89, double the figure for the period 1980-84. Bob Mason and Peter Bain, "Trade Union Recruitment Strategies: Facing the 1990s," *Industrial Relations Journal* 22, no. 1 (spring 1991).
62. Edmund Heery and John Kelly, "Do Female Representatives Make a Difference? Women Full-Time Officials and Trade Union Work," *Work, Employment & Society* 2, no. 4 (December 1988).
63. Ibid.
64. See Ed Snape, "Reversing the Decline? The TGWU's Link Up Campaign," *Industrial Relations Journal* 25, no. 3 (summer 1994), for the best account of this campaign.
65. Martin Upchurch and Eddy Donnelly, "Membership Patterns in USDAW 1980-1990: Survival as Success?" *Industrial Relations Journal* 23, no. 1 (spring 1992).
66. John Kelly and Edmund Heery, *Working for the Union: British Trade Union Officers* (Cambridge: Cambridge University Press, 1994), 88-89.
67. Upchurch and Donnelly, "Membership Patterns in USDAW."
68. Tom Sibley, head of research at MSF, interview by author, 18 November 1992.
69. "HRM in the Workplace: The Union Activists' View," *IRS Employment Trends* 567 (September 1994).
70. For a good survey of trade union responses to new management practices, see Miguel Martinez Lucio and Syd Weston, "The Politics and Complexity of Trade Union Responses to New Management Practices," *Human Resource Management Journal* 2, no. 4 (summer 1992).
71. John Storey and Nicholas Bacon, "The 'New Agenda' and Human Resource Management: A Roundtable Discussion with John Edmonds," *Human Resource Management Journal* 4, no. 1 (autumn 1993), 64.
72. TUC, *Quality Circles* (London: TUC, 1981).
73. TUC, *Human Resource Management: A Trade Union Response* (London: TUC, 1994).
74. John Edmonds, quoted in Storey and Bacon, "The 'New Agenda,'" 69.
75. For the best articulation of this approach, see the speech by John Monks, "Renewing the Unions," delivered at the *Unions* 95 conference (London, TUC Congress House, 18 November 1995).
76. "TUC Proposes 'Modern' Industrial Relations," *TUC Press Release*, 2 May 1996.
77. "Towards Industrial Partnership: A New Approach to Management Union Relations," IPA consultative document, September 1992.
78. Paul Willman, *Technological Change, Collective Bargaining and Industrial Efficiency* (Oxford: Clarendon Press, 1986).
79. W.W. Daniel and Terence Hogarth, "Worker Support for Technical Change," *New Technology, Work and Employment* 5, no. 2 (autumn 1990).
80. TUC, *Flexibility: A Trade Union Response* (London: TUC, 1985), 5.
81. CBI, *Pay and Performance 1988-89: The Road Ahead* (London: CBI, 1988).
82. Peter Ingram, "Ten Years of Manufacturing Wage Settlements: 1979-89," *Oxford Review of Economic Policy* 7, no. 1 (spring 1991), 96-97.

83. Paul Rathkey, "Trade Unions, Collective Bargaining and Reduced Working Time: A Critical Assessment," *Employee Relations* 8, no. 1 (1986).
84. This account is based on information from Gavin Laird, general-secretary of the AEU, interview with the author, 12 November 1992; and Allan McKinlay and Des McNulty, "At the Cutting Edge of New Realism: The Engineers' 35 Hour Week Campaign," *Industrial Relations Journal* 23, no. 3 (autumn 1992).
85. The CSEU unions were divided on goals and tactics. In order to win support from MSF, which organized white-collar workers in engineering, the AEU pressed for a reduction to a thirty five-hour week (white-collar workers already worked fewer hours than blue-collar workers) in two stages, from thirty nine to thirty seven, and then from thirty seven to thirty five. In practice, the goal was thirty seven hours during the 1989-91 campaign. Some unions also wanted to wage the campaign through industry bargaining with the EEF and, if need be, a national strike.
86. Ray Richardson and Marcus Rubin, "The Shorter Working Week in Engineering: Surrender without Sacrifice?" in *New Perspectives on Industrial Disputes*, David Metcalf and Simon Milner, ed. (New York: Routledge, 1993).
87. John Edmonds, speaking at the GMB Congress, June 1992.
88. For an expanded version of this argument, see Chris Howell, "Trade Unions and the State: A Critique of British Industrial Relations" *Politics & Society* 23, no. 2 (June 1995).

Chapter 3

EVERY WHICH WAY BUT LOOSE

German Industrial Relations Since 1980

Stephen J. Silvia

Introduction

For over forty years, a wide variety of observers and practitioners from both inside and outside of Europe considered Germany's economic institutions and practices to be among the most effective in the world. The virtues ascribed to the "German model" have been numerous; they include low inflation, steady advances in real incomes, rising productivity, export prowess and social peace maintained principally through negotiation rather than force.[1] German employers' associations and trade unions have served as central pillars supporting the postwar German "model." Unlike much of the rest of Europe, "social partners" have managed to maintain their hegemony over the labor market, and unions have even been able to score several victories at the bargaining table, on the picket line, and in politics.

Despite this impressive record, serious problems have begun to afflict both trade unions and employers' associations in the Federal Republic. Germany's dominant labor confederation, the German Trade Union Federation (*Deutscher Gewerkschaftsbund*, DGB), lost over one-

Notes for this section begin on page 120.

quarter of its membership (i.e., 3.2 million) between 1991 and 1997.[2] This decline produced a severe financial crisis that has triggered a sweeping reorganization of the German labor movement. Times for German employers' associations have been no less trying. Discontent among rank-and-file employers has mushroomed within the peak confederation of employers' associations, the Federal Organization of German Employers' Associations (*Bundesvereinigung der Deutschen Arbeitgeberverbände*, BDA), and its member organizations. Unprecedented recruitment and retention problems for many employers' associations – particularly in the five eastern states – have precipitated serious financial hardship, personnel cuts, and an ongoing wave of organizational consolidation.[3]

This complex and contradictory confluence of organizational deterioration with continuity in influence and outcome raises three questions that serve as the *Leitthemen* of this chapter: (1) Why have the social partners, in particular the trade unions, experienced increasing internal organizational difficulties since the 1980s? (2) How have these institutions been able to retain their influence in the economy and society despite their rising problems? (3) How will organized labor's position in German society change in the future? This chapter begins with two snapshots of the German trade union's place in society. The first is of the early 1980s and the second of the latter half of the 1990s. The objective of this comparison is to distinguish habitual difficulties from more recent ones in order to delineate the trajectory of the German labor movement.

The German Labor Movement Past and Present

The German labor movement reached an apex along a wide variety of indicators in the early 1980s. Between 1968 and 1981, union membership expanded by over 20 percent. In 1981, the combined total membership of all West German unions peaked at 9.7 million, 7.96 million of which were members of DGB unions. The unionization rate reached a twenty-five-year high of 36.2 percent in 1979.[4] Union density, however, inched downward during the 1980s, drifting from 35.7 percent in 1981 to 33.8 percent by 1989.

The traditional strongholds of organized labor in Germany have been chemical manufacturing, construction, iron and steel production, metalworking, mining, printing, and the public sector. Every third member of a DGB union (i.e., 2.6 million) in 1980 belonged to the Metalworking Employees' Industrial Union (*Industriegewerkschaft Metall*, IG Metall). The Public Service, Transportation and Transit Employees'

Union (*Gewerkschaft Öffentliche Dienste, Transport und Verkehr*, ÖTV) was the DGB's second largest union in 1980; it had 15 percent of total DGB membership (i.e., 1.1 million). The chemical and construction workers' unions ranked third and fourth within the DGB in 1980, with 8 and 7 percent of the total membership respectively (i.e., 661,000 and 533,000). The combined membership of the ten smallest DGB unions accounted for only 21.5 percent of the peak confederation's ranks.

Since the establishment of the German labor movement over a century ago, union members have disproportionately been males from blue-collar occupations. Several demographic and occupational categories have habitually been underrepresented within the rank and file. In 1980, the female unionization rate was 20.6 percent, which was fifteen percentage points lower than overall union density and only half as large as the 1980 female labor force participation rate. White-collar unionization amounted to 17.7 percent in 1980. This was more than five percentage points higher than in 1970, but again, it was less than half of the share of white-collar employment in the workforce. The unionization rate for employees age twenty-five and under was only 11.7 percent in 1980.[5]

At first glance, Germany's postwar industrial relations regime appears highly decentralized, but this is deceptive. Collective bargaining typically takes place across approximately fifty separate sectors; and most unions and employers' associations rely on a formally federal negotiating structure. In practice, however, the contract results from a few key sectors (typically the metalworking industry and occasionally the public service sector or chemical manufacturing) set the pace for all of the others. Similarly, within each sector, one or two districts usually serves as a "pilot" for all the others. As a result, all sectoral agreements closely adhere to the pattern set by the lead sector; regional contracts within each sector vary only at the margins. This system of "loosely centralized" collective bargaining creates a series of *Flächentarifverträge* (comprehensive collective bargaining contracts) that establish sectorally specific compensation minima throughout the economy.

The 1949 Collective Bargaining Act (*Tarifvertragsgesetz*, TVG) protects collective agreements from potential freeriders by requiring that any firm leaving an employers' association continue to be bound by the contracts concluded while it was a member for as long as those contracts remain in force. The TVG also permits the German federal labor minister to issue a "declaration of universal applicability" (*allgemeine Verbindlichkeitserklärung*, AVE), otherwise known as an *erga omnes* decree. An AVE declares an existing collective agreement covering a single region and sector to be legally binding on *all* firms in that sector and jurisdiction for the duration of the agreement including those that are not even members of the relevant employers' association, so long as at least a majority of the employees from that sector and region are already covered under it. Until German unification, a high and widespread degree of organization among the *employers* meant that virtually the entire German economy met the prerequisites for an AVE. On average, at least five hundred AVEs have been in force at any given time.[6] Thus, during its heyday, this network of contracts dampened wage competition at the sectoral level and reduced income differentials across the entire economy. In essence, West Germany had a "leakproof" solidaristic wage, since it was all but impossible for any firm to operate beyond the confines of a collective agreement.

The high degree of coordination in collective bargaining has contributed to holding the number of strikes to a minimum. During the 1980s, an average of 28 days per 1,000 employees were lost annually owing to strikes in the Federal Republic, placing it among the countries with the lowest frequencies of industrial action.

Until the 1980s, German labor has had at best a secondary interest in trade union affairs abroad. Since the German unions were the wealthiest in Europe, the presidents of DGB unions were frequently named as president of their sector's corresponding European Industrial Federation (EIF). Nevertheless, German labor leaders saw these European posts principally as honorifics and rarely became any more than perfunctorily engaged in European labor affairs. When German labor leaders did act in Brussels, it was most often either to protect or to extend the German industrial relations model at the European level, rather than to pursue a distinctly European agenda.

In summary, during the first three decades of the Federal Republic, the social partners served as central pillars supporting an economically successful *Modell Deutschland*. Although collective bargaining and industrial conflict were undertaken in all earnestness, the larger framework of the German industrial relations order, which the German state assiduously maintained, ensured that industrial conflict seldom disrupted the economy and that the fruits of the German economic success would be widely distributed among the employed. Yet there were obvious dark clouds on the horizon in the early 1980s. Sustained economic turbulence was just beginning, driving unemployment dramatically upward. An end to the center-left "social-liberal" governing coalition was becoming increasingly discernable; strains were rapidly intensifying between the German Social Democratic Party (*Sozialdemokratische Partei Deutschlands*, SPD) and the liberal Free Democratic Party (*Freie Demokratische Partei*,

FDP). Still, since the postwar German labor movement had weathered hard economic times and unfriendly governments in the past, most were confident that it could withstand arduous conditions again.

The German Labor Movement in the 1990s

When the 1990s began, it appeared that German unification would produce an unprecedented opportunity for trade unionists to strengthen their position in the economy, but the decade actually turned out to be the most difficult one for organized labor since the 1950s. In 1990, the economic, political, social, and even geographic contours of the Federal Republic of Germany changed abruptly, but the institutional framework of the German economy and politics remained remarkably the same. Why? In light of Germany's traumatic history during the first half of the twentieth century, the "victorious" western Germans, with substantial eastern support (at least initially), concluded that the least risky means to unify Germany would be simply to extend eastward all of West Germany's laws, organizations, and institutional arrangements (including the entire industrial relations complex) without any changes, since they have proved successful. Simply absorbing eastern Germany into the Federal Republic avoided experimentation and averted the need to revise the elaborate networks of economic, political, and social arrangements that were the product of forty years of incremental conflict and compromise in western Germany. In practice, however, this institutional transfer has proved extremely problematic. Many western institutions, some of which had already demonstrated significant shortcomings even before unification, were ill suited not only to the radically different circumstances in eastern Germany, but also to the new, far more heterogenous "Berlin Republic."

The German trade unions and employers' associations continued to play their traditional role of coordinating compensation within and across sectors in western Germany, but found it increasingly challenging to do so. The unification boom of 1990-1991 reduced western unemployment briefly, but the subsequent economic downturn of 1992-1993 and the slowdown of 1995-1997 brought underlying tensions back to the surface in a far more malevolent form.

Some western labor leaders initially considered merging with their eastern counterpart(s), but ultimately only one union, the Chemical Employees' Industrial Union (*Industriegewerkschaft Chemie-Papier-Keramik*, IG Chemie), actually did. Most rejected that option because union officials feared that a merger would designate the western unions as the legal, moral, and political successor of the eastern labor movement – one which had been totally subservient to the dominant Marxist-Leninist political party of the German Democratic Republic (GDR), the *sozialistische Einheitspartei Deutschlands* (SED, German Socialist Unity Party) – and thereby leave the western unions liable for the past actions of the eastern labor movement. Most western unions instead indirectly coordinated the liquidation of their "equivalent" union in the East and then recruited eastern members from scratch. This approach, although prudent, did have costs. It deprived most western unions of the former eastern labor movement's property, much of which had belonged to the prewar Christian and Social Democratic trade unions.

Initially, western German trade unions had great success recruiting new members in the former GDR. By the end of 1991, 3.9 million eastern members signed up. Many easterners initially joined unions because in the GDR union membership was a prerequisite for access to a wide spectrum of benefits; many easterners mistakenly assumed that the same would be true under the new industrial relations order. Large numbers of easterners also believed that union membership might increase the odds of saving their jobs.

The unification boom stimulated western business, producing a short-lived hiring spurt that in turn helped to raise western membership by 400,000. All told, the initial impact of unification swelled the ranks of German organized labor by 45 percent. The DGB expanded by 50 percent, from 7.9 million in 1989 to 11.8 million in 1991 (8.3 million in the west). By the end of 1991, union density in eastern and western Germany reached 47.8 and 33.2 percent, respectively.

Since 1991, union membership has dropped precipitously throughout Germany. Once it became clear that union membership was not necessary to attain amenities and did not guarantee job security, other easterners allowed their membership to lapse. By the end of 1997, total eastern membership had fallen to 1.9 million (i.e., less than one-half of the 1991 peak); eastern density slid to 29.0 percent. The central cause of this decline was the collapse of the eastern German labor market. The western unionization rate dropped between 1991 and 1997 by six full points to 29.8 percent (cf. a 1.8 percentage-point slide during the 1980s). A lackluster economy, the advent of deindustrialization in eastern and western Germany, a modest rise in the service-sector share of total employment, and the deterioration of the working class *milieu* all help to explain this plunge. The overrepresentation of blue-collar occupations among the members when compared to the economy as a whole became more pronounced in the 1990s. The number of young union members fell by over one-half between 1991 and 1996. Youth employees comprised 13 percent of the workforce but only 6 percent of DGB membership in 1996. The 1990-96 strike rate in Germany fell to its lowest level in the postwar era. An average of only 17 days per 1,000 employees were lost annually owing to industrial action.

Relations between labor and management became increasingly contradictory in the wake of unification. On the one hand, the representatives of employers' associations and trade unions pulled together with the Kohl government in a common effort to aid in the social and economic transformation of the former GDR. The institutions representing German business and labor have remained wedded to the existing system of collective bargaining, despite the problems that both organized labor and management were having in attracting and maintaining membership. On the other hand, wrenching economic change and strategic errors made the relationship between the social partners harsher at times than it had been in years.

The German collective bargaining regime, which had been leakproof in 1980, began to develop cracks in the 1990s. The metals sector retained its preeminent institutional position in the collective bargaining order, even though it accounted for an increasingly smaller share of total employment. Employers' associations were far less successful than the trade unions in attracting and retaining members east of the Elbe. Recent estimates place membership in most eastern employers' associations well below the 50 percent employment threshold required to trigger eligibility for a declaration of universal applicability. In western Germany, "association flight" (*Verbandsflucht*) and "association avoidance" (*Verbandsvermeidung*) became increasingly common, as a growing minority of employers, particularly small ones, began to reject the postwar cooperative German industrial relations order. The share of the workforce covered under collective agreements, although still high, started to slide.

Erosion has not been confined to the institutions of collective bargaining; Germany's much praised system of codetermination (*Mitbestimmung*) has also begun to wear along the edges. German unionists have become increasingly concerned that the steady shrinkage in the iron, coal, and steel industries, as well as the newly fashionable strategy of reorganizing enterprises into a series of independent holding companies, threatens to water down codetermination. Although codetermination is anchored in German law, employees must take active steps to convert this right into a reality. In the mid 1990s, only 24.5 percent of German private-sector employees worked at firms that provided "double codetermination" (i.e., both works council[s] and employee representation on the corporate board of directors [*Aufsichtsrat*]);[7] this was six percentage points lower than in 1984. The share of employees with neither component of codetermination increased from 50.6 to 60.5 percent during the same time period.[8] Although German labor law draws a sharp distinction between works councils and trade unions, union officials have learned to use codetermination's legal privileges and protection to extend their shopfloor presence and to protect their organizations during hard times.[9] The shrinking presence of codetermination in the German economy has not appreciably weakened organized labor so far, but if codetermination continues to erode unabated, it would inevitably impair the trade unions too.

To recapitulate, the two central pillars of the German industrial relations order – the employers' associations and trade unions – have developed discernible fissures during the 1980s and 1990s, but they have not crumbled. The employers' association, labor and governmental establishments have pulled together, despite their differences, to counter the centrifugal forces battering the incumbent German industrial relations regime.

With our two snapshots of German trade unions in hand, the following section shifts focus to the larger environment to help account for the changing place of labor in German and European society.

The Changing Environment for German Labor

Change in the environment for German labor has been uneven. The geopolitical and economic environment has shifted considerably over the past two decades, but the institutional framework for industrial relations – state support of the status quo and social partnership – have retained a remarkable degree of continuity. This section briefly recounts recent economic developments and profiles labor's relationship with its main external interlocutors, the employers, the state, and recent governments.

The Economic Environment

The Federal Republic was one of the few European countries for which, at least at first, the upper manifestation of the "double shift"[10] proved to be economically advantageous. Deepening economic integration since the early 1970s within Europe and among Europe, Japan, and North America provided upscale German niche producers with a relatively large market of affluent consumers who have been willing to pay high prices for quality goods. The undervaluation of the *deutsche Mark* (DM) during the first half of the 1980s – especially versus the dollar, sterling, and yen – enabled firms to expand West Germany's traditional trade surplus. Export success in turn permitted West Germany to retain a sizeable manufacturing sector (and as a result, its labor movement) at a time when most other industrialized countries first succumbed to deindustrialization. Indeed, Germany's export success during the 1980s came, at least to some degree, at the *expense* of manufacturing elsewhere in Europe and the United States.

Participation in the European Monetary System (EMS), which began operating in 1979, enabled the Federal Republic to enjoy, if not the best of both worlds in terms of inflation and employment, at least a better result than otherwise would have been the case. During the 1980s West Germany was an island of monetary restraint within a somewhat more expansive Europe, which allowed the Federal Republic to expand its merchandise trade surplus from DM 19 billion in 1980 to DM 140 billion in 1988 and 1989. The rise in exports kept West German unemployment at a manageable, if not ideal, average annual rate of 7.9 percent for the decade. While West Germany was racking up record export surpluses during the 1980s, a serious economic problem arose. Productivity growth slowed to an annual average of only 1.7 percent; that is, roughly one-half of the Federal Republic's performance in the 1970s. Between 1990 and 1997, western productivity growth has rebounded partially, averaging 2.1 percent each year.

Unification sent the German economy into a series of severe gyrations from which it has still not yet fully recovered. Unity initially fueled a short, sharp boom in the west. Western Germany's gross domestic product spiked upward, expanding by 5.7 percent in 1990 and 5 percent in 1991, before decelerating to 1.6 percent in 1992 and then shrinking by 2 percent in 1993. From 1994 to 1997, the real yearly growth rate of the western German gross "regional" product (GRP) averaged a lackluster 1.8 percent. Western German employment in the 1990s mirrored the halting growth record. The unification boom slashed western unemployment from 7.9 percent in 1989 to a ten-year low of 6.3 percent in 1991, but the 1992-93 recession and subsequent economic slowdown reversed this trend, driving up the western jobless rate to 9.8 percent by 1997 (11.4 percent for all of Germany). Between 1992 and 1997, the number of jobs in western Germany fell by over 1.5 million.

The decline in the share of employment dedicated to goods production picked up considerable momentum during the early 1990s as deindustrialization finally reached western Germany. During the 1970s and the 1980s, the manufacturing sector's share of employment declined each year on average by 0.4 percent; this contraction accelerated to 0.7 percent annually in the 1990s. Nonetheless, 34.0 percent of the workforce was engaged in goods production in 1997, which still is high in comparison to other western industrialized countries.

In 1981 the net flow of foreign direct investment (FDI) turned negative for the first time in the postwar era. From 1983 to 1989, German firms made more net new direct investments abroad than foreign firms invested in Germany by amounts ranging between DM 11 and 18 billion. The net outflow of new FDI accelerated steadily during the 1990s. Between 1990 and 1997, a *net* total of DM 234 billion new net direct investment flowed out of Germany, DM 47.3 billion (i.e., 1.3 percent of GDP) in 1997 alone, an all-time record, in spite of the initial massive new investments undertaken by both foreign and domestic firms in eastern Germany.

Economic developments in eastern Germany present a substantially different story than those in the west and are replete with even sharper gyrations, as would be expected from a region making a transition to market practices. Economic and monetary unification and the collapse of traditional central and eastern European economies precipitated an economic crash east of the Elbe. The gross regional product of the former German Democratic Republic dropped by 13.4 percent in 1990 and 31 percent in 1991. The GRP rebounded between 1992 and 1994, growing at an average annual pace of 9 percent, before tailing off once again to 5.2 percent in 1995, 1.9 percent in 1996, and 1.6 percent in 1997. The 1997 eastern GRP growth rate was particularly distressing because it was actually lower than the western growth rate for the same year. The transition from central planning also had a devastating impact on the labor market. Employment in eastern Germany fell by 30.7 percent between 1990 and 1997, from 8.8 to 6.1 million, and the official unemployment rate rose from 2.6 percent in 1990 to 18.1 percent in 1997. Industrial production in eastern Germany fell to one-third and industrial employment to one-fourth of pre-unification levels. Before unification, the majority of the workforce produced goods. By 1997, this had dropped to 16 percent, or roughly half the western percentage.

Without any special programs, the eastern German unemployment rate would have topped 40 percent, but three developments kept the unemployment rate down. First, the German government expanded and enacted a series of active labor market policies. These included subsidized early retirement, training programs, employment promotion and structural development corps (*Arbeitsförderung, Beschäftigung und Strukturentwicklung Gesellschaften*, ABS Gesellschaften), and employment creation measures (*Arbeitsbeschaffungsmassnahmen*, ABM). At their height in 1991, these programs absorbed two million workers and directly created 400,000 jobs at a cost of 23 percent of the GRP (cf. western German peak expenditures of 2 percent). Almost 50 percent of the eastern German working population had participated in at least one active labor market policy if short-time payments are also included. Second, 1.4 million eastern German employees have either moved to West Germany or commute there. Since only 372,000 western employees have gone in the opposite direction, the net outflow equals slightly more than one million.

Third, women in eastern Germany were systematically pressured out of the working world. Eastern women had a labor force participation rate of 85 percent in 1989, which was almost as high as the rate for eastern men and was much higher than that of western women (55 percent). Although many women worked in production jobs, most performed numerous staff and support roles, such as operating daycare centers and providing for an extensive set of social activities for employees. Once westerners began to take over the management of eastern enterprises, one of the first things they did was dismantle these ancillary undertakings, thereby eliminating a disproportionately high share of the jobs performed by women. Moreover, when most eastern German production units laid off redundant line workers, the managers and works councilors usually retained married males over females. As a result, two-thirds of the eastern German unemployed have been women, and eastern women have an unemployment rate twice as high as that of eastern men.[11]

Labor productivity has advanced at a rapid pace in the five new eastern states, but it still has some way to go before it reaches the western German level. In 1989, the GDR's labor productivity equaled approximately 25 percent of the western German level. A combination of mass layoffs and substantial public and private investment has in the interim almost doubled eastern German relative labor productivity, advancing it in 1997 to 57.7 percent.

Germany did manage to restore a large export-surplus soon after unification despite the massive diversion of western output from the export market to eastern Germany since 1990. Western Germany's trade surplus dropped from an all-time high of DM 135 billion in 1989 to DM 22 billion in 1991, but it rebounded to DM 61.9 billion by 1993 and reached DM 121.7 billion in 1997. Germany's "chronic" trade surplus is actually an indication of economic weakness rather than strength. It is the result of mediocre domestic demand owing to high unemployment and fiscal austerity in preparation for the introduction of the euro. Germany's current account balance, in contrast, performed poorly during the 1990s. Between 1991 and 1995, Germany ran an annual current account deficit of DM 30 billion. Service-sector imports, travel abroad, and remittances are the deficit's primary causes. Germany's current account deficit only began to subside toward the end of the 1990s. It amounted to DM 19.7 billion in 1996 and DM 10.1 billion in 1997.

Atypical employment has increased in the Federal Republic since 1980. Part-time work expanded between 1980 and 1997 from 7 to 15.9 percent of all the jobs in the labor market, but this was still relatively low by international standards. Part-time employment is sharply segmented along gender lines in the Federal Republic. In 1997, women held 88 percent of all part-time jobs. German trade unionists are divided in their attitudes toward part-time work. Traditionalists reject it, but other prominent unionists, including DGB president Dieter Schulte, have actually complained that a shortage of part-time jobs, particularly secure well-paying ones, limits the life choices of German employees.[12]

To summarize, problems with *Modell Deutschland* began to develop beneath the surface during the 1980s, but they manifested only under the extraordinary strain of German unification. The German collective bargaining regime continued to deliver moderate real wage increases in most years for those who held full-time jobs, but the numbers excluded from the regime increased steadily. A comparatively egalitarian social structure, which has been a hallmark of the Federal Republic, has thus increasingly been giving way to a "variable geometry" of segmentation that has proved particularly harsh on women, eastern Germans without jobs and their dependents.

The State and Government

The legacy of National Socialism continues to preclude direct attacks by the state against trade unions in the postwar era. This is not to say that individual governments and the labor movement have never clashed over particular policies, but that no postwar government has ever challenged the legitimacy of the industrial relations regime, dismantled the numerous means by which the postwar German state has undergirded organized labor and management, or excluded trade unions. Without exception, the German state has accepted collective bargaining autonomy, extended the coverage of collective agreements via *erga omnes* provisions, and promoted employee participation in boardrooms and workplaces through codetermination. German labor and management representatives also participate with government officials on the myriad of tripartite bodies that pervade the Federal Republic, which secure the social partners at positions squarely in the center of the economy, polity, and society. In addition, labor courts serve not only to reduce the number of instances when disputes lead to industrial action, but also to anchor organized labor and management firmly in German jurisprudence.

The conservative coalition – comprised of the Christian Democratic Union (*Christlich Demokratische Union*, CDU), its Bavarian sister party, the Christian Social Union (*Christlich Soziale Union*, CSU), and the FDP – which governed the Federal Republic from 1982 to 1998, respected the central principle of collective bargaining autonomy, even if many government officials made clear from time to time that their sympathies lay primarily with the employers. Helmut Kohl (CDU), who as federal chancellor headed the conservative coalition, summarized his view of the proper role of organized labor and industrial relations in a speech before the 1994 DGB convention:

> The German unions and the *Deutscher Gewerkschaftsbund* have a firm place in the society and economy of our land ... Thus understood, unions in my opinion have always been a part of a living democracy; they are an essential sphere of the social market economy. We – and I say this as one who in his life has had enough controversial disputes with the DGB among others – therefore also need strong unions in the future, [unions] that are ready and actively willing to shape change in the economy and society.[13]

Helmut Kohl and his governments took this supportive approach toward the industrial relations order for three reasons. First, few in the Kohl government considered Germany's postwar set of social and political institutions to be irretrievably broken. Second, a cardinal principle of German Christian Democracy is Catholic social teaching. This corporatist tradition is in many respects far closer to the policies of Social Democracy than to the laissez-faire ideology that predominates in Anglo-Saxon right-of-center parties and in Germany's FDP. Third, the CDU and CSU have a joint labor wing within their parties known as the *Christlich Demokratische Arbeitnehmerschaft* (CDA, Christian Democratic Employees' Group). Although the CDA is relatively small, it acts as a moderating force on CDU and CSU policies.

The most significant example of the Kohl government's active support of the status quo was the decision in 1990 to introduce the western German industrial relations regime virtually unaltered to eastern Germany. Throughout the initial years of unification, Helmut Kohl and his top officials regularly consulted with unionists and employers' association officials regarding virtually every major step that the government took in the five eastern states. The leadership of the state-owned *Treuhandanstalt* (THA, Trust Holding Agency), the body tasked with reorganizing and privatizing the economic holdings of the East German state, actively bolstered the eastward spread of employers' associations by agreeing (with government approval) to cover the membership fee of any enterprise under THA control and by using the going collective bargaining rates for each sector to set the compensation for all Treuhand employees. The

German government also played an activist role in the eastern economy in a bid to save eastern Germany's "industrial cores."

More recently, the former federal labor minister Norbert Blüm (CDU) worked tirelessly with the Construction Agriculture and Environmental Employees' Industrial Union (*Industriegewerkschaft Bauen-Agrar-Umwelt*, IG BAU)[14] and the two construction employers' associations to attain a special minimum wage for foreign construction employees posted to German sites as a way to help prevent "wage dumping" from undermining the *Flächentarifverträge* in the construction sector.[15]

Helmut Kohl's commitment to a German-style, corporatist industrial relations regime extended to the European level. Kohl and Blüm made good on a pledge to see that the European Union approve the compromise directive on European works councils while Germany presided over the European Council during the second half of 1994, despite BDA objections to some of the details of the directive as it was written. Norbert Blüm also worked hard at the European level in the mid 1990s to attain a posting directive to regulate foreign construction employees working in the Federal Republic.[16]

Kohl was not completely passive when it came to marginal alterations of the regime. He took small steps toward making the German labor market more flexible (e.g., the 1985 *Beschäftigungsförderungsgesetz*, [Employment Promotion Act] liberalizing atypical work, the 1992 addition of article 249h to the *Arbeitsförderungsgesetz* [AFG, Work Promotion Act] to create a temporary second tier in the eastern German labor market, the 1996 liberalization of the law regulating sick-pay [*Lohnfortzahlung*], and the 1997 reduction of subsidies for early retirement [*Arbeitsteilzeit*]), but Kohl did not fundamentally alter the substance of the industrial relations regime, with one exception: the amendment of AFG article 116, which declared that employees who were laid off owing to shortages resulting from a strike in their industry but in a different region, were ineligible to receive unemployment benefits.

Immediately after IG Metall won the 1984 strike to reduce the workweek, employers clamored for a change in article 116, which took place after much controversy in 1986.[17] Despite the change of law, German trade unions have won several industrial conflicts since 1986 simply by adjusting tactics. The amendment of article 116 has therefore not proved debilitating to organized labor.

The Employers

Of all the components that comprise *Modell Deutschland*, the employers' associations have come under the most stress in the past two decades. This is particularly threatening to the status quo, because the high density of employers' associations has been the single most important factor preventing a significant non-union sector from developing in the Federal Republic.

The *Gesamtverband der metallindustriellen Arbeitgeberverbände* (Gesamtmetall, General Association of Metal-Industry Employers' Associations) is by far the most important member of the BDA. Gesamtmetall has consistently accounted for at least 40 percent of the employees of all the enterprises belonging to BDA affiliates. Hence, trends that develop in Gesamtmetall invariably affect the BDA as a whole as well. The membership rates of Gesamtmetall's western affiliates have been declining since the mid 1980s. In 1980, 56 percent of all workplaces in the western German metalworking industry, employing 73 percent of all employees, belonged to a Gesamtmetall affiliate; density in terms of employment peaked in 1984 at 75 percent. Yet, by 1994, these measures of association density had slipped to 43 and 65 percent respectively. Thus, the evidence clearly indicates that density in employers' associations has declined considerably in the western German metalworking sector since 1980, assessed either in terms of workplaces or employment.[18]

The situation in eastern Germany is even more dire. As part of the German government's effort to promote the spread of western institutions eastward, the *Treuhandanstalt* encouraged all of the managers running the workplaces under its control to join business associations by paying any membership dues. This subsidy helped Gesamtmetall's eastern affiliates attain a density of 57.4 percent in terms of employment in 1992. Two years later, however, the THA had already divested almost all its holdings and therefore was no longer covering dues payments. Hard times and a controversial strike in the metalworking and steel industries combined with the end of the dues subsidy to reduce density in the eastern metalworking industry to 35 percent. Membership in the Saxon metal industry employers' association deteriorated so badly that in late 1994, IG Metall began a fruitless campaign to recruit new members for the *employers'* association.[19] Employers' association density plummeted throughout the eastern economy. By 1998, three-quarters of all manufacturing firms were not members of an employers' association.[20]

Why has employers' association membership dropped in western Germany? Some blame the impact of German unification,[21] but the evidence does not support this. Employers' association density peaked well before unification. The catalyst that transformed inchoate employer dissatisfaction into actual association avoidance was the successive collective bargaining agreements to reduce the workweek from forty to thirty-five hours, which were first concluded in the metalworking and printing industries in 1984. Weekly working time reduction raised costs for small firms disproportionately higher than for larger ones, thereby permanently upsetting the fragile balance between large and small firms from the same sector around a single minimum compensation package.[22]

Besides contract negotiations, many small- and medium-sized employers were disappointed with the quality of the legal and personnel advice they received from their association. Many complained that the associations had become "encrusted bureaucracies" that were primarily oriented toward larger companies from traditional industrial branches.[23] Voice in employers' association also arose as an issue for small- and medium-sized enterprises. The repeated use of peak-level "summits" between the heads of Gesamtmetall and IG Metall during the 1980s, which culminated in the conclusion of multiyear contracts to reduce weekly working time, angered much of the rank-and-file membership of the regional associations that comprise Gesamtmetall. These summits circumvented the traditional decision-making process in the metalworking sector, which relies on regional affiliates rather than Gesamtmetall to negotiate the actual contracts. Managers at smaller enterprises complained that the summits allowed the giant metalworking companies, which had a strong preference for continuing production, to influence the ultimate agreements unduly, to the detriment of the rest of the sector and the economy.[24]

Out of the mass of small- and medium-sized employers who were systematically frozen out of the corporatist power structure, a handful of dissidents began to congregate in associations for smaller firms, such as the *Arbeitsgemeinschaft Selbständiger Unternehmer* (ASU, Working Group of Independent Entrepreneurs). These dissidents cooperated loosely with a small circle of like-minded intellectuals and journalists, to develop an increasingly trenchant critique of the postwar industrial relations system, which they denounced as a "collective bargaining cartel."[25] Despite the rise in disgruntlement and the development of alternative models, the leadership of the German employers' associations remained firmly committed to the postwar collective bargaining order. In 1989, the BDA issued a joint declaration with the DGB stating that a decentralization of the postwar bargaining regime could spark "ruinous competition" among employers and employees; the BDA has held to that line ever since.[26] Nonetheless, discontent has continued to bubble beneath the surface in the employers' camp.

Although German unification offered a perfect opportunity to amend the industrial relations order, none of the top officials in employers' associations proposed any changes. To the contrary, in the spring of

1990 the leaders of Germany's business associations came out jointly in favor of a quick unification of the two Germanies and an extension of the existing industrial relations infrastructure in an unaltered form to the east. When it became clear after the 18 March 1990 GDR election that unification would indeed proceed quickly under the auspices of CDU-led governments in both east and west, the business associations worked closely with the trade unions and the government to extend eastward the full range of institutions and practices that had become standard in the Federal Republic, including comprehensive multiyear collective agreements.

On 9 March 1990, the BDA and DGB issued a joint declaration on the economy of the German Democratic Republic. The declaration stressed the necessity of embracing social-market principles in order to become successful economically and hailed the Kohl government's intention to achieve a quick economic, monetary, and social policy union as a positive step. The declaration also called for the creation of a comprehensive set of regulatory structures and policies (*Ordnungspolitik*), including an industrial relations regime compatible with that found in the Federal Republic.[27] The then BDA president Klaus Murmann "strongly urged" Helmut Kohl during the early months of 1990 to adopt exchange-rate parity for eastern wages as a part of German monetary union and publicly committed German employers to the objective of wage-and-benefit parity between eastern and western Germany as quickly as possible within the confines of the existing western industrial relations regime. On 18 September 1990, the BDA and DGB issued another joint declaration on employment in the GDR that called on the government to use active employment policies to curb joblessness with the ultimate aim of placing individuals in private-sector employment.[28]

The first comprehensive round of wage negotiations for eastern Germany took place in the spring of 1991. This series of sectoral talks set eastern wages as a percentage of the western *contractual* rate, which was in line with the conservative policy of organized labor and management to extend the status quo. In a few cases, most notably in the eastern metalworking sector, the social partners even concluded – at the *employers'* urging – multiyear, step-by-step contracts that set a timetable for attaining contractual wage parity.[29] These multi-year contracts immediately became controversial among employers, however, because of the rapid pace they set for attaining parity.

When the German economy began to falter in 1992, dissatisfaction within the ranks of many employers' associations rose to acute levels, particularly in eastern Germany, prompting the leadership of some of these organizations to resort to extreme actions that challenged the sanctity of collective bargaining contracts and the integrity of the comprehensive collective agreements *(Flächentarifverträge)*. In early 1993, Gesamtmetall and the Steel Industry Employers' Association shook the very foundations of the postwar German collective bargaining order when they took the unprecedented (and by most assessments illegal) step of canceling their three year eastern wage-agreements with IG Metall two years before they were due to expire. At the urging of Gesamtmetall, the eastern metal-industry employers' associations unilaterally instituted a 9 percent wage increase for 1993 instead of the 26 percent set out in the multiyear contract and said 1994 would be open for negotiation.[30]

This act of brinkmanship provoked a bitter industrial dispute, which culminated in a two-week strike throughout Saxony and Brandenburg in May 1993. IG Metall exhibited substantial resolve by successfully mobilizing an inexperienced eastern membership to strike under extremely difficult economic and political circumstances. IG Metall forced the employers to rescind the cancellation of the 1991 contracts, but the union agreed to renegotiate the agreements in return. The ensuing talks resulted in not only DM 6 billion in wage concessions for the employers (by extending the time frame set to reach wage parity with the west), but also the introduction of a "hardship" clause into the eastern collective bargaining agreements. This clause permits troubled firms and works councils to petition the collective bargaining parties to consider a reduction of wages and benefits below the contractually established minimum pattern.[31]

Recruiting members to join employers' associations in eastern Germany remains extremely difficult for several reasons. Since the official unemployment rate in eastern Germany has hovered between 15 and 20 percent for over five years, eastern employers do not need mutual aid to keep a lid on labor costs the way they have in western Germany. Thus, perhaps the single most important incentive for firms to join an employers' association is absent in the east. Even if adequate density made it legally feasible to resort to *erga omnes* declarations to enforce minimum compensation rates in several flagship sectors of eastern Germany, the political propriety of doing so would be dubious, since it would cause additional plant closures and unemployment. On the other side of the coin, eastern employers' association officials are under tremendous pressure to accommodate the rising demands of eastern members for more "flexibility," even when this means violating legally binding contracts. For example, hundreds of firms in the Saxon metalworking sector alone have tacitly colluded with their employees to reduce compensation below the contractual minimum set in comprehensive collective agreements in exchange for preserving employment. The president of the Saxon metal industry employers' association, Dietrich Haselwander, admitted that only two-fifths of all his members in Saxony respect all of the minima set in the collective bargaining agreement.[32] Although these types of illegal arrangements are not unheard of in crisis sectors in western Germany, such as textile and apparel production, it has never has been so widespread in the west as it is in the east.

Thus, unification has created the first viable domestic "exit option" from the collective bargaining regime for most employers. Eastern Germany has become a new frontier where operating without being a member of an employers' association is, at least for the moment, possible. The end of the Cold War and German unification have opened new possibilities for German business to act more aggressively against labor because the new geopolitical configuration has all but eliminated the pressure to demonstrate the superiority of capitalism. Still, the preponderance of top officials in all Germany's firms and business associations publicly support a reformed version of the current collective bargaining order, including the *Flächentarifvertrag*.[33]

To recapitulate, the environment for organized labor in the Federal Republic of Germany has become more difficult since 1980. Dissension among the employers' ranks, markedly weaker economic performance, and the complications of German unity have all made the terrain for trade unionists far more challenging than it has been in some time. It is equally important to point out, however, that in most instances organized labor, the employers' associations, and the state have pulled together to defend the existing industrial relations order against a growing periphery of unemployed workers and disgruntled *petit bourgeois* employers.

Union Responses

The remainder of this chapter assesses the perceptions and actions of the German labor movement within a changing environment since 1980. It is organized into four topical sections: politics, collective bargaining policy, organizational structure, and recruitment and representation. Each section details the policy debates, the measures taken, and the results.

Organized labor has traditionally proceeded quite cautiously in Germany and in most instances has endeavored to shore up the status quo. The last two decades of the twentieth century have proved to be no exception. By the end of the 1990s, however, it appeared that internal immobilism had become increasingly debilitating.

In the 1980s, trade unionists responded to a surge in unemployment by refurbishing an old strategy, namely, weekly working time reduction to permit the continuance of hourly wage gains while at least appearing to address the issue of unemployment. German labor succeeded in reducing the workweek, but victory came at the heavy price of disrupting the delicate internal balance within the employers' camp.

By the start of the 1990s, German labor leaders increasingly came to the realization that always doing the same things in the same old way does not guarantee perpetual success. Labor leaders therefore began to plan top-down organizational reform. Although there has been widespread agreement within the German labor movement that reform is necessary, consensus frequently broke down when it came to the direction and the details. Disagreement repeatedly produced gridlock at the confederational level. Consequently, the largest four individual unions have been pursuing their own reforms, which have focused principally on union mergers to counterbalance declining membership. This conservative strategy of German labor has proved relatively successful in the short run in preserving the status quo, but if participation and coverage continues to decline in the postwar industrial relations regime, the risk of a slow slide into irrelevance becomes increasingly likely. Squaring the contradiction between preserving the *Flächentarifvertrag* and introducing greater grass-roots participation will be the principal dilemma with which German unionists must grapple if they are to survive and even prosper in the twenty-first century.

Politics

The German state still plays an active and effective role in sustaining the postwar industrial relations order. This has allowed organized labor in the Federal Republic to focus attention beyond immediate existential concerns to more strategic and long-term matters, which in turn has helped to account for the relatively successful record of the German labor movement and German dominance in setting the strategic direction for the European labor movement.

The collapse of "real existing socialism" in central and eastern Europe disoriented many German trade unionists and damaged the reputation of the labor movement. Few postwar German unionists were ever Communists, but many were Marxists, and the events of 1989 and 1990 severely tarnished their long-held utopian goal of a socialist society. Many western German unionists quietly continue to cling to socialism as a goal today, if for no other reason than the want of an acceptable alternative. This has, however, only contributed to the transformation of labor's image in German popular opinion since 1980 from one of modernizer to dinosaur. In eastern Germany, the vast majority of the rank and file have no interest in resuming the pursuit of a socialist vision, although some express nostalgia for elements from the GDR years. This shift in opinion regarding socialism is extremely important, because it has subtly eroded the ability of trade union leaders to influence public policy.

The ending of the Cold War did perform a service for the German labor movement by bringing to an end the often exaggerated internal ideological debate between the so-called accommodationist unions, such as *Industriegewerkschaft Bergbau, Chemie, Energie* (IG BCE) and IG BAU, that endorsed "social partnership" with employers, and "militant" or "activist" unions, such as IG Metall and Media Employees' Industrial Union (*Industriegewerkschaft Medien*, IG Medien), whose leaders depicted their organizations as a "countervailing" force to capitalism.[34] In practice, this distinction was more often a matter of style than of substance. Activist as well as accommodationist unions regularly concluded collective bargaining agreements, confronted employers when necessary, and cooperated with them when it was for the greater good of their members. It was principally when the unions addressed the greater issues of the day over which they had no control, such as foreign policy, that the differences became most pronounced. The end of the Cold War finally provided unionists from both sides with the opportunity to jettison this distinction without a difference that produced little other than division and rivalry within the ranks of organized labor.

Until the late 1990s, fealty to the principle of "unitary and non-partisan unionism" (*Einheitsgewerkschaft*) precluded any explicit support of the SPD. Nonetheless, there has always been substantial cooperation between the German labor movement and the SPD. The preponderance of postwar labor leaders have been SPD members as well, and the DGB has worked closely with the SPD in numerous ways that it has not done with any other party.

Over the past thirty years the DGB has come full circle in its relationship with the German Social Democratic Party. During the first two decades of the Federal Republic, the DGB suffered from a "state fixation," which was in large part the product of the inability of the SPD to attain power. DGB leaders presumed that an SPD-led government would solve its major problems by strengthening the labor and codetermination laws, creating a lavish welfare state and implementing Keynesian demand management. Once the SPD finally came to power in the Federal Republic for the first time in the latter half of the 1960s, union officials were sorely disappointed. In particular, the policies of the SPD-

FDP governments during the 1970s and early 1980s fell far short of organized labor's expectations. By 1980, however, years of frustration and disappointment with SPD-led governments led many unionists to dismiss the efficacy of government and instead begin to explore the extent to which the labor movement could "rely on its own power" (i.e., use collective bargaining and social mobilization) to achieve economic and social progress without the SPD.[35]

The formation in 1982 and subsequent longevity of the coalition between the CDU/CSU and the FDP at first served to reinforce labor's relative shift away from government and more toward direct action. Union leaders during the 1980s often described the campaign to reduce the workweek as a direct means for labor to reduce unemployment, which was necessary because the government was unwilling to use active labor market policies. Yet, by the late 1990s, the limits of labor's own power had become apparent. Despite the reduction of the average workweek by more than two hours since 1984, the jobless rate had climbed to record postwar highs and real incomes had begun to ebb. The surge in unemployment was concentrated in manufacturing, the stronghold of organized labor. Hence, the increased joblessness not only undercut German labor's negotiating strength at the bargaining table, but also was a prime cause of union membership declines.

Union officials had also become increasingly frustrated with the longevity of Helmut Kohl's chancellorship, not least because it precluded more active labor market intervention. Consequently, the DGB executive committee, in coordination with the heads of the individual unions, decided in October 1997 to set aside DM 8 million to launch a nationwide advertising campaign entitled, "Your Voice for Jobs and Social Justice." This six-month campaign, which ran from April to September 1998, included public posters, print advertisements, cinema spots, flyers and public demonstrations. The campaign's stated objective was to promote a "change of policy" at the federal level to one more favorable to employees, but in practice it was a thinly veiled effort to campaign for the replacement of the Kohl government with an SPD-Alliance '90/The Greens coalition in the 27 September 1998 federal elections.[36]

The open acceptance of the Alliance Greens at the 1998 DGB congress marked the culmination of a long and often difficult rapprochement. In the 1970s, both right and left within the union movement judged the Greens antithetical to labor. Leftists denounced the Greens as reactionary and *petit bourgeois* because they challenged materialism and stressed individual rights. Traditional unionists decried the Greens as utopian extremists whose naïve proposals would destroy jobs. Initially, both wings of the labor movement mistakenly dismissed the Greens as just a passing fad among upper-and middle-class college graduates.[37] A lasting relationship between the German labor movement and the Greens only unfolded in the 1990s, a good decade after the alternative party first appeared on the national scene. German unification and leadership change leavened attitudes within both movements. The Greens became considerably more moderate, particularly after unification when many from the fundamentalist wing left the party. A wave of retirements in the labor movement allowed a younger generation that better understood the Greens to rise to prominence. The appearance of the SED successor, the Party of Democratic Socialism (PDS), on the political landscape in the 1990s also made the Greens look relatively benign by comparison.

Union engagement in partisan politics is commonplace in most countries, but not in Germany owing to the *Einheitsgewerkschaft* principle and a political debacle dating back to the early years of the Federal Republic. In 1953, the DGB chose "Vote for a Better *Bundestag*" as a federal electoral slogan. Since the incumbent chancellor was Christian Democrat Konrad Adenauer, this slogan was a none-too-subtle endorsement of the SPD. The strategy backfired. The SPD actually lost seats and many blamed in part the DGB's partisan campaign.[38] After the 1953 election, the DGB regularly limited its electoral activity to issuing a set of "electoral touch stones" (*Wahlprüfsteine*) a few months before each federal election to serve as a voters' guide. The electoral touch stones were invariably far closer to the positions of the SPD than any other party, but Christian Democrats within the German labor movement did not judge this to be a violation of the principle of *Einheitsgewerkschaft*. In 1994, the DGB under its newly elected president Dieter Schulte again issued electoral touch stones but supplemented them with a position paper on job creation entitled *Five-Way Strategy to More Employment*, which it promoted heavily during the campaign.[39] Once again there were no objections to this more active involvement in the federal election campaign because it did not explicitly endorse any candidate or coalition.

Leading trade unionists argued that the 1998 Jobs and Social Justice campaign was also not a break from the nonpartisan tradition of *Einheitsgewerkschaft* because it called for a change in *policy* – which, in theory at least – any political configuration could do. In practice, however, organized labor campaigned aggressively for the SPD candidate for chancellor, Gerhard Schröder, and a "red-green" coalition. German labor leaders transformed the 1998 DGB congress into little more than a five-day electoral rally for Gerhard Schröder. The DGB even had the Düsseldorf convention hall decorated in red and green. Then labor minister (and IG

Metall member) Norbert Blüm and Helmut Kohl criticized the DGB for staging this partisan electoral extravaganza. In his speech to the convention delegates, Helmut Kohl stated that he continued to support *Einheitsgewerkschaft* as a principle and that he found the DGB's abandonment of nonpartisanship to be an "unhappy development." Kohl then added, "I would be a bit more careful … I think in this disagreement … that we should maintain at least a few standards."[40]

Unfortunately, the unrelenting focus on the 1998 federal election left many difficult organizational issues unresolved, such as reforming the structure of the DGB (including its articulation to the member unions) and a new means to attract younger employees.[41] This left many delegates despondent; even the DGB's own information service quoted one lamenting, "I have been to funerals that were more fun. I feel no trace of a breakthrough mood."[42] Thus, in the late 1990s, the German labor movement broke from its postwar tradition of nonpartisanship to embrace a political strategy that amounted to little more than "praying" for a friendly government, despite labor's dismal track record elsewhere in Europe with this approach during the 1980s.[43]

On 27 September 1998, the DGB's prayers were answered. The German electorate voted a red-green government into power. The new government quickly expressed its gratitude to the DGB. It repealed most of the Kohl government's labor market reforms and IG Metall vice president Walter Riester – a man widely judged to be the most creative and capable strategist in the German labor movement – became the new federal labor minister. As promised, Schröder put Riester in charge of constituting an "alliance for jobs" (*Bündnis für Arbeit*) forum to bring together a small circle of top representatives from organized labor, management, and the federal government to develop initiatives to reduce unemployment.

Collective Bargaining

In the postwar era, the German labor movement's core task has been collective bargaining. Since 1980, the economic and social environment for collective bargaining has become increasingly difficult. Nevertheless, German unions have managed to defend the standard of living of the *employed* during the 1990s. Deep-seated problems have increasingly come to overshadow immediate incremental successes, however.

Real gross wages and salaries per employee grew by 0.7 percent each year on average in West Germany during the 1980s and 0.9 percent from 1990 to 1997. This pales in comparison to the 3.8 percent average annual increase of the 1970s. The gap between the 1970s and 1980s widens further when benefits are taken into consideration. On the one hand, this comparison slightly understates labor's success in advancing wages and salaries since the 1970s because the data are calculated on an annual basis and therefore do not reflect the hourly increases employees received as part of the agreements to reduce weekly working time (i.e., averaging approximately 0.3 percent per year). On the other hand, real nonwage benefits grew by approximately 6 percent per year on average in the 1970s, but by only 1.3 percent per year in the 1980s. The growth rate in terms of total compensation was roughly the same in the 1990s as in the 1980s because working time reduction continued, and nonwage costs advanced at roughly the same rate as wages and salaries in the 1990s. Growth in real compensation in the 1980s and 1990s did not outstrip labor productivity as it had in the 1970s. The gross adjusted employees' share of the national income, which peaked in 1982 at 72.5 percent, dropped sharply until it bottomed out at a more than thirty-year low of 64.5 percent in 1990; it has since fluctuated between 65 and 68 percent.

Organized labor has scored several victories through collective bargaining. In the spring of 1984, IG Metall won an arduous six-and-one-half week strike over weekly working time reduction that was the largest and most expensive labor dispute in German history.[44] Once IG Metall had broken through the forty-hour barrier, the other DGB unions also began to press for weekly working time reduction, but only IG Metall and IG Medien actually attained a 35-hour workweek by the mid 1990s.[45]

The ultimate impact of the drive to obtain weekly working time reduction on the German industrial relations order was more negative than positive, however. IG Metall and IG Medien did manage in the short run to reassert the primacy of their unions over the works councils and to turn back the disintegration of pattern bargaining in their sectors, but at a tremendous cost. By the end of the 1980s, reducing the workweek had inadvertently disrupted the delicate economic balance among employers in several sectors that had sustained the system of *Flächentarifverträge*.

The politics behind working time reduction are complex. Officials in the media and metalworkers' unions embraced cutting weekly working time principally for two reasons, neither of which has anything to do with the publicly stated explanation (i.e., to reduce unemployment). First, the drive for working time reduction enabled each union to preserve their dominant structural position over works councils. Raising the demand for weekly working time reduction made the entire issue of the deployment of labor a topic of collective bargaining. This allowed union leaders to reassert control over an increasingly salient issue that had previously been the province of the works councils, thereby shoring up union hegemony within the German industrial relations regime.

Second, the policy of weekly working time reduction allowed the unionists to make a grand gesture to the unemployed while actually advancing the *wages* of the members further than if the unions had simply pursued straightforward wage negotiations. How? It is important to note that an essential component of weekly working time reduction, as union strategists have formulated and pursued it, included an *increase* in the hourly wage in order to ensure that the weekly wage remained the same. Union theorists relied on the Keynesian notion of preserving aggregate purchasing power to justify *voller Lohnausgleich*, or "full wage-compensation" for weekly working time reduction. In practice, this component of working time reduction actually gave German unionists a second avenue to pursue wage increases that was far less vulnerable than direct pay rises to the right-wing charge that wage increases produced additional unemployment. Unionists even insisted that full wage compensation actually *increased* rather than decreased employment, because of its Keynesian countercyclical effect.[46] From 1983 (i.e., the year before IG Metall broke through the forty-hour barrier) to 1993, the real weekly wage increased by 15.2 percent, but the real hourly wage advanced by 26 percent, that is, by almost three-quarters more. This hourly rise compared favorably to sectors that did not pursue shortening the workweek as aggressively. Thus IG Metall was able to have its cake and eat it too; union officials were able to make the *rhetorical claim* that they were working toward reducing unemployment (although most evidence indicates that working time reduction did little to secure jobs)[47] while actually increasing the hourly wages of their members.

The 1992-93 recession, which hit the metalworking industry particularly hard, forced trade unionists and employers to draft creative contracts and to compromise in order to save jobs, firms, and comprehensive collective bargaining. A 1993 Volkswagen accord served as a model for a special two-year supplementary collective agreement covering the entire western German metalworking sector signed in 1994. This agreement permitted firms in financial trouble to reduce the workweek to thirty hours *without* compensatory increases in the hourly wage in exchange for a firing freeze.

German unification and the decade-long campaign to reduce weekly working time consumed so much time and effort that it produced an "issue blockage" *(Regulierungsstau)* in many other areas of collective bargaining.[48] In particular, the social partners in most sectors had neglected to update the overarching framework for collective bargaining, which is codified in a series of sectoral "skeletal" and "framework" contracts *(Manteltarifverträge and Rahmentarifverträge)*. Both labor and management agree that the multiyear skeletal and framework accords, which in many sectors are three to four decades old, are in desperate need of revision. Some of these contracts, which are a throwback to the heyday of Fordist mass production, contain provisions for occupations that no longer exist, such as computer card hole punchers, but provide little guidance regarding compensation for new positions (e.g., webmaster). Few provide guidance for compensating employees engaged in new forms of work, including group work, project work, satellite-office work, telecommuting, or new organizational forms, for example, pay for performance and internal contracting.

An additional anachronism is the division between blue- and white-collar employees. Blue- and white-collar employees typically have separate contracts; firms pay blue-collar workers by the hour or piece, and white-collar employees receive monthly salaries. Over the past twenty years, the distinction between blue- and white-collar work in factories has virtually collapsed, yet most existing framework agreements compensate white-collar workers substantially more for doing essentially the same tasks. Large segments of both the business and labor communities have proposed replacing the separate blue- and white-collar framework agreement with a unitary compensation framework contract *(einheitliche Entgelttarifvertrag)*.[49]

Despite the common acknowledgment of the need for collective bargaining reform and the agreement regarding the areas needing attention, trade union leaders, employers' association representatives and the business establishment in general have all publicly stated that the advantages of the *Flächentarifvertrag* system still outweigh the disadvantages.[50] Change has been slow and uneven because building a consensus around a particular set of alternatives has been far more difficult than acknowledging the inadequacy of the status quo. For example, the sticking point stalling the creation of a unitary compensation framework contract in most sectors is not the concept in general, but the decision whether to increase blue-collar wages or decrease white-collar salaries in real terms to reach parity. IG BCE is one of the few unions that has a unitary compensation framework contract because it agreed in the late 1980s to a complex multiyear framework contract that constrains the income growth of some white-collar employees in the chemicals sector.[51] Other unions have not wanted to risk alienating their white-collar constituency or to forego the opportunity to advance blue-collar incomes.

Expanding flexibility in compensation and in working time has been especially difficult to negotiate. Both sides accept the idea of replacing the traditional fixed-percentage increase with options, but differ over what those options should be. IG BCE and the chemical industry employers' association have taken the lead in this area as well; during the mid 1990s, they added to their contracts a weekly working time "corridor" of thiry to forty hours and a compensation "corridor" that allows a firm experiencing economic hardship to undercut the collective bargaining rate by as much as 10 percent if it agrees to a firing freeze.[52] IG Metall, in contrast, prefers a collective bargaining "menu" and a "hardship clause" to corridors. A collective bargaining menu would fix the total compensation cost, but permit employers to assemble compensation packages from a variety of "building blocks." IG Metall's eastern contracts already contain hardship clauses. They permit economically troubled firms to petition the collective bargaining parties to consider a reduction of wages and benefits below the contractually established minimum.[53] Employers prefer something resembling the arrangement in the chemical industry. They also favor making the payment of some benefits, such as Christmas bonuses and vacation pay, contingent on the economic well-being of the firm, as well as using arbitration more often to settle disputes. IG Metall, for its part, would prefer that employees be paid according to their education and training rather than the specific requirements of the jobs they are doing.[54]

In late 1997, Gesamtmetall and IG Metall made substantial headway toward completing a reform of the *Flächentarifvertrag* system, but the parties paused in early 1998 because they did not wish to bargain during the months leading up to the September federal election. They resumed discussions after the election, but the place remained glacial. Significant differences still remain, so a quick agreement is by no means guaranteed. Nonetheless, both sides see themselves on the road toward enacting a reform of the *Flächentarifvertrag* system that will provide each firm with a limited set of opportunities to tailor compensation to meet company needs and to allow less profitable firms to reduce labor costs in a controlled fashion.[55] In other words, in order to preserve legitimacy and stem flight, the stewards of the unitary "leakproof" German collective bargaining regime are in the throes of converting it into a controlled two-tiered system in a bid to preserve its comprehensive coverage.

Although the process and structure of collective bargaining are on the verge of significant change, the substance has remained remarkably the same, particularly in the metalworking sector. In April 1997, IG Metall president Klaus Zwickel proposed the thirty-two-hour, four-day workweek as IG Metall's next collective bargaining objective. Zwickel's proposal proved controversial both inside and outside of the metalworkers' union. Many local union officials objected to further working time reduction because they knew most of their members would rather receive more money. IG Metall "modernizers" also wished to avoid repeating the dogmatic debate over working time of the 1980s, particularly under the dramatically different economic circumstances of the 1990s. The modernizers would have preferred a far more flexible policy of working time reduction in keeping with current trends (for example, the use of "time accounts" into which employees can "deposit" overtime hours that they can later "withdraw" with interest to fund an extended leave or early retirement) rather than simply demanding an even shorter fixed workweek for all.[56]

Zwickel's proposal also divided unionists outside of IG Metall. DGB president Dieter Schulte, a former IG Metall executive committee member, at first rejected but then ultimately embraced Zwickel's proposal. Schulte even went so far as to proclaim the twenty-five-hour workweek as a long-term goal of the labor movement at the 1998 DGB convention. ÖTV president Herbert Mai and the heads of many other public and service-sector unions supported the thirty-two-hour week as a goal, whereas IG BCE president Hubertus Schmoldt dismissed setting a single weekly working time as anachronistic.[57] If nothing else, Klaus Zwickel's proposal to reduce the workweek to thirty-two hours demonstrated the lack of consensus among German trade unionists regarding the future content of collective bargaining.

Collective bargaining concerns in eastern Germany have been more existential. When the Federal Republic of Germany and the German Democratic Republic united economically in July 1990, eastern wages equaled approximately one-third of the average western wage, the official workweek was forty-three hours and forty-five minutes, eighteen annual vacation days were standard, and eastern productivity equaled roughly one-quarter of the western rate. By 1997, eastern wages had risen to 77 percent of the western average, most eastern employees received twenty-eight vacation days, and the average workweek had fallen to 39.5 hours. Eastern productivity in 1997 amounted to only 57 percent of the western level. Between 1991 and 1993, eastern unit labor costs as a percentage of western unit labor costs fell from 150.7 to 133.5 percent. The relative unit labor costs then remained stubbornly high as wage increases kept pace with productivity gains until 1997 when they dropped to 123 percent of western unit labor costs.

The desolate situation in eastern Germany has produced desperate measures. In early 1998, the metal industry employers' associations of Saxony, Saxony-Anhalt, and Thuringia with the blessing of Gesamtmetall founded a new, subsidiary employers' association called "Ostmetall."

The eastern metal industry employers' associations designed Ostmetall to be an alternative association for those firms that had refused to join the eastern Gesamtmetall members because the *Flächentarifvertrag* was too expensive or for those firms who were contemplating quitting because of IG Metall's aggressive demands.[58] IG Metall refused to bargain with Ostmetall because the union judged the subsidiary employers' association to be both a bargaining tactic and a threat to the *Flächentarifvertrag* system.

In May 1998, however, Ostmetall concluded a five-year agreement dubbed "Phoenix" with the tiny *Christliche Gewerkschaft Metall* (CGM, Christian Metal Employees' Union). The CGM is not a part of the DGB. It is a confessional union with no party affiliation that claims a total of only 110,000 members throughout Germany and 7,500 in the area covered by the contract. The Phoenix contract provides a single compensation structure for blue- and white-collar employees, an annual "working time corridor" of 1,800 to 2,200 hours (i.e., thirty-one to forty-two hours per week, excluding holidays and thirty vacation days), a liberal hardship clause, mandatory profit sharing, and compulsory mediation in industrial disputes. Three-quarters of the metal industry workplaces in the area covered by Ostmetall are legally eligible to adopt the Phoenix contract immediately, since they do not belong to an employers' association, but few have in practice.[59]

Never before in German postwar collective bargaining history have there been competing *Flächentarifverträge* in the same sector and region. IG Metall's response has been to denounce Phoenix as a "phantom contract" because the CGM has so few members, and to challenge the legitimacy of the CGM as a union in court.[60] In other words, labor is relying on the state to protect the postwar German collective bargaining regime. The ultimate potency of Phoenix as a threat hinges on the court's ruling.

In summary, through hard work and several struggles, German unionists during the 1980s and 1990s have managed to avert the worst possible outcome in the realm of collective bargaining, that is, the collapse of the *Flächentarifvertrag*. This accomplishment sets the German labor movement apart from many others in the industrialized world that have lost comprehensive and sectoral bargaining; but even in Germany, the days of the uniform sectoral collective bargaining agreement are numbered. The slowly emerging compromise package for reforming the collective bargaining order introduces elements of flexibility and choice into collective bargaining contracts. In the short run, it is likely to contribute significantly toward stemming at least some of the erosion of employer participation in the traditional manufacturing sectors of western Germany. A successful reform of the system of *Flächentarifverträge* may even persuade a sufficient number of eastern managers operating outside of the postwar collective bargaining regime to join it, thereby making the reformed collective bargaining order viable in eastern Germany. A successful reform of the *Flächentarifvertrag* system would not be able to reverse the long-run structural and demographic trends working against organized labor, however. A successful reorganization of the labor movement itself is also necessary.

Organizational Responses

The German labor movement is currently undergoing its first thoroughgoing organizational reform since its reestablishment half a century ago. Many in the labor movement hoped that restructuring the German labor movement would be a synoptic, cooperative endeavor based on a new strategic vision of what trade unions should be in the twenty-first century. In practice, the reform effort deteriorated into a piecemeal power struggle for institutional and personal survival among union elites. Financial crisis rather than strategic planning has been the most powerful force shaping the reorganization of the German labor movement. Between 1995 and 1997, union mergers cut the number of DGB affiliates from sixteen to twelve. Union leaders have already agreed to an additional round of mergers that will bring the independent *Deutsche-Angestellten Gewerkschaft* (DAG, German White-Collar Employees' Union) into the DGB as a part of a massive service employees' union and reduce the number of DGB member unions to seven by the year 2000.

For decades, German unionists attempted to mask these structural problems with superficial and ad hoc measures designed to preserve the status quo, but this conservative approach proved insufficient to the challenges that had arisen by the early 1990s. A spate of jurisdictional disputes and the high cost of expanding eastward served both to accentuate the German labor movement's existing organizational imbalances and to exacerbate financial shortcomings. The simultaneity of the shock added to the complexity of the enterprise, but it also offered the possibility of a more comprehensive reorganization. The reform discussion focused on two points: how should the DGB member unions reorganize themselves and what should be the division of labor between the individual member unions and the DGB?

The debate over the reconfiguration of the individual unions has been fractious. Broadly speaking, two competing blueprints came to the fore in the mid 1990s: an IG Chemie plan to create approximately half a dozen self-sufficient "multibranch" unions and two proposals from the smaller DGB affiliates and the public-sector unions simply to coordinate activities more closely. IG Chemie officials argued that unions would only survive in the twenty-first century if they became high quality, self-sufficient service providers for an increasingly sophisticated, nonideological, professional clientele. Trade union self-sufficiency would raise "brand loyalty" among members. Consequently, all services the DGB provided directly to union members, such as legal aid and group discounts, should be done by individual unions. In order to obtain the full economies of scale required to provide a full set of professional services at a reasonable cost directly to members, each multibranch union would need a membership of at least one million. The only way to achieve this would be through a series of union mergers that would eliminate the smaller unions.[61] The IG Chemie leadership added that one million member multibranch unions would also have far more leverage in Berlin and Brussels.[62] IG Chemie officials held up their own organization as a model. It was in the midst of merging with *Industriegewerkschaft Bergbau und Energie* (IGBE, Mining and Energy Employees' Industrial Union) and *Gewerkschaft Leder* (GL, Leatherworkers' Union) to form the one-million-member-strong *Industriegewerkschaft Bergbau, Chemie, Energie*.

IG BAU and IG Metall have pursued a strategy similar to IG Chemie's, albeit in a quieter fashion. IG BAU merged with the Agricultural, Forest and Garden Employees' Union in 1995. IG Metall absorbed *Gewerkschaft Textil-Bekleidung* (GTB, Textile and Apparel Employees' Union) in 1997, and *Gewerkschaft Holz und Kunststoff* (GHK, Wood and Plastic Workers' Union) agreed to merge with the metalworkers' union at the end of 1999.

Self-sufficient multibranch unionism has had numerous detractors, however. Five objections stood out. First, many accused IG Chemie of promoting a stark version of industrial unionism simply as a tactic to force recalcitrant smaller unions into mergers with larger ones by depriving them of the common DGB services (e.g., office space and legal services) upon which they depend for survival. Second, IG Chemie's plan combines unions in a haphazard fashion. Personal feuds among union leaders and staff pay scales of potential suitors have played a far greater role in determining mergers than any organizational or economic logic.[63] Third, the IG Chemie proposal strengthens industrial unionism and its underlying logic (one workplace, one union) precisely at a time when the organization of work is moving in the opposite direction. Fourth, some have pointed out that the sheer size of the multibranch unions would make recruitment, retention, and representation difficult in many sectors. A massive, impersonal, and bureaucratic apparatus running a trade union would most certainly alienate not only large numbers of potential members who would fear that such an organization would be incapable of addressing their individual needs, but also its officials who would have trouble identifying with it as "their" organization. Large size would make organizing particularly difficult in smaller workplaces and sectors where shared skills and allegiance to a profession are extremely important.[64] Finally, critics are concerned that multibranch unionism would narrow the political horizon of the organization solely to the problems of jurisdiction, decreasing the likelihood that unions would be interested in cross-sectoral solidarity beyond their union during strikes and other campaigns.[65]

Two groups of union heads initially proposed an alternative to IG Chemie's vision of multibranch unionism, which they called "cooperative unionism." One was comprised of the five traditional public sector unions: ÖTV, the German Railroad Employees' Union (*Gewerkschaft der Eisenbahner Deutschlands*, GdED), the German Postal Employees' Union (Deutsche Postgewerkschaft, DPG), the Police Officers' Union (*Gewerkschaft der Polizei*, GdP), and the Education and Scientific Employees' Union (*Gewerkschaft Erziehung und Wissenschaft*, GEW). The other was an alliance among four moderate-sized private-sector unions known as the "four little tigers": the GHK, GTB, IG Medien and the Food, Restaurant, Hotel Employees' Union (*Gewerkschaft Nahrung-Genuss-Gaststätten*, NGG).

The plans of both these groups were sketchy on details and gave no indication of the extent to which cooperation could actually cut costs. Neither plan proved viable in practice, and the two groupings quickly fell apart. Three of the four little tigers merged with much larger unions; only the fourth, NGG, remains independent. The independent white-collar employees' union, DAG, and five of the DGB public-sector unions agreed to a provisional "policy platform" that lays out a timetable for forming a single massive public and private service-sector union with over 3.5 million members by the fourth quarter of 1999.[66] The new union would become the largest DGB affiliate (displacing IG Metall), and the largest single union in the world. If all the planned mergers come to fruition, the German trade union landscape of the twenty-first century will look starkly different. It will consist of seven DGB affiliates: four multibranch unions (the "policy platform" service-sector union, IG Metall, IG BCE, and IG BAU), two small public sector unions (DPG and GdED), and the private service-sector NGG. Whether this new configuration will prove to be more efficient, effective, influential, or successful in attracting new members remains to be seen.

Throughout the 1990s, the DGB served as center stage in the internal struggle over the future direction of the German labor movement. In November 1990, just six months after being elected DGB president,

Heinz-Werner Meyer, a former president of the miners' union, gave the keynote address at the "Hattingen Forum," a newly created venue for trade unionists and intellectuals to exchange ideas for renewing the German labor movement. Meyer consciously chose this occasion because a research team comprised of union and academic experts was presenting its findings from an exhaustive study on the political, ideological, and structural weaknesses of the labor movement entitled, *Beyond the Resolution Register*. Meyer endorsed the study's central conclusion that unions needed to launch a thoroughgoing and wide-open "discourse" within their ranks and to introduce a wide variety of decentralized and participatory reforms if they were to remain a viable force in the twenty-first century.[67]

DGB officials decided to write a new Basic Program stating the ideological understanding and the policy goals of the German trade union movement from scratch rather than simply amending the existing program, as had been done in the past. DGB staff members began drafting the program by posing a set of ten "guiding questions" *(Leitfragen)*,[68] which they invited unionists and nonunionists alike to discuss through a series of written contributions,[69] meetings, and open fora.[70] Despite the DGB's best efforts, little debate ensued, except among top union officials and a handful of sympathetic academics.[71]

The final result of four years of intensive labor was a new Basic Program, which the DGB approved in Dresden on 16 November 1996. Whereas the new Basic Program is a substantial improvement over previous programs, it suffers from two problems that often plague these types of documents. It ratifies current practice far more often than it breaks new ground, and it frequently resorts to the language of compromise, which blurs its focus. The most controversial element of the Basic Program is its acceptance of the social market economy as a system that has proven superior to socialism for achieving the objectives of working people. It does point out that the social market economy is far from perfect: it has not prevented mass unemployment or produced social justice. It concludes, however, that the benefits of the social market economy far outweigh its flaws. The Basic Program also calls for a greater integration of economic and environmental objectives, greater co-shaping *(Mitgestaltung)* of the society and economy for trade unions, more thoroughgoing equality for women, and a socially responsible and democratic Europe.[72]

The DGB leadership had originally planned to approve a comprehensive reorganization of the DGB at the Dresden convention as well, but this did not take place because the document was nowhere near completion. By 1996, the dispute between IG Chemie and its critics, which was in full gear, and the onset of financial crises throughout the German trade union movement slowed progress regarding an organizational reform to a standstill. Much of labor's financial crisis was a product of German unification. German trade unions and the DGB spent substantial sums extending their organizations eastward in 1990 and 1991. At first, labor leaders hoped that these expenditures would pay off. Expectations ran high that the addition of large numbers of eastern members would help alleviate the financial problems that had bedeviled the labor movement during the 1980s – these included the collapse in scandal of several cooperative ventures, including the Co-op supermarket chain and the largest housing authority in western Europe, *Neue Heimat*. It soon became apparent, however, that labor's hopes would not be realized.

The eastward expansion of the labor movement proved expensive. The DGB and its member unions had to hire, to transfer, and to deploy new staff throughout the east. They also had to rent offices and equipment and to set up a communications network from scratch under extremely primitive circumstances. Anticipation of inevitable job losses led many labor leaders (particularly those from manufacturing sectors) deliberately to build organizations that could service far fewer members than the initial numbers belonging to their eastern branches. Until the shakeout came, however, these unions were hopelessly understaffed. Other union leaders, particularly those in the public and service sectors, established a large apparatus in the five new states in the belief that the initial employment and membership levels in their sectors would remain stable because the former GDR had such a disproportionally small service sector. Yet, the number of job losses far outstripped even the most pessimistic estimates from 1990 and 1991, so all unions suddenly found their eastern offices overstaffed. Lower eastern wages and a lower ratio of full-time employees to members held the average eastern per capita monthly dues payment to between 50 and 60 percent of that in the west. Thus, almost every union spent far more money setting up and maintaining operations in eastern Germany than it collected in dues.

All of the DGB member unions, save the police officers' union, suffered significant eastern membership declines that have pinched finances to a greater or lesser degree. A few unions, such as HBV, ÖTV, and DAG, had to cut back severely, sell property, and dip into their strike funds during the mid 1990s in order to close annual budget deficits exceeding between DM 20 and 70 million. Most others, including the metalworkers' union, implemented hiring freezes and pared back perquisites in order to close deficits ranging from hundreds of thousands to a few million *deutsche Mark*.[73]

The DGB receives over 90 percent of its income from a contribution of 12 percent of the gross dues of each affiliate union. Hence, when membership declines, so does the DGB's income. The financial crisis hit the DGB particularly hard. It forced the DGB to cut its operating budget by DM 59 million (i.e., 17 percent) between 1992 and 1997. Over the same period, the DGB trimmed total staff by 625 to 2,075, including a reduction at the Düsseldorf headquarters from 330 to 210 officials.[74]

Declining membership was not the only development draining the union confederation's coffers during the mid 1990s. The massive job losses in the former GDR have produced a colossal wave of expensive unfair-dismissal litigation. Even the most basic case of this type can easily cost DM 10,000. The litigation boom prompted the DGB, which handled most legal matters directly for the unions, to increase its staff of legal experts by 150 (i.e., 40 percent) between 1989 and 1993 in order to meet the demand in the five eastern states (cf. the former GDR accounted for only 25 percent of total DGB membership in 1993). The cancerous growth of DGB legal services helped to push up the share of the DGB budget consumed by personnel costs between 1991 and 1994 from 55 to 72 percent.[75]

The 1994 Berlin DGB convention amended DGB statutes an unprecedented forty-two times, in most cases instituting some form of austerity. In tandem with the overall DGB employment reductions in the national, state-district, and local offices discussed earlier, the delegates cut the size of the DGB Managing Federal Executive Committee *(Geschäftsführender Bundesvorstand)* from eight members to five, the DGB convention from 600 delegates to 400 (starting in 1998), the DGB Federal Committee *(Bundesausschuss)* from 100 representatives to seventy and the DGB state district boards *(Landesbezirksvorstände)* from three members to two. The Berlin convention also decreased the required number of DGB Federal Committee meetings per year from two to one, reduced the size and authority of the DGB departments for collective bargaining, education, foreign employees, handicrafts, and technology, and eliminated DGB departments for civil servants, white-collar employees, and blue-collar workers. The convention did spare the DGB women and youth departments, so as not to send the wrong signal regarding labor's commitment to these groups.[76]

Financial crisis increasingly came to dominate the debate over the organizational reform of the German labor movement, which worked to the advantage of the supporters of multibranch unionism. As dues income plummeted and expenses soared, the DGB shed increasing numbers of programs and personnel to balance its budget. These cuts were ad hoc rather than planned, but they amounted to a de facto organizational reform, namely, a sharp decline in the DGB's relative importance.

In July 1997, the unrelenting financial pressures forced the smaller unions, which had been dependent on DGB lawyers to provide legal services for their members, to accept a complex plan to detach legal services from the DGB and to devolve their provision largely to the individual unions. In practice, common legal services had always subsidized the small unions at the expense of the big ones. The new arrangement pared back the subsidy drastically, freeing up funds for the supporters of multi-branch unionism to begin to offer their own legal services, while undercutting both the financial viability of the smaller unions and further eroding the relative power of the DGB.[77]

Deadlock over organizational reform persisted into 1998. The delegates to the 1998 DGB congress were supposed to complete the long-delayed organizational reform (as well as discuss new means to recruit younger union members), but union leaders instead concentrated almost exclusively on promoting the candidacy of Gerhard Schröder for the federal chancellorship, leaving the project once again unfinished. As a quick fix, the DGB leadership submitted a resolution asking the congress to delegate authority over organizational reform to the DGB Federal Committee, but skeptical delegates, many of whom felt bruised in the recent battles over legal services and DGB budgets, voted down the resolution. As a result, organizational reform of the German labor movement remained stalled and the DGB continued to waste away by default.[78]

Deadlock plagued progress at the European level as well. German union officials rarely miss an opportunity to embrace Europe rhetorically because it resonates well with the anti-nationalistic leanings of the German left. In practice, however, most German union leaders (in particular, IG Metall) have repeatedly tried to use the European trade union apparatus simply to pressure unions in other countries to adopt German collective bargaining priorities. Incompatibilities between the "Latin" trade union structure, which vests ultimate authority in the confederation, and the "Teutonic" model, in which the sectoral unions are the dominant players, perpetually complicate the European activities of the German labor movement because the European Trade Union Confederation (ETUC) is largely organized along Latin lines. For example, German unionists have not been wholly hostile to the "social dialogue" at the European level as spelled out in the social protocol to the Maastricht Treaty, but they have gone to great lengths to ensure that the social dialogue does not cede any collective bargaining authority to the DGB or the ETUC.

At the sectoral level, IG BAU, IG BCE, and IG Metall have chosen strikingly different European strategies, yet all share a common defensive goal: the protection of the national *Flächentarifverträge*. During the 1990s, at the urging of IG Metall, the European Metalworkers' Federation (EMF) initiated a series of conferences on coordinating collective bargaining. IG Metall used these conferences primarily to attempt to convince other EMF members to adopt weekly working time reduction and other German objectives as their collective bargaining goals. The EMF has demonstrated a flair for declaring with much fanfare repackaged versions of the status quo constitute substantial progress.[79]

IG BCE has taken an alternative approach toward relations among European unions. It has promoted the co-mingling of organizations through bilateral exchanges between unions. In February 1993, IG BCE's predecessor, IG Chemie, concluded an unprecedented "partnership agreement" with the British General, Municipal and Boilermakers' Union (GMB). The Irish Services, Industrial, Professional, and Technical Union (SIPTU) joined shortly thereafter.[80] The accord calls for language training and the comprehensive exchange of information and personnel among the unions. The objective is first to allow the relationships based on practical cooperation to develop gradually according to their own logic rather than forcing them to follow a master plan. The European Commission has looked favorably on this cooperative approach. Since 1993, it has regularly provided funds to offset the majority of the project's cost.[81] In 1997, the GMB and IG BCE deepened their cooperative effort by offering reciprocal membership access to all union services for each other's members. Although this reciprocal membership accord only covers about 120 members, IG BCE president Hubertus Schmoldt stated that it represented a step toward the goal of "the creation of joint membership at the European level to be able to achieve minimum standards on collective bargaining agreements for all workers."[82] A year later, the GMB and IG BCE concluded a third agreement. This accord expanded the exchange of information and personnel, and established a schedule for regular meetings between the heads of the two unions.[83]

The European Federation of Building and Woodworkers (EFBWW) has cooperated more closely with its opposite number in Brussels, the European Federation of the Construction Industry (*Fédération Industrielle Européenne de la Construction*, FIEC), than any other EIF. The activities of the EFBWW and FIEC have focused on gaining more control over the labor market in the European construction industry.[84]

In summary, the forces promoting multibranch unionism have won the war over the reorganization of the German labor movement. Red ink and internal jockeying have been a far more powerful force than superior reasoning or comprehensive planning in guiding the German labor movement's organizational reform. Similarly, defending the national status quo rather than creative thinking has dominated German labor's approach toward Europe.

Recruitment and Representation

The German labor movement neglected recruitment and representation until well into the 1990s and is still struggling to improve its glaring weaknesses in these areas. German unions have traditionally relied on class solidarity and peer pressure to recruit new members. They have no paid professional organizers and rarely hold membership drives. Union recruiting departments are invariably small and considered a backwater within the organization.[85] The old recruitment methods, however, are proving inadequate. As the decades have progressed, the power of class solidarity has ebbed. The increased affluence of many skilled workers enabled them to leave traditional, tight-knit, working-class neighborhoods and move into the far more socially heterogeneous suburbs.[86] When traditional appeals to solidarity struck little resonance, many union organizers were quick to blame the very people they failed to organize for having insufficient class consciousness rather than reassess the traditional recruitment methods.[87] Employment trends have worked against organized labor. Job creation in Germany has taken place disproportionately in small firms and the service sector, two areas in which unions the world over have immense difficulty organizing. Moreover, the cornerstone principle of the DGB, namely, industrial unionism, is unattractive to most white-collar employees, particularly those in staff positions, because it inevitably leads to blue-collar domination of unions.

Since a large share of the employees in the business information-systems sector are the white-collar service-sector professionals destined to become the skilled workers of the twenty-first century, this field provides good examples of the problems and possibilities for union recruitment and representation in the future. At the start of the 1990s, the business information-systems sector was not a fertile ground for labor. Skilled technicians earned twice the median German income and had substantial on-the-job autonomy. Fewer than 5 percent belonged to a union. The 1992-93 recession triggered the first big wave of layoffs in the sector. The cases of Digital Equipment Corporation (DEC) and IBM-Deutschland are particularly instructive because labor successfully recruited much of the skilled core technicians in the former, but became ghettoized in the blue-collar workforce in the latter.[88]

The most important reason why IG Metall succeeded in making inroads only in DEC was, ironically, because DEC did not belong to an employers' association. DEC's independent status led IG Metall to focus on the individual concerns of DEC white-collar employees, unencumbered by a *Flächentarifvertrag*, giving employees the opportunity to participate *actively* in crafting specific solutions to their particular problems. When IBM-Deutschland reorganized into a holding-company structure in the early 1990s, it used the occasion to escape the jurisdiction of IG Metall. IBM segregated its production from its service activities. The production subsidiary stayed in the metalworkers' employers' association, but all the other service subsidiaries negotiated a set of weak contracts with the DAG. IG Metall responded by asking employees to defend the *Flächentarifvertrag* and force IBM to extend it to all of its subsidiaries. This approach failed to resonate with most skilled technicians who often found IG Metall's standard contract ill-suited to their work.[89]

These two examples illustrate that the German labor movement's recruitment problems are increasingly the result of a clash between pattern and participation. The heart of the German postwar industrial relations regime, the *Flächentarifvertrag*, can often be a barrier to attracting skilled white-collar employees because it precludes active participation, which these types of employees prefer.

Conclusion

In the years since 1980, the postwar German industrial relations regime has weathered challenges of unprecedented number, variety, and intensity. Germany's system of social partnership has shown signs of stress, but – unlike many other industrialized countries – the essential elements of the Federal Republic's postwar labor relations order remain intact. Why has *Modell Deutschland* exhibited such exceptional resiliency? Will German social partnership be able to survive for much longer given the mounting internal and external pressures working against it?

Germany's historical legacy and dense institutional infrastructure greatly help to explain the longevity of the postwar industrial relations regime. The nightmare of National Socialism still serves as a formidable hurdle that thus far has precluded the amassing of a political majority in the Federal Republic favoring a systematic elimination of organized labor's influence. Can historical memory sustain the postwar industrial order forever? Probably not; these taboos remain powerful today, but they are not nearly as significant as they once were. Memories fade. Economic, political, and social conditions continue to diverge from those of the immediate postwar years.

More than historical legacy has helped to sustain the status quo in postwar German industrial relations. Several mutually reinforcing institutional features have also contributed to its duration. A broad guarantee of collective bargaining autonomy in the German constitution, collective agreements that are legally binding, declarations of universal applicability, and legally sanctioned works councils have combined to serve as a strong foundation for the postwar industrial relations order even in the most tempestuous of times. Moreover, the considerable resources of organized labor and management in Germany – including secure finances and large professional staffs – also contribute to the durability of the labor regime.

The single most important explanation for the endurance of the postwar German industrial order, however, is the degree to which core German *employers* still depend on it to achieve ends that otherwise would be exceedingly difficult to accomplish. German employers rely on the rigidities of the labor relations regime to dampen domestic wage competition, to minimize labor strife, to promote and to standardize a high level of training, and to maintain a harmonious environment in the work place. Continuing employer dependence on the industrial relations regime distinguishes Germany from most other industrialized countries; it also helps greatly to explain the exceptional institutional continuity of labor relations in the Federal Republic.

Furthermore, most German employers have remained committed to the postwar industrial relations system because it would be exceptionally difficult to dismantle such a comprehensive system for enforcing minimum standards without abandoning the prevailing postwar business strategy of concentrating on high-end, niche markets for manufactured goods worldwide. Most alternatives to the postwar social partnership would be hard pressed to preserve labor peace or the current system of vocational training. Hence, despite rising employer complaints about the cost of some recent collective bargaining settlements and a surge of employers' association avoidance, few German employers – particularly those at the core of the economy – support loosening the postwar industrial relations system as a credible solution to their problems. Employers' association officials in particular have a strong vested interest in preserving the current highly mediated status quo. Although unions could survive a decentralization of collective bargaining to the plant level, such a transition would largely eliminate the need for employers' associations as they are now constituted in Germany.

German politicians, regardless of party, find themselves in a comparable position. Politicians have greatly benefited from the economic and social stability provided by the postwar industrial relations order. Leaders of all political persuasions, moreover, tend to be conservative when it comes to change capable of redistributing power and resources away from them and toward others, both inside and outside of their parties. As a result, there has never been more than a small minority in the *Bundestag* that has ever supported a loosening of the postwar industrial relations status quo.

The social partners and politicians have therefore typically responded to challenges to the postwar labor relations regime by defending the status quo as best they could. This is not to say that there have been no disputes among labor, management, and the government during these years. Still, this parallel (if not always concerted) shoring up of the German postwar industrial relations order has largely preserved not just the practices, but also the exclusive place of organized labor and management within the regime.

The mutual defense of the industrial relations status quo has not succeeded without a price. Although the leakproof structure of postwar German industrial relations has produced a high degree of equity among its participants, it has managed this only at the *expense* of those outside of the regime, in particular, the unemployed, early retirees, women and others who find themselves involuntarily out of the labor market. Mass unemployment has been chronic since the early 1980s, in large part because of a vicious cycle plaguing the German economy that is in part a byproduct of the postwar labor relations regime. Small- and medium-size enterprises have found it increasingly difficult both to fulfill the requirements of the world's most generous collective labor agreements and to pay exorbitant payroll taxes to support the rising numbers of pensioners, early retirees, the disabled, and the unemployed. More firms go out of business as a result of these high labor costs, which in turn increases the tax burden on those that remain. On the employees' side, those lucky enough to have a job must turn over an increasing share of their paycheck to the state in the form of payroll taxes in order to fund transfer payments to those not participating in the labor market. This expanding tax burden depresses hiring and labor market participation. Since fewer people are working, payroll taxes increase again.

Furthermore, the many efforts undertaken by unions, employers, and the government since 1980 to shore up their individual positions within the postwar industrial relations regime have, ironically, at times had a deleterious effect on other parties, weakening the industrial relations order as a whole. For example, the introduction of lean production and decentralized personnel strategies by business in many sectors posed a challenge to the pre-eminence of the trade unions over works councils. The unions' campaign to reduce working time, which was in part a response to "works council egoism," in turn heightened tensions within the employers' camp between supplier and assembler firms, producing association avoidance and flight.

These often unintended detrimental repercussions have produced a growing minority of dissidents on the periphery of the German industrial relations regime who have begun to question its efficacy. More managers are questioning whether the benefits of comprehensive collective bargaining are truly worth the escalating labor costs. Women, easterners, foreign workers and service employees have increasingly found that the traditional institutions' rigid control over the German labor market may produce considerable affluence and equity among skilled native-born western males, but all too often it disadvantages them. Moreover, as the size of the periphery has grown, critics have increasingly accused trade unions and employers' associations of acting more like members of a special interest cartel than the representatives of all employees and employers.[90]

Many analysts have depicted labor's problems worldwide as principally the product of "globalization" against which unions and individual firms can only react.[91] In Germany, however, employers, government, and organized labor have more often produced problems by selecting policies that have exacerbated underlying internal tensions in the postwar system of social partnership. An obvious example is labor's drive to reduce the workweek mentioned above. Other observers point to the heavy emphasis on hierarchy and formal expertise in German firms, which has hindered the adoption of new production techniques like simultaneous engineering, as well as the one-sided anti-inflationary policy of the *Bundesbank*, which until the second half of the 1990s increased the comparative costs of producing in Germany by driving up the value of the *deutsche Mark* versus most other currencies.

A new German synthesis for maintaining a monopoly over wage determination is gradually arising out of a combination of incremental negotiation and controlled industrial conflict. Although all the details of this new synthesis have by no means been settled yet, its general form can be sketched. The central objective of this new synthesis for German industrial relations remains the same, namely, the preservation of a high-skill/high-wage economy through a heavily mediated labor market. The contours of the labor market, however, are changing radically. The Federal Republic's unitary labor market simply produces too much unemployment and capital flight to persist unamended.

Successive collective agreements since the mid 1990s have been gradually and incrementally constructing a "managed two-tier labor market." Germany's emerging two-tier labor market does have a core and a periphery. Unlike most other dual labor markets, however, the lower portion of the labor market is *not* an informal sector, but is *also* regulated by organized labor and management. The objective is to create a less expensive compensation package for weaker firms in order to stanch association avoidance among employers and to absorb a good share of the unemployed back into the labor market without completely abandoning control over wage competition.

Examples of a managed dual labor market are appearing with increasing frequency throughout much of the German economy. The employment security pacts of the mid 1990s agreed to in most manufacturing sectors, which exchanged reduced hours and compensation for job security, were precursors of this development, as was the de facto pause in progress within many sectors toward wage parity between eastern and western Germany. Since the postwar German system of social partnership primarily evolves incrementally, the precise contours of the secondary labor market are only emerging gradually out of successive rounds of collective bargaining and industrial conflict. Ultimately, however, the trend toward incorporating opening clauses and other special employment arrangements in German collective bargaining agreements, far from a temporary or exceptional phenomenon, is gradually producing a managed two-tier labor market that may ultimately resemble Denmark or the Netherlands.

It is highly unlikely that the postwar German industrial relations regime will suffer a sustained attack. Hollowing out is a far greater risk. The German industrial relations order has weathered almost a decade of declining union membership and fifteen years of employers' association defection. Even if organized labor, management, and government all agree that they wish to continue to work together to police the German labor market, they can only do so if the social partners continue to represent a significant share of their respective constituencies. If membership attrition continues, however, the established social partners inevitably lose both their economic leverage and social legitimacy.

A managed two-tier labor market may successfully prolong the hegemony of the established social partners in the postwar industrial relations regime by stemming association avoidance and reducing unemployment. Maintaining two classes of members within the same trade union or employers' association would prove challenging to manage, however, especially if the lower tier were disproportionately concentrated in eastern Germany or if it were disproportionately comprised of women.

Nonetheless, majorities within organized labor and management judge the alternatives to a managed two-tier labor market – that is, either preservation of a unitary labor market (and with it high unemployment) or comprehensive deregulation – as even less appealing.

A simple defense of the current unitary status quo may appear more prudent in the short run, since it husbands resources and does not risk failure, but it would not prevent the German labor movement from slowly sliding into irrelevancy as the traditional union strongholds in manufacturing and public service become an ever smaller share of the labor market. German unionists should not count on even a highly successful red-green coalition to solve their problems for them either. As the United States under Bill Clinton and the United Kingdom under Tony Blair have demonstrated, neither a (moderately) friendly government nor a buoyant economy is sufficient to reverse declining union density. The recent move toward multi-industrial unionism within the DGB does address many immediate financial problems related to economies of scale, but it does not resolve the larger problem of attracting the skilled employees of the twenty-first century to join a union.

Many German union officials acknowledge the vexing problem of recruiting and retaining members in an increasingly technical and individualistic society. German labor's success in organizing Digital Equipment Corporation employees shows that recruiting young software writers and computer technicians is possible so long as they are given ample opportunity to participate. Nonetheless, fealty to pattern over participation has impeded the general application of the lessons from DEC elsewhere. Labor's long-run place in German society, however, ultimately depends on resolving this fundamental contradiction between pattern and participation in a way that makes unions attractive to nontraditional members.

Notes

1. For example, Lowell Turner, *Democracy at Work: Changing World Markets and the Future of Labor Unions* (Ithaca, New York: Cornell University Press, 1991).
2. The source for all of the quantitative data in this chapter, unless otherwise noted, is Statistisches Bundesamt, *Statistisches Jahrbuch für die Bundesrepublik Deutschland*, various years.
3. Stephen J. Silvia, "German Unification and Emerging Divisions within German Employers' Associations: Cause or Catalyst?" *Comparative Politics* 29, no. 2 (January 1997): 187-208.
4. The unionization rate is calculated by dividing the data on *actively employed* members by those for wage and salary earners. This method differs from the German trade unions' estimation because it *excludes* retired and unemployed members, who are not a part of the workforce.
5. Deutscher Gewerkschaftsbund, *Geschäftsbericht des Bundesvorstandes des Deutschen Gewerkschaftsbunds* (Frankfurt/Main: Union-Druckerei), various years.
6. Reinhard Bispinck, "Daten und Fakten zum bundesdeutschen Tarifsystem," *WSI-Mitteilungen* 46 (August 1993): 529-30.
7. Three different models of codetermination exist for employee representation on corporate boards. The strongest version is known as *Montanmitbestimmung* because it is exclusively for the coal, iron, and steel industries. Firms with 2,000 or more employees fall under the second strongest form of codetermination, which is set out in a law from 1976. The third and weakest form of codetermination covers companies with between 500 and 999 employees (Leo Kissler, *Die Mitbestimmung in der Bundesrepublik Deutschland. Modell und Wirklichkeit* [Marburg: Schüren, 1992]).
8. Bertelsmann Stiftung and Hans-Böckler-Stiftung, ed., *Mitbestimmung und neue Unternehmenskulturen – Bilanz und Perspektiven. Bericht der Kommission Mitbestimmung* (Gütersloh: Verlag Bertelsmann Stiftung, 1998), esp. 52-54.
9. Kathleen A. Thelen, *A Union of Parts: Labor and Politics in Postwar Germany* (Ithaca, New York, 1991), 2-5.
10. See Chapter 1 for a discussion of the "double shift."
11. Wilhelm Adamy, Gerhard Bosch and Matthias Knuth, "Arbeitsmarkt," in *Gewerkschaftsjahrbuch 1993. Daten – Fakten – Analysen*, Michael Kittner ed., (Cologne: Bund, 1993), p.!331.
12. Dieter Schulte, "Arbeitsgesellschaft am Ende? Herausforderungen aus der Sicht des DGB," *Gewerkschaftliche Monatshefte* 45, no. 12 (December 1994): 762.
13. Deutscher Gewerkschaftsbund, *Protokoll. 15. ordentlicher Bundeskongress. Berlin, 14. Juni 1994* (Frankfurt/Main: Union-Druckerei, 1994): 84-85.
14. IG BAU is the product of a 1995 merger between The Construction Employees' Industrial Union (*Industriegewerkschaft Bau-Steine-Erden*, IG BSE) and the much smaller Garden, Agricultural and Forestry Employees' Union (*Gewerkschaft Gartenbau, Land- und Forstwirtschaft*, GGLF).
15. *Süddeutsche Zeitung*, 15 and 17 July 1997.
16. *tageszeitung*, 4 June 1996; and Bruno Köbele, "'Europäischer Arbeitsmarkt. Grenzlos mobil?' Eröffnungsrede," *Dokumentation der Konferenz 'Europäischer Arbeitsmarkt. Grenzlos mobil?* 6-8 March 1995, Bruno Köbele and Gerhard Leuschner ed., (Baden-Baden: Nomos, 1995): 11-16.
17. Stephen J. Silvia, "The West German Labor Law Controversy: A Struggle for the Factory of the Future," *Comparative Politics* 20, no. 2 (January 1988): 164-165.

18. Silvia, "German Unification," 192-193; Walther Müller-Jentsch, "Das (Des-)Interesse der Arbeitgeber am Tarifvertragssystem," *WSI-Mitteilungen* (August 1993): 501; and Wolfgang Schroeder and Burkard Ruppert, "Austritte aus der Arbeitgeberverbänden. Motive – Ursachen – Ausmass," *WSI-Mitteilungen* 49, no. 5 (May 1996): 319.
19. *metall*, March 1995.
20. *Frankfurter Allgemeine Zeitung*, 18 May 1998; and *Welt*, 28 May 1996.
21. For example, Birgit Mahnkopf, "The Impact of Unification on the German System of Industrial Relations," Discussion Paper FS I 93-102, Wissenschaftszentrum Berlin für Sozialforschung, 1993.
22. Silvia, "German Unification," 194-198.
23. *tageszeitung*, 13 June 1996.
24. Wolfgang Schroeder, "Die Unternehmerverbände: Programmatik, Politik, Organisation," *Gewerkschaftsjahrbuch 1992. Daten – Fakten – Analysen*, in Michael Kittner ed., (Bonn: Bund, 1992), 672-73.
25. Arbeitsgemeinschaft Selbständiger Unternehmer, *Mehr Marktwirtschaft am Arbeitsmarkt* (Dortmund: Rhein-Ruhr Druck Sander, 1985).
26. For example, *Süddeutsche Zeitung*, 2 March 1998.
27. Bundesvereinigung der Deutschen Arbeitgeberverbände and Deutscher Gewerkschaftsbund, "Gemeinsame Erklärung zur Wirtschaft der Deutschen Demokratischen Republik," 9 March 1990.
28. Bundesvereinigung der Deutschen Arbeitgeberverbände and Deutscher Gewerkschaftsbund, "Für mehr Beschäftigung in der DDR." Gemeinsame Erklärung zur Sozial- und Wirtschaftseinheit Deutschlands, 18 September 1990, printed in *arbeitgeber*, 5 October 1990.
29. The mood in Germany in early 1991 was so exuberant that IG Metall representatives at first *resisted* the employers' offer of a multiyear, step-by-step contract leading to wage parity because unionists feared being locked into a long-term agreement could actually slow progress to wage parity if unification progressed faster than had been anticipated (*Frankfurter Allgemeine Zeitung*, 2 March 1991; *Handelsblatt*, 11 March 1991; and Johannes Göbel, "Tarifanpassung Ost-West. Eine Zwischenbilanz [I]," *arbeitgeber* 46, no. 19 [7 October 1994]: 655).
30. *Handelsblatt*, 19 February 1993.
31. Stephen J. Silvia, "'Holding the Shop Together': Old and New Challenges to the German System of Industrial Relations in the mid 1990s," *Berliner Arbeitshefte zur sozialwissenschaftlichen Forschung*, no. 83 (July 1993).
32. *Quelle*, June 1995.
33. *Frankfurter Allgemeine* Zeitung, 28 March 1996; and Bundesverband der deutschen Industrie, *Für ein attraktives Deutschland in einem weltoffenen Europa* (Cologne: BDI, 1998).
34. Andrei S. Markovits, *The Politics of the West German Trade Unions: Strategies of Class and Interest Representation in Growth and Crisis* (Cambridge: Cambridge University Press, 1986), 20-21.
35. Andrei S. Markovits and Christopher S. Allen, "Trade Unions and the Economic Crisis: The West German Case," in *Unions and Economic Crisis: Britain, West Germany, and Sweden*, Peter Gourevitch et al. ed., (London: George Allen & Unwin, 1984), 164.
36. Deutscher Gewerkschaftsbund, "DGB Kampagne & Jugendbündnis. Materialien – Dokumente – Planungen," *Einblick*, no. 9802 (1998); and Dieter Schulte, "Statement zum Start 'Deine Stimme für Arbeit und soziale Gerechtigkeit,'" DGB press conference transcript, Düsseldorf, 14 April 1998.

37. Markovits, *The Politics*, 445.
38. Ibid., 82-83.
39. Deutscher Gewerkschaftsbund, Bundesvorstand, *Fünf-Wege-Strategie zu mehr Beschäftigung. Positionen des Deutschen Gewerkschaftsbundes* (Düsseldorf: DGB, 1994).
40. *tageszeitung*, 12 June 1998; and Helmut Kohl, "Rede von Dr. Kohl vor dem 16. ordentlichen Bundeskongress des Deutschen Gewerkschaftsbundes," Düsseldorf, 10 June 1998, 6.
41. *Handelsblatt*, 11 June 1998; and *Welt*, 11 June 1998.
42. Deutscher Gewerkschaftsbund, *Einblick*, 11 June 1998.
43. *Frankfurter Rundschau*, 13 June 1998; *Handelsblatt*, 12 and 15 June 1998; *Süddeutsche Zeitung*, 12 June 1998; and *tageszeitung*, 12 and 13 June 1998.
44. For a history of the strike, see: *Gewerkschaftliche Monatshefte* 35, no. 7 (July 1985).
45. *Süddeutsche Zeitung*, 17 December 1986.
46. For example, Hans Janssen, "Die Arbeitszeitpolitik der IG Metall – Notwendigkeiten und Perspektiven," in *Perspektiven der Arbeitzeitverkürzung. Wissenschaftler und Gerwerkschafter zur 35-Stunden-Woche*, Hans Mayr and Hans Janssen ed., (Cologne: Bund, 1984).
47. This issue is controversial. Union representatives assert that reducing the workweek from forty to thirty-seven hours created or saved a total of 200,000 jobs, whereas Gesamtmetall experts claim that it created and saved at best 20,000 jobs. Academic studies indicate that working time reduction had a positive but very small impact on employment. See: Peter Hampe, ed., *Zwischenbilanz der Arbeitszeitverkürzung*, Tutzinger Schriften zur Politik no. 1(Munich: von Hase and Koehler, 1993).
48. Walter Riester, "Diskussion zu dem Referat von Walter Riester, 'Tarifpolitik im Umbruch,'" *Gewerkschaftliche Monatshefte* 45, no. 3 (March 1995): 161.
49. Wolfgang Hromodka, "Arbeiter und Angestellte im Arbeits- und Versicherungsrecht," *Neue Zeitschrift für Arbeitsrecht* 9, no. 1 (1992).
50. *Handelsblatt*, 20 January and 8 June 1998; *Süddeutsche Zeitung*, 2 August 1997; and *Wirtschaftswoche*, 6 November 1997.
51. Gottlieb Förster and Peter Hausmann, "Der Bundesentgelttarifvertrag der chemischen Industrie. Geschichte, Erfahrungen und Perspektiven," *WSI-Mitteilungen* 46, no. 12 (December 1993): 782-98.
52. IG Chemie-Pressedienst, 19 March and 7 April 1997; *Spiegel*, 9 June 1997; *Süddeutsche Zeitung*, 5 June 1997.
53. Silvia, "'Holding the Shop Together.'"
54. Gesamtmetall, "Den Flächentarifvertrag jetzt reformieren," *Gesamtmetall Informationen für Presse, Funk und Fernsehen*, no. 21/1997, 17 November 1997.
55. *Handelsblatt*, 20 January 1998; and *tageszeitung*, 7 March 1998.
56. *Spiegel*, 14 April 1997.
57. *Handelsblatt*, 11 April 1997; and *Welt*, 16 April 1997 and 11 June 1998.
58. *Handelsblatt*, 11 April 1998.
59. *Frankfurter Allgemeine Zeitung*, 18 May 1998; *Handelsblatt*, 18 May 1998; and Christliche Gewerkschaft Metall and Ostmetall, *Die Metall- und Elektro-Industrie im Wandel. Phönix – eine Chance für den Flächentarifvertrag* (Dresden: Ostmetall, 1998).
60. *Süddeutsche Zeitung*, 18 May 1998.
61. *Wirtschaftswoche*, 7 September 1990.
62. Hermann Rappe, "Die Rolle der Gewerkschaften in der modernen Industriegesellschaft," in *Für eine Politik der Vernunft. Beiträge zu Demokratie und Sozialpolitik*, Hermann Weber ed., (Cologne: Bund, 1989), 276-84; Hermann Rappe, "Wir werden

Beispiel setzen. Gespräch mit Hermann Rappe über die Fusionspläne von IG Chemie-Papier-Keramik und IG Bergbau und Energie," *Gewerkschaftliche Monatshefte* 43, no. 1 (January 1992): 8-13; and Seppel Kraus, "Bausteine für eine DGB Reform," *Gewerkschaftliche Monatshefte* 44, no. 5 (May 1993): 284-93.

63. *Handelsblatt*, 14 May 1993.
64. *Quelle*, November 1993, 13.
65. Hans-Hermann Hertle and Jürgen Kädtler, "Die industriepolitische Wende der industriellen Beziehungen. Gewerkschaftspolitik unter dem Primat der Industriepolitik am Beispiel der IG Chemie, Papier, Keramik," *Soziale Welt* 21, no. 2 (1990): 183-205.
66. Deutsche Angestellten-Gewerkschaft, Deutsche Post Gewerkschaft, Gewerkschaft Erziehung und Wissenschaft, Gewerkschaft Handel, Banken Versicherungen, IG Medien and Gewerkschaft Öffentliche Dienste, Transport und Verkehr, "Entwurf der 'Politischen Plattform' zur Neustrukturierung der gewerkschaftlichen Interessenvertretung im Dienstleistungsbereich, in der dienstliestungsnahen Industrie, im Medien-, Kultur- und Bildungsbereich durch die Gewerkschaften DAG, DPG, GEW, HBV, IG Medien and ÖTV," Stuttgart, 24 February 1998.
67. Jürgen Hoffmann et al., ed., *Jenseits der Beschlusslage. Gewerkschaft als Zukunftswerkstatt* (Cologne: Bund, 1990), 17-26.
68. The ten framing *Leitfragen* are:
    1. Paths to social unity
    2. The future of the welfare state
    3. The structuring of the economy
    4. The future place of work in society
    5. Education and training for the future
    6. The emancipation of women
    7. European cooperation
    8. Migration and social integration
    9. The environment, peace, and development
    10. The future of trade union interest representation

    (Deutscher Gewerkschaftsbund, Abteilung Grundsatz, politische Planung, ed., *Leitfragen zur Programmdebatte* [Düsseldorf: DGB, 1993]).
69. For example, Heinz-Werner Meyer, ed., *Aufbrüche – Anstösse. Beiträge zur Reformdiskussion im Deutschen Gewerkschaftsbund und seinen Gewerkschaften*, vol. 1 (Cologne: Bund, 1994).
70. Wolfgang Uellenberg von Dawen, "Organisations- und Programmreform des DGB," *Gewerkschaften heute 1995*, in Michael Kittner ed., (Cologne: Bund, 1995), 97-112.
71. Rudi Schmidt and Rainer Trinczek, "Fusion und Konfusion. Gründe und Hintergründe für die Reorganisation des DGB," in *Reform des DGB. Herausforderungen, Aufbruchspläne und Modernisierungskonzepte,* Thomas Leif, Ansgar Klein and Hans-Josef Legrand ed., (Cologne: Bund, 1993), 84-85.
72. Deutscher Gewerkschaftsbund, Bundesvorstand, *Die Zukunft gestalten. Grundsatzprogramm des Deutschen Gewerkschaftsbundes* (Düsseldorf: DGB, 1996).
73. *Deutsche Presse Agentur*, 8 January 1995; *Focus*, 28 May 1995; *Gewerkschafter*, February 1994; and *ÖTV-Intern*, 18 March 1994.
74. Deutscher Gewerkschaftsbund, *Einblick*, no. 9803 (1998); *Quelle*, March and September 1994; *Reform Raster*, no. 2-94 (3 February 1994); and Deutscher Gewerkschaftsbund, *Geschäftsbericht des Bundesvorstandes des Deutschen Gewerkschaftsbunds* (Frankfurt/Main: Union-Druckerei), various years.

75. Deutscher Gewerkschaftsbund, *Geschäftsbericht des Bundesvorstandes des Deutschen Gewerkschaftsbunds* (Frankfurt/Main: Union-Druckerei), various years.
76. Deutscher Gewerkschaftsbund, *Protokoll. 15. ordentlicher Bundeskongress. Berlin, 13.-17. Juni 1994* (Frankfurt/Main: Union-Druckerei, 1994).
77. Deutscher Gewerkschaftsbund, Bundesvorstand, "DGB macht Rechtschutz organisatorisch selbständig," *DGB-Pressemeldung*, PM 138, 1 July 1997.
78. *Handelsblatt*, 12 June 1998; and *Süddeutsche Zeitung*, 12 June 1998.
79. European Metalworkers' Federation, "Collective Bargaining Policy in a Changing Europe: Statement of Principle on Collective Bargaining Policy by the European Metalworkers' Federation," paper for the EMF Collective Bargaining Policy Conference, Luxembourg, 11-12 March 1993.
80. IG Chemie-Papier-Keramik and GMB, *Partnership Agreement between GMB and IG Chemie-Papier-Keramik*, Brussels, 3 February 1993.
81. *Umschau*, December 1994; and Industriegewerkschaft Chemie-Papier-Keramik, *Flagge zeigen für ein soziales Europa: Europäischer Betriebsrat* (Hannover: Buchdruckwerksätten Hannover, 1992), 24-28.
82. *Financial Times*, 4 March 1997.
83. Industriegewerkschaft Bergbau, Chemie, Energie, *IG BCE-Presseinfo*, 3 March 1998.
84. Jan Cremers, "Europäischer Arbeitsmarkt in Bewegung," in *Europäischer Arbeitsmarkt. Grenzlos mobil?* Dokumentation der Konferenz, 6. bis 8. März 1995, Bonn, Bruno Köbele ed., (Baden-Baden: Nomos, 1995), 17-23.
85. For example, *Gewerkschafter*, September 1994; and Gudrun Hamacher, "Projekt Mitgliederentwicklung (ME) der IG Metall," Frankfurt/Main, 13 July 1993.
86. For example, Ulrich Beck, *Risikogesellschaft. Auf dem Weg in eine andere Moderne* (Frankfurt/Main: Campus, 1986).
87. *Quelle*, February 1995; and Gewerkschaft Öffentliche Dienste, Transport und Verkehr, *Werben mit System. Mitgleiderwerbung in der Kreisverwaltung: Von der täglichen Werbearbeit zur Werbeaktion. Arbeitshilfe Organisations- und Werbearbeit* (Stuttgart, Courir, 1994).
88. Witich Rossmann, "Industrial Relations in West Germany in the 1990s: The Computer Industry as an Example," paper presented at a conference on The Political Economy of the New Germany, Cornell University, 14-15 October 1994, 7-8.
89. *Digital IG Metall Tarif-Information*, no. 1, February 1994.
90. For example, Roman Herzog, "Aufbruch ins 21. Jahrhundert." Rede zur Eröffnung des Hotels Adlon, Berlin, 26 April 1997.
91. For example, William Greider, *One World, Ready or Not: The Manic Logic of Global Capitalism* (New York: Simon and Schuster, 1997).

Chapter 4

"YESTERDAY'S MODERN TIMES ARE NO LONGER MODERN"

Swedish Unions Confront the Double Shift[1]

Rianne Mahon

Introduction

The Swedish union movement has stood as the exemplar for "power resource" theorists.[2] During the Golden Age, Swedish unions proved particularly successful in accumulating resources in the bargaining arena, through politics and, more broadly within civil society. Centralization of collective bargaining helped establish the paramount position of the peak organization for blue-collar workers, LO (Landsorganisation i Sverige), vis-à-vis its affiliates[3] and allowed it to pursue its policy of solidaristic wages bargaining[4] with considerable success. Its close relationship with the Swedish Social Democratic Party (SAP) enabled LO to influence public policy, and it often acted as the source of important policy innovations. The unions could thus draw strength from reforms instituted by successive social democratic governments, notably economic policies focused on maintaining full employment, and a comprehensive welfare state, constructed along universalistic lines. LO was also able to develop

Notes for this section begin on page 162.

a hegemonic working-class identity within civil society. The alliance-building role of social democratic reforms has often been stressed,[5] but LO was also able to assert its hegemony in the labor market where the burgeoning strata of white-collar workers early embraced a working-class-friendly "wage earner" identity.[6]

Yet even the Swedish unions have discovered that "yesterday's modern times are no longer modern"[7] and power resources accumulated in the past are not immune to devaluation. In fact, their very successes have contributed to forces undermining the unions' position. Industry rationalization, favored by the LO-SAP's economic policy model, and the development of the social democratic welfare state, with its characteristic comprehensive, high quality public services, have contributed to the relative growth of white-collar and public-sector employment which helped undermine the coordinating function played by LO-SAF negotiations. Perhaps more importantly, the very export-led growth on which the unions' postwar gains depended, fueled the development of large multinational firms. The latter have become a powerful force behind "globalization" and Sweden's integration into the new Europe. They have also been the main force behind the decentralization of collective bargaining.

The first section of this chapter sets in bold relief the changes to the unions' position since 1982. It will be argued that for most of the 1980s, the Swedish unions seemed to be shaken by the crisis but remained intact. Yet the semblance of continuity simply masked profound changes which were slowly eroding their resources. By 1995 the unions and their state were in crisis and disarray. In the next section, the forces behind the change will be examined, with particular emphasis on the transformations with which the unions were belatedly forced to grapple. These two sections provide the backdrop to the main story which explores the unions' responses to these challenges. Here the stark contrast drawn in the first section will be adjusted to reveal a movement intensely engaged in a process of strategic and organizational renewal.

The Swedish Model: A Daliesque Portrait

As the 1980s opened in Sweden, the Golden Age seemed tarnished but not over. Union density continued to rise, reaching 85 percent in 1986. Union membership was high not only in classic areas of union strength – those organized by unions affiliated with the LO *(Landsorganisation)* – but also among white-collar workers. The unions affiliated with the TCO *(Tjänstemännens Centralorganisation)* or with the smaller association of professional unions, SACO *(Sveriges Akademikers Centralorganisation)* had been very successful in organizing the growing cadre of white-collar employees. To be sure, the broader picture looked less rosy. The Social Democrats had been out of office since 1976, and the governing coalition of bourgeois parties had begun to abandon full employment. Moreover the industrial relations system had been shaken by a series of escalating conflicts, culminating in the "great conflict" of 1980.[8] Nevertheless the Social Democrats returned to office in 1982 committed not only to restoring full employment and maintaining the welfare state but also to introducing the wage earner funds which the LO had proposed at the height of its 1970s campaign for industrial and economic democracy.[9] It is thus not surprising that the Swedish unions saw little need for strategic reorientation.

There were, of course, signs that the times were changing, but the unions seemed to have taken these in stride. The growth of white-collar occupations and the service sector had altered the relative weight of different unions within the LO as well as the balance between it and the white-collar unions. Although membership in LO unions had doubled between 1950 and 1985, TCO and SACO had expanded even more rapidly. Within both LO and TCO, moreover, the relatively rapid growth of public-sector employment led to shifts in the relative position of affiliated unions. Thus by 1977 the powerful metalworkers' union, Metall, had lost the number one position to Kommunal, the union representing blue-collar employees of municipal and county governments. SF, which organized the blue-collar employees of the central government, became the third largest LO union. Coincident with the growth of both private and public services was the rise in female labor force participation rates. By 1980, 74 percent of working age women were in the labor force, and women's labor force participation continued to rise throughout the decade – although over two-fifths of the female workforce worked less than full time. In Sweden this change in labor force composition was quickly reflected in union membership. In fact, unionization rates for women in areas organized by both LO and TCO came to surpass men's in the 1980s.

These developments certainly resulted in modifications to the Swedish industrial relations system. Thus in 1982 LO and SAF, the peak organization of Swedish employers, still negotiated the master agreement for blue-collar workers in the private sector, but since 1973 similar negotiations had become the norm between SAF and the then-new cartel of white-collar workers, PTK. The impetus for centralization outside the LO-SAF area had come from the public sector: when workers in the latter were granted full bargaining rights in 1966, only cartels and union confederations were recognized as negotiating parties. This not only prompted a merger movement in LO; it also sparked the formation of the first cartel for white-collar employees of the central government, TCO-S. County and municipal employees unions followed suit, forming KTK and SACO-K.[10] The formation of white-collar cartels and increased cooperation among public-sector workers made it difficult for LO-SAF agreements to set the pace in a manner consistent with the need for stable growth on which the unions' broader economic strategy hinged. Ironically, the very acceptance of LO's principle of wage solidarity by TCO unions undermined support for the principle within the ranks of LO's private-sector affiliates who watched their position decline relative to the lower rungs of white-collar workers. It also fueled employer interest in decentralization, a point to which we shall return.

Nevertheless it is easy to understand why the unions, and LO in particular, felt that nothing fundamental had changed: the restoration of their social democratic partners to office would allow the necessary, but incremental, adjustments to be made as they had before. In order to make it attractive to all wage earners, the Swedish welfare state had been reformed in the 1960s with the introduction of the income replacement principle to social insurance. The spate of labor law reforms in the 1970s had in part been designed to cement this cross-collar alliance by appealing to wage earners' common interest in industrial democracy.[11] Finally, important changes to family policy recognized that wage earners increasingly came in two sexes.[12]

If in 1982 the unions' complacency was understandable, by 1992 it had become abundantly clear that the old model was in crisis. Union density was still relatively high, but the unions had been shaken by the first decline (to a "low" of 82 percent) since the 1930s. The biggest drop, moreover, had occurred in the main urban areas and was concentrated among younger workers – the unions' future. While density levels began to rise again in the 1990s, the unions had little cause for jubilation. The "flight back" could be attributed to the dominance of union-administered unemployment insurance and the unions' role in representing employees facing layoffs, but the legal basis for both of these was being challenged by the Bildt government (1991-94). Unions had also been hit by cuts in government funding for union education, the elimination of tax writeoffs for union dues, and increases in own-contributions to social insurance, including the union-administered unemployment funds.

The Social Democrats' return to office in 1994 initially aroused hopes that something would be done to restore the old order, but such hopes were quickly dashed. The new government seemed no more capable than the Bildt government of tackling unemployment which had risen to European levels. High unemployment, in turn, fueled the deficit, which left the Social Democrats vulnerable to pressures to restore Sweden's credit by cutting social expenditures. Coming in the context of an accord between the SAP government and the Center Party, long a proponent of flat-rate benefits, these cuts have fed concerns that the income replacement principle is in jeopardy. Worse still, on the eve of LO's 1996 congress, the SAP government introduced changes to the labor code which reintroduced flexibilities that the employers had sought – and, in part, won – from the Bildt government. As a result, the historic alliance between LO and the SAP, which was under strain in the 1980s, is now seriously frayed.

The LO has also been forced to face up to the end of the old system of coordinated bargaining in which it had played such a pivotal role. While the Swedish industrial relations system's reputation for labor peace had been shaken by waves of wildcat strikes in the 1970s, since then legal strikes have become more frequent, rising to a peak in 1995 when there were more strikes and industrial actions than at any time since the great conflict of 1980.[13] The drive by the key engineering employers association, VI,[14] to decentralize bargaining has added to tensions within LO. Thus in 1983 VI drew Metall away from the LO fold. By 1990 it had succeeded in persuading SAF to abolish its bargaining secretariat and then to terminate agreements that obliged it to collect comprehensive wage statistics. In 1993 the leading engineering firms attempted to avoid participating in national bargaining altogether. While the unions managed to defend the principle of national bargaining, LO not only lost its direct role in bargaining, it also found it increasingly difficult to establish a common norm for its affiliates, let alone for the labor market as a whole.

Thus it is no longer possible to avoid the conclusion that things have changed. If the Swedish industrial landscape appeared somewhat altered after the first decade of crisis, today it looks like a painting by Salvador Dali: the familiar figures can still be discerned, but they are rapidly losing their characteristic shape. Restoration of the traditional Swedish model no longer seems possible, and the unions now recognize the need for strategic renewal.

A New Context: Globalization, Decentralization, and Flexibilization

Like their counterparts elsewhere, the Swedish unions have had to learn to act in circumstances quite different from those of the Golden Age. The new circumstances are simultaneously the product of long-term changes and the result of the interaction of employers, governments, and unions pursuing strategies that aim to enhance or mitigate the effects of structural tendencies. While globalization can be seen primarily as a long-term trend which the Swedish model supported, decentralization and flexibilization are best understood as developments initiated by the big engineering firms. Although the Swedish labor movement has long stressed the importance of exports and of trade liberalization, the first few decades of growth over which the Social Democrats presided resulted from rising demand in both the export and home markets. From the late fifties on, however, exports came to play an increasingly important part.[15] Concomitant with the rising importance of exports has been a shift in export markets. Although the U.S. remains an important market, the European Union's share has grown substantially.[16]

Changes in the composition of Swedish exports contributed to globalization. During the 1970s, it had become clear that new suppliers of timber and iron ore posed a serious challenge to the industries which had long shaped Sweden's export profile. The declining competitiveness of these staple industries adversely affected related branches like basic steel, shipbuilding, pulp and paper. Crises in the older export industries in turn increased Sweden's dependence on the engineering branch and on the large transnational firms that dominated production of capital goods and consumer durables. Export growth has been particularly strong in the engineering branch.[17] By 1980 the largest engineering firms – Electrolux, Ericsson, Asea, and Volvo – already accounted for one-quarter of Swedish exports, and these firms were becoming less and less reliant on home market sales, and thus on the national economy.

Foreign direct investment by Swedish-based firms grew even more dramatically than exports during the later years of the Golden Age. The real acceleration, however, occurred in the 1980s when Swedish foreign investment increased by 800 percent.[18] The large engineering firms again accounted for the lion's share.[19] The tight labor market undoubtedly contributed to the outflow, but the announcement of "Europe 1992" constituted a major draw as the EC countries absorbed a growing share of the total. There has also been a significant rise in foreign investment in Sweden since a social democratic government eliminated restrictions on foreign ownership of shares traded on the Swedish stock exchange. Over one-third of Swedish industrial workers are employed by foreign-owned firms.[20]

The growth in international financial markets has also served to tie the Swedish economy into the emergent global financial network.[21] In Sweden as elsewhere, the internationalization of the financial market was fueled by the rapid growth of nonbank financial institutions, including internal finance companies set up by high profit engineering firms like Volvo and Asea.[22] These innovations reduced the efficacy of financial regulations in all national economies irrespective of the previously existing differences among them and Sweden has been no exception.

Employer interest in decentralization has been fuelled by structural change. The importance of R and D to the now-dominant branches of Swedish industry, combined with the turbulence generated by the integration of financial markets, has prodded Swedish firms to rely increasingly on retained earnings and equity, a preference reinforced by the high interest rates of the 1980s. This gave them a structural reason no longer to accept the modest profit levels assumed in the LO-SAP Rehn-Meidner economic policy model.[23] It has also spurred their desire to put an end to the policy of solidaristic wage bargaining that formed part of that model.

The drive for decentralization has also been fed by industrial rationalization. Earlier industry rationalization followed a typically Fordist path – a concentration of industrial capacity designed to reap economies of scale, a bias in favor of labor-displacing machinery, and the deskilling of jobs. Yet direct and indirect worker resistance also encouraged large Swedish employers to undertake precocious experiments with new forms of work organization.[24] The separation of white- and blue-collar workers, each with their own collective agreement, made it more difficult to implement the new strategy, not the least because Metall's adherence to solidaristic bargaining meant that pay increases for skilled metalworkers led to the spread of pay rises across the blue-collar collective.[25] This contributed to VI's determination to decentralize bargaining.

Industrial restructuring has also meant a decline in employment in the goods-producing sector and a concomitant rise in service- sector employment. The social democratic welfare state left its imprint on the latter as growth occurred especially in public services, such that the public sector now accounts for nearly 40 percent of total employment. Yet job growth has not been confined to the public sector. Producer services now account for nearly 10 percent of total employment,while 14 percent work in the consumer service sector.

These developments have also fed VI's interest in decentralization. As the new players adopted solidaristic bargaining, gains in the lead branches were transmitted across the economy. In the 1960s, SAF was prepared to accept this,[26] but since the end of the 1970s, it has worked to decouple the two sectors. Its success in this regard has posed a major challenge to union solidarity. The potentially divisive effects of decoupling appear even greater when the gender dimension is factored in – i.e., the concentration of men in the shrinking but economically central export sector and of women in the expanding service sector. Distributional conflicts between the two contributed to the emergence of a gender-based politics in the late 1980s.[27]

Gender is not the only new element in Swedish politics. An important cultural shift seems to be underway from a society-centered to a more individualist perspective in which "self-realization" and "individual difference" take priority over traditional collective identifications like family, region, class, and nation. The shift in Swedish values tracked in a larger study of changes in Europe was particularly marked among blue-collar workers, the backbone of the old social democratic order.[28] Thus in politics as in industrial relations, the large collective actors that once dominated the scene appear to be melting, leaving behind a more fluid system of representation.

In different ways these developments have changed the context of action for Swedish employers, the Swedish state, and the unions. At the same time, these structural tendencies are the result of choices made by actors. Thus at the microlevel, employers have contributed to globalization by raising their stake in the export market, by investing in overseas facilities, and by joining the play in the burgeoning international financial market. As managers, they have experimented with new forms of work organization and they have spunoff specialized activities which have fed the growth of the producer service sector. These actions have contributed to changing the microfoundations of employer interests.

Engineering the Shift

Opposition to Sweden's entry into the EU did force employers to deploy collective resources supporting the "yes" option, but on the whole collective action has been less necessary in favor of globalization than it has been for decentralization. Firm-based actions – including those that resulted in the sudden outflow of capital in the fall of 1990 precipitating the Social Democrat's decision to apply for membership – have often been enough to change the context of action. Collective action has played a much more critical role in the struggle over decentralization. Here two actors are of especial importance, SAF and VI. While the former played the leading role in the heyday of the Swedish model and has remained an important figure on the scene, VI has been the chief protagonist in the struggle to dismantle the old model in favor of a highly decentralized alternative.

VI's interest in decentralization is intimately bound up with the drive for flexibility associated with the new forms of work organization:

for core workers, the functional and temporal flexibilities stemming from broader job classifications, new skill mixes and wage systems, as well as more permissive rules governing work time; for the rest, numerical flexibility or the growth of a pool of "just in time" workers. Flexibility on the terms sought by VI required fundamental changes to the Swedish model, and to bring these about, collective action aimed at transforming the very terms of discourse in civil society was undertaken.[29] It also entailed escalating political demand aimed at gutting the labor code reforms of the 1970s, transformation of the welfare state, the imposition of neo-liberal macroeconomic objectives, and the destruction of the once much-vaunted labor market policy. Their relative success on the political front will be examined in the next section. Here the focus is on VI's attempt to transform the collective bargaining regime which SAF, along with LO, had once helped to establish.

SAF began to develop its new wage policy in 1979 in response to VI's increasingly vociferous dissatisfaction. The new policy aimed to replace the old regime's macroeconomic calculus, which was concerned with aggregate demand, with one more suited to the employers' microeconomic interests. The new policy line also represented a clear renunciation of the principles embedded in the EFO formula of the 1960s, which accepted the legitimacy of diffusing the benefits of productivity gains in the most efficient industries throughout the national economy. Now the relevant unit was to be the individual plant where productivity would be promoted by introducing performance-based pay systems. Contra the norms embedded in LO's wage solidarity policy, SAF also argued that wage differentials needed to rise to encourage individuals to master a wider range of tasks.

In 1979 SAF and VI were still prepared to incorporate this micro-oriented wages policy within a bargaining framework that remained national in scope, albeit decentralized to the branch level. It proved difficult, however, to convince key elements within SAF's own ranks – notably the large, domestic-market-oriented HAO (retail employers association) but also the export concerns in the forestry industry – to leave the central bargaining table.[30] LO too fiercely resisted the move to decentralized bargaining. Nevertheless, the profitable engineering firms were able to use high levels of wage drift to undermine support for the old model. By 1990, VI had persuaded SAF to abolish its negotiating secretariat. In the subsequent round, a government-appointed commission, named after Rehnberg, its chair, played a central role. As Kjellberg argues, the Rehnberg round simultaneously meant a super decentralization (the elimination of local negotiations left the local details a matter for local management) and supercentralization (most agreements fell within its terms).[31] The Rehnberg round thus eliminated wage competition while allowing greater scope for pursuit of firm-specific wage policies. The two-year contracts arising out of these agreements were also innocent of the earnings guarantee clauses that had become anathema to VI.

By 1993, it was clear that VI had lost all interest in bargaining at the national level. It aimed to conclude cross-collar agreements at the firm or even divisional level, eliminating national contracts altogether. Once the unions recognized this, however, new cross-collar alliances were formed – at the level of national unions – to resist and this they did with success.[32] Instead, a group of state mediators, backed by LO's successful coordination of its affiliates and, perhaps more importantly, the economic situation, managed to reproduce a level of national coordination equivalent to the Rehnberg commission. In 1995, however, neither LO nor the government-appointed Edin commission were able to curb the increases employers in the booming export sector, led by the pulp and paper industry, were able and willing to grant. As Kjellberg notes, the 1995 round was "the most conflictual for many years, with an overtime ban in engineering, strikes in retail trade, transport, hospitals etc."[33]

The struggle over decentralization is far from over. A more decentralized system has been accepted by the majority of employers and also by the unions, but exactly how decentralized and under what rules has yet to be determined. The leading engineering firms are clearly committed to the establishment of enterprise bargaining to support the formation of a group of core workers who are able and willing to take on a wide range of tasks and motivated to do so by individualized wages, set through a one-on-one dialogue with local management. As we shall see, the unions remain equally determined to ensure that local negotiations occur within a framework that continues to be set by national agreements. Nor is decentralization the only trend, in that the state has, in various ways, stepped in to fill the vacuum created first by the inability of LO-SAF agreements to play their former pace-setting function and, more recently, the elimination of trans-sectoral bargaining. This has made the transformation of the state an especially important part of VI-SAF's strategy.

The State's Contribution

There were important differences between the strategies chosen by the social democratic government of the 1980s (the "Third Road") and that of the bourgeois coalition government of 1991-94 (the "only road"). The former aimed to restore full employment and repair the damage done to the welfare state by earlier bourgeois governments (1976-1982). The Bildt government explicitly set out to engineer a system shift: macroeconomic policy was given a marked neo-liberal orientation, and deregulation of the labor market was clearly on the agenda. Yet both governments contributed to the processes of decentralization, flexibilization and globalization.

The Social Democrats' Third Road sought to steer a course between the monetarism of Thatcher and the Keynesian policies initially pursued by the first Mitterrand government. It aimed to raise demand for Swedish exports through an aggressive devaluation – and during its first term of office, the strategy appeared successful as exports rose and unemployment fell. During the latter half of the 1980s, however, the government lost control of the economy. Financial deregulation certainly contributed to this. While, as a small open economy, Sweden may not have had a choice as to whether to deregulate, it could decide on when and how it would occur, and it is the latter set of decisions that have come under fire. Credit ceilings were lifted in November 1985 before changes were made to the tax system to eliminate the incentive for private borrowing (1990) and before regulations on foreign investment were lifted. Thus, a credit boom centered on domestic real estate and construction was added to the stimulus which devaluation gave the export sector,. The resulting inflation eroded the export sector's competitive edge and helped destroy the old system of collective bargaining.

Although the Third Road contributed to Sweden's success in maintaining full employment while much of Europe abandoned it, it inadvertently supported VI's drive to decentralize bargaining. While the government initially was able to convince the unions not to recoup the wages lost through devaluation, the loss of macroeconomic control resulted in wage drift which frequently exceeded contractually agreed increases for both blue- and white-collar workers in industry. Such high levels of drift spread to other sectors via earnings guarantee clauses and thus helped VI to convince the rest of SAF that the old system had to be replaced. It also undermined rank and file confidence in the national unions just when the big engineering companies had intensified the campaign to win the hearts and minds of "their" workers.

It would be unfair to suggest that the Social Democrats intended to support VI's drive to decentralize bargaining. In fact, they showed a willingness to use a variety of instruments – concessions; the "renewal funds," which gave unions some leverage over company investment in training; political pressure and, when all else failed, the attempt to impose an incomes policy in 1990 – to regain macroeconomic balance. When the latter failed, the finance minister pressed the reluctant parties to accept the Rehnberg Commission. Upon their return to office in 1994, the Social Democrats set up the Edin Committee, a committee comprised of economists from all labor market parties, to establish a wage norm for the 1995 round. More recently, the Öberg commission was appointed to look into ways of strengthening the powers of the national conciliation service in order to ensure that society's general interests would prevail in collective bargaining.

Even the Bildt government supported the maintenance of some form of national wage policy, albeit for different reasons. Decentralization, which effectively put an end to solidaristic wage bargaining, had led to the widening of the gender pay gap in the 1980s. This did not go unnoticed by the renascent Swedish women's movement, and, given the latter's growing political importance, the Bildt government could not afford to ignore their demands for pay equity. Aided by the impending decision to join the EU where pay equity legislation was stronger, Liberal leader and then social minister, Bengt Westerberg, picked up on an earlier Social Democratic initiative to strengthen the 1970s equal opportunity legislation. The resulting reforms accorded the equity ombudsman the kind of proactive role missing from the earlier legislation. The subsequent Social Democratic government similarly showed a preparedness to act, establishing an important commission to look into ways to close the gender wage gap and, more broadly, to increase women's economic power.

As employers, various governments have also given mixed signals, but the main trend has been decentralization. The Social Democrats tried to restore the private sector's pace-setting function by using various means to get the public sector to follow the former's lead.[34] At the same time, they helped sever the connection between the export and public sectors. Thus in 1986 the government successfully fought to eliminate earning guarantee clauses from public-sector agreements. Local managers were given more leeway in order to attract (or keep) those with skills in high demand, and more and more room was made for individual, results-based increments. In the 1990s, the private-sector practice of establishing "potts" to be distributed through local negotiations was introduced to public-sector bargaining.

Decentralization has also been supported by the drive to increase labor market flexibility, a goal which governments of both stripes have pursued since the mid-1980s. One of the areas where flexibility has been sought is in the rules governing working time. Here a marked shift has occurred from a concern with the gender implications of various work-time arrangements to the subsequent fixation on flexibility. In 1988 the Social Democrats chose to campaign for a sixth week of vacation instead of the six-hour day demanded by the Social Democratic Women's League (SSKF). To appease the latter, the SAP established DELFA which was directed to examine the gender distribution of working time and explore the consequences of various work-time arrangements for gender equity. DELFA's final report focused instead on labor market flexibility, raising the idea of regulations based on the number of hours worked per annum rather than the weekly limits specified in the 1970s law on working time. The next (Larsson) commission was established with the express purpose of exploring this option.

The issue came up again as the export sector began to emerge from the depths of the recession. After the 1992 devaluation, overtime leapt to nearly 5 percent of hours worked in manufacturing. The now "lean" firms in the export sector were clearly meeting the surge in demand less by new hires than by increasing hours worked by the remaining core. The Bildt government appointed a new commission on worktime to look into the adjustments to Swedish law required by membership in the EU and the broader questions raised in the Larsson report. Under the Social Democrats, the commission's mandate was broadened to consider whether work-time reductions could contribute to job creation. Increasingly, however, the issue has come to be seen neither as a way of achieving gender equality[35] nor full employment, but rather as part of a negotiated exchange between employers and unions whereby the unions gain (modest) reductions in annual working time in exchange for increased flexibility of the working day or week.[36]

The achievement of greater functional flexibility also forms part of the agenda. Although Swedish active labor market policy, with its strong emphasis on training, has long been held up as a model for others, by the mid-1980s there were signs that the old system was no longer adequate. Of particular concern was the growth of firm-based training, which escaped the regulatory reach of existing legislation. In 1989 the Social Democrats set up a national commission for skills which was asked to propose ways to stimulate (and regulate) employee training at the firm level. Received by the Bildt government, the final report revealed a deep division between the majority, who favored a training tax combined with locally negotiated training agreements, and the SAF representative, who opposed state intervention of any sort. SAF's opposition helped ensure that the report was shelved. For the remainder of its term in office, labor market policy focused on trying to deal with the growing number of unemployed through various make-work initiatives. Training remains on the agenda, but the efficacy of once-hallowed Swedish labor market policy has come openly into question.[37] The current debate focuses on the question of whether, and how, broader societal concerns are to influence an increasingly enterprise-driven system.[38]

Labor legislation is another area of contestation which bears directly on the issue of on whose terms greater flexibility is to be achieved. Here too the terms of the debate have changed markedly over the last decade. Like the 1970s labor law reforms, the first commission, set up by the Social Democrats in the late 1980s, aimed to strengthen the unions' position in the workplace, especially on issues like work organization and training. The Bildt government changed the commission's mandate in line with SAF's demand for the elimination of the "work environment bureaucracy" which impeded the implementation of its vision of the flexible workplace. Its report again revealed the depth of the cleavage between the labor market parties. Lack of consensus – plus the veto which the Social Democrats claimed for their support of the Bildt government's September 1992 crisis package – allowed the social liberals in the Cabinet to ignore some of the harsher SAF-inspired recommendations, but changes were introduced which aimed to increase numerical flexibility by lengthening probationary and temporary appointments. Seniority rights were attenuated as employers were allowed to exempt two people per seniority list.[39] While the Social Democrats reinstated the old legislation, they did so on the understanding that the labor market parties negotiate a new accord which would introduce greater flexibility. When a new agreement was not forthcoming, the government introduced its own legislation. While the latter made some improvements to the rights of replacement and part-time workers (a main concern of public-sector unions), it increased the length of time firms are allowed to employ temporary workers. More importantly, it made it possible for union locals to conclude agreements on the rules governing the hiring of temporary workers and exemptions from seniority, without first seeking the approval of the national office. This clause angered the unions who want to ensure that decentralization and flexibilization occur within a framework set by national agreements or laws.

Both social democratic and bourgeois governments have tried to tackle the issue of the general terms under which flexibility is to be introduced. In 1989 the Social Democrats set up the Productivity Delegation. Several volumes produced for the Delegation focused on the productivity gains to be made by breaking with Fordist forms of work organization and did so in ways that highlighted the common interest of employers and unions in such changes. Although Swedish firms had precociously experimented with alternatives to Fordist production lines, the 1980s had marked a retreat, albeit with some notable exceptions.[40] While the emphasis on the requalification of work was consistent with the unions' emergent policy of "solidaristic work" (see next section), the final report favored the employers' preferred vision of flexibility, recommending, inter alia that wage differentials be allowed to rise to reflect the lower productivity of youth and the firms' desire to create a core workforce by increasing pay differentials.

A broader attack on the institutional underpinnings of the Swedish model was launched by the Social Democrats' Power Project, whose report reflected the position of the head of the research team, Olof Petersson: "Old institutions are transformed into empty shells, though many of these institutions continue to survive for many years ... Nostalgia and a lag in self-understanding legitimize old organizations, while state subsidies, security of employment and monumental buildings freeze and preserve social movements."[41] These themes were subsequently taken up and developed by the Bildt-government appointed Lindbeck commission which used public choice theory to attack Swedish corporatism and peak level bargaining.

The unions constituted an important point of resistance to SAF's neo-liberal project, and it was their capacity to resist that the Bildt government worked to undermine. Tax writeoffs for union dues were eliminated, and employee contributions to unemployment insurance were substantially increased. The latter made it more difficult for cash-strapped unions to raise dues because unemployment insurance contributions go to union-administered funds. The Bildt government also introduced legislation designed to end the unions' "monopoly" on UI funds, an institutional arrangement considered critical to the achievement of high density levels in Sweden. Neo-liberal policies such as the growth of contracting out and privatisation have created problems for the unions too, given the way Swedish unions are structured along sectoral (i.e. public-private) lines.

Social democratic and bourgeois governments have facilitated globalization. At the beginning of the 1980s, the Swedish state possessed the institutional requisites for a national economic policy. A good part of the story of the Third Road is the story of how these controls were dismantled, increasing the country's vulnerability to continental and global developments. Such vulnerability, in turn, became the standard rationale for unpopular decisions in the 1990s.

In 1985 the Social Democrats gave up the instruments through which the Swedish state had regulated the financial market. It also announced that it would not borrow abroad to finance the debt. In 1989 foreign exchange controls were dismantled. The Social Democrats also set in motion the liberalization of controls on foreign direct investment in Sweden, a policy shift completed by the Bildt government. In response to a sudden outflow of capital in the fall of 1990, the SAP government announced that Sweden would apply for membership in the EU – a move rejected in 1973 by a social democratic government as incompatible with Sweden's long-standing policy of international neutrality. In May of 1991 the Swedish currency was pegged to the ecu, which replaced a currency basket heavily weighted toward the U.S. dollar. Although Sweden has decided to defer entry into the EMU, the social democratic government continues to do its best to meet the Maastricht criteria.

Unions Charting a New Course

Globalization, decentralization,and flexibilization are thus three important tendencies,reshaping the terrain on which Swedish unions act and challenging them to strategic innovation. Globalization, and the premium it puts on competitiveness, has spurred a search for new forms of labor market flexibility, but the terms under which the latter is being introduced have yet to be settled. The rules favored by the leading engineering firms put a premium on decentralization not only to the workplace, but to the individual employee. The Swedish state has been more ambivalent. Many initiatives have supported VI's neo-liberal line, but even the Bildt government could not afford completely to ignore the resistance mounted by the unions nor the demands of an increasingly vociferous women's movement.

These changes have also generated tensions within the unions which have further intensified the pressures for renewal. Thus the changing balance between white- and blue-collar workers contributed not only to the decentralization of collective bargaining but also to the reduction of LO's weight within the labor market and electoral arenas. High profits have not only fueled tensions between the unions in the export and domestic sectors, they have also severely tested the unions' egalitarian ideals. Employer experiments with new forms of work organization have pressed on the collar line and thus challenged one of the foundations of the Swedish union movement. More broadly, the search for flexibility has put in question the very underpinnings of union power.

The Swedish unions were slow to recognize the need for change. Throughout the 1980s, LO continued to fight a rearguard action to restore the bargaining regime through which it had so successfully pursued its policy of wage solidarity. And LO leaders were often left to splutter in frustrated anger as successive social democratic governments charted a course which increasingly diverged from theirs. Beneath the surface, however, forces for change were at work. The unions' most encompassing response to these challenges has been a strategy of "solidaristic work." The latter shares a commitment to wage earner solidarity with the earlier strategy, and, like the Rehn-Meidner policy, it aims to combine equity and efficiency. In an effort to counter the employers' move to decentralize bargaining under neo-liberal rules, however, solidaristic work shifts the center of gravity away from the macroeconomic and national focus of the Rehn-Meidner policy to the workplace. The Rehn-Meidner policy combined a modified Keynesian economic policy, active labor market measures coordinated by the national government, and national wage bargaining aimed at securing growth, stability, and solidarity. These elements worked to encourage microeconomic efficiency but only indirectly through pressure on inefficient firms or industries to rationalize. The new version of solidarity focuses directly on the workplace where one interpretation of solidaristic wages – equal pay for work of equal value – is to be grafted onto a post-Fordist productivity dynamic. In this respect, the unions have followed the employers in moving to a more decentralized system.

For the unions, however, the existence of an appropriate national framework remains at least as important as it was in the past. Union strength in negotiating new wage systems, worktime agreements, and training schemes at the local level depends on both national agreements and supportive labor legislation. Full employment and a high quality, universalistic welfare state remain crucial to the maintenance of solidarity. Without these supports, the new strategy will do little to check the tendency toward labor market polarization associated with neo-liberal versions of post-Fordist restructuring. To some extent the unions are aware that "solidaristic" decentralization is contingent upon the existence of supportive mechanisms at the national level. As we shall see, innovations in bargaining strategies, modes of representation, and organizational forms are designed to develop local capacities while retaining mechanisms for national coordination. Less attention has been paid to the question of what sort of resources the unions need from the state and how to secure these – not surprisingly, because until recently the unions could take the latter for granted.

This is not to say that there has been no political innovation. The other important development is LO's embrace of wage earner feminism, and LO's new self-representation as Sweden's largest women's organization is more than mere rhetoric. It has entailed important organizational changes and has left its marks on the unions' bargaining agenda. There has also been considerable effort to harness the energies generated by wage earner feminism to the struggle for solidaristic work, but the attempt to combine the two strategies has given rise to tensions that the unions have found hard to manage, especially as the gender divide in the highly segregated Swedish labor market too neatly coincides with the division between the export and the domestic sector. This divide has become all the more salient due to the elimination or weakening of many of the traditional mechanisms for sharing the results of productivity rises in the export sector.

Bargaining: Solidaristic Work for Gendered Co-workers

Union bargaining strategies have developed in the context of a protracted struggle with employers over the terms under which decentralization and flexibilization are to be implemented. The unions have come to accept the need for greater decentralization and, with this, increased differentiation. Yet they have also sought new ways to assert the interests of workers or wage earners as a collectivity against the employers' drive to individualize the relationship, and to maintain a national framework for local negotiations against the employers' move radically to decentralize the bargaining regime. Solidaristic work is the unions' main strategic response to these challenges. The strategy involves the development of new systems of job classification to give (autonomous) work teams an enriched bundle of tasks; new wage forms that encourage workers to take on these tasks; rights to training which enable everyone progressively to master the new tasks; and new worktime arrangements that address the firms' needs arising out of just-in-time production while meeting the workers' (varying) needs.

Not surprisingly, the union behind the new strategy, Metall, was one of the earliest exposed to the consequences of management's new production concepts. When the big engineering firms experimented with new forms of work organization in the 1970s, Metall experienced a loss of members to SIF.[42] Metall's decision to break ranks with LO in the 1983 bargaining round – the first crack in the unions' resolve to resist decentralization – needs to be seen in this light: the move to branch level bargaining was a price Metall considered worth paying for the addition of a high skill wage classification. Yet ending solidaristic wage bargaining was not a realistic option for Metall. Its own ranks include many low-waged members in dead-end assembly jobs. The union also had a symbolic stake in the maintenance of solidarity: Metall is credited as the source of the unions' ideal of wage solidarity. Metall had, therefore, to try to resolve the tension. It began to do this at its 1985 congress, where it adopted the outlines of a policy that would come to form the core of the new strategy.

Solidaristic work is not Metall's alone, however. In 1988 the LO committee, set up to rethink the 1970s economic and industrial democracy strategy, began to flesh out a strategy of solidaristic work for unions in all sectors. The document contained contributions not only from Metall but also from Kommunal, the largest public-sector union, and from Handels, the largest LO union in the private sector. At its 1991 congress, solidaristic work was adopted as LO's official strategy. TCO also embraced a policy in line with solidaristic work at its 1989 congress, and many of its unions, from major unions like SIF and SKTF (Metall's and Kommunal's counterparts) to smaller ones like the pharmacists' union, are actively committed to it.

It is not easy to transform unions used to a more centralized bargaining process, into unions capable of pursuing solidaristic work, however. As a Metall report noted, "a congress decision in Stockholm and a book of a couple of hundred pages are not enough to translate a broad strategy into daily union work."[43] Solidaristic work requires the local clubs and their members to assume a key role and upper levels of the unions to develop the support mechanisms needed. This is a reversal of the postwar order where the national office increasingly assumed responsibility for the main tasks, leaving to local clubs the job of negotiating piece rates consistent with nationally set guidelines. Some, like Kommunal, have been more successful than others in developing the kinds of support needed.[44]

This is not to suggest that the national level is no longer important. As we have seen, the employers want to eliminate national bargaining and to confine the benefits of core "co-worker" status to a relatively privileged few. Although it is clear that master agreements between SAF and LO are no longer on the agenda, the unions are determined to preserve national agreements at the branch level and to maintain a degree of interbranch coordination. Although LO hoped to be able to play the lead role here, it has been less effective as the affiliates have developed new forms of cross-collar alliance at the branch level. The latter were formed to preserve the principle of national agreements against the threat posed by VI's attempt to eliminate national bargaining by enticing workplace clubs into cross-collar "co-worker" agreements. The latter exposed a weak point in the unions' defenses – the way the Swedish union movement institutionalized the old Fordist division of labor . Yet the new alliances are more than simply defensive. The unions are working together to negotiate collective agreements that reflect their common interest in solidaristic work.

Cross-collar collaboration really took off in the 1993 bargaining round when Metall began to work closely with SIF and CF (the SACO engineers union) to conclude agreements that moved a considerable distance toward the elimination of cross-collar differences in wagesetting practices. The three unions also work together on issues of worktime and training.[45] Perhaps the boldest vision of the new cross-collar coalitions, however, was the cooperation agreement between the two old rivals in the retail and commercial sector, Handels (LO) and HTF (TCO). In the course of yet another attempt to arrive at a tenable boundary agreement, the two unions agreed to the establishment of a permanent coordinating body, with subgroups to deal with questions like wage negotiations, training, and union activities at the international level. What was particularly innovative was the commitment to work toward the formation of the "third union – a union for the future." Avoiding the premature and perhaps unnecessary step of outright merger, the third union allowed for the formation of joint workplace clubs at sites where co-worker agreements were on the agenda.

Inconceivable in the 1980s, these embryonic cross-collar alliances may provide the outlines of the future industrial relations system. They do, however, face considerable obstacles, not the least of which are the reemergence of old rivalries. Thus the third union has proved difficult to put into practice, and tensions have surfaced periodically in the engineering branch. Tensions have been greatest in the municipal and county government sector where SHSTF broke off its cooperation with Kommunal over the restructuring of work, opting to raise the professional status of its members at the expense of Kommunal's. Although it had been willing to work with Kommunal and SKTF, in 1995 SHSTF, the other large TCO union in this branch, went its own way, demanding a wage increase well above the rest. SHSTF's demands in fact highlight one of the main areas of conflict between the unions' solidaristic work strategy and their commitment to achieving gender equity.

By international standards the gender wage gap is relatively low in Sweden. Solidaristic wage bargaining and the old earnings guarantee clauses contributed significantly to these results, but when these mechanisms for sharing out the productivity gains of the export sector were undermined in the 1980s, the gap began to widen. The 1988 nurses' strike was the first to call renewed attention to the gender wage gap which was especially marked in the healthcare sector (women's wages were equivalent to 75 percent of the average male salary in this branch). That same year a group of women from all three trade union centrals launched their own study. Their 1990 report sparked an important debate within the union movement and in society at large.

Despite the tough economic conditions, in 1993 Kommunal, SKTF and SHSTF joined forces – with the silent support of the larger SACO unions, SSR (social workers) and LSR (physiotherapists) – determined to make a breakthrough on pay equity. They were ready to draw on a range of techniques toward this end, notably the revaluation of women-dominated occupations and the establishment of a special "pott" dedicated to the elimination of discriminatory wage differentials. On the surface, all unions agree on the need for gender wage parity. Yet it is not so easy to turn agreement in principle into accepted practice. Unions like Metall can agree on the desirability of special increments for the lowest paid but have more difficulty with a special "women's pott," not the least because this is seen to jeopardize the export sector's norm-setting function.

These tensions were very apparent in the 1995 round. LO thought it had worked out a compromise that addressed the issues of special concern to the export unions while also pushing for a special pott to be distributed according to the percent of women within each bargaining group. Kommunal and Metall had accepted this but the compromise fell apart at the February meeting of the bargaining council where, for the first time since coordinated bargaining had begun, several unions indicated they would not endorse the recommendation. The paperworkers union in particular gave voice to the tensions between the two conceptions of "just wages," one based on class and the other on gender. While the old principle of solidarity had allowed the establishment of special potts for low-waged workers (many of whom were women, but not singled out as such), the idea of a gender-specific pott was more difficult to accept. The real concern, however, was that the two-year norm proposed by LO would allow the big paper companies to use the extra profits gained from the unions' restraint as they had in the 1980s – to award huge increases to top executives and to invest abroad.

The surfacing of tensions between the two conceptions of wage earner justice – one centered on a class based definition of solidaristic work, the other on gender equity – highlights an important problem posed by the formation of cross-collar alliances at the branch level. What trans-sectoral mechanisms are there for working out principled compromises between the two? Until recently the LO unions have been careful to argue that their participation in branch level alliances in no way precluded coordination through the LO. This may have been the case in 1993, but LO's ability to secure acceptable compromises has been put in question. Solidaristic work may thus turn out to be a project shared by all (or most) co-workers but it is unlikely to be the project of a hegemonic LO as its predecessor (solidaristic wages) was. This is not a problem in and of itself as long as the emergent constellations of co-workers develop a means of settling the intersectoral differences that have gained an extra salience with the rise of wage earner feminism.

Mobilizing for Solidarity, Redefining the "We": Recruitment and Representation

By the late 1980s, it had become clear that Swedish unions faced a deepening crisis of representation. For the first time since the 1920s, union density fell, and this was especially marked within the private sector, where density levels for blue-collar workers dropped from 84 percent in 1986-87 to 77 percent in 1991, and among blue-collar workers in large urban areas. In addition, more and more workers were taking advantage of the fact that they could subscribe to a union-administered UI fund directly without having to join the union.[46] The membership figures were but one sign of the crisis. There were others, like the "Dala revolt," a movement which began among local trade union activists in the engineering branch in the mid-1980s and spread to other sectors.

The crisis can be interpreted in different ways, however. The malaise has been attributed to the independence of the younger, educated, and secure individuals, the "children" of decades of social democratic reforms. For some, this was interpreted to mean the rise of the narrow self-interested individuals celebrated in SAF's neo-liberal discourse. Accordingly, the unions needed to respond by turning to "service unionism.[47] Others held that these new individuals might eschew the old class identity of their parents, but this did not mean the end of solidarity. Rather, the new individuals favored the more fluid commitments of social movement politics. The rise of wage earner feminism can be seen as one response to this, as Swedish feminism has long represented women (and men) as individuals with the "right to be human," but new ways of addressing youth also follow from this interpretation. In a different way, solidaristic work recognizes the rise of individualism within the working class but argues that class (or wage earner) solidarity remains necessary if individuals are to be empowered at the workplace.

To establish these new discourses, the unions have turned to dialogical unionism – the constitution of collective identity through an open, yet structured, dialogue involving leaders, local activists, and the rank and file.[48] Such dialogue can take diverse forms, from study circles and local conferences to the use of modern survey techniques. The key is not the specific technique used but how it is used. For instance, surveys are not used simply to ascertain what the members think but rather as part of a broader effort to structure a dialogue that fosters the formation of a particular collective identity and mobilizes support for the set of demands associated therewith. Swedish unions have their own term for dialogical unionism: the concept of "anchoring":

> When LO members speak of anchoring their decisions with the membership, they do not mean simply soliciting members' opinions and then being responsible to them; convincing members of the official union position also plays a large role. Thus the congruence between rank and file and the representatives' opinion is not simply a measure of representative democracy, but of the officials' persuasive skills as well.[49]

A substantial part of this anchoring process is aimed at organizational reform, a topic to be taken up in the next section. Here we shall concentrate on the set of dialogues that aim simultaneously to anchor the new definition of wage earner solidarity and to give the latter a gendered identity.

In the 1990s, Metall engaged in an intense effort to renew rank and file commitment, developing new way of working that placed considerable stress on the union's character as a "talking organization." One of the expressions thereof is an interesting combination of survey and face-to-face discussion, "*Metallträff*" (Metall Meetings), which deliberately reach beyond those who normally participate in the union's local and regional structures. The *Metallträff* were designed to organize a structured yet open dialogue with rank and file members about union bargaining priorities as well as broader policy questions. Kommunal has similarly worked to develop a sustained dialogue around its 1997 Manifesto. In addition to more traditional techniques, the union has recognized the way newer forms of electronic communication can be put to dialogical uses.[50] Dialogical forms have also been deployed to develop support for cross- collar alliances. Thus in the crucial 1993 round, Metall, SIF and CF developed a common questionnaire, "How do we want it?" which was distributed to their local clubs who used it to generate discussion and then fed back the results to national headquarters. The unions were able to use the results to develop and sustain a common position – "contract 2000" – a model national agreement for all three unions which covers issues like training, worktime, and new wage systems.

While these examples all refer to the use of various techniques to develop member support for solidaristic work, LO has similarly made good use of surveys to launch a discourse in which women and youth are represented as forces for union renewal. Of particular import is the survey of union members (both white- and blue-collar) whose results are analyzed and published in LO's series *Voices from the Union and the Job*. *Voices* has worked to establish a clear link between the interests of women and youth and other strategies for renewal, notably solidaristic work and organizational reform. Thus the substantial increase in women's labor force participation was identified as one of the most important changes of the last decades to which the unions had to respond. The main message was that women, especially younger women who were identified as the most radical of all workers, appeared as a force to be mobilized for solidaristic work: "one can also track an impatience especially among the young LO women who want the local union to have more say at the workplace and who also think that the unions should push questions like training and development on the job and greater influence for employees over their work."[51]

The survey also took issue with the view of youth as free-floating individuals no longer interested in old social movement politics. *Voices* took care to point out that although union density was lower among young people, it had increased by 10 percent since the mid-1970s. Youth were represented as interested, even active, in the union, but turned off by traditional forms of communication, especially formal meetings. Thus the problem was not their detachment from traditional class identities but rather the unions' failure to move beyond the formal modes of representation, which better fitted earlier conceptions of democracy, to more direct and engaging forms of contact. In other words, "voice" need not be replaced by "exit" but rather amplified by establishing new, and more engaging forms of dialogue.

The discursive representation of women and youth as forces for union renewal has become increasingly embedded in union practice. Thus unions like Metall and SIF have created special youth memberships and Metall and SF (now SEKO) have organized meetings with youth at the regional level. The construction workers union set up regular youth conferences where two young members from each local would get together to discuss contemporary issues. This male- dominated union also arranged joint summer and winter courses with Kommunal, a union with a high proportion of women members. As part of its contribution to the SAP's 1994 electoral campaign, LO organized a youth parliament which provided those in attendance with an opportunity to grill the trade union and party leadership. Some initiatives, such as rock concerts sponsored by Metall and LO (the latter on Walpurgis Eve, a celebration of spring and youth that occurs on the eve of May Day), reflect a traditional view of "fun-loving" youth. Yet some of the leadership have made the connection which *Voices* sought to establish. This is reflected in LO's youth oriented magazine, *Union*, which offers a lively mix of pop culture, international issues, and articles exploring issues high on the unions' priority list.

In the 1990s, LO also began to produce *Clara*, a magazine devoted to women which, like *Union*, is a lively yet serious publication. LO, TCO, and many of their affiliates have also been involved in various projects designed to increase women's participation in union activities, including the development of special courses and course material for women. In line with the contemporary women's movement's slogan, "half the power, all the wage," direct efforts have been made to increase the representation of women in the unions' upper echelons. LO has been particularly active in this regard.[52]

These initiatives indicate that wage earner feminism is taking root in the Swedish trade union movement. This has not been an easy process, however, nor is it complete. Historically, the struggle for equality of the sexes has at best been subsumed under the class struggle. Although women now make up nearly half LO's members – and more than half of TCO's – old habits die hard. It may have become fashionable to be "for" equity and thus even to support affirmative action, but there is still a tendency to treat women as workers *tout court*. The move to equitable representation in the ranks of union activists and officials is thus important, but representation in the deeper sense – i.e. that goes to the heart of how who "we" are is defined in word and in deed – is even more critical. As a leading spokesperson for wage earner feminism within LO noted:

> The political discourse of the labor movement describes ... class conflict and the way that class oppression gets expressed. When it is a question of gender conflict, the latter has simply not existed as an important problem. Nor is there even a word for gender oppression. This has created a sense of homelessness among many women, for only a part of their experience is described in political terms .... If the sense of isolation is to be broken and the experience of masses of women are to be allowed to come to the surface, that reality must be described .... Oppression must also be named.[53]

Thus the ideological/identity dimensions of the re-presentation of the Swedish unions are as critical as the changes in the sex (and age) profile of union officials.

Finally, dialogical unionism also characterizes LO's (belated) response to SAF's campaign to gain ideological hegemony. This began as the "justice project," launched in 1991. The justice project was designed as a multilevel campaign dialogue engaging leadership, rank and file, the most marginalized in Swedish society, and critical voices from outside the union movement. An important component was the sponsorship of some 2,500 study circles across the country. Local groups were provided with material which raised questions linking both solidaristic work and gender equality to the concept of justice. Participants were asked to voice their view of justice – and on what needed to be done to make Sweden a just society – as well as directly to engage in local activities within their union, the local SAP organization, and municipal politics. In doing so, the project utilized both traditional channels and newer networks built up by those most active in the campaign to engage women and youth. To put a human face on existing injustices, LO chose Per Holmberg, who had been closely associated with the commission (the low-income commission) credited with having rekindled the drive for class and gender equality in the 1960s. Working with popular journalist Maj Gull Axelsson, Holmberg conducted a series of in-depth interviews with some of the most marginalized in contemporary Sweden. The third component was a series of more formal dialogues which aimed to open LO activists to the broader debate about the kind of society Sweden should become.[54]

The justice project served to frame the discussion of wage policy, training, worktime, employment and social policy, and democracy at LO's 1996 congress,[55] but its aim was broader than this. Its goal was to counter the right's gains in ideological struggle by anchoring a common conception of solidarity and justice, one that brought together the discourses of wage earner feminism, solidaristic work, and the democratisation of the union, prefigured in the discourse on youth. Those in charge of the project were able to convince the LO leadership that this goal could not be accomplished through a five-year campaign, no matter how intensive. Accordingly, LO dedicated funds to its continuation in the form of the "LO idea debate," which deploys the same creative mix of local study groups, network building, seminar and film series, and publications as that pioneered by the justice project.[56]

An Organizational Kaleidoscope

The renewal of dialogue is critical to the restoration of the Swedish union's hegemonic capacity. The campaign will mean little, however, if the LO cannot resolve the apparently more mundane organizational challenges it faces. These include not only the working out of a new internal relationship, appropriate to the more decentralized environment in which the unions must operate, but also new ties with LO's white-collar counterparts. If the latter cannot be achieved, the Swedish unions will not have the means to resolve the intersectoral tensions to which the cross-collar coalitions at the branch level give voice. Solidaristic work, co-worker alliances and the various attempts to revitalize the links between leadership and the rank and file all imply organizational reform. The unions' financial problems, exacerbated by the Bildt government's initiatives, provide additional impetus.

Organizational reform thus constitutes a very important part of the story. In fact, the whole structure of the Swedish union movement is in a state of turmoil, and it is by no means clear where – and even whether – the kaleidoscope will stop. This section focuses on a number of important developments: the reemergence of "craft clubs" within large vertical unions; widespread experimentation with a new organizational paradigm; the development of interunion cooperation at the level of the transnational corporations; and efforts to reorganize the peak associations. To put these changes in perspective, a picture of the organizational landscape once so familiar to students of Swedish industrial relations is needed.

At the national level, LO had come to occupy the leading position vis-à-vis the white-collar unions, especially TCO and its affiliates. Its national headquarters on Norra Bantorget – a kind of architectural counterpart to SAF's headquarters on Blasieholm – housed its influential research department and provided the meeting point for key bodies like the Secretariat[57] and the council of union leaders which hammered out LO's bargaining strategy.[58] At the level of individual unions, Metall provided the exemplar, at least for unions in the private sector, with its combination of workplace-based clubs and strong national organization.[59] Until recently, however, public-sector unions remained quite centralized and the workplace organizations of the white-collar unions, including SIF, have never been as strong as Metall's. Moreover, even in unions like Metall, many smaller units do not have workplace clubs, relying instead on the union's local branch office.

Union organization in part reflected the structure of collective bargaining. While LO was signatory to the master agreement with SAF (from 1956 on), the national unions were party to agreements regulating wages and conditions of employment at the branch level. In the private sector, local units retained a role in recruitment and piece rate negotiations. For most of the postwar period, however, the national unions were paramount. The unions' national boards retained the authority to determine whether, when and how strikes would be conducted. The relationship between national leadership and the base was governed by the rules of representative democracy, but delegates to representative organs above the workplace normally were selected by indirect election. The wave of unrest that culminated in the wildcat strikes of the early 1970s signaled that the balance had tipped too far in the direction of centralization, but the cure sought – the labor law reforms of that period – is now widely regarded as having contributed to the further bureaucratization of workplace unionism. This is one of the outcomes the current reforms aim to avoid even while they seek to address the complex set of challenges that have occurred in the unions' environment.

Two of the innovations are closely related to solidaristic work: the renewal of a form of craft unionism in the heart of large industrial unions and the implementation of a new organizational paradigm. The first can be seen as the revival of the strategy Metall adopted at the turn of the century for holding onto its skilled crafts while building an industrial union.[60] Then, craft- or occupation-specific units coexisted with the workplace-based clubs that were to become the primary unit of organization. The recombination of craft and industrial unionism has assumed a new relevance as solidaristic work involves unions in negotiating about production-related concerns.[61] In other words, unions need to be able to speak to their members as people with particular skills whom management wants to draw into the restructuring – on its terms. Such a targeted dialogue gives the unions a means to compete more effectively for the loyalty of their members by showing that they recognize their skills and will support their efforts to continue to develop them.

While craft clubs remain an option in Metall's statute books, the current interest in craft clubs comes from other large vertical unions, notably SIF, SKTF, and Handels. Between 1987 and 1990 SIF ran a special project which sought to tap occupational identities as a basis for developing support for the union's emergent solidaristic work strategy. The project involved preparation of material on changes to the work environment, personnel training, terms of employment, and other issues related to the restructuring of work as they affected particular occupational groups. SKTF has also chosen to sharpen its profile as a union combining the benefits of occupational and industrial unionism. It concluded cooperation agreements with over thirty occupational associations and established a special service to act as a link between these and its regional offices.

The new organizational paradigm is even more explicitly related to solidaristic work. If the union is to advance its solidaristic work strategy, it has to be able to reach into the place where it is to be implemented; the workplace is the locale where the main negotiations over new wage systems, job classifications, the organization of production, and training regimes, will occur. Union organization thus needs to be turned on its head. If the national office constituted the centerpoint of the old model, the workplace, and individual members within, have now become primary sites. The aim is not to build yet another layer of bureaucratic experts at the local level, but to form new local leaders – "all-rounders" who can be consulted on questions of job classification and evaluation, new wage systems, equal opportunity, or even what the company is up to in other parts of the world. In this context, the exercise of leadership means functioning as kind of *animateur* who can activate, educate, and empower. The new union official is also more likely to do union work on a part-time basis, with the remainder spent on the shopfloor.

The third development forms an important part of the Swedish unions' response to globalization. The formation of union organizations that cut across both occupational and workplace units, to bring representatives together at the level of the transnational corporation (KFS)[62] was first developed in response to the employers' use of new corporate forms to evade the unions' solidaristic wages policy. Thus the basis for KFS in Volvo was established in the mid-1950s when the clubs discovered that the company was trying to establish different rates for the same job in its various divisions.[63] As the corporation-based clubs came to see that they were dealing with firms that were increasingly transnational in scope, they began to establish links with their counterparts in other countries.

During the 1980s, Swedish unions tried unsuccessfully to secure transnational codetermination rights within the Nordic region. As with the 1990s drive supported by the European Commission under Delors, the aim was to enable unions representing workers from all subsidiaries of a multinational corporation to meet with management once a year at the latter's expense. For Swedish unions, however, the key is to use these rights to lay the basis for international solidarity. They are thus generally opposed to the idea that full time union officials play a central role, insisting instead that local clubs send their representatives. They also reject the idea that the agreements be signed by the international or European branch organizations. The emphasis on local union involvement is consistent with the new organizational paradigm, but, taken too far, it poses a threat to a broader conception of wage earner solidarity. There is a real danger that KFS will support the firms' strategy of replacing (national) wage earner solidarities with identification with the (transnational) firm. In other words, while local representatives do have an important role to play, national unions should also be at the table.

Craft revival, the new paradigm, and KFS are all relatively innovative responses to the challenges posed by decentralization and globalization, but Swedish unions have also tried more traditional solutions like mergers. The restructuring process has upset the organizational balance within the union movement. Thus industrial decline has taken its toll on unions like the miners and clothing and textile Workers. More recently, contracting out, deregulation, and privatization have eroded the boundary between public and private services, contributing to a rising number of jurisdictional disputes. In its 1991 report to Congress, LO took up a number of these questions, recommending a reorganization of boundaries, including the elimination of the public-private distinction in favor of a broader one between goods-producing and service-sector unions. It also recommended that mergers be explored by a number of the smaller unions. Three of the recommended mergers did take place – the merger of the Clothing and Textile Workers Union with the Factory Workers Union to form Industrifacket with some 160,000 members; the Miners' Union with Metall; and the Seafarers with the national government workers' union, SF, which is comprised primarily of unions in the transport and communication sector, to form SEKO (Service and Communications Union).

None of the mergers proved easy to bring about. At what was to have been their last congress, the Food Workers Union pulled out of the planned merger with the Clothing and Textile Workers' Union and the Factory Workers Union, despite the strong endorsement by their outgoing and highly regarded President, and despite the enormous amount of work that had gone into making Industrifacket a model of the new unionism. The merger of the Miners Union and Metall was nearly derailed when a storm blew up over the "golden parachutes" provided to retiring members of the Miners' Union executive. The merger of SF and the Seafarers Union succeeded, but it has not expanded, as LO originally hoped, to include the Transport Workers Union. The two TCO unions affected by similar changes – ST and SIF – seem to have been somewhat more successful in that they quite literally moved in together. There was talk of a merger there too, which might have included SKTF, but nothing has come of this, in part because for both SIF and SKTF, the cross-collar alliances have been more important. This raises the question of whether mergers should take place among unions that belong to the same peak organizations or whether it would be useful to cut across the collar line in ways prefigured by the "third union" experiment in the retail and commercial branch. This, in turn, raises the larger question of the future of the peak organizations themselves.

In the past, LO played a critical part in maintaining interbranch coordination. Contemporary developments, however, seem to be drawing the national unions increasingly into a dialogue with their members at the local level, their white-collar allies at the branch level, and their counterparts in other countries. These relationships are certainly necessary if the unions are to meet the challenges they face, but they do raise questions about the role of the peak associations. Although there are some informal mechanisms of cooperation that cross both branch and collar divides, these are not enough. There is still a need for some form of cross-cutting organizations with the authority to work out differences between unions, especially where these touch on the gendered divide. Thus the peak associations too need to change if solidarity is to survive.

Although the need for a more fundamental rethinking of the structure of Swedish unions was raised in the late 1980s, the prospect seemed too much for the embattled LO leadership, leaving the debate to take place underground, within the LO and its unions. Some openly argued that LO should merge with TCO and that core service functions (union education, research) should be hived off to semi-autonomous agencies. Others argued that LO constitutes the soul of the Swedish unions and must remain strong if the spirit of solidarity and justice is to survive. The deadlock between the two was apparent in the report of the first Persson Committee whose task it was to lay out LO's place in a changing environment. The latter not only failed to endorse changes within LO, it also avoided any mention of the need for a new, closer relationship with TCO. The second Persson Committee made a breakthrough on a number of questions. The structural reforms it recommended fit well with the trimmed down structures of the new paradigm.[64] It also acknowledged the end of the era in which LO played a critical role in coordinating collective bargaining and recognized the need to broaden and deepen cooperation with TCO. Another committee made important recommendations concerning the relationship between regional and local structures within LO. Both of these documents formed the underpinnings of the organizational changes adopted at LO's 1996 congress. Similar debates, leading to internal organizational reforms, have taken place within TCO.

These processes of internal reform are certainly producing leaner organizations, but they have done little to deepen the connection between LO and TCO. To be sure, at LO's 1996 congress, a motion from Metall was passed which committed LO to developing an action plan for more effective cooperation with TCO. By this time, however, TCO had decided to develop its relationship with SACO. In the fall of 1996, TCO and SACO signed a cooperation agreement and shortly thereafter announced the formation of a joint legal services company. At its 1997 congress, TCO endorsed the move toward a merger with SACO.

In part the move to embrace SACO is easier for TCO than creating closer formal ties with LO because both white collar union organizations remain committed to a nonpartisan stance whereas LO has retained an official connection with the SAP. There is also a sense that pooling their research capacity would improve their capacity to intervene in national and European politics. This, however, assumes a common white-collar employee identity, and, in the past, SACO and TCO were often divided by TCO's identification with the solidaristic values espoused by LO whereas SACO affiliates embraced a form of business unionism more compatible with its liberal-professional values. The question is, is SACO moving closer to TCO or is the latter moving away from union values of solidarity and embracing SACO's liberal professionalism?

Certainly some TCO unions, notably the nurses' union, SHSTF, have moved in the latter direction but others, including SIF and SKTF both of which are important players within TCO, retain the union identity formed in the period of LO hegemony. Moreover, some of the large and powerful unions within TCO, notably SIF, are not keen on the rapprochement with SACO. TCO itself remains ambiguous. While it is closer to SACO on the issue of what role the state should play in collective bargaining, it is closer to LO on other key policy issues (see below). Moreover, it made it clear that the decision to move toward a merger with SACO did not rule out closer cooperation with LO.

Unions, Party and State: A Post-Saltsjöbaden Accord?

The Swedish unions have traditionally seen political exchange as particularly important. For LO, such exchange was very much shaped by its relationship to the SAP. Since its foundation in 1898, LO has seen itself as one wing of the labor movement and the party as the other. From the 1930s, LO was able to look to its political counterpart to obtain resources complementary to those gained at the bargaining table. Thus although the 1938 Saltsjöbaden Accord between LO and SAF is rightly seen to have established the principle of centralized self-regulation in collective bargaining, LO's willingness to enter into the accord was linked to the labor movement's broader goal of implementing a Keynesian full employment policy. LO's embrace of solidaristic wages bargaining in the 1950s was, in turn, premised on the willingness of the social democratic government to adopt the rest of the Rehn-Meidner package. Active labor market policy was designed to ensure that those who lost their jobs through restructuring would be able to move to areas of job growth and/or to obtain the new skills required.

Although TCO and SACO have officially held to the principle of nonpartisanship, under the Social Democrats, the state also played an important role in giving a material basis to the notion of common wage earner interests that cut across the collar line. Thus earnings-related social insurance plans were added to the original Beveridge style program in the 1960s, making the Swedish welfare state attractive to white- and blue-collar workers alike. The labor law reforms of the early 1970s, undertaken in the name of industrial democracy and equal opportunity, sought to address the common interests of Swedish wage earners of both collars and sexes. In this sense, all Swedish unions learned to rely on a friendly state.

The relationship between the Social Democrats and the unions however came under increasing stress in the 1980s.[65] Relations between LO and the SAP improved somewhat during the Bildt government's term of office but even then the SAP's involvement in the autumn 1992 crisis agreements[66] lent additional support to the growing chorus of voices arguing that the unions should rely more on collective bargaining than political exchange. The unions' strategy when the SAP returned to office – to negotiate a post-Saltsjöbaden accord – reflected this view.

The strategy recalled aspects of the model from the unions' Golden Age, with adjustments to reflect the demands for flexibility, decentralization, and internationalization. Like the earlier accord, the unions hoped to negotiate a set of rules to govern union-management relations in the labor market and at the workplace. Also like the earlier accord, the aim was to establish a set of rules that were beyond politics – a set of rules that would not be subject to change with electoral outcomes. The unions' vision of the new accord allowed for a more decentralized form of self-regulation but recognized the need for a mechanism to establish an overall rate of increase consistent with macro-economic balance. Thus, while the earlier accord paved the way to coordinated bargaining at the national level, a new accord would recognize that national agreements only set the parameters, leaving to local parties to negotiate new job classifications and new wage systems. Firm-based training would be regulated by national agreements, again leaving the details for local parties to work out.

Although this strategy placed greater weight on the unions' capacity to negotiate appropriate agreements with the employer(s), the unions assumed that the state would continue to play the supportive role it had in the past. Thus the SAP government was expected to restore full employment, to encourage the labor market parties to work out training agreements, and to maintain the welfare state. They hoped that labor legislation would continue to provide employment security while doing more to strengthen the rights of individuals at the workplace. They wanted stricter regulation of temporary help agencies and rights for part-time workers to fulltime jobs. The unions thus assumed that political exchange would continue to function as it had during the Golden Age when they could count on their special relationship to the governing party. This assumption has been severely tested.

In the face of continuing pressure from the global financial community to deal with the deficit, the government broke its promise to restore social insurance rates to their former level. Compensation rates were dropped to 75 percent in January 1995, and in April of that year the SAP made a surprise agreement with the Center Party, long an advocate of returning to Beveridge-style social policies. The agreement not only extended the cuts in compensation rates to unemployment insurance but also introduced measures to curb municipal spending. Although compensation rates were raised to 80 percent in 1998 and the SAP government increased transfers to municipalities, the cuts left their mark. Thus reductions to social insurance rates prompted a rash of private-sector agreements offering supplemental insurance to those with the market power to claim it. The curbs on municipalities which, along with the counties, are the main providers of social services, made it increasingly difficult to maintain social services without recourse to user fees, lower staff-client ratios, and rising unemployment in the very branch which, in the 1980s downturn, helped counteract the general rise in unemployment. This time, unemployment in the public services continued to rise even as industry began to recover.

Although the Social Democrats met the unions' demand for a clear commitment to reduce unemployment, this was made contingent on the willingness and ability of the labor market parties to agree on new rules to replace the 1970s law on employment security (LAS) and a new wage-setting system capable of combining macroeconomic stability with decentralization. This seemed compatible with the unions' goal – a post-Saltsjöbaden Accord – but when the agreement was not forthcoming, the Social Democrats introduced legislation that went a considerable way to meeting the employers' demands.[67] On the very eve of LO's 1996 congress, the SAP government announced legislation which lengthened the term of temporary employment contracts and made it possible for local union organizations to conclude agreements without first seeking the national union's approval. This is in marked contrast to the 1970s labor legislation which supported the national unions' right to prevent locals from entering into agreements which worsened the terms of employment.

Discontent had already been brewing with the polls showing a steady drop in support for the SAP and a concomitant rise for the Left and Green parties. In the 1996 fall election for the European Parliament, 58 percent of LO voters stayed home and of those who voted, more chose the Left Party and the Greens (46 percent) than the SAP (35 percent). At the LO congress, the government's "betrayal" sparked a heated debate on the issue of continued financial support for the party and while the majority voted to maintain the connection, a number of unions substantially cut their financial support. Several major demonstrations were organized by union locals (especially those associated with the LO maverick, the Transport Workers Union) as well as by networks of the unemployed. Although some in the LO leadership supported the demonstrations, TCO seemed to have less difficulty endorsing the protests than LO, which was constrained by its official ties to the governing party.

The protests did not stop the new labor legislation which was introduced in January 1997 but they did persuade the Social Democrats to withdraw the proposed changes to the system of unemployment insurance and, in its spring proposition, to put money back into social services. At the SAP congress in the fall of 1997, the government also gave in to LO and agreed to increase child allowances, to raise compensation rates to 80 percent, and to reduce the period of sick leave paid by the employer to the original level. The preliminary report of the SAP- appointed commission on the role of the national conciliation service also favored LO's position. As a new election loomed, dissident LO unions returned to the fold.[68] This suggests that even if the relationship is not what it once was, not enough has changed to lead either the party or LO to seek divorce. LO members still account for a substantial part of the electorate and the party tie still seems to offer better terms of exchange than LO, as an interest group, could exact from a bourgeois government, especially given the paramount position which the neo-liberal Moderate Party have assumed within the bourgeois bloc.

The issue of Europe has also proved divisive, and in the referendum which saw a narrow majority support membership in the EU, two-thirds of LO members ignored the party line[69] and voted no. Nevertheless, the tensions here are less between the party and the unions, than reflective of the gender divide. Unions where women predominate, like Handels and Kommunal have thus been prominent Euro-skeptics whereas those in the male-dominated export sector, like Metall and the Paper Workers Union, look to Europe to shore up the waning capacities of national states. In the referendum on EU membership, moreover, Handels and Kommunal were successful in forcing LO to maintain a position of official neutrality, despite the wholehearted engagement of unions like Metall on the yes side. LO's inability to bridge the gap on this issue thus provides further evidence of its hegemonic decline.

Conclusions

If, in 1982, Swedish unions looked forward to a restoration of the Golden Age, by the end of the century it has become clear that new strategies were needed. The unions have focused on meeting the challenges which became visible in the 1980s: decentralization and flexibilization on the one hand; the feminization of the labor market and politics on the other. Solidaristic work attempts to meet the first by elaborating a solidaristic alternative to the employers' vision of the new workplace. Decentralization and flexibility are accepted, but, for the union, local negotiations over new job classifications, wage systems, training, and worktime regimes, must continue to take place under the umbrella of national agreements. Wage earner feminism addresses the second by taking up the demands of the recharged women's movement for pay equity and parity. In both instances, the unions, especially LO, have assumed they could rely on their connection with the Social Democrats to secure the needed political resources.

Both strategies address some of the major challenges the unions face, but each raises new problems for a union movement used to operating (with great success) in a very different environment. Neither takes certain changes – the end of full employment and, more broadly, globalization – adequately into account. Moreover while the new strategies are not, in principle, incompatible, the deepening economic divide between the male-dominated export sector and the "sheltered" sector where most women work, is generating tensions that make them hard to pursue in practice.

Solidaristic work developed in response to employer-induced changes to the industrial relations regime. The unions' bargaining strategy aims to maintain a distinct wage earner identity at the workplace, backed by cooperation at the national level. It aims to meet demands for decentralization and flexibility by accepting broader job classifications, multiskilling, and flexible worktime arrangements but asserts a critical role for unions in negotiating such changes at the local and national levels. The unions are trying to anchor this redefinition of solidarity among the membership by turning to dialogical unionism, by experimenting with the new organizational paradigms and by reviving craftlike organizations within large industrial unions. The hope was that the successful conclusion of a post-Saltsjöbaden Accord would provide the broad regulatory framework within which the unions and their locals could work out the details. Such an agreement has thus far proved elusive.

Each of these initiatives is important but none will be easy to implement. First, solidaristic work means that union structures have to be turned on their heads. The unions recognize this, but, as the critical report to Metall's 1995 congress suggested, these new ways of working are harder to put into practice. Second, the flexible reorganization of production challenges the collar line which has been one of the Swedish unions' foundation stones. The emergence of embryonic cross-collar alliances begins to rectify this, but, again, it is not always easy to put into practice. Although progress has been made at the branch level, the peak associations do not seem to have grasped the challenge. LO and TCO have been intensely involved in internal organizational change, but LO has been slow to recognize the need to approach TCO not as the hegemonic big brother, but rather as an equal. Under these circumstances, it is not surprising that TCO has turned to SACO. The key question here is whether the balance of forces within LO and TCO will change in time or whether solidarity will be replaced by liberal professionalism, as a new center of gravity is built around a newly merged TCO-SACO and LO is pushed to the margins.

Wage earner feminism is the unions' response to the marked rise in women's labor force participation rates and to the strength of a recharged women's movement. It has meant that the unions, notably the female-dominated public-sector unions, have placed pay equity firmly on the bargaining agenda. The unions have also moved to represent women wage earners in the double sense of representation: moving toward parity in union structures and redefining the "we" to bring gender into a class-centered discourse. The changes are impressive, but they have not come easily to a union movement where class solidarities have long taken priority over others. And their task has not been made easier by the growing divide between the export and sheltered sectors.

Given the marked segregation of the Swedish labor market, any move to close the gender pay gap must involve some form of trans-sectoral coordination, whether by the labor market parties on their own or only with the help of the state. Yet the peak associations, especially the once hegemonic LO, have been weakened, as became all too apparent in the 1995 bargaining round when LO failed to forge agreement around a common set of demands which included the special women's pott. LO was also unable to neutralize internal tensions in the debate over Sweden's entry into the EU. The unions in the export sector were quick to see the value of the EU's support for KFS and have also been more inclined to see in the EU an opportunity to counter the power of transnational capital. Unions in the sheltered sector have been more skeptical of the possibility of maintaining the Swedish model in a Europe where the welfare state is weaker and where, following Maastricht, the fight against inflation has had priority over all other macroeconomic goals.

It is not difficult to understand why Swedish unions have responded as they have. New strategies usually emerge out of critical reflection on the past, and solidaristic work and wage earner feminism try to address the challenges that appeared in the 1980s when Sweden seemed exempt from the corrosive effects of the return of mass unemployment. It is perhaps less easy to understand why the unions believed that the reelection of the Social Democrats would mean a restoration of the old patterns of political exchange. To be sure, this is in a sense what happened in 1982: the "Third Road" may have broken some of the principles of the Rehn-Meidner policy, but it did help secure full employment and preserve the welfare state. As the twentieth century draws to a close, however, it seems clear that national states have ceded much of their capacity to manage national economies. Even the Swedish Social Democrats have proven unable to crack the problem of unemployment and, as a result, have found it increasingly difficult to maintain the social democratic form of the welfare state. In this respect it is surprising that Swedish unions have continued to act as if the return of full employment capitalism were just around the corner.

Notes

1. Research for this project was partly funded by the Social Science and Humanities Research Council of Canada. The Swedish Institute for Working Life Research provided an excellent venue for the research time in Sweden. I would also like to thank Ann Britt Hellmark, Rob Ryan and Jennifer King for their research assistance and various colleagues/friends for their comments on the numerous drafts.
2. Walter Korpi's *The Working Class in Welfare Capitalism: Work, Unions and Politics in Sweden* (London: Routledge and Kegan Paul, 1979) launched this approach to class relations that focused on the kind of power resources which the working class could develop and deploy in capitalist societies See also Andrew Martin, "Is Democratic Control of Capitalist Economies Possible?" in *Stress and Contradiction in Modern Capitalism*, ed. Leon Lindberg et al., (Lexington, Mass: D.C. Heath, 1976); John Stephens, *The Transition from Capitalism to Socialism* (London: Macmillan, 1979); and Gösta Esping-Andersen, *Politics against Markets: The Social Democratic Road to Power* (Princeton, Princeton University Press, 1985). For a more critical perspective see Göran Therborn, "Why Some Classes Are More Successful Than Others," *New Left Review* 138 (1983).
3. See James Fulcher, *Labour Movements, Employers and the State: Conflict and Cooperation in Britain and Sweden* (Oxford: Clarendon, 1991) and Peter Swenson, *Fair Shares: Unions, Pay and Politics in Sweden and West Germany* (Ithaca: Cornell University Press, 1989) for more detail.

4. The policy has two dimensions: the general reduction of wage differentials and payment according to the job one has, rather than where one works or for whom. During the 1960s and 1970s, collective agreements focused on the former.
5. See Esping-Andersen, *Politics against Markets*
6. See Tommy Nilsson, *Från kamratföreningen till facklig rörelse: de svenska tjänstemännens organisationsutveckling 1900-1980* (Lund: Arkiv, 1985)
7. The quotation, from which this chapter takes its title, comes from a report produced by a joint union-management working group in the engineering branch: NAV Project Group (VI, Metall, SIF, and CF), "Nya allmänna anställningsvillkor – NAV" (1994)
8. The latter refers to a combination of strikes and lockouts affecting both public- and private- sector workers. For details see Andrew Martin, "Trade Unions in Sweden: Strategic Responses to Change and Crisis" in *Unions and Economic Crisis*, ed. P. Gourevitch et al. (London: Allen and Unwin, 1984).
9. The original Meidner version was adopted at LO's 1976 congress but in the course of subsequent negotiations, was considerably watered down. See Jonas Pontusson, *The Limits of Social Democracy: Investment Politics in Sweden* (Ithaca: Cornell University Press, 1992).
10. Anders Kjellberg, "Sweden: Can the Model Survive?" in *Industrial Relations in the New Europe*, ed A. Ferner and R. Hyman, (Oxford: Basil Blackwell, 1992).
11. These included the law strengthening the position of shop stewards (1974), the law on employment security (LAS, also 1974), the codetermination law (MBL, 1976), and the Work Environment Act (1978)
12. See Rianne Mahon, "Child Care in Canada and Sweden: Policy and Politics" *Social Politics* 4, no 3 (fall 1997).
13. Anders Kjellberg, "Sweden: Restoring the Model?" in *Changing Industrial Relations in Europe*, ed A. Ferner and R. Hyman, 2d ed. (Oxford: Blackwell, 1998), 95.
14. Until the 1990s the industry had a trade association and a separate organization to represent it vis-à-vis its employees. The two have merged to produce VI. The latter will be used throughout this chapter for purposes of simplicity.
15. Exports rose from 26 percent of sales in 1960 to 47 percent in 1988 Pontusson, *The Limits of Social Democracy*, 102.
16. The EU's share (minus Denmark, which forms part of the Nordic economic area) rose from 42 percent in 1970 to nearly 50 percent in 1990 Thomas Andersson, "Sveriges utrikeshandel i en förändrad omvärld" *Stockholm: Institute for Economic and Social Research* Paper #323, 1992. Figure 5:30.
17. Andersson, "Sveriges utrikeshandel" 19, Table 6
18. This excludes the effect of inflation and foreign investment in real estate. Thomas Andersson, "Sveriges utrikeshandel," 16.
19. Thomas Andersson, "Sveriges val, EG och direkt-investeringar" *Bilaga 7 til EG- konsekvensutredningen* Stockholm IESR number 1412, (1993): 45, fig. 3.6.
20. *LO Tidningen* 17 February 1995.
21. Peter Englund, "Financial Deregulation in Sweden" *European Economic Review* (1990).
22. Gregg Olsen, "Labour Mobilization and the Strength of Capital: The Rise and Stall of Economic Democracy in Sweden" *Studies in Political Economy* 34, (1991), 128 It is not only the large Swedish multinationals that have contributed to the outflow of portfolio investment. LO, TCO, and several of their affiliates have taken advantage of the liberalization to invest in stocks traded abroad. *Svenska Dagbladet* 27 November 1994 and 30 November 1994.

23. In the early 1950s, two LO economists, G. Rehn and R. Meidner, came up with an economic policy model which aimed, through a combination of a modified Keynesian macroeconomic policy, active labor market measures, and solidaristic wage bargaining, to improve the terms of the full-employment-price stability and growth-equity trade-offs. See Lennart Erixon, "What's Wrong with the Swedish Model?" Meddelande no. 12, 1985, Institute for Social Research, University of Stockholm.
24. See Christian Berggren, "New Production Concepts in Final Assembly – the Swedish Experience" in *The Transformation of Work?* ed S. Wood (London: Uwin Hyman: 1989); Thomas Sandberg, *Work Organisation and Autonomous Groups* (Lund: Liber, 1982); and Åke Sandberg, *Technological Change and Co-determination in Sweden* (Philadelphia: Temple University Press, 1992).
25. Tommy Nilsson and Åke Sandberg, *Rörelse över gränser* (Lund: Arkiv, 1988), 99.
26. This was one of the assumptions embedded in the EFO formula named after three economists, Edgren of TCO, Faxen of SAF, and Odhner of LO. Although the formula was never officially adopted, it was taken as an accurate description of bargaining outcomes even into the 1980s. Christian Nilsson, "The Swedish Model: Labor Market Institutions and Contracts" in *Labor Market Contracts and Institutions: A Cross-National Comparison*, ed. J. Hertog and I. Theeuwes, (Elsevier, 1993), 258.
27. See J. Jenson and R. Mahon, "Representing Solidarity: Class, Gender and the Crisis of Social Democratic Sweden," *New Left Review* 201 (1993).
28. Thorleif Pettersson and Kalle Geyer, *Värderingsförändringar i Sverige: Den svenska modellen, individualismen och rättvisa* (Stockholm: LO, Samtal om rättvisa nr 4, 1992) The shift to individualism should not be equated with a move toward neo-liberalism. Bo Rothstein provides evidence that Swedish individualism remains marked by a strong element of solidarity. See "Social Capital in the Social Democratic State: The Swedish Model and Civil Society, paper presented at the eleventh International conference of Europeanists, Baltimore, Md, February 1992, 27.
29. See S. O. Hansson and A. L. Lodenius, *Operation högervridning* (Stockholm: Tiden, 1988) and Victor Pestoff, "The Demise of the Swedish Model and the Rise of Organized Business as a Major Political Actor," paper presented at the Society for the Advancement of Socio- Economics, Stockholm, 1991.
30. See Jonas Pontusson and Peter Swenson, "Labor Markets, Production Strategies and Wage- Bargaining Institutions" *Comparative Political Studies* 29, no. 2 (1996).
31. Anders Kjellberg, "Sweden: Restoring the Model?," 90
32. See R. Mahon "Wage-Earners and/or Co-Workers? Contested Identities," *Economic and Industrial Democracy*, 15. no. 3 (1994) and below for more detail.
33. Kjellberg, "Sweden: Restoring the model?," 92
34. See Nils Elvander, "Income Policies in the Nordic Countries" *International Labour Review* 29, no. 1 (1990) 16.
35. The SSKF continues to raise this issue but they are pretty well alone in this. The women- dominated unions in fact are pushing for the right of parttime workers (mainly women) to fulltime positions.
36. The 1990s have seen the negotiation of a plethora of such local agreements, and in the 1998 round, such clauses were written into the national agreements covering important export sectors like engineering and pulp and paper
37. SAF may have been the first to launch the attack, but real impetus was given to the critique by two sets of studies done by foreign experts. See D.G. Blanchflower, R. Jackman, and G. Saint Paul, "Some Reflections on Swedish Labour Market Policy", Stockholm: SOU 1995, 39 and the series of studies conducted for SNS under the joint

leadership of Richard Freeman of the U.S. and Uppsala economists A. Björklund and A. Forslund.

38. In the 1998 round, key private-sector unions like Metall and Handels negotiated agreements which set aside a certain portion of the wage sum at the local level for training.
39. As there were separate contracts for blue-collar, white-collar, and professional workers, in any plant each would have its own seniority list
40. See Metall, *Solidarisk Arbetspolitik för det Goda Arbetet* (Stockholm: Metall, 1989) and E. Landell and J. Victorsson, *Långt kvar Till Kunskapssamhället* (Stockholm: Allmänna förlaget, 1991).
41. Olof Petersson, "Democracy and Power in Sweden" *Scandinavian Political Studies* 14, no. 2 (1991): 188.
42. Scott Lash, "The End of Corporatism: The Breakdown of Collective Bargaining in Sweden" *British Journal of Industrial Relations* 22, no. 2 (1985).
43. Metall, *Rapportbok – Väx, Tryck, Våga,* Metall, 1995, 55-56
44. Kommunal has a program, "*kom an då*" which trains local cadre to lead solidaristic work projects. It also regularly brings local activists together to learn from each other's experience.
45. The three-year agreements signed in 1998 included a (very modest) provision for worktime reduction and a collective agreement allocating a certain percent of the wage increase to firm-specific training funds. Handels' agreement similarly included a provision for training but also added the proviso that if the firm did not use the fund to invest in training, the money would be distributed as a general increase.
46. Anders Kjellberg, "Sweden: Can the Model Survive?," 119. For more detail see Anders Kjellberg, *Fackliga Organisationer och Medlemmar i Dagens Sverige* (Lund, Arkiv: 1997).
47. See Kristina Ahlen, *Unions Facing Change: Changing the Value of Union Membership with MarketplaceBbenefits* (Stockholm: ALC, 1990).
48. This concept is derived from Claus Offe and Helmut Weisenthal, "Two Logics of Collective Action," *Political Power and Social Theory* 1 (1980).
49. Kristina Ahlen, "Unfulfilled ambitions: Democratic Legitimacy in Swedish Labor Unions" (Stockholm: ALC, 1994), 145
50. It is by no means alone in this but its website – www.kommunal.se – is a particularly good one.
51. LO, *Röster om Jobbet och Facket* (Brevskolan, 1989), 74-75
52. See Rianne Mahon, "Women Wage Earners and the Future of Swedish Unions," *Economic and Industrial Democracy* 17 no. 4 (1996), 558-562.
53. Ann-Sofie Hermansson, *Arbetarrörelsen och Feminismen* (Stockholm, Brevskolan: Samtal om rättvisa serier no. 11, 1993), 9
54. This involved the organization of a high profile seminar series and the publication of a number of monographs on feminism, the future of the welfare state, and democracy in the union and in Swedish society.
55. See Rättviseutredningens rapport to LO's twenty-third congress, *Rättvisa,* September 1996, for more detail.
56. Idea Debate thus remains, along with the gender equality network, an important ginger group within LO. It has worked to maintain contacts with local union activists, including the informal networks which grew up to protest the Social Democrats lack of action on the employment front, as well as with university students and leading intellectuals.

57. The Secretariat is composed of four members of the executive (the President, the two Vice-Presidents and the Secretary) plus eleven union leaders selected from the affiliates, usually the largest. The Secretariat reports to the representative council, LO's highest official decision-making body between congresses (held every fifth year).
58. On the development of professional staff in LO and its key affiliates see Inga Hellberg, *Det Fackliga Förtroendet: en Studie av Ombudsmän och Experter 1950-1991* (Stockholm: Atlas, 1997).
59. Anders Kjellberg, *Facklig organizering i tolv länder* (Lund: Arkiv, 1983)
60. James Fulcher, *Labour Movements, Employers and the State: Conflict and Cooperation in Britain and Sweden* (Oxford: Clarendon Press: 1991), 49.
61. On this issue, see Wolfgang Streeck, "Interest Heterogeneity and Organizing Capacity: Two Class Logics of Collective Action" in *Social Institutions and Economic Performance: Studies of Industrial Relations in Advanced Capitalist Economies* (London: Sage, 1992).
62. KFS stands for *koncernfackligt samarbete.* The usual English translation – codetermination in multinational corporations – is misleading because it focuses on union-management relations rather than what the Swedish unions see as the prior task of developing inter(national) union dialogue and cooperation (samarbete) that would build cross-national solidarity.
63. Bo Stråth, "Verkstadsklubbarna vid Volvo och SAAB: Facklig politik i två företagskulturer," *Metall 100 År* (Stockholm: Metall, 1988) See also Klas Levinson, *Medbestämmande i strategiska beslutsprocesser: facklig medverkan och inflytande i koncerner* (Uppsala: Dept. of Business Studies, Uppsala University, 1991).
64. These recommendations included shortening the period between congresses from five to two years; that the Representative Council and Conference of Union Presidents be abolished and that the Secretariat, which would become the decision-making body between congresses, be enlarged to give the remaining union presidents the right to attend and speak (but not to vote).
65. Collective affiliation to the party was ended in 1990 For more on these strains see Jonas Pontusson, "At the End of the Road: Swedish Social Democracy in Crisis," *Politics and Society* 20, no.3 (1992).
66. These attempted to defend the fixed exchange rate policy initially introduced by the Social Democrats. Through these agreements, the SAP claimed a de facto veto over the labor law reforms which the Bildt government was planning to introduce.
67. See Rianne Mahon, "From Paradigm Exemplar to Hollow Shell? Swedish Unions at the End of the Twentieth Century," *Sociologie et Societe,* special issue on unions, fall 1998.
68. The Social Democrats suffered a setback in the 1998 election, dropping to 38 percent of the vote. The Left Party got 12 percent, however, and together with the Greens (4.6 percent) this gave the Social Democrats sufficient support to remain in government.
69. Since the SAP's embrace of Europe in 1990, the EU has not been an issue dividing the two blocs Membership in the EMU has, however, become a "class" issue with SAF leading the campaign to sign on.

Chapter 5

THE HOLLOWING OUT OF FRENCH UNIONS

Politics and Industrial Relations After 1981

Anthony Daley

Introduction

French unions have faced many of the same challenges confronting their counterparts in Europe over the last two decades – high unemployment, aggressive employers, a liberalizing state, and a changing labor force. While they have had left government for over half the period, they have watched their mainstream parties become convinced of the necessity to liberate market forces, and the "interventionist state" has become more market friendly. But French unions have also contributed greatly to their own problems. Inter- and intra-union political maneuvering has depleted membership, thereby weakening the ability of French labor to confront economic and political changes and aggravating their effects. The damage has been stunning. French unions lost half their members after the late 1970s. Near silence reigns where local unions once displayed vibrancy. Although locals could once wield resources effectively against individual employers, the balance has now shifted to management, and union organizations have disappeared in some industries. Where national unions could once influence political parties, labor's con-

Notes for this section begin on page 213.

cerns are increasingly less reflected in political agendas. The age-old capacity to mobilize discontent and force concessions from state authorities has been depleted, the November-December 1995 strikes notwithstanding. Even employers complained of the absence of bargaining partners! With few members, weak organizations, and competition among themselves, French unions have had to cling to the remaining legal protections for their very survival. Internal and external dynamics have hollowed out the French labor movement.

This essay examines the causes and consequences of organizational decay. It suggests a serious erosion of the French model of industrial relations which has traditionally focused on a state capable and willing to provide resources for unions and to structure working-class representation, if only to maintain social peace. It then explores the economic forces after 1980 that have threatened the viability of this model by prioritizing investment decisions over social control. Finally, the essay shows that most current strategies of French labor still reflect a logic derived from the traditional model. Even the most innovative strategies at the local, national, or European level have failed to reverse decline.

A Changing Portrait of French Unions

The French model of industrial relations developed several distinctive features in the thirty-five years after World War Two. Its unions were short on members and long on rhetoric, more willing to lead protests than negotiations. Managerial inflexibility and a potentially unfavorable local balance of forces encouraged employers to shun collective bargaining at the company level. In response to state cajoling, weak employer associations bargained over minimum wages at the sectoral or regional level for a precise set of job categories defined by the state. The state served as puppet master, prodding the bargaining partners to negotiate and compensating for bargaining failures by elaborating a corpus of labor law that detailed the mechanics of employment, training, and employee representation.

The implications for French unions were clear: organizational resources were less consequential than elsewhere in Europe. Density peaked at 35 percent in the immediate postwar period and dropped to 20 percent by the 1970s, but it was always uneven – low in the private sector, higher in the civil service, and highest in nationalized industries. Organizational ties were based more on loyalty either to individual militants or a worldview than on the provision of services. As long as a critical mass of membership existed, then, local unions could instill fear in employers and encourage state intervention. Elections for workplace representative institutions – plant delegates, works councils, conciliation boards, and bipartite administrative committees in the public sector – were occasions either to wield individual charisma or choose among competing ideas. They also tended to substitute for membership, and the unions consequently lacked resources.

As of 1980, the French labor movement was splintered into competitive organizations divided by politics and strategy. The largest of them, the *Confédération Générale du Travail* (CGT), engaged in class confrontational rhetoric tempered with bargaining pragmatism. The *Confédération Française Démocratique du Travail* (CFDT) was the second largest organization, closing in on the CGT after breaking with the passivity of Catholic unionism in 1964 and developing a militant social Catholicism afterwards. *Force Ouvrière* (FO), which had split from the CGT in 1948 to pursue an American-styled business unionism, eschewed grand ideas for bargaining leverage, but was a serious competitor mainly in the public sector. The largest public-sector union, though, was the teachers' union, the *Fédération de l'Education Nationale* (FEN).[1] Smaller players included the *Confédération Française des Travailleurs Chrétiens* (CFTC) and the *Confédération Générale des Cadres* (CGC) representing mid-level managers and engineers. Independent unions existed by company or economic activity, especially within the public sector.

Historically French unions depended on political parties to implement many of their ideas. Unions and parties shared worldviews but had mixed records in cooperation. The CGT enjoyed a close relationship with the largest party on the left (until the 1970s), the Communist Party (PCF). The CGT-PCF linkage was cemented organizationally by joint membership at the leadership level and culturally by the overt class conflict characterizing French society. In contrast, relations between FO and CFDT on the one hand and the Socialist Party (PS) on the other were informal and ambiguous. The CFDT had an affinity of ideas with one faction of the PS. The FO's anti-communism (cementing its internal political mosaic) made it susceptible to a loose alliance with the broad centrism of the precursor to the PS, the SFIO. At times the CGC flirted with Gaullism.

Unions were largely decentralized. Each confederation has been organized by occupation within industrial federations and geographically within cross-industrial *(inter-professionnel)* departmental unions (UDs). The federations (after 1968) organized workplace units (*sections syndicales d'entreprise* or SSEs) while the UDs organized local unions (ULs) within individual towns. The SSEs had wide discretion to set agendas and formulate strategies within broad guidelines. The UDs were the eyes and ears of the confederation in the provinces. Industrial and geographic structures were balanced at the confederal level. In theory, these two levels of organization worked together to ensure job-based representation and intraclass mobilization. In practice, confederal imposition of political positions created tension. Competitive unionism affected collective bargaining.[2] Any union declared "representative" by the Ministry of Labor – the five major confederations, the FEN, and independent unions for individual sectors – could sign contracts even when unions representing the majority of workers were opposed. Any union, in turn, could strike against that contract. The result was workplace contentiousness, aggravated by an authoritarian streak within French management. Because of management's unwillingness to bargain over substantive issues, industrial conflict was separated from contract demands. With lean organizations, unions appealed to the political sphere for what they could not attain in the labor market.

After 1945, the French state used an array of policy tools to monitor industrial relations, offer incentives to create jobs at the local level, and decree a vast array of social policies. By the 1970s, policymakers had used these tools to construct a national industrial relations system that strengthened the role of the confederations, strong-arming employers and unions to negotiate at the national level about problems of employment, quality of work, and training. This gave workers what union organizations could not obtain for themselves. The Ministry of Labor set minimum wages to boost salaries at the low end and push up salary scales. It extended favorable bargaining agreements to larger jurisdictions. It decreed policy on vacations, retirement, and working time. It defended employees threatened with dismissal. It stimulated bargaining by threatening to act unilaterally in the absence of agreement between social partners. In general, the state-centric arrangements substituted public policy for union bargaining and devolved very little power to the peak organizations of labor or capital. Unions had little incentive to increase membership or improve collective bargaining. State intervention in the labor market encouraged unions to seek returns from parties. Capturing the state became more important than incremental labor market reforms, reinforcing the tendency to neglect organization for ideas. State intervention, even for the less partisan FO, tempered intransigent employers, compensated for bargaining weaknesses, and equalized bargaining outcomes. The result was a highly politicized labor movement, inextricably tied to state intervention.

The Socialist administration that began in 1981 initially aggravated these political reflexes. The left came to power pledging to increase the democratic control of the economy through nationalizations and new employee rights. It also promised an economic stimulus package to raise incomes and create jobs. These initiatives and the new openness of Parisian ministries gave hope to unions that their organizational deficiencies could be overcome through state intervention, further validating the political approach to union mobilization. The left reforms gave the unions very few new resources.

Policy reversal in 1983, therefore, demoralized French unions. The unions were grossly unprepared for the changes taking place within the economy. Leaders tended to wait for state action rather than accumulate organizational resources. Given the high expectations for the left's agenda, the U-turn in economic policy divided the political left and aggravated interunion relations: the CGT reverted to political oppositionalism that closely followed the arguments of the PCF; the CFDT supported the Socialists even as its members deserted it; and FO lambasted both the governing left and Communists in the labor movement. Individual unions were at a strategic dead end. The constant politicking – either continued affiliation with a left government that reversed its campaign promises or interunion maneuvering – encouraged membership defection.[3] There was a larger systemic problem, however, that was aggravated by the changes within the political turnaround. The structure of French industrial relations had given labor leaders little incentive to overcome fragmentation. State mandates for employee representation had created administrative structures at the firm and alongside government that provided crucial resources to the short-term interests of union organizations. In the long term, though, these institutions not only failed to alter the environment facing unions, but also weakened the very foundations of the labor movement because they discouraged organizational renewal.

The U-turn bumped unemployment into double digits by 1985 where it has hovered since. Economic policy focused on the strength of the currency and a ruthless attack on inflation. Governments scaled back industrial subsidies to save employment, favored investment over consumption, and budgetary restraint over employment generation. A strong franc was maintained by aggressively reducing costs, including the price of labor, to levels below those of trading partners. The core of economic policy after 1983 ran counter to the dominant union strategy – negotiating wages. French unions had reason to be deeply pessimistic by the 1990s.

Meanwhile, membership decline further undermined union presence at the workplace. The CGT was hardest hit with its bastions – male production workers in heavy industry – deeply affected by the changes taking place in the economy, and its gains among white-collar employees could not compensate.[4] Table 5.1 shows the membership losses suffered by the major French unions. By 1995, French union density was under 9 percent, the lowest among OECD countries.[5] Along with membership decline has come a reconfiguration of the labor movement. The once powerful CGT metalworkers' federation dropped from over 400,000 members in the 1970s to 70,000 in the early 1990s. Once one of the most important federations in the CFDT, the federation of textile, clothing, and leather workers (*Hacuitex*) lost 80 percent of its members in the twenty years after its peak year of 1973 and has become marginalized in the confederation. In contrast, white-collar unions in FO and the CFTC have gained members. At between 23 and 31 percent, the unionization rate for white-collar, knowledge-intensive employees dramatically exceeds those for clerical and production workers.[6] Table 5.2 confirms a substantial equality between the CGT and CFDT in election for works councils, while Table 5.3 shows rough parity among those two unions, FO and the FEN, in results for public sector administrative commissions. Election results also show disaffection with all the large confederations who have received a diminishing overall vote, while abstention rates have been higher.[7]

Table 5.1 Membership in French Unions (in thousands)

	CGT	CFDT	FO	CFTC	CGC	FEN	others
1970	1830	605	389	65	186	428	165
1980	1320	672	471	102	216	520	180
1993	639	473	370	93	111	300	135

Source: Dominique Labbé, *Syndicats et syndiqués en France depuis 1945* (Paris: L'Harmattan, 1996), 132

Table 5.2 Works Council Elections in France (percentage of all votes cast)

	CGT	CFDT	FO	CFTC	CGC	others	Non-union
1978	38.5	20.4	10.0	2.7	6.6	5.2	16.3
1979	34.4	20.5	9.7	3.1	5.8	4.8	21.2
1994	22.4	20.3	12.7	4.1	6.0	6.2	28.4
1995	19.7	20.5	12.3	5.1	6.4	6.2	29.9

Note 1: Because elections are held every two years and results are aggregated on an annual basis, observers compare elections on two-year intervals – odd-to-odd and even-to-even.
Note 2: Before 1985, the data did not include elections in the national railway (SNCF).
Source: Ministère du Travail, de l'Emploi et de la Formation Professionnelle

Table 5.3 Elections for Civil Service Administrative Commissions in France (percentage of all votes cast)

	CGT	CFDT	FO	CFTC	CGC	FEN	FSU	others
1978-80	20.6	16.3	15.3	2.8	3.8	29.9	—	11.3
1993-95	16.7	15.2	15.7	2.6	2.0	18.1	14.7	15.0

Note 1: Elections in the *Fonction Publique* are held every three years. Because they are held at different times, the best measure is a three-year average.
Note 2: The *Fédération Syndicale Unitaire* (FSU) was created in 1993 from a split in the FEN.
Source: Ministère de la Fonction Publique

The free fall of the CGT in membership and workplace elections offered new opportunities to other unions. By the mid-1980s, the CGT confronted works council alliances between the CFDT and FO or some combination of smaller unions. As employers felt freer to circumvent the CGT in collective bargaining, the game of competitive unionism intensified, continuing to alienate the workforce. Membership drain, however, eventually affected the organizations of all unions. While full-time staff has always been meager, organizations relied on a minimal local presence to mobilize larger groups of workers. Membership decline began to impair the ability to lead such mobilization, however. Local union officials needed to assume even larger responsibilities because of the lack of members and because changes in French labor law gave them new responsibilities. The decline in dues revenue forced unions to rely more on public subsidies for its press, training, participation in representative institutions, and even for its full-time officers.[8]

As elsewhere in Europe, strike rates have dropped precipitously in the last fifteen years. Between 1979 and 1994, hours lost to work stoppages dropped from 3.6 to 0.75 million days – a fall of 75 percent, although it blipped to 5.9 million days in 1995.[9] An increasing percentage of strikes in France occurs in either civil service or nationalized companies where employees are more protected from management retaliation. The private sector is virtually quiescent. Given the traditional importance of strike activity to precipitate political response and compensate for organizational weakness, such quiescence is maybe more consequential to the French movement than analogous trends elsewhere.

The collapse of the old model has forced unions to innovate. An inability to rely on political parties to capture the state and "change society" has encouraged unions to rely more on their own capacities. They have tried recruitment strategies in small companies and have used works councils to bargain over employment. They have experimented with work organization, working time, and even the organization of the unemployed. The loss of members reached its trough and memberships increased slowly by the early 1990s. But a sustained recovery of French unions depends on their ability to adapt to a new model of industrial relations.

In the late 1990s, French industrial relations looked very different from twenty years earlier. Where the unions, led by the CGT, once denounced class exploitation and profitmaking, they now almost universally seek to make incremental changes in the lives of members and potential members. Where they protested, they now negotiate with management. Where companies once feared firm-level bargaining for its potential to politicize labor relations, they have become its ardent defenders. Where managers once ran an authoritarian workplace, they are now more open to employee participation. This conversion from confrontational bargaining to permanent negotiation has been incomplete and uneven, but it constitutes a dominant tendency. Unfortunately for the unions, the change has taken place largely on employer terms. Individual companies set the agenda for negotiation, while unions largely react to employer demands. Changes taking place in the economy and polity outpaced the ability of unions to adapt.

The Economic Challenge for French Unions

The French economy has changed dramatically in the last twenty years. French producers focus increasingly on Europe for trade, investment, and alliances while producing in increasingly smaller units and expecting bargaining to devolve as well. The more the French state met business needs and engaged less in redistributive policy, the more French unions were disadvantaged.

Until the 1980s, state actors and company managers had favored increasing centralization of production on a *national* level. Public policy encouraged economies of scale within mass production industries.[10] While policymakers had used the European Coal and Steel Community and the Common Market to force timid French capitalists to become more competitive, a national champion policy envisioned national production for French employment and income. The nationalization program of the victorious Socialists in 1981 extended this policy with an import substitution strategy to "reconquer the domestic market."[11]

After the early 1980s, however, economic activity became markedly more international both within and outside of Europe. Transborder mergers and strategic alliances rose as did levels of both exports and import penetration. As European credit markets opened up, large French producers could borrow abroad and escape the restrictions of government credit policy. Another indicator of internationalization was foreign direct investment. Long a net recipient, France witnessed a turnaround in the mid-1980s, although net outflows had tapered off by the mid-1990s. And European investment as a percentage of total foreign investment increased from 23 percent in 1981-83 to 64 percent in 1988.[12] Business and political elites concluded that companies needed greater scale, market share, and presence in foreign markets. The internationalization of operations both immunized business against union mobilization and weakened governmental reflexes to industrial conflict.

Simultaneously, French business decentralized both production and collective bargaining. Average plant size decreased. Between 1981 and 1993, the percentage of the workforce employed in plants with over 500 employees dropped from 17.3 to 11.3, while the percentage of those working in plants with under fifty employees increased from 47.8 to 54.9.[13] Production decentralization brought firm-level bargaining. Encouraged by government labor policy to rethink past practices, French employers embraced company-level collective bargaining with the zeal of converts. The Socialist labor reforms (the "Auroux Laws" after Minister of Labor Jean Auroux) were at first bitterly contested by the business community but came to facilitate labor flexibility. Employers were obliged to negotiate wages with union representatives on an annual basis, although they were not required to reach agreement. That same law also permitted firm-level accords which downgraded agreements made at the sectoral or national levels.[14] This right of "derogation" enabled employers to make sectoral agreements more flexible. By strengthening works councils at the expense of union organizations, the second Auroux Law further met firm- level needs.[15] Plant-level agreements increased rapidly after the early 1980s, jumping from 1955 total agreements in 1983, to 6496 in 1990, and 9274 in 1996.[16] Thus, bargaining initiatives have shifted to management since the mid-1980s, and the terms of agreement reflect company needs.

Firm-level bargaining complemented accords at higher levels and fed an overall increase in collective bargaining. After declining in the early 1980s, sectoral bargaining stabilized and increased slightly by the early 1990s.[17] One of the many ironies of French industrial relations is that despite low union density, bargaining coverage is high.[18] This has been stimulated from above: the Auroux Laws gave the Ministry of Labor authority to impose agreements on individual sectors, thereby inducing employers to negotiate. As a result, sectoral *conventions collectives* covered

25 percent of private-sector employees in 1981 and over 95 percent by the mid-1990s, although the terms of such agreements often varied little from minimum legal standards.

High unemployment rates have put downward pressures on wages and changed the character of bargaining. Employers could insist on the bare minimum of sectoral agreement or even derogations from salary scales. With a small pie to divvy up, unions and employers searched for other issues on which they could agree. Consequently, bargaining over working time, job classifications, training, and the right of expression became more important. By the mid-1990s, collective bargaining at the sectoral level addressed almost as many nonsalary as salary issues. The increasing nonwage focus of bargaining is even clearer at the firm level where clauses concerning working time exceeded those of salary matters by 1996.[19]

Along with job reductions came a changing labor force. Manufacturing was hit much more severely than the service sector, and within manufacturing, unskilled jobs have declined while technical fields have expanded. Both trends offered women new employment opportunities, and female labor force participation rates reached 59.7 percent by 1995.[20] Programs to ease workers out of the labor force targeted older workers, typically male and between the ages of fifty and sixty. Meanwhile, the drop in the legal retirement age to sixty in 1982 made participation rates of workers over sixty the lowest in the OECD area. Historically high unemployment rates have been bunched into two categories – long-term and youth – amplifying a dualistic labor market. Weak labor markets have also translated into an increase in atypical work. The vast majority (eight out of nine in 1988) of new jobs created are limited term, part-time, or temporary.[21]

Workforce changes have affected the labor movement in several ways. Employees who work on permanent contract (the standard before 1980) have become a new "labor aristocracy." Rightly or wrongly, unions have been accused of *corporatisme* – the desire to protect this closed community at the expense of wider social solidarities. The difficulty of organizing workers in atypical employment is evident in the unionization rates among those workers under twenty-four years who tend to be disproportionately in such jobs – 1 percent in 1990 down from 9 percent in 1981.[22]

The Labor Code has mitigated the effects of decentralization by providing a uniformity of treatment not always available through negotiation.[23] It has established floors for pay issues (minimum wage, sick pay, vacation time, and retirement pay), the design of representative institutions (works councils, plant delegates), the terms of employment contracts, and the conditions of work. Although underfunded and understaffed, the labor inspector has a responsibility to ensure compliance with all provisions of labor law. Employers must abide by the minimum standards of sectoral agreements if no union signs a derogation agreement, and procedures for abrogating sectoral agreements are tedious. Not surprisingly, employers have sought to modify this legal framework.

The Changing Role of the French State

After the U-turn in 1983, policy elites liberalized economic policy. Liberalization *à la française* has involved expanding the market for French firms from a national to a European dimension and encouraging companies to bargain at the local level. State actors have not been free market crusaders, however. Constrained by institutional legacies and political alliances, they have maintained a critical role for the state in developing French capitalism. In gradual and sometimes contradictory ways, the state has changed its focus from redistribution to investment.

The architecture of economic policy begins with Europe. Socialist President François Mitterrand was a key actor in expanding the European policy arena. His decision to abandon economic stimulus policies in 1983 maintained France in the Exchange Rate Mechanism of the European Monetary System. Subsequently, France promoted completing the Single European Market, a project facilitated by the appointment of Jacques Delors as Commission President. Likewise, Mitterrand worked closely with the Germans in forging the Maastricht Treaty and EMU in 1991. After 1983, the Socialists and the right decided that economic policy would prioritize the external constraint. Governments defended the value of the currency with high real interest rates. Currency stability would encourage managers to contain costs and facilitate foreign investment. The policy, however, dampened domestic demand and tied monetary policy to the Bundesbank. Despite an overvalued currency, no French government has devalued the franc since 1983.

The most effective way to maintain the currency's value was to dampen cost pressures. Slow growth in budgetary expenditures reduced inflationary pressures. The disindexation of public-sector wages in 1983 helped public-sector firms to contain costs, and this reverberated throughout the rest of the economy, lowering wage claims. Wage growth in France was the second lowest (to Greece) in the European Community after 1985.[24] This policy of "competitive disinflation" reduced the inflation differential with Germany (France's largest trading partner) by the mid-1980s. It eventually restored equilibrium to the trade balance with Germany, and it improved the overall commercial balance. Most importantly, it brought high profit levels, especially important for foreign investment.[25]

Efforts to reduce budget deficits to comply with EMU convergence criteria squeezed redistributive policies. High unemployment and the selective exoneration from payroll taxes as an incentive to hire new employees had put enormous pressure on the welfare system. In 1995, the government of Alain Juppé attempted to balance the books by cutting costs, lowering benefits, transferring the financing from payroll to income taxes, and eliminating special public-sector pension programs. These actions triggered the mass social mobilization in the fall of 1995, which, although it forced the government to back down on public-sector pension reform, failed to modify the overall reform. Higher payroll taxes and lower benefits reduced the market-softening effects of the pension system, national health care, and unemployment compensation. With a temporary increase in business taxes to meet the budget target, the left government of Lionel Jospin, elected in June 1997, moderated the tendency to pay for EMU out of the social wage.

Budgetary stringency also brought a reorientation of industrial policy. Wholesale subsidies of traditional sectors (coal, steel, shipbuilding, textiles) had protected employment in the 1970s. The first two years of left government suggested that the state would actively finance industrial restructuring. The U-turn, however, altered the dominant thrust of industrial policy. Nationalized companies were in the forefront of labor shedding in the mid-1980s. These were union bastions and the employment reductions dramatically increased deunionization. This is not to suggest a new state dispassion for industrial intervention. Even in the mid-1990s, the European Commission complained about Parisian bailouts.[26]

Budgetary concerns also encouraged a rethinking of the public sector. The government of Jacques Chirac (1986-88) began to undo the nationalizations of 1982. It privatized some firms until the 1987 crash, and Chirac's defeat in the 1988 presidential elections put a damper on further action. Between 1988 and 1993, Socialist governments acquiesced to selloffs and stock dilutions to raise capital, facilitated by a buoyant stock market. After March 1993, the center-right government of Edouard Balladur (1993-95) resumed the privatization program by targeting twenty-one groups in the public sector (twelve of which were from the 1986 list). In the aftermath of the Chirac presidential victory in 1995, the government of Alain Juppé (1995-97) resumed the work of its predecessor.[27] Even the Jospin government continued to privatize state enterprise, albeit with less missionary zeal.

Policy in the 1980s actively encouraged state and private companies to invest in each other. Cross-shareholding was intended to establish a "hard core" *(noyau dur)* of stable investors, which, by implicating the banking sector, would provide the basis for long-term access to capital and prevent hostile takeovers. Such market structuring ran into several obstacles, however. The financial sector overextended itself in speculative investments. The crisis of French banks was evident in the mid-1990s with the massive losses of the state-owned Crédit Lyonnais and Gan, and rescue operations have included divestiture of industrial assets. Networks of interlocking directorships reinforced the power of upper management to the chagrin of partisans of shareholder capitalism. Governments undermined a strategy of cross-investment by allowing foreign direct investment in over half the shares of such companies as Total, Elf Aquitaine, and Pechiney.[28] Still, a web of business alliances remains largely in place, enabling companies to remain independent and tying business to banking.

Reluctance to engage in knee-jerk liberalism can be seen in policies toward state monopolies where changes have been far from uniform. Governments have defended a French conception of *service public* as one based on universal service vis-à-vis the liberalizing impulses of the European Commision. The state-owned electrical utility, Electricité de France (EdF), used concerns over universalism to fight the Commission over competition in the domestic market for electricity. In contrast, the state rail system run by the Société Nationale des Chemins de Fer (SNCF) has reduced service to small towns and focused efforts on both the major lines and the *trains à grande vitesse*. The ill-fated attempts to restructure the SNCF in the fall of 1995 came from an attempt to cut state subsidies and to meet objections of European competitors. Nonetheless, the Juppé government assumed over half the debt of the company in 1996, and the Ministry of Transportation continues to handle this dossier with kid gloves. Governments have pushed harder to reform telecommunications. The Socialists separated telecommunications from the postal services in 1990, freeing the new company France Télécom to enter global markets and to forge alliances with other long distance carriers and equipment manufacturers. The Juppé government removed France Télécom's monopoly in business services in 1996. It also changed the company's statute and converted it to a joint stock company, which facilitated a future privatization, a decision later approved (at least in partial form) by the Jospin government. Governments have also opened up the telecommunications market to comply with Commission directives.

Governments have been slower to restructure the civil service *(fonction publique)*. After the expansion of state employment in the early

1980s, budgetary austerity has limited job growth, and an incomes policy for state employees (tying salary increases to predicted levels of inflation) has put a cap on wage growth. Municipal governments began contracting out some services. The Juppé government used preparation to meet the budgetary criterion of EMU to force through deeper cuts in state expenditures in 1995 and 1996, although it planned small salary increases for 1997 to forestall industrial unrest. During the late 1980s and early 1990s, the employment contraction combined with a loss in purchasing power encouraged job actions by public-sector workers, and union militancy has delayed reorganization.

Policymakers have gradually assumed control of the French welfare state. Unique in Europe, the system (pensions, medical insurance, and unemployment compensation) was funded by payroll taxes and administered by unions and employers. Such funding became increasingly difficult after the mid-1980s given a shrinking workforce and labor market policies that exempted employer contributions and increased burdens on other employers. Because governments covered deficits, however, policy change came increasingly from above after the mid-1980s. As employers balked at paying the highest payroll taxes in Europe, a consensus developed among the Socialists and the right that universal funding was a necessary path to forestall endless deficits. The reforms of the Juppé government ignited the massive protests in November-December 1995, but they were made into law the following year. The Jospin government completed many of the reforms in late 1997 by phasing out employee contributions almost entirely for the most expensive budget item, health care, and increasing funding from a universal tax.

The French state has developed an aggressive labor market policy. The size of efforts to counter unemployment has been stunning: nearly half of all French jobs depended on state policy by the early 1990s.[29] While some policies lowered employment costs, others encouraged the improvement of human capital. Many of the employment programs required employers to include on-the-job training. The second Mitterrand administration (1988-95) developed an individualized voucher system to enable school-leavers and all unemployed workers to retool their skills. Training became a right available to all employees. The Jospin government pledged to create 700,000 new jobs in both the public and private sectors.

Creating long-term skilled jobs has been difficult, as all governments have discovered. Attempting to forestall even greater unemployment, governments have created hundreds of thousands of nonpermanent jobs – either temporary so-called training programs at low wages that actually involve more work than training or private-sector employment with exemption for employers of payroll taxes. Between 1985 and 1992, youth employment schemes doubled to almost one million short-time jobs.[30] Some programs paid young people subminimum wages, while others subsidized employer payroll taxes. Programs for the long-term unemployed also subsidized payroll costs. By the mid-1990s, three-quarters of the unemployed had spent time in temporary jobs or state programs.[31] Anecdotal evidence suggests that companies took training subsidies to hire workers they otherwise would have hired on their own. Likewise, vouchers were neither promoted nor funded sufficiently to make a significant impact.

Governments have tried to make labor markets more flexible and have sought to spur collective bargaining to accomplish that goal. The ability to derogate from a sectoral accord requires agreement between the employer and union representatives. In this light, employer complaints of an absence of union organizations become more understandable. After the Chirac government ended the practice of requiring state approval for layoffs in 1986, new legislation encouraged unions and employers to bargain over the terms of layoffs rather than requiring the approval of the departmental labor inspector. In the 1990s, the Ministry of Labor has encouraged unions and employers to negotiate working time reduction as a way to hire more workers. The encouragement of bargaining has sometimes circumvented the unions. In a serious breach in the legal basis of union representativeness, legislation in 1996 allowed companies without union representatives to bargain with works councils on wages, although any agreement would have to be approved by a joint union-employer committee at the sector level.

The absolute priority given to the external constraint, however, made lowering labor costs an overriding goal. The Five-Year Employment Law of December 1993 increased workplace flexibility. It gave companies easier recourse to the system of short-time work. It also changed the standard for full-time employment to an annual calculation so employers could vary hours according to fluctuations in demand. Public-sector incomes policy has been copied by the private sector. For those with jobs, total compensation rose only slightly in real terms. Between 1980 and 1995, labor costs as a percentage of national product fell from 56.0 percent to 51.7 percent.[32]

The only positive experimentation in the public sector that the unions could find has been in European social policy. The Socialists encouraged French multinationals to embark on European consultation procedures, facilitating the development of European works councils.

Thomson, Elf-Aquitaine, Bull, Péchiney, Rhône-Poulenc, Renault, Saint Gobain, and BSN (now called Danone) embarked on Europe-wide consultation procedures from the mid-1980s to the early 1990s. Not surprisingly, the first six belonged to the public sector; Saint Gobain had only recently been privatized; and the head of BSN/Danone, Antoine Riboud, was a strong supporter of the Socialists. French governments of left and right have also been in the forefront of a Europe-wide social policy.

Overall, French unions felt squeezed by public policy. Strike actions could postpone certain policies – and even bury some minor ones – but the unions held little sway over the architecture of policy. And the logic of state action seems to guarantee a harsh future for organized labor. Retrenchment in national defense and a quasi reintegration into NATO promise tens of thousands of layoffs at state armament plants. Moreover, the end of conscription puts additional pressure on labor markets for young people. The right's flirtation with tax cutting – nipped in the bud by defeat in 1997 – had the potential to whittle away at funding for public- sector services. The development of private-sector pension plans will erode the state retirement system. Thus, while governments have shown a mixed record on involvement in the economy, policy has contributed to the Europeanization and localism that have weakened French unions.

New Activism by French Employers

Few would have thought that the environment after 1981 would have been friendly to French business given their own competitive difficulties, the Socialist discourse of a "break with capitalism," and the reforms of the left government. Since the U-turn, however, French business has been as dynamic as any counterpart in Europe. Ironically, both the changes in ownership and reform of French labor law strengthened French firms. Business self-confidence has weakened the ability of unions to influence company policy.

French companies were in a vise by the early 1980s. Mass producers were more vulnerable to low-wage mass production from newly industrialized countries. Knowledge-intensive industries were stumbling over managerial inefficiencies and capital shortages. Moreover, the Ministry of Labor had strong-armed employers to limit private-sector layoffs to address the onset of mass unemployment. And state industrial policy had shifted from channeling investment to achieve scale economies to extending subsidies to small and large firms alike, both of whom suddenly found themselves in competitive difficulties.[33] The results were weaknesses in competitiveness and a demoralization of the business community. Productive investment fell after 1974, companies queued up for state subsidies, and labor relations remained rigidly hierarchical.

The left program turned into a boon for business. Shareholders forced to sell to the state were compensated above market value. State control of these companies facilitated changes that would have been more difficult in private hands. Activist industrial policy in the first years of left governance reorganized the diversified groups into core activities. Loss-takers received large infusions of capital first to cover ongoing losses and then to recapitalize. After the U-turn, these companies shed employees much faster than their private-sector counterparts. Evidence for the financial success of nationalization could already be found in the high profit levels for public-sector companies by the mid-1980s. Moreover, the elimination of price controls gave companies more discretion in product markets. The liberalization of financial markets – elimination of exchange controls, removal of state allocation of credit and new securities markets – enabled companies to tap new sources of investment funds. While French firms were the most indebted in the world in 1980, they were the least indebted by the early 1990s.[34] French companies were also among the most profitable in the world by the early 1990s.[35]

As corporate giants restructured to core activities, they depended more heavily on suppliers. And the emphasis on quality production has forced important changes in subcontracting relationships: an arms-length relationship has been replaced by greater cooperation between large companies and their suppliers.[36] Also, the heavy labor-shedding and withdrawal from certain markets in the mid-1980s facilitated the entry of small startups in previously large-firm-dominated niches. Both trends have contributed to a new dynamism in small- and medium-sized enterprises where the new jobs were being created and where the unions were absent.

The most innovative changes for the employers, however, have taken place in human resource management. Before 1980, enterprise culture was characterized by rigid authority relations, a strict division of labor, and a high level of workplace conflict. Employers equated participation with collective bargaining and preferred to engage in minimal bargaining at the sectoral level to keep unions away from workplace decisionmaking. Spurred by the Auroux Laws, however, they embraced employee input – minus, however, the unions. Employers experimented with various forms of "participative" management. The nonunion expression groups mandated by the Auroux Laws facilitated employee input on work processes and enabled company experimentation with work reorganization. In 1986 France had more quality circles than all the other countries in the European Community.[37]

Such participative management techniques were the rage of the business press and business school curricula in the 1980s, although debate exists over both their extent and their success.[38] The mantras came in different forms – "Toyotism" to break down production rigidities, autonomous work teams, job rotations, skill upgrades, etc. These approaches had in common an attempt to break down hierarchy, to eliminate production bottlenecks, to increase productivity, and to lower costs. While the quality circle fad mushroomed and withered by the 1990s, managerial emphasis on quality remained. That, in turn, has brought a new concern for coordination and communication. Successful work reorganizations have been those designed for the long term and oriented toward productivity enhancements, involving a large percentage of the workforce. To the extent that firms have recourse to less-than-permanent staff, work reorganization becomes harder. Some studies suggest that the authoritarianism and rigid production practices that characterized authority relations under mass production have been recast with new information technologies.[39] By the early 1990s the same business press that had lauded the new forms of management was complaining that it no longer seemed effective, especially in the midst of a difficult recession.

Employers have individualized the employment contract as much as possible. They have used profit- and gain-sharing programs to tie pay more closely to firm performance.[40] There are increasingly more attempts to tie salary increases to skill and performance levels. Renault provided a path-breaking example with its 1989 agreement that tied pay to employee initiative in developing skills.[41] A Ministry of Labor study found a high level of performance-based pay through 1993, although unemployment had reduced overall salary increases.[42]

The circumvention of unions has also been discernible in the recent usage of employer-sponsored referenda to garner legitimacy for painful actions. As part of its reorganization, for instance, Air France reduced the workforce, froze pay, and blocked promotions. It then called a referendum of the workforce in April 1994 with the implication that a negative vote would bring further reductions. (Given the earlier attempts at downsizing, major strikes in fall 1993, and the resignation of the CEO, the implication of crisis facing the airline was not very subtle.) The referendum won overwhelmingly with 83 percent "favoring" management's plans. Similar referenda have taken place at other firms.

French employers have also become much more politically aggressive, raising topics that were taboo only a few years ago. For instance, several trade associations have called for either the abolition or the weakening of the minimum wage. Such sentiment was behind the ill-fated proposal for a subminimum youth wage, and the Balladur government withdrew the bill after massive protest in March 1994. Beginning in the early 1990s, employers attacked the traditional seniority bonuses to secure greater workforce flexibility, and sectoral agreements were signed in toys, automobile repair, retail trade (among others) that tied bonuses to skill levels. Some employers pushed for works council wage bargaining, a version of which was made law in fall 1996. Others question openly whether French unions are still "representative" of the workforce. Most employer groups have not engaged in full frontal attacks, preferring instead for individual firms to derogate from the *convention collective*.[43]

The peak employer association, the *Confédération Nationale du Patronat Français* (CNPF), has done a poor job in aggregating interests. Disunity is evident in conflicts between those firms willing to take wages out of competition and those competing on the basis of wages. (Unions complain that some trade associations have had difficulty enforcing even minimal agreements.) The search for cost savings or "subsidy chasing" publicly disrupted employer unity in the 1990s. Despite strenuous objections from the CNPF, member firms were signing deals with the state after 1996 to exchange working time reduction for partial exoneration of payroll taxes. While French multinationals (and state planners) speculate about the high performance, integrative "factory of the future," capital mobility has encouraged labor-intensive firms to disinvest from national production. The decision to "exit" French markets contradicts the goals of employers who preach "voice." The most spectacular display of disunity, however, was the resignation of Jean Gandois from the presidency of the CNPF in October 1997. After Jospin announced legislation for a thirty-five-hour workweek, Gandois undoubtedly saw himself squeezed between the hardliners on his board who did not want to negotiate with a left government and those companies willing to work with a prime minister who preached bargaining but instead resorted to legislation.

Union Strategies

A liberalizing state and activist employers have made the environment much more treacherous for French unions. Governments have given companies more freedom to maneuver, and they have made labor markets more flexible. Employers have been active in reorganizing the workplace. In a short space of time, French unions have had to shift their cognitive frameworks and overhaul their strategic orientation.

Political Strategies

The combination of external forces and internecine warfare has pushed French unions to experiment with different political strategies. The labor movement has long been shaped by its relationship to politics. Unions have historically had close ties to political parties, and they tried to influence government policy through persuasion or, more frequently, strike activity. Egged on by regular workplace elections, interunion competition has been yet another political practice.

State intervention in industrial development and industrial relations had convinced the unions that governments held the keys to economic change. Moreover, the state had frequently been the laboratory for innovations in industrial relations. Unions looked to the state to counter the authoritarian reflex of employers. Although unions spoke out consistently on policy issues, union decentralization made strike actions or the threat thereof the primary mechanism to influence policy. Politicians and civil servants were susceptible to the extent that they shared a mistrust of employers, believing them to be risk-averse and unwilling to share power outside the family. The state pressured firms to be more accommodating in industrial relations.

The 1970s had been expectant political years for French unions. Labor market unity between the CGT and CFDT dating from 1966 was complemented by political alliance between the communists and socialists in 1972. The expectations of left victory fed hopes that a new left government would intervene more actively on behalf of labor. The split between the PCF and PS before the legislative defeat in 1978, however, encouraged fissiparous tendencies within both confederations briefly to downplay party allegiances and experiment with labor market strategies. Each developed "propositions" to save employment by restoring competitiveness in beleaguered companies – a strategy more focused on the economics of the firm than on the benevolence of the state. This "proposition-force" unionism contrasted with the class-based "oppositionalism" that had earlier characterized the CGT and, to a lesser extent, the CFDT. While oppositionalism entailed the development of extreme positions designed as much for public consumption as for negotiating with management, propositionalism sought to reorient industrial development and to extend the boundaries of collective bargaining from wages to investment and employment.[44] Within a year, however, both confederations backed off and moved in different and more conflictual directions. In the CGT, those wedded to confrontational strategies or close alliance with the PCF succeeded in marginalizing reformers. In the CFDT, partisans of propositions quietly lapsed into a rhetoric of bargaining over wages and a disdain for political projects. Meanwhile, FO asserted its independence from political parties, maintained its faith in business unionism, and disdained infringement on managerial responsibility. This upheaval in union thinking set in motion a newly bitter rivalry that has since divided the labor movement.

The years between 1978 and 1984 were devastating for the CGT and CFDT in terms of membership.[45] The initial cordiality between left government and the unions failed to translate into organizational resources. After the left won in 1981, French unions failed to coordinate an agenda, partially because the program and the policy initiatives of the first two years of government made the need for such coordination less apparent, since they dovetailed with union demands for more purchasing power and greater public control of the economy. Yet, the unions worked at cross purposes and divided on key policies. The CGT supported Keynesian stimulation, although it pushed for more; it applauded the increase in public-sector employment, but was cautious about the Auroux Laws. The CFDT supported the labor laws (it had been the prime intellectual force behind them) but timidly supported Keynesian macroeconomic policy and worried publicly about inflationary tendencies. FO welcomed the injection of purchasing power, but attacked aspects of the Auroux Laws and had difficulty working with a government that included communists. Until 1983, however, lack of union unity was tempered by concerns not to disrupt the work of the left government.

Political disappointment after the U-turn reawakened oppositionalism within the CGT. The PCF quit the government in 1984 and entered active opposition, stridently opposing the socialists. Discord within the left initially tightened union partisanship. The CGT took the policy shift as a betrayal and attempted to mobilize against layoffs. Its actions toward the closure of Renault-Billancourt were revealing: instead of recognizing the need for the company to retool, the CGT mounted a massive public relations campaign to martyrize the ten unionists fired and prosecuted (they received a later presidential pardon) for both vandalism and assault against other union militants during a demonstration to protest the closure.[46] This was an unwinnable fight that consumed enormous resources.

No new relationship developed after the U-turn between the governing socialists and the other unions, although the CFDT applauded the policy shift and the FO praised the exit of the communists. The socialists tried initially to rely on friendly relations with the CFDT, but found an organization beset by inner turmoil. While the leadership embraced the firm and preached the "modernization" of the economy, its membership was upset by the new market situation. And FO was no longer waiting in the wings to act as a responsible bargaining partner. The decline in purchasing power and mounting unemployment encouraged the confederation to pursue a more militant posture.

The continued decline of the Communist Party finally convinced the CGT to overhaul its strategy. Beginning in 1992, it withheld its political endorsement in national elections, although this was nuanced by leaders stating their own opinions. The CGT has been stymied by the reluctance of most of its leaders to relinquish overlapping leadership roles. Only in 1997 did Secretary General Louis Viannet step down from the Political Bureau of the PCF. Moreover, it is ideologically difficult to separate union from party: CGT members have been more loyal to the PCF than have been members of either the CFDT or the FO to the PS.[47]

Partisanship has been less divisive for the CFDT and FO. The latter has long used its formal neutrality as a weapon against the CGT. The liberalizing policies of the PS in power helped the CFDT move toward neutrality, and it declared its impartiality for the 1986 legislative elections and afterwards. Two years later it even dropped references to socialism from its program. With the left linkage dropped, the CFDT became the key negotiating partner of the center-right Balladur and Juppé governments, a role which it tried to sustain with the Jospin government after mid-1997. Its leadership risked vituperative internal criticism for supporting the social security reforms in 1995 but it continued along this line nonetheless.

The new political climate also forced the big three unions to become more modest in attempts to influence public policy. By the mid-1980s, the CFDT was attempting to influence the labor market instruments used to ease workers out of heavy industry. Part of this innovation came during collective bargaining sessions, but a large portion came through direct negotiations with the Ministry of Labor. The CGT and FO were much more ambivalent about participation in labor market programs, as they feared assuming managerial responsibility. In contrast, all three confederations pressed governments to adhere to a French version of *service public* – universal access to public services. This message had the advantage of appealing to the public-sector workforce and the wider public. Individual unions varied in their emphases. FO warned against the labor market dangers of deregulation to both employee and consumer. The CFDT pressed the right governments to use the guarantee of universal access as a lever to serve the public interest. The CGT sought to lower costs and to improve the delivery of services to customers.[48] It departed from its counterparts, however, in its emphasis on central government services, government-owned utilities, and nationalized companies, bordering on, but backing away from, wholesale condemnation of change in the public sector. The significance given to the public sector has helped unions build support for memberships which are overwhelmingly from the public sector. To the extent that job actions by public-service employees have not been resented by the wider public, the unions have succeeded in using this issue as a wedge to confront a liberalizing state.

By the 1990s, welfare state policy had became a litmus test for interunion politics. Participation in the administration of welfare benefits had long been a union principle: co-managing with employers the social security administration had been a way for the unions to maintain visibility and mildly influence redistributive policies. The Juppé plan in fall 1995 revealed the cleavages separating the unions, however. The CGT and FO resisted bitterly, claiming that the center-right threatened benefits, while the CFDT, CFTC, and CGC were willing to trade a diminished role in decisionmaking for universal funding and coverage. FO paid for its opposition to the reforms: in 1996 it was ousted from the presidency of the important national health care fund – that it had held for thirty years – to the benefit of the CFDT. In jockeying for the leadership of regional funds, CFDT representatives sided with employer representatives rather than FO.

The collapse of union organization has made protection by the state even more important. Less tangible than employment or wages, the legal framework is necessary for survival. The legacy of the interventionist state is the Labor Code that protects employees, forces employers to recognize unions, promotes collective bargaining, and maintains representative institutions (for instance, works councils) that can compensate for union organizational deficiencies. The unions have fought to prevent a weakening of labor law. They have pressured governments to limit the amount of workplace flexibility. Prime Minister Chirac ended the administrative authorization of layoffs in 1986, for example, but the unions succeeded in strengthening informational and consultation requirements. They lost some attempt to restrict workplace representation, but they succeeded in convincing the center-right in 1996 to allow unions to nominate representatives *from the outside* in small firms for the purpose of negotiating voluntary worktime reductions. Because the state frequently codifies or extends collective bargaining agreements, bargaining strategies can become legal strategies.

In their alliances with other social movements, the unions continued along their separate paths. The CGT has long worked with organizations, such as the peace movement, associated with the PCF, but those alliances had more to do with party than union concerns. For the last twenty years, the CFDT has forged national and local alliances with new social movements involving gender and environmentalism. In general, the unions realize that they no longer have the clout to alter political agendas alone, and they now back away from heavy-handed attempts to direct social mobilization. Cooperation with social movements has succeeded best when tied to specific issues. All three confederations worked with student groups to mobilize against a subminimum wage that resulted in its subsequent withdrawal in 1994. In the mobilization of the unemployed for higher benefits in winter 1997-98, however, the unions diverged in their support: the CGT quietly backed the various groups while the CFDT and FO opposed them.[49]

Weak labor markets and union division have made industrial conflict a less viable political tool. The capacity to mobilize still exists, especially in the public sector, but the unions cannot necessarily initiate such actions, nor can they use them strategically to influence public policy. The problem can be summarized as "strike for what, strike against whom?" The increasingly crusading spirit of governments in favor of market-conforming or market-opening reforms makes them less likely to intervene in private-sector disputes. In the public sector, most strike "victories" have been fleeting. While industrial action stalled reorganization at Air France in 1993-94, for instance, the eventual plans were implemented with equal ferocity *and* the legitimacy conferred by a company-wide referendum. Likewise, strike activity in fall 1995 forced the government to abandon temporarily its plans to harmonize public-sector pensions, but it failed to alter the additional tax to achieve solvency or the transfer of control to the state.

The confederations vary in their willingness to spearhead such actions. When CFDT Secretary General Edmond Maire declared the strike an archaic union tool in 1985, he sent a clear signal to local unions that the confederation valued bargaining over striking without reservation. Likewise, the call to work during the civil servant strike in 1989 was an attempt by the CFDT leadership to demonstrate its responsibility to the government. In contrast, the CGT still relishes conflict, and FO has become increasingly more willing to act combatively. This was brought home clearly in the 1995 mobilization when the CGT and FO were in the forefront of the militancy and the CFDT leadership called for an end to the strikes.

Political strategies have gradually included a European dimension – varying by confederation – although a deep-seated national ambivalence about European integration has helped delay the shift of organizational focus (and resources), and it remains unclear exactly what Europe can offer French unions that they do not already have. Protection of the

Labor Code may be more effective in helping individual employees than pressuring the European Commission to forward a particular directive.

The CFDT has taken the lead on Europe. Its Europeanism has rested on the belief that an expansion of bargaining was necessary to keep up with increased capital mobility and the argument that labor rights could be delivered on the European level. Its enthusiasm was fortified by one-time member and then Commission president Delors. The deputy secretary general of the European Trade Union Confederation (ETUC) came from the CFDT. Its union for engineers and supervisory personnel has the presidency of the Council of European Professional and Managerial Staff (FIET). A former researcher for the confederation was central in drafting the Social Charter.

In contrast, the CGT remained suspicious of European integration, displaying little faith that Euro-cooperation would provide the basis for spearheading change in European institutions or bargaining. That position began to change slowly in the 1990s as the confederation increasingly saw the utility of transnational cooperation for information and mobilization.[50] It belonged to some European sectoral committees (printers and entertainers) and had applied to join others. Its policy positions have dovetailed with other European unions (IG Metall and the UGT), and it cooperates with cross-border activity in European multinationals.

FO is the most perplexing to outside observers. With its origins in the Cold War divisions, it has long had a pro-Europe bias. Yet, the confederal leadership wanted little to do with the European initiatives on European works councils, preferring to leave management to management. (This was not true of federations, such as the metalworkers, which opposed the positions of Secretary General Marc Blondel.) As a way of reconciling diverse tendencies within the confederation – Blondel rules uneasily over a strange combination of Trotskyists, Gaullists, and old-line supporters of "Bergeronism" (the anti-Communist former secretary general) – FO remains fixed upon a bread-and-butter wages and hours unionism which, for treaty reasons, cannot exist at the European level. Thus, it is more and more a reluctant member of the ETUC.

These different perceptions on the utility of Europe for French labor manifested themselves in the ratification of the Maastricht Treaty in September 1992. The CFDT adopted an unambiguously positive position, arguing that competitiveness and employment would increase with a common currency and that the social clause in the treaty would strengthen European collective bargaining. The opposition of the CGT was based almost exclusively on the deflationary character of the convergence conditions. While the argument overlapped that of the PCF, nearly half the electorate also agreed; and the confederation consistently emphasized the concrete economic effects and not vague notions of national sovereignty. Because of the referendum's divisiveness, FO refrained from endorsing either position.

High unemployment has made any political vision of Europe difficult for the unions. The European project is most frequently associated with market liberalization, and unionists have fears of social dumping and capital mobility that were only aggravated by the Hoover affair in 1993.[51] Even the CFDT's enthusiasm for a European political strategy began to crumble in the 1990s in the face of opposition from some federations and its own realization that it had political costs. The absence of the CGT in ETUC also made mobilization over European issues more difficult. The CGT had been excluded because of vetoes from FO and CFDT who long claimed that membership in the World Federation of Trade Unions (WFTU) was incompatible with the free collective bargaining held up by the ETUC. Under the leadership of Secretary General André Bergeron who retired in 1989, this was an article of faith for FO. The political feud after 1979 explained the CFDT's opposition, for previously it had favored CGT membership. With the breakdown of communist regimes, however, the WFTU disintegrated, and the CGT distanced itself progressively until it quit in December 1995. Only in 1999 did the CGT join the ETUC: the CFDT concluded that European economic change necessitated a more inclusive organization and that the CGT had made sufficient internal modifications. French competitive unionism thus acquired European dimensions.

French unions continued to be highly politicized after the profound changes in their political context. Partisanship has diminished but not disappeared. Cold War cleavages have hardened into organizational ones, and two generations of union militants have known only competitive unionism. Dependence on the state remains high, although it is less for new gains than for protection of older ones. Unfortunately, the French state promises to be increasingly less accommodating. While political strategy before 1980 had coherence – unions tying their future to a state to deliver goods and to parties that shared ideals – its current political practice seems incoherent at best and undoubtedly dysfunctional to the long-term interests of the unions.

Organizational Strategies

In the context of deunionization, French unions have had to make choices over the allocation of shrinking resources. Conflict over organizational approaches was obscured first by political fights. Only later did modest change take place in organizational practices.

The defeat of propositionalism in the CGT delayed organizational innovation. At issue was a worldview – how to conceptualize changes within the business community, at the workplace, within political parties *and* how to organize around such a conceptualization. The CGT metalworkers federation was a tragic victim. After the late 1970s, it lost 80 percent of its members, became more white collar and more female, and shifted its base toward electronics. Attempts to steer the federation away from demoralizing losing battles and toward more flexible bargaining strategies led to forced resignations. In organizational terms, however, inertia was the norm within the CGT. The confederation had difficulty translating ideological orthodoxy into organizational change. Dues collection was controlled by the federations, not the confederation, and local unions mostly enjoyed wide autonomy. Attempts to alter this financial independence to strengthen the central offices were defeated in the 1982 and 1992 congresses, although the federations agreed to reallocate funds to aid individual unions or federations which had become impoverished through membership losses.

Even before the 1980s, the CFDT had experimented with ways to circumvent the decentralization bred into French unions. The tradition of Catholic unionism put less emphasis on balancing interests and more on developing coherent organization.[52] In contrast to the CGT or FO, the founding statutes of the CFDT from 1964 gave the confederation first crack at revenue from member dues. Organizational reforms in 1970 made leadership circles less responsive to the federation and UD by giving the Executive Commission more autonomy. They also created a new cross-industrial layer between the UD and the confederation, the regional union (UR), which was intended to transcend narrowly based local action and to stimulate a "societal unionism" capable of addressing issues outside the workplace. However, the confederation never established a clear division of labor between the UD and the UR, and the latter became transmission belts from the leadership.[53] Attempts to dissolve the UDs were rebuffed by the delegates at the 1992 congress. Centralization remained incomplete.

These organizational debates passed by FO. Largely because of its internal mosaic of forces, FO could not consolidate control in the confederation. Anti-communism was a glue that held them together, but it could not be used in a centralizing fashion. The fall of the Berlin Wall made that anti-communism much less effective. Instead, the leadership was in constant negotiation with its federations and locals who remained jealous of their independence. While former Secretary General Bergeron was enormously popular and stayed in power for twenty-six years, he never dominated his federations and departmental unions. This was most evident in December 1984 when the team around Bergeron, who had been overwhelmingly reelected secretary general the previous month, agreed to sign a multi-industry bargaining agreement over workplace flexibility and was overruled in the National Confederal Committee. Even by the mid-1990s, the confederation did not have a national research office due to both an anti-intellectualism and fears that it would be wielded by one group against another.

Settling political scores could continue to take place while the unions denied the challenges they faced. Membership drain continued for more than a decade before its scale was even acknowledged. This was partially an organizational problem: monthly dues collection gave local militants a monopoly of information over true membership and it was difficult to centralize that information. All levels have incentives to exaggerate to gain organizational power inside the confederation and establish bragging rights outside. Yet, once the weakness was acknowledged, it became necessary to analyze the patient to find a cure. The CFDT published reliable figures only in 1988. The CGT followed suit four years later. FO had still not published believable figures by the mid-1990s.

Organizational torpor was jolted by the development of extra-union assemblies of workers, *coordinations*. These impromptu localized structures developed mainly among public- sector employees. Because they were founded in workplace identities and forwarded narrow demands, universalistic unions had difficulty making sense of them. The organization of *coordinations* placed great weight on the intrinsic worth of direct democracy and self-learning, contrasting with the tendency of unions to rely on the expertise of Parisian federations. Like the Italian COBAs, they also had a high percentage of participants gravitating from the far left.

The confederations were embarrassed at their inability to perform in analogous ways. The CGT attempted to direct movements, FO tried to ignore them, and the CFDT denounced some for the participation of Trotskyists. When locals sought to cooperate in *coordinations*, they risked the wrath of their confederations. The CFDT expelled several locals in health care and the postal service in 1988. Those nurses and aides who were expelled formed their own union, which has been strong in the Parisian area. The postal locals formed a separate union with organizations in most of France's departments. By the mid-1990s, it was the second largest union at France Télécom and the fourth largest at the Post Office. Yet, the unions learned from this experience. Since the early 1990s, central offices have been quick to lend logistical support without imposing discipline. In the Air France strike of 1994, the public sector strikes of 1995, and the truckers conflict in 1996, the confederations permitted a wide latitude at the local level. In the case of the CFDT, this pitted local unions against confederal leadership.

Simultaneous to these fissiparous tendencies were efforts to find an organizational solution to competitive unionism. In the late 1980s, the CFDT tried to create a self-defined "reformist" pole of non-CGT unions – the CFDT, FO, CFTC, and CGC. Such a large federation, thinking went, would force changes and undermine the CGT. This strategy depended on the participation of FO, however, and its leadership remained reticent about such an explicitly political maneuver. By the late 1980s, it viewed the CFDT's policies on the workplace as overly collaborative and criticized its willingness to reach agreements with employers. As a profoundly anticlerical organization, it also had difficulty cooperating with the CFDT whose roots were in social Catholicism. Finally, it is conceivable that the new leadership under Blondel was secretly hoping to reunify with the clearly weakened CGT. In any case, the FO rejected participation and by the 1990s was sparring with the CFDT even more than its traditional rival, the CGT.

Instead of grouping unions together, such maneuvering resulted in another split, this time in the FEN. The teachers union had long been debating ways to forge labor unity.[54] Yet, it was quickly embroiled in partisan fights. At its founding, the FEN promised to transcend the Cold War divisions and to tolerate diverse political perspectives with the understanding that neither the CGT nor FO would field rival federations. That truce was broken in the 1980s by FO and in the early 1990s by the CGT. The former used the argument that the FEN had acquiesced too readily to state salary constraints, while the latter argued against a newfound "reformism." Indeed, the leadership of the FEN was considering an alliance with the "social Catholics" within the larger "social democratic" federation just discussed. To gain organizational approval for such changes, it needed to marginalize its communists. Therefore, it changed its statutes to stress its new "reformism" and forced a loyalty oath from those unions dominated by the communists. An ambivalent response forced exclusion.

By the early 1990s, therefore, French unions were becoming even more fragmented. Those unions excluded from the FEN formed a new federation, the *Fédération Syndicale Unitaire* (FSU), which claimed 150,000 members by April 1993. The December 1993 workplace elections immediately transformed the FSU into the largest vote-getter among teachers. In the aftermath, the FEN forged a confederation – the *Union Nationale des Syndicats Autonomes* (UNSA) – by grouping autonomous unions representing policemen, supervisory personnel on the railroad, Parisian metro workers, artists, and agricultural workers. UNSA served as an umbrella organization that could ally with other "reformist" unions. It constituted the fourth largest confederation with 400,000 claimed members, and received national representative status in 1994.

By the early 1990s, the CGT and CFDT realized to varying degrees that centralization, intraunion political conformity, and interunion rivalry were having a disastrous impact on morale. For the CGT, this was impelled by the realization that the drain on membership was creating a unionism of elected officials; a secretary of the metalworkers federation complained in 1993 that too many local unions "live with only elected members as dues paying members."[55] It also discovered that 60 percent of all wage earners had either never known or no longer knew a CGT member.[56] For the CFDT, this was an organizational admission that its own militants chafed at central control and sought the local flexibility necessary to keep abreast of increasingly innovative employer negotiating demands.

A desire to de-emphasize the center, however, did not mean that local unions would immediately pick up the slack. Local organization needed to be constructed. Before the 1980s, union locals (either SSEs or ULs) had insufficient staffing, funding, and recognition from employers. Strengthening the local level had been on union agendas since the early 1980s, but attempts to localize organization were uneven. The CGT and the CFDT paid lip service to local action throughout the 1980s, yet it was never clear how many extra organizational resources they were willing to commit or how much they would relinquish attempts to ensure political conformity. Thus, the highly publicized desire by the CGT confederation to prioritize the local unions in the aftermath of the Forty-fourth Congress of January 1992 was followed by considerable discussion but few organizational resources. Leadership relied instead on moral suasion.

Local organization developed instead alongside SSEs. Since the early 1980s there has been a devolution of union authority and even organization to works councils. The combination of membership loss and the annual obligation to bargain propelled by the Auroux Laws transformed works councils from administrators of social activities (company canteens, holiday parties, and summer camps for employees' children) to bargaining partners. Mandated since 1945, works councils have significant budgets which they can disburse for several services. They must also be consulted in the event of redundancies or impending technological change, and the Auroux Laws enabled them to hire independent experts to examine company restructuring.

Such prerogatives confused workplace representation between unions and works councils, especially where unions were weakly implanted. By 1989, 50 percent of all firms in France lacked any union presence.[57] This confusion was all the more pronounced to the extent that firms invested in human resource management to build enterprise loyalty. For instance, works councils have signed agreements with firms even when union delegates – the only representatives legally entitled to sign contracts on behalf of the workforce – have been present. Especially in small firms, works councils have substituted for union organization. Yet, even when unions are present, an activist works council can detract from the socialization functions that unions typically perform. A study conducted by the CFDT chemical workers federation found that its union sections spent on average 60 percent of their time on works council activity, leaving little time to nurture the union.[58] The focus for many union sections is simply electioneering.

Works council bargaining put the unions in a bind. On one hand, they have long pressed for more works council rights, and the major confederal unions place their members on works councils. Once elected, council members can dispose of budgets exceeding several million francs, and it is not uncommon for them to fund union activities. On the other hand, the confusion of responsibilities has submerged the functions of the SSEs into the well-being of the firm and weakened the capacity of SSEs to forge workplace identities and ULs to aggregate local issues.

The unions have split in their perspectives. Most of the unions in the CGT and FO differentiate union from works council activity and view the latter as a tool of the former. In contrast, in the early 1980s the CFDT (and FO metalworkers) began to see works councils as institutions capable of subsuming union representation. The CFDT developed a network of associations not only to link works councils and provide expertise (both of which are provided by similar networks in the CGT and FO) but to encourage collective bargaining agreements.

One way to bind centrifugal localism via works councils has been to control and disseminate information. The development of specialized knowledge became a practical necessity given the emphasis on competitiveness, the reality of job loss, and the explosion of firm-level negotiation. Union decentralization has led to compartmentalized knowledge, and information about structures and strategies is not always widely diffused. Experts hired by works councils were frequently economists and consultants either within or close to the confederation. Although the numbers of permanent officials in UDs, federations, or confederations have remained stable or slightly declined, they receive a higher level of training than did their counterparts a generation ago. Likewise, the unions have much more data now at their disposal. Both the CGT and CFDT have set up confederal structures to aggregate bargaining data from local unions.[59]

The professionalization of union staffs has been a double-edged sword. While necessary to balance the centrifugal forces of decentralization, stay abreast of activist employers, and monitor public policy, it also risked separating union officials from membership. In the absence of members, union officials were being asked to perform more responsibilities. In the process of becoming experts in workplace issues they lose touch with members and potential members.[60]

Between center and local have been the federations. At the sectoral level, French unions have not needed to engage in a massive merger movement to coordinate activities, although some aggregation has taken place. The development of industrial unionism in the early twentieth century had already reduced the number of federations within each confederation. By 1981 each confederation had between twenty and thirty-six federations and UDs in each of the ninety-six departments. Still, in the face of membership loss federations have had to adapt their organizational structures to a changing workforce *and* the construction of a critical organizational mass. An illustration of the former was the creation by the CGT of three new federations in the early 1980s to cover workers in growing service sectors – social work, financial services, and scientific research. A good example of the latter was the CFDT metalworkers absorbing the troubled mining federation in 1984. Changes in federational organization have had limited effects in terms of industrial relations, although they can have political repercussions within the confederation.[61] The reconfiguration of individual federations has not dramatically affected abilities to mobilize or bargain. Given the legal notion of representative unionism, employers have to deal with the other unions anyway.

An uneasy relationship remains between the central offices and local unions, as local attempts to circumvent confederal divisions have created even greater fractionalization. The confederations seem to be increasingly relegated to political duties and service provision for the local practitioners of industrial relations. Decentralized bargaining favors greater autonomy for local unions. And the most vibrant institutions at the local level are works councils, not unions.

The unions know very well, however, that their survival continues to depend on state-supported representative institutions. Before the SSEs were created in 1968, elected works council members and plant delegates were surrogates for the union at the workplace. Although plant delegates have declined with the implantation of the SSEs, the works councils received greater powers. With the decline of union memberships, they provide financial benefits in firms where unions are present and a presence where they are absent. While they make union organizational work difficult, they also magnify the importance of the unions.

Politics have clearly constrained union organizations, and it is hard to find a change or proposal for change that is not laden with deeper political significance. Those structures can hardly be invigorated in the absence of members. The unions can position structures to respond better to employer, government, or European initiatives, yet without an infusion of new blood they risk a high level of entropy.

Recruitment and Representational Strategies

The historical indifference to membership constituted a powerful legacy for French unions to overcome. Labor law discouraged recruitment. Works councils already provided services for the company workforce. Representing all workers, plant delegates addressed specific grievances. Contracts cover all workers and not just unionized ones. These features of French industrial relations have either remained constant or become more pronounced in the last fifteen years. Thus, altering organizational cultures has been a Herculean task, especially given the persistent politicking that has alienated existing members and discouraged potential ones.

After 1980, French unions became electoral machines. Running in elections required fewer resources than recruiting members, although more members brought more votes and a different conception of the union's role. Even under the best of circumstances, an active recruitment campaign would be difficult to mount given the poverty of the unions. A member-oriented strategy therefore introduced conflict over resource allocation within unions. Given these impediments, the unions initially had to make basic choices about organizational strategies.

For the CGT, defending bastions was more reliable for electoral fortunes, and it dovetailed with oppositionalist reflexes. After the U-turn, its rhetoric focused on the destruction of jobs. It forwarded unrealistic wage claims designed to embarrass other unions or put the employer on the defensive. This strategy enjoyed some localized success: while overall electoral fortunes dwindled, they increased in steel, mining, shipbuilding, and engineering – sectors hit hardest by restructuring. The CGT also engaged in a range of spectacular actions to emphasize its militancy, portray itself as victim, and vilify the other unions for lack of support and management for insensitivity.[62] These were appeals to core workers who were threatened by the increasing flexibility of labor markets and had few options. Oppositionalism was a smaller vote-getter for it typically increased the payoffs to redundant workers, but it had long-run negative results, as redundant workers, however well compensated, became ex-union members.

The CFDT and FO were more reluctant to engage in suicidal spectaculars. Yet, an insistence on bargaining over the consequences of deindustrialization was also a weak recruitment tool. While it may have improved exit options, it provided no venue for the introduction of new blood into either organization.

The first concrete attempts to address deunionization focused on deepening the financial commitment of existing members. In the early 1980s, the CGT and the CFDT introduced a system of automatic withdrawal of union dues from member bank accounts. While this stabilized finances, it also sapped one strength of French unionism – the contact between militant and member necessitated by the collection of monthly dues. It has been adopted unevenly by local unions and remains a bone of contention. Local officials retain a strong attachment to face-to-face contact, especially given the organizational pressures toward greater expertise.

In attempts to attract new members, local unions made explicit deals with employers to lower the cost of membership. An agreement signed at the Axa insurance group in 1990 provided for employee vouchers worth several hours of pay that could be redeemed monthly by the union of choice. This "union check" was intended to replenish union coffers and thereby strengthen collective bargaining. At the Gan insurance group, management agreed to pay the union according to its votes in works council elections. Similar agreements were signed at SNECMA, Péchiney, Elf-Aquitaine, and the Casino retailers. The CFDT has been the force behind these ideas, although it has provoked dissent. The policy was censured by over 40 percent of the delegates at the 1992 confederal congress. Meanwhile, FO at the confederal level strongly opposes this strategy for the dependency on the firm it creates, but its metalworkers have been more acquiescent. The CGT has also been mildly averse to depending on employers to bolster the ranks. Still, CGT and FO union locals have signed agreements to gain leverage over implementation.

The unions have provided new services to attract members. At the local level, both the CFDT and FO have negotiated discounts with merchants for individuals holding union cards. The regional CFDT union of the Lorraine offered nonworkplace services, such as marital counseling, estate planning, and legal advice, to employees in small companies. In other cases, the unions have sought to generalize services, such as vacation planning, that can be obtained through works councils in large companies. Other services are more national in scope. The white-collar union of the CFDT has assembled a service to match students looking for work with union members, while the CGC has developed an employment placement service for those members seeking work. Service unionism has provoked bitter fights within each confederation since it evokes one of the core historical conflicts of the French labor movement – between nineteenth-century employment exchanges (*bourses de travail*) and idea-centered industrial unionism.

The CFDT has been the most innovative in thinking through ways to represent employees in small business. The confederation was the leading force in negotiations on training with artisanal producers in 1985. In Lorraine and Aveyron, it has negotiated with small firms to put in place regional delegates who could simultaneously represent employees in several firms. In the Var, it even participated in a nonprofit organization that lent funds to small businesses for local job creation. Generalizing these experiments, however, has been difficult, and their effect on total membership or workplace elections seems limited.

All unions have attempted to address new audiences – supervisory personnel, women, youth, atypical workers, and immigrants – but the task has been daunting. The unions have lacked basic information about their own organizations. As of September 1994, neither the CFDT nor the CGT knew how many young people were members.[63] Yet, they also needed effective communication tools and a discourse that addressed each group. In the tradition of idea-based unionism, such claims tend to be dismissed as narrow *(catégoriel)*, which still grates on the universalism of French unions. Thus, each target of opportunity became the focus of tensions between the generalization of demands and the specificity of individual constituencies.

This tension between universalism and particularism has been evident in the case of middle management and supervisory personnel. In part because of the changing economy, this has been a growth area for the three large confederations. Each has separate transfederational organizations allowing supervisory personnel to maintain a separate identity. Before 1980, they tended to focus on maintaining firm-level status differentials, although that was a tough sell within their respective confederations.[64] Since then, they have become increasingly sensitive to the financial squeeze on supervisory personnel as firms downsize and reorganize production. Both the CFDT's *Union Confédérale des Cadres* and the CGT's *Union Générale des Ingénieurs, Cadres, et Techniciens* have mobilized around the degradation of work. In the late 1980s FO's *Union des Cadres et Ingénieurs* sought more continuous training. The CFDT and FO have benefited from the mistakes of the CGC whose historic promanagement strategies found a shrinking audience.

Union efforts at recruiting women have been difficult. Confederations remain overwhelmingly male, although individual federations – health, commerce, and postal workers – have majorities of women. One study found that union density among men is twice that of women.[65] In its 1994 self-study, the CGT found that only 25 percent of its members were women.[66] This is both an economic and an organizational issue. As elsewhere in Europe, French women have worked in low-wage and part-time employment, difficult areas to organize. Yet, the organizations have a number of choices within their control. They could encourage female leadership, and they could address gender-specific issues – equal pay, childcare, parental leave, working time, and sexual harassment. Not surprisingly, the unions have relied on state intervention for many gender issues. The reform push of the early Mitterrand presidency, spearheaded by the Ministry of the Rights of Women, encouraged political solutions to labor market issues. The CFDT, in particular, worked with ministries in forging laws on professional equality (1983) and sexual harassment (1992) for which the confederation received little credit.

The confederations diverged on subsuming gender into broader programs. The CFDT has been much more willing to address gender issues in isolation from other concerns, while the CGT and FO, by emphasizing the overwhelming effects of labor market instability, tend to treat them within the context of larger questions. This was evident in the manner in which the CFDT viewed working time flexibility. It championed the right of women to perform industrial work at night, and it recommended greater flexibility for Sunday work to provide more time to women workers. In contrast, FO suggested that neither men nor women should work abnormal hours. The issue of parental leave also drew out differences among the unions. The CFDT publicized an agreement it signed in October 1993 with the prepared meats manufacturer Fleury-Michon that used works council funds to cofinance paid parental leaves. The FO vehemently contested the legality of using such funds.[67] Because the leave-taking parents were to be replaced by temporary workers, the CGT argued that the agreement perpetuated unstable employment. The impact of issue isolation or broader linkage on recruitment remains uncertain.

The CFDT has been the most aggressive in thinking about the representation of women within its organization. The 1982 congress mandated that 25 percent of leadership positions be held by women. It used the elevation of Nicole Notat to secretary general in 1992 as a concrete indicator of possibilities in the confederation. Yet, the CFDT has not succeeded in leveraging quotas for the top confederal positions to increase participation at lower levels. The percentage of women delegates at all three confederal congresses stabilized at roughly 20 percent.

Perhaps the most recruitment enthusiasm, at least at the CGT and CFDT, has been directed at young people. Deunionization has been most evident among employees under twenty-five years. When they are employed (and the unemployment rate among the young has exceeded 25 percent), they tend to be in atypical jobs, the most difficult to organize. All three confederations realized to varying degrees that organizations held less appeal for this age cohort. The same slogan used by the CGT and CFDT ("enough blah-blah") suggests that previous youth programs were ineffective. The CFDT has been the most enthusiastic in devoting resources in this domain, partially motivated by the fact that, of the three confederations, it was the weakest within this category. In the aftermath of the 1992 congress, it assembled a group, "*Turbulences*," to examine methods of redressing the situation. That group, in turn, mounted a slick magazine of the same name in 1993 that sought to address lifestyle concerns as well as labor market issues but which downplayed the union affiliation. It also organized an assembly of 2000 young people in October 1994 which resembled more a festival than a union meeting. It has organized a network of twenty local *Turbulences* through the ULs. The CGT and FO have been less ambitious. The CGT has tried to cultivate a special image among the young. It started a youth magazine *(Espoir)* in 1990, which is much more union centered than its CFDT counterpart. The confederation devoted more funds to youth organizing. It has encouraged local unions to work with student and antiracist groups. Finally, it too has organized national-level meetings for young militants.

The most important representational work in the direction of young people has relied on the application of labor law. Some unions have sought to establish a union presence at work sites – especially those hiring temporary or seasonal employees – employing a large number of young people. Both the CGT and CFDT have gained recognition at MacDonald's. The CGT has organized seasonal workers in the Alps, while FO has publicized its local judicial services to encourage seasonal workers to learn their rights.[68] The unions have attempted to organize the temporary work sector with only meager success. The CGT has four union sections in temporary agencies – out of over 1000 locales.[69] Finally, all three confederations have both pressed for state regulation and negotiated company and sectoral protections for temporary workers. While these attempts to establish a presence in the world of unstable work receive considerable publicity, they pale in comparison to the increases in flexible work contracts.

Immigrants have always presented a contradictory challenge for the unions. They garner suspicion from native members, who nonetheless benefit from their organization due to their low-wage threat. The CGT, in particular, has a long tradition as an integration mechanism for waves of immigrants. In the 1970s, the CFDT championed immigrant rights as part of its mobilization of semiskilled workers. Still, since the 1980s, speaking to the nonnative community has been more difficult in the context of permanent unemployment and the apparent permanency of these workers once considered temporary.

The unions have pressed for equal rights within a labor market perspective. They have developed political strategies to press for nondiscrimination and equality of rights in and out of the workplace. The CGT and the CFDT have been in advance of public opinion in the recognition of cultural pluralism. For instance, the CGT pressed for workplace mosques at Renault already in the 1970s. The organizations have also been vocal against restrictions on immigration imposed by right governments in 1986 and 1993.[70] The CFDT has been more willing to recommend that local organizations work with antiracist social movements, although it has pulled away from cooperation with second-generation *beur* associations. The CGT has historically framed immigration issues within the context of the international trade union movement and the possibility of regulating international migratory flows. Workplace strategies have tended to subsume specific claims of the nonnative workforce into more global labor market demands.[71] Thus, job-related issues of privacy, religion, or language have been subordinated to a broader discourse on precarious employment. Still, in the cases of celebrated conflicts – the Peugeot plant at Sochaux in 1989, the auto-part manufacturer Chausson in 1990, and the shipbuilder La Ciotat in 1991 – the demands of a large nonnative community have been pressed with particular vigor.

Recruitment poses enormous challenges to French unions, not the least because the organizations have so few resources now to expend. Within this context, two experiments bore potential interest. First, the CGT announced in 1994 that it was targeting 200 work sites to show the extent to which local unions could be strengthened. Second, borrowing from American unions, the CFDT created the category of "organizer" and assigned 300 militants to increase memberships. The attempts show a commitment to forge of "unionism of members" (CFDT's slogan). They also suggest a top-down approach to recruitment, however, indicating that the center will continue to play a significant role. Moreover, even when the confederation is clear in its commitment, individual federations or UDs have been very uneven in their application of recruitment strategies. Local leaders have to balance the competing demands for their time, especially when a high percentage hold elected positions.

It is too early to pass judgment on these efforts, but the results do not seem overwhelming. While the CFDT has witnessed small annual membership increases since 1990, the CGT was losing members through 1994 and only stabilized its numbers in 1995. Numbers in FO are not known, but there seems to be no dramatic surge. The effects of membership decline and employment destabilization have forced the confederations to rethink what they do, how they do it, and the tradeoffs involved. However, the legal framework has been an impediment, and the decentralization of French unions guarantees that efforts will be uneven.

Bargaining Strategies

Nowhere have changes in union strategy been more evident than in bargaining. After the mid-1980s, local agreements skyrocketed. The impetus, however, came as much from the state and employers as from the unions. Unions sought to develop innovative bargaining positions, but this has been an uphill battle given the demand for greater workplace flexibility. The decline of the CGT has facilitated a new "bargaining culture" by enabling employers to exploit better the rivalry among unions. It encouraged the CFDT to pursue a much more consensus-oriented strategy in negotiations, and it permitted the development of collective bargaining within works councils, outside the purview of union organizations.

To the extent that multi-industry bargaining has taken place, the CFDT has taken the lead. Although the confederation prioritizes local bargaining, it sees this level as an opportunity both to set a framework for local negotiations and to head off state regulation. Ironically, the socialists tried to encourage peak concertation in the early 1980s only to have it fail over working time in 1981 and workplace flexibility in 1984. (Not only did the CGT and FO oppose the latter agreement, but so many federations and URs within the CFDT opposed the stance of their negotiators that the text was dropped.) In the late 1980s and early 1990s, the CFDT worked with the CNPF to develop a set of orientation agreements on the modernization of French companies.[72]

Sectoral negotiations have become increasingly more difficult. Employers sought refuge at this level before 1980 because they feared firm-level negotiations. The explosion of firm-level activity over the 1980s has made sectors less relevant. Most firms concede as little as possible at the sectoral level and want to guard maximum flexibility for themselves, especially on wages. (In low-wage sectors, the unions contend that some employers are opting out of agreements.) Rather than taking wages out of competition, sectoral bargaining now sets broad parameters for labor market competition.[73] The unions would like sectoral accords to compensate for weaknesses at the local level, but that would require a balance of forces that has not existed since the U-turn.

The diminished importance of the sector has altered the resources for individual unions. FO has traditionally found its strength in negotiating salaries at the sectoral level, and its federation officials had a lock on relations with employers – even to the point of concluding agreements at the sectoral level when it had few members locally. As the content of sectoral agreements moves increasingly away from salary issues, however, FO has become less of a bargaining leader. Between 1985 and 1994, the CFDT increased the number of agreements it signed by almost fifty percent, investing considerable intellectual energy in negotiating these accords. The CGT's reluctance to sign agreements can be partially explained by its disproportionate strength in large companies where sectoral accords are less important.[74]

Local strike actions no longer consistently initiate bargaining. Unions and employers are either legally required to meet (in the case of annual wage bargaining) or one side wants new contract language. This regularization of bargaining has eliminated a critical tool for organized labor. Because it glorified conflict for its own sake, however, oppositionalism had little to contribute to specific bargaining strategies in the context of sustained unemployment. For instance, the CGT at Renault mobilized under the slogan that "layoffs cannot be negotiated." Such a blanket statement, while electorally useful, created a situation in which the union could only lose in the face of a determined employer.[75]

The most durable defensive strategy has relied on French labor law. Unions have used bargaining requirements to open negotiations with recalcitrant employers. Likewise, they have sought to take advantage of legal difficulties in changing the terms of contracts. As employers became more active in reorganizing the workplace, the defense of previous agreements became a litmus test of union strategy. Among the confederations, only the CFDT argued for rethinking previous agreements in the face of economic change, although it is important to note that large variation has existed within each organization. The elaborate system for hiring and firing has provided important protection. For example, at IBM's French subsidiary, the five unions contested an agreement signed by an autonomous union that not only indexed a part of salaries on annual results but provided for immediate layoffs for those who refused to comply. They received a court injunction on the basis of unfair dismissal, and management was forced to negotiate dismissal procedures.[76] Likewise, at the crane manufacturer Potain, unions used court injunctions to force management to fulfill the terms of earlier negotiations and to cancel layoffs.[77] Unions can also use labor law as a wedge both to organize workers and force employers to bargain. The CFDT fought eight different civil proceedings in Lyons to force MacDonald's to treat its franchises as a single employment unit and therefore organize a works council and provide services to the unions.[78]

The unions (especially, but not exclusively, the CFDT) have broken new ground by engaging in "give-and-take" *(donnant-donnant)* bargaining. Here the emphasis is not simply negotiating tradeoffs but trading away past gains for future ones. The historic dominance of oppositionalism meshed well with a legal framework that demanded local agreements be consistent with those at higher levels. Even FO, whose strategy before the 1980s was based on permanent bargaining, relied on past practices and rarely acquiesced to explicit tradeoffs because of the legal difficulties in obtaining derogations and the negotiating ethos within the confederation. Militancy could hardly be used as a lever after 1980, however, and contemporary plant-level agreements frequently trade clauses at the sectoral level for local gains.

The explosion of firm-level bargaining since 1980 corresponds to changes in the issues over which labor and management negotiate. A permanent dialogue now exists on working time with countless variations on teamwork, flextime, part-time work, early retirement, annualized hours, and so forth. The movement away from salary negotiations and the willingness to tackle working time issues steer management and labor into subsidiary issues that include skilling levels, career mobility, and work organization. Moreover, an increasing number of agreements have social peace clauses tying the signatories to an arbitration process in the event of disagreement. Some agreements also specify time periods of two or three years. Because they tend to bundle both salary and work items, such contracts fall ambiguously between the unlimited terms of *conventions collectives* and the annual obligation to bargain. They are frequently accompanied by company-wide referenda to add legitimacy.

The emphasis on working time reduction for purposes of employment is new to the 1990s. Throughout the 1980s, the French state had taken the initiative to alter working time. The Socialist government decreed in 1982 that the legal workweek would be reduced from forty to thirty-nine hours. In 1986 it instituted more flexible working hours by increasing variations on the legal workweek. The Balladur government permitted employers to annualize working hours, thereby reducing the amount of overtime paid on a monthly basis and presumably enabling employers to hire more employees. The so-called Robien Law enacted by the Juppé government offered incentives to employers to negotiate (voluntarily) working time reductions to thirty-two hours a week. The Jospin government's law mandating the thirty-five-hour workweek subsidizes firms that negotiate working time reduction in advance of the year 2000 for large companies and the year 2002 for smaller ones.

The unions have had difficulty in articulating coherent positions, however. The stickler has usually been salary. Both the CGT and FO have opposed "work sharing" – working time reduction with loss of salary. At the confederal level, the CGT argues that such tradeoffs encourage a further labor market instability, that they discourage genuine job creation, and that they give incentives to employers to compete on the basis of wages.[79] FO has consistently opposed working time reductions if they result in loss of salary for the employed. FO's argument is twofold: first, lowering wages is unhealthy for the economy since employment levels will rise only with more purchasing power; and second, employers cannot be trusted to reinvest savings in new employees.[80] In contrast, the central offices of the CFDT have consistently argued for much greater solidarity with the unemployed and have been willing to trade salary for jobs, although the union refuses (for political reasons) to endorse work sharing.[81]

The disjuncture between Paris and the provinces has been large. In the early 1980s the confederations could attach symbolic importance to working time reduction while local unions bargained on salaries. A decade later, however, public pressures and employer activism have forced union sections into firm-level experiments. Most of these agreements have combined working time reduction with salary flexibility effectively entailing salary reductions. Sections from all three representative unions have signed such agreements.[82]

Bargaining over the introduction of new technologies is frequently placed under the rubric of working time negotiations, but it is analytically distinct at least partially because it rarely takes place within crisis conditions and because it invariably involves clauses on salaries, classification, and employment protection. A lively debate has existed for the last two decades in French industrial relations over the appropriate union strategies and the importance of such collective bargaining. The CFDT was frequently seen as willing to experiment, and the CGT and FO were perceived as more traditional and less willing to bargain. The transition from oppositional to bargaining unionism, however, has altered practice, although managerial reluctance to part with control of information prevents this from being fertile ground for union gains.[83]

In local bargaining, employers often negotiate with works councils (and occasionally with plant delegates) instead of the unions. Where a union delegate is present, the employer must by law negotiate with the union. Yet, because of the increased prerogatives given to works councilors and the regular contact, the employer has an incentive to negotiate with them and not the union. Moreover, works councilors tend to be more conciliatory than union actors. François Lagandré found that the majority of "illegal" agreements have to do with managing working time.[84] Unions only sometimes have the wherewithal to contest them. This is not to argue that all contractual irregularities produce concessionary negotiations. Works councils can reconcile different perspectives within the workforce. One study found instances of works councils creating jobs, working with local job placement, and creating training opportunities for the long-term unemployed.[85] Because of the personnel overlap, SSEs can work well with works councils.

The line between "give-and-take" and concession bargaining, however, could be difficult to discern. Local unions without the means to challenge employers (or with a sympathy for the employer's position) have signed agreements that derogate from the sectoral *convention collective* without guaranteeing much to the workforce. Locals from all the confederations have bargained in this manner, although it has been primarily the CFDT that has provided an intellectual justification. In the early 1990s, employers sought not only salary decreases (frequently in conjunction with working time reductions) but derogations from sectoral agreements. In exchange they promised not to reduce the workforce or to slow the reductions.[86] In the crisis dichotomy of signature or bankruptcy, most union sections tend to sign.

Until the 1980s, such agreements could be dismissed as the work of a "company union" or an aberrant local. Employment bargaining in the last fifteen years, however, has taken on a different hue. Autonomous unions still sign weak agreements, but the pressures on locals of representative unions have increased. In the face of high unemployment, the decrease in union membership, the difficulty in mobilization, and the context of competitive unions, it has been difficult to avoid at least one local pursuing this strategy.[87]

European bargaining had some potential for French unions if only to impose order on individual sectors. The unions, however, have extended their disagreements to a transnational scale. And the unwillingness of employers to bargain at that level has forced unions exclusively into negotiations over European works councils. Here the key issues seem to be the type of concertation – French or German – and the division of seats among the French unions. Even if the CGT is not a member of a European federation and is not part of negotiations, it must by French law be included in any representation scheme, although such representation is not always according to its strength in elections. The unions agree that European works councils can provide important information for future bargaining, but the consensus ends there. The CGT and FO oppose attempts to allow these EWCs to bargain over wages, while the CFDT is willing to explore this issue. In the final analysis, EWCs interest French unions less than their counterparts elsewhere in Europe because of the existing level of legal protection.

The volume of firm-level derogations, the local focus of bargaining over a wide array of issues, the professionalism of union staffs, the negotiating role of works councils, and the weakening of class solidarities have altered union activity. As a result, labor regulation depends much more on the integrative capacity of the firm and its own market position than on the welfare of the broader labor force. The conception of management and managed has become blurred, altering how unions conceive of their activity, their organization, and even their identity.

Conclusion

Public policy, economic change, and their own self-destructive impulses have hollowed out French unions over the last generation. Depopulated and resource-poor organization are being asked to negotiate on a regular basis. The unions were initially unprepared for the explosion of local bargaining, as they lacked the expertise and even the staff to fulfill employer expectations. Required to negotiate, employers have sought to bargain over firm-level flexibility. Where unions were not present, employers negotiated with works councils. Union strategic action has aimed to confront these new challenges. In the absence of new resources, however, local unions are much more influenced by their own histories, the individual employer, and the nature of the competitive challenge facing the company. Overall, unions are more willing to trade previous contractual guarantees for employment protection.

The identity of the French labor movement has been altered. The new need to focus on member-centered organization for the purpose of local bargaining threatens the charismatic idea-based unionism that sought broader social change. Local experimentation guarantees that transitions to new identities will be fragmented and difficult to discern. It is even questionable in the late 1990s the extent to which the term movement can still be used in France. There is little sense of common purpose and no collective political project within confederations, let alone among them.

The losses suffered in the previous decade weigh heavily upon French labor. The unions may have gained independence from left parties, but there is also no voice within the political spectrum for the types of redistributive public policies that would benefit members. Competitive unionism is still a reality: as political differences hardened into organizational identities, the cleavages among rival organizations have become even more rigid *despite* instances of sporadic cooperation and reminders from opinion polls that members and potential members are disgusted with such polemics. Glimpses of organizational creativity have not returned unions to the position they held fifteen years ago. The dramatic decline in membership has stopped, but there is no assurance that the meager increases of the last few years will continue. Bargaining has increased, but unions still face the unenviable task of negotiating away past gains. For every local success story, there appear to be several failures that are never told. Union pragmatism must be placed within the context of even more innovative employers and a liberalizing state. Far from removing wages from competition, French bargaining is pitting the workforces of individual companies against each other. Employer temptation to bargain with works councils threatens the very concept of union representativeness.

The events of November-December 1995 confirmed this trajectory. For several weeks, workers staged the largest mobilization since May 1968 to challenge the liberalizing reforms of the Juppé government. Unions had learned that local strikes needed to be run locally, that militants had to loosen their partisan and confederal collars. Despite the inconveniences caused by public transport stoppages, the strikes were largely supported by the French public.

The strikes, however, exemplified the inability of unions to translate mobilization into tangible results. Within weeks labor relations returned to "normal." The government had cobbled together the reforms in social security financing and public sector pension programs as well as the reorganization of the railroads, believing that unpopular reforms could be digested. The political miscalculation was evident – the combination provoked outburst as a sympathetic public supported angry public sector workers – but the core project of revising social security remained in place. The unions continued to fight each other afterwards, and each of the big three confederations was beset with serious internal divisions. Unemployment remained high.

The strikes had shown the changing dynamics of the labor movement, however, as the private sector remained quiet. Labor relies increasingly on the state for its resources. French unionism is now limited to a shrinking public sector, confederations struggle to maintain visibility, and unions depend on public-sector subsidies for their operations. These are not the indicators of good health.

State dependence was evident in the aftermath of the Socialist legislative victory in June 1997. The keystone of Jospin's program was the reduction of unemployment through job creation and the introduction of a thirty-five-hour workweek. To make the latter idea attractive to the unions, he promised no reduction in pay. While the new government initially hoped unions and employers could negotiate the terms of overall workweek reductions, it did not shrink from imposing them on reluctant employers. While the subsequent legislation required bargaining between unions and employers over implementation – providing possibilities for pay decreases – it was clear that once again the state had used leverage unavailable to the unions. Moreover, the government may have provided unions a critical entree into small business, as it allowed the confederations to nominate employees to bargain where no union organization existed.

Nonetheless, the choices for union strategic action appear limited. The constraints that have been constructed for the last generation now seem overwhelming. A powerful business community flexes its market muscle. Internal organizational cleavages frustrate the best attempts to innovate, while external fights between union organizations sabotage them. Labor law discourages membership, but without a growth in membership organizational renewal is stymied. Without renewed organization, local bargaining is condemned. Breaking out of this vicious circle will only come with a new political settlement, which would require both union unity and a break with the state. The former is unlikely while the latter would remove the very crutch that has so far prevented disaster.

Notes

1. Like FO, the FEN had broken off from the CGT in 1948, but it succeeded in balancing communists with other left forces until the 1980s.
2. Anthony Daley, *Steel, State, and Labor: Mobilization and Adjustment in France* (Pittsburgh: University of Pittsburgh Press, 1996).
3. Dominique Labbé, *Syndicats et syndiqués en France depuis 1945* (Paris: L'Harmattan, 1996).
4. Dominique Andolfatto and Dominique Labbé, *La CGT: Organisation et audience depuis 1945* (Paris: La Découverte, 1997).
5. See Organisation for Economic Cooperation and Development, *Employment Outlook* (Paris: OECD, July 1991).
6. Huguette Bouzonnie, "Audience syndicale," *Liaisons sociales*, series D, special issue, no. 68 (18 July 1991): 16.
7. The confederations dominate voting because labor law specifies that "representative" unions control nomination procedures for the first elections. If voting does not produce a quorum, then a second election must be held in which anyone can be a candidate.
8. Public-sector employees can continue to draw salaries while working for the union, thereby lowering personnel costs for cash-strapped organizations.
9. Data from the Ministère du Travail, de l'Emploi et de la Formation Professionnelle
10. André Gauron, *Histoire économique et sociale de la Cinquième République: Le temps des modernistes*, vol. 1 (Paris: La Découverte, 1983); and *Histoire économique et sociale de la Cinquième République: Années de rêves, années de crises (1970-1981)*, vol. 2 (Paris: La Découverte/Maspero, 1988).
11. Ministry of Research and Industry, ed., *Une politique industrielle pour la France: Actes des journées de travail des 15 et 16 novembre 1982* (Paris: Documentation Française, 1983).
12. See OECD, *Economic Survey: France, 1990/1991* (Paris: OECD, 1991), 104.
13. OECD, *Economic Survey: France*, various years.
14. According to French labor law, agreements made at one level must be consistent with those made at higher ones.
15. See Chris Howell, *Regulating Labor: The State and Industrial Relations Reform in Postwar France* (Princeton: Princeton University Press, 1992), 166-185.
16. Data from the Ministère du Travail, de l'Emploi, et de la Formation Professionnelle
17. In contrast, multi-industry bargaining slowed after 1980: there were forty-five agreements in the 1970s, for instance, and only eighteen in the 1980s.
18. See OECD, *Employment Outlook*, 1994, for a comparative analysis of bargaining coverage.
19. Data from the Ministère du Travail, de l'Emploi, et de la Formation Professionnelle
20. *OECD Economic Survey: France 1996-1997*, 165.
21. Guy Groux and René Mouriaux, "The Dilemma of Unions without Members," in *The Mitterrand Era: Policy Alternatives and Political Mobilization in France*, ed. Anthony Daley (London and New York: Macmillan and NYU Press, 1996).
22. Bouzonnie, "Audience syndicale."
23. Jean-Emmanuel Ray, *Droit du travail. Droit vivant*, 5th ed. (Paris: Editions Liaisons, 1996).
24. Dominique Taddéi and Benjamin Coriat, *Made in France: L'Industrie française dans la compétition modiale* (Paris: Livre de Poche, 1993), 51-52.

25. Pierre-Alain Muet, "Contraintes et gains de la désinflation compétitive," in *Entreprise France: Made in France*, vol. 2, eds. Benjamin Coriat and Dominique Taddéi (Paris: Livre de Poche, 1993).
26. For instance, the Commission overturned a 1996 sectoral plan for the textile industry.
27. The two center-right governments differed, however, in how they employed privatization receipts. Balladur used them to lower budget deficits while Juppé used them to pay off state debt.
28. Public policy has been inconsistent in terms of foreign ownership. For instance, it blocked the sale of Thomson Multimedia to Daewoo in 1996 in response to public concern.
29. This figure includes individuals participating in youth programs, working in subsidized jobs, enrolled in training programs, or receiving unemployment compensation, as well as those employed by central and local government, nationalized enterprises, and the armed forces.
30. Anthony Daley, "Socialist Employment Policy in France: 1981-1993," *Studies in Political Economy*, 42 (fall 1993): 24.
31. Ministère du Travail, de l'Emploi et de la Formation Professionnelle, *Premières Informations* 327 (31 March 1993).
32. See *OECD Economic Surveys: France*, various years.
33. Élie Cohen, *L'État brancardier: Politiques du déclin industriel (1974-1984)* (Paris: Calmann- Lévy, 1989).
34. Taddéi and Coriat, *Made in France*, 30-31
35. Bob Hancké and David Soskice, "Coordination and Restructuring in Large French Firms: The Evolution of French Industry in the 1980s," Discussion Paper #96-303, Wissenschaftszentrum Berlin für Sozialforschung, March 1996.
36. Bob Hanké, "Industrial Reorganization in France: Changing Relationships between Large and Small Firms," Discussion Paper #96-301, Wissenschaftszentrum Berlin für Sozialforschung, January 1996.
37. Françoise Chevalier, *Circles de qualité et changement organisationnel* (Paris: Economica, 1991).
38. See the following special issues of widely read journals: "Le management participatif ne fait plus recette," *Liaisons sociales. Mensuel*, no. 79 (May 1993); 'Le management participatif: Un problème plutôt qu'une solution," *Revue française de gestion*, no. 88 (March-May 1992).
39. Michel Cézard, Françoise Dussert, and Michel Gollac, "Taylor va au marché: Organisation du travail et informatique," *Travail et emploi*, no. 54 (1992).
40. Jacques Rojot, "Profit-Sharing and Gain-Sharing in France," *International Handbook of Participation in Organizations*, vol. 3 (Oxford: Oxford University Press, 1993).
41. "Renault: Développement de l'Accord à Vivre," *Liaisons Sociales*, series LS, no. 6866 (23 June 1993).
42. Valérie Douce, "L'Individualisation des salaires en 1993," *Premières synthèses*, no. 65 (16 August 1994).
43. François Lagandré, *Nouvelles relations de travail: Pratiques contractuelles et perspectives* (Paris: L'Harmattan, 1990), 188ff.
44. Jean-Pierre Huiban, "The Industrial Counterproposal as an Element of Trade Union Strategy," in *The French Workers' Movement: Economic Crisis and Political Change*, ed. Mark Kesselman with Guy Groux (London: George Allen & Unwin, 1984).
45. Labbé, *Syndicats et syndiqués*, chapter 3; *Le Peuple*, 9 December 1993, 32-37.

46. Virginie Linhart, "Les 'dix' de Renault-Billancourt: Les enjeux d'une mobilisation d'appareil, juillet 1986-décembre 1989," *Revue française de science politique* 42, no. 3 (June 1992): 375-401.
47. Frédéric Lemaitre, "Législatives: Le vote selon la sympathie syndicale," *Liaisons sociales. Mensuel*, 15 April 1993.
48. These confederal perspectives on the public sector should not obscure the fact that the public- sector federations for all three unions have mobilized against incomes policies and projected employment cuts.
49. The CFDT argued that the protest had targeted CFDT leadership of the unemployment compensation system, while FO claimed that only the unions could speak for the unemployed. The CFDT seemed to fear political hijacking by the far left, but the position of its leadership created considerable resentment at the base. Local works councils run by the CFDT, for instance, have long been active in diverting resources to bump up benefits for the unemployed.
50. Michel Guerre, "Quelle démarche unitaire de la CGT en Europe?" *Analyses et Documents Economiques*, no. 60 (June 1994): 27-31.
51. The American multinational transferred production from France to Scotland after playing one potential site against the other.
52. Guy Groux and René Mouriaux, *La C.F.D.T.* (Paris: Economica, 1989).
53. Pierre Eric Tixier, *Mutation ou déclin du syndicalisme? Le cas de la CFDT* (Paris: PUF, 1992), 162-170.
54. René Mouriaux, *Le syndicalisme enseignant en France* (Paris: PUF, "Que sais-je?" 1996), 94-102.
55. Bernard Lamirand, "Rapport d'activité et quitus," *Le guide du militant de la métallurgie*, no. 227 (October 1993): 66.
56. *Le Peuple*, 9 December 1993, 36.
57. Bouzonnie, "Audience syndicale."
58. Dominique Labbé and Maurice Croisat, *La fin des syndicats?* (Paris: L'Harmattan, 1992), 109-110.
59. Because of competitive unionism, these data centers do not follow bargaining where their confederal unions are absent, depriving such data collection of an important comparative dimension.
60. For an earlier view, see Gérard Adam, *Le pouvoir syndical* (Paris: Dunod, 1983).
61. For instance, the 1997 merger of chemicals and energy in the CFDT may challenge confederal policies, since each federation opposes the confederation's reformism.
62. In the case of the "Billancourt 10," this strategy became an all-or-nothing attempt to back management into a corner on the restructuring of Renault and was bound to lose, thereby revealing the increasing weakness of the union.
63. Both the CGT and the CFDT undertook internal surveys in fall 1994 to garner more information about memberships.
64. The CFDT was an exception in its call for wage compression in the late 1970s.
65. Bouzonnie, "Audience syndicale," 18.
66. *Le Peuple*, 28 September 1995.
67. After the company organized a referendum on the issue, and it won with a bare majority, FO eventually acquiesced to the accord.
68. *Force Ouvrière Hebdo*, 24 June 1992.
69. *L'Hebdo de l'Actualité Sociale*, 10 December 1993.
70. See *Syndicalisme*, 1 July 1993.

71. See Chantal Rey, "Des pistes pour l'action syndicale," *Analyses et Documents Économique*, no. 44 (February 1991): 51-52.
72. Among those agreements signed were procedures to handle technological change in 1988; the flexible organization of working time, working conditions, and gender equality in 1989; temporary hires in 1990; and occupational training in 1991.
73. Dominique Meurs, ed., *Négociations salariales: Le lien branche-entreprise* (Paris: Documentation française, 1996); Dominique Dieppedalle and Hubert Puel, *Les négociations salariales de branches* (Paris: Documentation Française, 1992).
74. According to the Ministry of Labor, in 1994 the CFDT signed 73 percent while the FO signed 73 percent, the CFTC 61 percent, the CGC 59 percent, and the CGT only 30 percent of all sectoral agreements.
75. See Daniel Labbé, "Renault: Les trois âges de la négociation," *Travail*, no. 26 (autumn 1992): 86.
76. See *Le Monde*, 21 June 1994; *La Tribune Desfossés*, 18 February 1994.
77. See *Le Monde*, 20 May 1994; *La Croix*, 22 December 1993.
78. *Syndicalisme*, 15 July 1993.
79. *L'hebdo de l'actualité sociale*, 10 March 1995, 25-29.
80. *Force Ouvrière Hebdo*, 1 March 1995.
81. *Syndicalisme*, 2 March 1995; *Syndicalisme*, 16 February 1995.
82. It is difficult to predict which unions will sign which local agreements, although there are broad tendencies. When they are present in a firm, the CFDT, FO, and CFTC sign almost 90 percent of all agreements, the CGC in excess of 90 percent, and the CGT signs over 75 percent.
83. Mark Kesselman, "French Labour Confronts Technological Change: Reform That Never Was?" in *The Mitterrand Era*, ed. Daley.
84. Lagandré, *Nouvelles relations de travail*, 194.
85. Daniel Labbé, "Des comités d'entreprise au service de la solidarité," *Management et Conjuncture Sociale*, no. 444 (3 October 1994): 9-22.
86. As in the Potain example, employers do not or cannot always keep such promises, thereby reinforcing union skepticism.
87. The third Auroux Law allowed unions representing a majority of employees to veto such agreements. Yet, such a veto usually requires coordination of local unions. And the Labor Ministry can override vetoes. Finally, the organization of referenda by employers made union challenges more difficult.

Chapter 6

THE RESURGENCE OF ITALIAN UNIONS?

Richard M. Locke and Lucio Baccaro

Introduction

Over the last five years, Italian unions have experienced a remarkable resurgence. After more than a decade of declining political power, membership loss, and significant inter-and intraunion conflicts, Italy's three major union confederations, the *Confederazione Generale Italiana del Lavoro* (CGIL), the *Confederazione Italiana dei Sindacati Lavoratori* (CISL), and the *Unione Italiana dei Lavoratori* (UIL) have reemerged as key actors in Italy's political economy.[1] How did this turn-around occur and how stable is the new position of Italian labor? We argue that changes in Italy's political environment, specifically the demise of the old party system, and various strategic changes by the Italian unions themselves brought about this reversal of fortune; it promises to be much more stable than previous efforts at recasting Italian labor relations.

The Turnaround

The 1980s were difficult years for Italy's labor movement. Following the demise of the Government of National Solidarity in 1979 and the defeat

Notes for this section begin on page 259.

of the powerful metalworkers' union at the Fiat strike in 1980, Italian unions experienced an erosion of their political, economic, and organizational power. The center-left government coalitions of the 1980s were much less responsive to union demands and, over the course of the decade, promoted a series of policies (e.g., austerity, liberalization of the labor market, privatization of state-owned enterprises) which negatively impacted the unions. The collapse of tripartite bargaining in 1984 spelled the end to both union participation in income policies and union unity as the three major confederations once again split (along partisan lines) over this issue.

Increased isolation in the political sphere was mirrored by growing weakness in the labor market as a result of the radical restructuring of the Italian economy in these years. National industry bargaining stagnated, local and/or regional deals proliferated, and some powerful employers' federations began demanding the replacement of collective bargaining with more individualized negotiations between employees and employers. Finally, the unions' organizational troubles were exacerbated by declining membership (going from 49.3 percent in 1980 to 38.8 percent in 1990) and growing competition from rival workers' organizations, like the *Sindacati Autonomi* (autonomous unions) and the *COBAS*. In short, twenty years after the Hot Autumn struggles of 1969, Italian unions appeared to be once again organizationally weak and divided, having squandered much of their hard-earned political capital with few lasting gains to show for it.

Yet, since the early 1990s, Italian unions have bounced back. Although still declining, membership seems to have stabilized and unions enjoy renewed legitimacy among rank-and-file workers. Today, Italian unions once again participate in national economic policymaking (i.e., income policies) and bargain with employers both at the national level, through periodic national industry contracts, and at the company level. They have also been involved in major reform efforts (e.g., pension reform). This regained influence is the byproduct of changes in Italy's political landscape, several legislative efforts to reform Italian industrial relations, and significant reforms in the unions' own organizational structures. For example, with the recent changes in Italy's party system (i.e., the disappearance of the Christian Democratic and Socialist Parties and the reform of the Italian Communist Party, now called the Party of the Democratic Left [PDS], the political cleavages and tensions among the three major union confederations, which in the past had undermined various reform efforts, including past efforts to introduce neo-corporatist bargaining,[2] have been attenuated. In addition, several institutional reforms, including the 1990 law regulating the right to strike in essential public services, the 1992 "privatization" of public- sector employment relations, and the 1993 reconfiguration of collective bargaining arrangements, have all enhanced the position of Italy's unions vis-à-vis rival organizations and strengthened their position with regard to employers. Finally, the unions' own organizational reforms, aimed at revitalizing their plant-level structures, democratizing their internal decisionmaking processes, and thus enhancing their ability to aggregate and represent diverse interests, have also reenergized the Italian unions.

Certainly, this is not the first time Italy has tried to reform its industrial relations arrangements. Throughout the 1970s and 1980s, a variety of attempts aimed at remaking Italian labor relations in the image of other, supposedly more "mature" national systems were promoted. The reform of Italian labor law through the *Statuto dei Diritti dei Lavoratori* (a comprehensive labor code modeled on the American Wagner Act) in 1970, the attempt by *Confindustria* (Italy's major business association) and the three major labor confederations, the CGIL, CISL, UIL, to forge a Swedish-like Basic Agreement through wage indexation in 1975, and experiments with neo-corporatist "concertation" in the late 1970s and again in 1983-84 were all designed to recast Italian industrial relations in the image of other, more "mature" national systems. Yet all of these initiatives failed. Instead of promoting greater centralization, standardization, and quiescence, these reform efforts unleashed a series of intraorganizational struggles that resulted in the further decentralization and fragmentation of Italian labor relations.

Given this record of repeated failure, caution is required in assessing whether recent reform efforts constitute a fundamental break with the past or merely a continuation of Italy's long-standing process of chaotic and contradictory institutional reform. Nevertheless, we argue that because these most recent reforms have been accompanied by significant shifts in both Italy's political system and the unions' own organizations, they stand a better chance of succeeding than previous reform projects.

The remainder of this chapter develops our argument by first providing a highly stylized reconstruction of the shifts the Italian industrial relations system underwent between the late 1970s and the early 1990s. We then examine the changes in the unions' environment: changes in state policies affecting unions and the labor market, and changes in the employers' attitudes vis-à-vis both unions and collective bargaining. Then we analyze the unions' response to these changes. We focus on the most recent efforts to redesign the framework for Italian industrial relations in the early 1990s. We conclude by speculating on how the composite of reforms recently introduced in Italy is likely to evolve when faced with future changes, both economic and political.

The Changing Portrait of Italian Unions

Italian unions faced the same challenges that other labor movements described in this volume faced. But these challenges were exacerbated by Italy's overly politicized,[3] and poorly institutionalized [4] system of industrial relations. Until the Hot Autumn, the period of intense social and labor mobilization that began with the student demonstrations and mass rallies over pension reform in 1968 and lasted until the 1970 contractual round,[5] Italian unions were politically divided and weak. For example, until the late 1950s – early 1960s, Italian labor had no formal legal protection. The old fascist legal codes remained in force, and prefects, judges, and magistrates interpreted them to the disadvantage of workers. Moreover, until the establishment of the Constitutional Court at the end of the 1950s, it was impossible to revise these fascist codes since nobody was empowered to judge them unconstitutional. In this context, factories became a legal no-man's land with management free to persecute union activists, strikers subject to severe sanctions, and collective agreements not enforceable.

Employers took advantage of the unions' precarious legal standing to circumvent labor market regulation and undermine the unions' presence within their plants. In fact, unionization in industry decreased from 47 percent in 1950 to 19 percent in 1960,[6] and remained concentrated primarily in large industrial enterprises in the North. Moreover, organized business used its power to pursue a low-wage, export-oriented growth strategy. This strategy not only generated enormous profits for individual firms but also created the conditions for Italy's postwar economic "miracle."[7] For instance, during these years, *Confindustria* insisted on highly centralized collective bargaining since this worked to the advantage of employers. *Confindustria* would set wages and working conditions to the most backward and unproductive sectors of the economy (such as agriculture) and then generalize these terms to all of industry. Because the unions were themselves highly centralized and also weak in both the labor market and the political arena, they were unable to resist the low-cost, labor-sweating strategy.

All this changed with the Hot Autumn, which overturned almost all of the social, political, and economic patterns established in the postwar period. For example, increased collaboration among the three confederations led to partial reunification in 1972 in the form of the *Federazione Unitaria* CGIL-CISL-UIL. At the same time, factory councils – elected by and composed of union and nonunion workers alike – were established and gained substantial power in a number of large industrial enterprises. The unions used their new found power to demand greater wages, eliminate overtime, regulate layoffs, restrict internal mobility, and slow down the pace of work. These changes had substantial consequences for industrial output, profitability, productivity, and labor costs. Between 1970 and 1974 unit labor costs increased 64.15 percent, as opposed to annual increases of 8.5 percent between 1963 and 1969. During the first half of the 1970s, the number of hours worked per employee decreased 12 percent.[8]

Turbulent industrial relations accentuated these problems as Italy experienced more strikes and strike days during these years than just about any other industrialized democracy.[9] Finally, unions used their newly acquired power in the labor market to push for a number of social and political reforms (e.g., schools, pensions, housing, the South) as well.

Responding to this potentially explosive situation, a number of Italian political, business, and unions leaders began working on rebuilding Italian industrial relations by promoting a series of major institutional reforms in labor law and collective bargaining. By the end of the 1970s, it appeared as if Italy had truly remade itself. New or reformed institutions, such as the[10] *scala mobile*, and the *cassa integrazione Straordinaria* [11] had been introduced over the course of the decade and provided industrial workers, as well as Italy's three major union confederations (CGIL, CISL, and UIL), with a set of legal rights and social benefits. All of these institutional reforms sought to institutionalize and stabilize Italian industrial relations. Moreover, between 1977-79 CGIL, CISL, and UIL also engaged in "concertative" bargaining with the *Confindustria* (the major employers' association) and the government on various industrial and labor market policies.[12] Italy's new industrial relations system appeared to be a radical break with the previous pattern of labor management relations in Italy, characterized by union exclusion and managerial unilateralism.

All of these institutional reforms, to one degree or another, were inspired by other national systems (with the sole exception of the cassa integrazione, which is an Italian peculiarity). The Statuto was modeled after the American Wagner Act, the 1975 *scala mobile* accord after the Swedish Basic Agreement,[13] and the various experiments with social concertation after analogous arrangements in central and northern Europe. Yet all of them failed to recast Italian industrial relations along the lines of these seemingly more "mature" and "stable" foreign systems.

Instead, by the end of the 1980s, it was clear they had actually accentuated the long-standing fragmentation and decentralization of Italian industrial relations.[14]

Thus, by the end of the 1980s, Italy was still coping with its long-standing woes of poorly formalized collective bargaining arrangements, politically divided trade unions, and high levels of industrial conflict, only this time in the service sector. Economic concertation had collapsed in 1984, and with its demise, ideological divisions among the confederal unions resurfaced. No clear architecture of collective bargaining existed, so the same issues were often negotiated at more than one level. Moreover, the fortunes of the main confederal unions had declined considerably. The three confederal unions no longer seemed capable of representing entire segments of the labor force, their bargaining power in the political arena had diminished substantially, and new unions, particularly in the public sector, had emerged to contest their representational monopoly. These unions, called *Sindacati Autonomi* (autonomous unions) and *Comitati di Base* (COBAS) (grass-root committees), often succeeded in reopening already negotiated collective agreements through frequent strikes. This, in turn, contributed to Italy's high rates of inflation – higher than all major international competitors[15] – and further augmented the anarchy of Italian industrial relations.

Why did the institutional reforms of the 1970s, which were clearly modeled after the supposedly more "mature" neo-corporatist systems of central and northern Europe, not only fail to produce *Statuto dei Lavoratori*, their anticipated results, but also perhaps even contribute to the organizational fragmentation and political divisions already plaguing Italian labor relations? The answer lies, we argue, in a particular combination of unintended consequences of the reform efforts and the changes provoked by the simultaneous globalization and segmentation of the Italian economy.

The new industrial relations system of the 1970s was conceived primarily as a response to an "internal shock," the Hot Autumn strikes and their consequences. Accordingly, the various reform projects of these years were based on a compromise between labor and management. The unions offered stability at the workplace and self-restraint in industrial conflict, while employers and the state assured income security from inflation and industrial restructuring, through a cost of living escalator (i.e. the scala mobile) that provided almost 100 percent wage protection against price increases, and a state-funded unemployment insurance scheme (the cassa integrazione) which guaranteed 80 percent of workers' wages in the case of layoffs. In short, the various reform efforts were based on the assumption that Italy's political-economic problems derived mainly from the absence of a uniform and coherent "national model" of industrial relations. They thus tried to recreate in Italy the institutional preconditions for a new national model, inspired by neo-corporatism, which at the time appeared to be the most efficient regulatory system among the advanced industrial nations.

However, as the Italian economy began to change, these new institutions unraveled: the globalization of the economy decreased the relevance of national institutions, while decentralization provided employers with new strategic opportunities to challenge the unions' newly acquired rights and power, particularly at the company and plant levels. These changes led to a fundamental shift in the balance of power between labor and capital, thereby undermining the compromise on which the new industrial relations system had been erected.[16] In the early 1980s the Italian economy went through a massive wave of industrial restructuring.[17] The unions appeared unable to negotiate, let alone protect their membership against, the consequences of this restructuring. Moreover, in this new economic environment, the various institutional reforms aimed at enhancing the efficiency and predictability of the industrial relations system either collapsed or provoked unintended but nonetheless negative consequences. As a result, inflation rates remained higher than all major international competitors; unit labor costs increased; capital accumulation decreased; unemployment grew (particularly among youth and Southerners); and the public debt ballooned.[18]

Now Italy is once again attempting to construct a coherent "national system." A more activist state has recently passed a number of laws that regulate industrial conflict in the service sector and rationalize labor relations in the public sector. With the recent abolition of the scala mobile and the introduction of a formalized structure for collective bargaining, the resuscitation of tripartite, neo-corporatist collective bargaining is being attempted. At the plant level, employers and unions collaborate on issues like restructuring, the introduction of new technology, training, and work reorganization. These developments are by no means entirely consistent. For example, although the majority of trade union cadres espouse responsibility and moderation, a sizable minority within the CGIL (the *Essere Sindacato* faction) and the COBAS still espouse a rhetoric of class conflict and political intransigence; and other nonconfederal ("autonomous") unions defend the particularistic interests of small professional groups. Similarly, although most employers recognize the unions as partners in workplace management, some of them seek to exploit the changing balance of power with labor to restore managerial prerogatives and moderate union demands.

Yet, in spite of these inconsistencies, the preconditions for a new, more flexible and democratic industrial relations system may be emerging. Increased competition from rival organizations like the COBAS and other autonomous unions, and growing dissent from within, have forced the confederal unions to reexamine several of their organizational strategies and become more responsive to the needs and interests of their membership. Recent changes in workplace representation structures (i.e., the *Rappresentanze Sindacali Unitarie*) promise not only to render the factory councils more democratic but also, by permitting participation of the COBAS and the autonomous unions in elections for the new councils, to eliminate a primary source of labor conflict in Italy.

In sum, although the evidence is still fragmentary and even ambiguous, a new approach to political-economic regulation seems to be emerging in Italy – one that avoids the usual tradeoffs between centralization and standardization on the one side, and decentralization and flexibility on the other. Thus, the 1992-93 reforms that established a more centralized system of wage negotiations did not preempt the possibility for experimentation and democratic participation at the local level.

The next sections seek to document first how changes in the unions' environment contributed to undermine the economic viability of the Italian industrial relations system of the 1970s, and then how the unions developed a set of strategic responses to these challenges and relaunched themselves.

Fragmentation in a Turbulent World

In the 1980s, the simultaneous internationalization and decentralization of the economy undermined the bases of the "class compromise" on which Italy's "new" industrial relations system had been erected. While technological innovations and industrial restructuring transformed the workplace, the locus of control over some of the major macroeconomic variables – for example, exchange rates, interest rates, and money supply – moved away from national economic institutions and toward a supranational monetary regime, the European Monetary System (EMS).

The decentralization process was linked to the crisis of Fordist forms of work organization in Italy's large firms.[19] Already after the first oil shock, the introduction of new, flexible technologies considerably reduced the comparative advantage of these larger firms. Between 1971 and 1981, the shape of Italian industry changed significantly. The number of small- and medium-sized firms (up to ninety-nine employees) increased by 21 percent, while employment within these firms rose almost 29 percent.[20] These firms outperformed their larger counterparts in terms of growth of value added, investment, employment, productivity, and even growth of income per employee.[21] Absenteeism and industrial conflict were also lower in small- and medium-sized firms.[22] These trends continued well into the 1980s.[23]

After the second oil shock, Italy's large firms began to restructure as well. This new phase of industrial adjustment was characterized by the further decentralization of production, increased capital intensity, and the radical reorganization of work.[24] During these years, big companies regained the lead over smaller firms in terms of productivity, profitability, and ability to innovate, particularly by adopting flexible manufacturing systems.[25] Throughout the 1980s, the organizational structures of big companies like Fiat (autos), Olivetti (computers), Montedison (chemical products), Falck (steel), and Italtel (telecommunications) came to resemble closely those of smaller firms in industrial districts. These companies dismantled their bureaucratic and hierarchical administrative structures, transformed themselves into holdings surrounded by semi-autonomous profit and cost centers, and restructured their supplier networks, retaining internally only certain critical phases of the production process and the development of key technologies.[26]

In the early 1980s, Italy's large companies also increased their investments abroad. In the first four years of the decade, Italy' stock of foreign direct investment (FDI) nearly doubled, growing from U.S.$ 6.9 billion in 1980 to U.S.$ 13.27 billion in 1984.[27] Although the degree of internationalization of the Italian economy remained negligible vis-à-vis other European economies of comparable size – for example, in 1984 Great Britain's FDI constituted 15.5 percent of world's total, as opposed to Italy's 2.1 percent – in the early 1980s Italy became a net capital exporter.[28] Italy's FDI was particularly concentrated in three sectors: engineering, including motor vehicles, rubber, and oil. Each of the sectors was dominated by single industrial groups: Fiat, Pirelli, and AGIP, respectively. A survey of Italian multinationals found that cost reduction was not the main determinant for their FDI. Other motivations, including market penetration, hedging against protectionism, and acquisition of international experience, were more prominent. However, twenty of the seventy-five companies in the sample declared that the need to reduce costs played an important role in their decision to invest abroad.[29]

As a result of these various restructuring efforts by Italian companies, industrial employment fell,[30] and union membership declined from 49 to 39 percent throughout the 1980s. Between 1980 and 1986 employment in larger firms declined by 6.1 percent. In the same period, the number of workers supported through the state-funded redundancy fund (cassa integrazione *guadagni*) increased from 3.8 percent of the work force in 1981 to 10.1 percent in 1984.[31] Net real wages ceased to grow as they had done in the years immediately following the Hot Autumn, when they rose 24 percent between 1974-78. Instead, between 1978-85 net real wages remained constant.[32] This, coupled with a considerable rise in labor productivity, led to a substantial growth of gross profits from 26.4 percent of value added in 1977 to 35.9 percent in 1985 – a figure even higher than those experienced during the so-called "economic miracle" of the 1950s.[33]

State Policies

The Italian government tried to respond to the new challenges resulting from shifts in the economy through a variety of strategies including more rigorous and restrictive monetary and fiscal policies, privatization of state-owned enterprises, and a variety of labor market reforms.

Macroeconomic Reforms and European Monetary Union

Italy's shift in macroeconomic policy was marked by Italy's entry into the EMS in 1979. Before Italy entered into the EMS, the country had pursued a unique, "national" response to the supply shocks of the early 1970s – one considerably different from the standard stabilization policies pursued, for example, by the United Kingdom in the early 1980s.[34] Giavazzi and Spaventa[35] described this prior, unorthodox response as a "peculiar blend of supply side measures, inflation, and exchange rate depreciation." Unwilling or unable to deflate the economy *tout court*, Italy's economic authorities focused instead on first restoring firm profitability, and then, slowly reducing the country's inflation rates.

Profits were increased through the subsidization of social security contributions paid by employers (the so-called *fiscalizzazione degli oneri sociali*), which decreased from 39.3 percent to 29.7 percent of gross wages from 1976 to 1980.[36] This was partly financed by fiscal drag resulting from steeply progressive marginal tax rates – introduced in 1974 with strong union support. Fiscal drag also raised the tax burden on industrial workers by almost 9 percent between 1974 and 1980. Frequent currency devaluations were also employed to prevent Italy's growing inflation from cutting into the international competitiveness of Italian exports as well as to assure that the reduction in demand by increased taxation was offset by exports. Exports grew at an average real rate of over 9 percent between 1976-80; GDP real growth was 4.3 percent per year in 1977-80, well above most international competitors; and the share of gross profits in manufacturing increased 7.9 percent in 1977-80.[37]

This policy had costs in terms of higher inflation rates than other advanced industrialized nations, and a growing public debt.[38] Moreover, the use of fiscal drag to finance increased public expenditures was of clearly limited duration, because the unions began to demand indexation of tax brackets. Consequently, when inflation soared again in the late 1970s, Italy's government tried to curb inflationary expectations by joining the EMS. Basically, with this decision the Italian economic authorities hoped to gain credibility vis-à-vis domestic and international investors by binding Italy's monetary policy to Germany's – a country with a solid reputation for anti-inflationary monetary policies.

This shift from flexible to semifixed exchange rates implied that Italy as well had joined other industrial nations in adopting a new "macroeconomic regime" which privileged price stability over full employment. Restrictive monetary policies were accompanied by restrictive fiscal policies. To enhance the Central Bank's control over money supply, a "divorce" was celebrated in 1981 between the Bank of Italy and the Italian Treasury. This freed the Bank from its requirement to purchase unsold state bonds, which had provided the government with unlimited financing,[39] and reasserted the Central Bank's autonomy and control over money supply. However, it was for many years an "Italian-style divorce" or a divorce among "*separati in casa*," (which means that both partners pretend they are divorced but continue to live together). In other words, by the time the Bank of Italy regained its autonomy, the secondary market for treasury bonds (which it had helped create) was so well developed that bonds were practically as liquid as money and earned significant interest. As soon as the Bank stopped financing government spending with the creation of money, interest rates on treasury bonds increased in order to guarantee their sale on the market. Their high interest rates plus tax-free status (which the government granted), suddenly made treasury bonds very attractive. As a result, the government easily continued to finance its deficits and was in no way constrained to reform its spending practices.

The consequences for Italian public finances, however, were disastrous. Since the growing stock of short-term treasury bonds expired at very short intervals (between six and twelve months), the government had to frequently refinance its debt through the issuance of even more bonds. Moreover, in order to sustain the market for treasury bonds, very high interest rates had to be paid. As a result, the government dug itself into an ever-deeper hole as its basic debt, and the costs of servicing it, continued to grow. In short, the Bank of Italy's regained independence actually contributed to the creation of a huge cumulated public debt, which today continues to threaten Italy's macroeconomic stability and its place within the European Union.

Joining the club of European nations participating in the second phase of the EMU is today one of the Italian government's main political goals. To the surprise of many, this goal was achieved in May 1998. Italy succeeded in meeting four of the five qualifying criteria: an inflation rate lower than the average of the three most "virtuous" countries + 1.5 percent; long- term interest rates not exceeding the average of the three best performing nations + 2 percent; no currency devaluations for the past two years of permanence within the EMS; and finally (but by far most importantly) a ratio of public deficit to GDP not exceeding 3 percent. This last convergence criterion was the most difficult to reach given that public deficit was 10.2 percent of GDP in 1991 when the Maastricht Treaty was signed.

Italian efforts to catch the "European train" were far from linear. For quite a long time, in fact, there was debate among the country's political and economic elite over whether Italy should try to participate in the single currency and particularly, whether the country should go through the severe process of fiscal consolidation needed to meet the convergence criteria. It was, to be sure, a covert debate, mostly taking place among economists and top level politicians – the Italian public being overwhelmingly in favor of the single currency. But as a result of this debate, Italy firmly embraced EMU relatively late (in the summer of 1996).

The Berlusconi government (which held power in 1994) was quite clearly Euro-skeptical. It had no intention of joining EMU from the very beginning because it believed the short-term costs were too high. The Berlusconi government wanted to negotiate, instead, a delayed entry into a two-speed Europe together with other countries of the so-called Club Med, i.e., Spain and Portugal. This position was in accord with the advice of key Christian Democratic politicians in Germany, including Karl Lamers and even Helmut Kohl, between 1994 and 1996. Lamberto Dini, the head of the technocratic government which followed the Berlusconi government, also made no attempt to join EMU. Its *Documento di Programmazione Economico-Finanziaria* (DPEF), a three-year macroeconomic plan presented yearly by the government to parliament, explicitly indicated that the 3 percent deficit/GDP ratio would be reached only at the end of 1998, i.e., too late for admission to EMU.

In 1996, the new Prodi government, at the beginning of its mandate, also sought to negotiate Italy's delayed entry within EMU. Again, Prodi's Documento di Programmazione Economico-Finanziaria (DPEF), presented in June 1996, specified that Italy would reach the 3 percent deficit/GDP ratio only at the end of 1998. In fact, as a result of this proposal, a verbal fight developed between Prodi and Mario Monti (Italy's chief representative to the European Commission): Monti accused Prodi of deliberately keeping Italy out of Europe, and Prodi replied that his government intended to enter Europe but with a living as opposed to dead country. In the summer of 1996, something changed, quite unexpectedly, in Italian policy vis-à-vis the EMU. The informed Italian public believes that this change has much to do with Prodi's visit to Spain to negotiate the terms of the delayed entry of both Italy and Spain into EMU. Aznar's response was that Spain had no intention of waiting for Italy. It was determined to join the first group of countries. This trip to Spain provoked a major turnabout in the Italian government's policy. A few weeks later, the Prodi government launched the so-called Eurotax, aimed at reducing Italy's public deficit.

In accomplishing this shift to a pro-EMU policy, the Prodi government was supported by the union movement, which persevered with wage moderation and engaged in unpopular welfare state reforms, but not by organized business. In fact, the *Confindustria* never espoused a clearly pro-EMU line: one of the few people in Italy (apart from the leader of the Communist Refoundation Party, Fausto Bertinotti) to publicly take an anti-EMU stance was Cesare Romiti, the president of Fiat. Why did he do so? Probably because he feared the recessionary consequences of fiscal consolidation, since Fiat (like other big Italian companies) primarily operates on the domestic market. We will return to a more detailed examination of employer strategies below, but now let us examine other government efforts to respond to the "double shift" of the Italian economy.

Privatization

In the early 1980s, after joining the EMS, the Italian government undertook another step toward the restoration of monetarist orthodoxy by privatizing various state-owned firms. Beginning in 1983, IRI and ENI (Italy's two major state holdings) privatized between four and five major firms per year, including well-known giants like Alfa Romeo and Lanerossi.[40] Privatization not only helped IRI and ENI emerge from their financial difficulties, but also helped the managers of these companies to increase their autonomy from the government. During the 1970s the state holding companies had placed themselves in a vicious cycle in which their growing dependence on government financing had forced them to give up much of their operational autonomy. In order to regain their independence and return to their original institutional mission, IRI and ENI sold off major components of their holdings.[41]

Although privatization was beneficial in many respects, the Italian experience, when compared with other national efforts, appeared quite modest. For example, between 1980 and 1986, IRI privatized twenty-five companies with 50,968 employees. During roughly the same period, British firms employing 400,000 people were denationalized. Similarly, funds realized from the sale of state enterprises in Italy during the first half of the 1980s amounted to only a fifth of the income nine French privatizations generated in one year (1986-87).[42] Moreover, because privatization efforts in Italy followed no set legislative or administrative guidelines, the state holding companies could not be assured that their intentions to sell off individual firms would be realized. Thus, although IRI successfully privatized Alfa Romeo, it was blocked in its efforts to sell off SME, a much smaller food business.[43] Recently, however, the government has sought to reduce the sizes of IRI and ENI and has once again pushed for the privatization of several large entities including the ILVA (steel), TelecomItalia, and two of Italy's major banks, Credito Italiano and Banca Commerciale.

Labor Market Reforms

Alongside these privatization efforts, the Italian government also sought to restore market signaling in the allocation of resources through the gradual deregulation of the labor market. During the 1970s the confederal unions had pursued a strategy of rigid control over labor supply by abolishing apprenticeship programs, imposing a system of anonymous hiring from special, union-controlled, placement lists (*liste di collocamento*), and transforming all "atypical" labor contracts (part-time, fixed-time, seasonal contracts, etc.) into full-time jobs.[44] As a result of this strategy, the degree of labor mobility, both "external" (i.e., among different firms) and "internal" (within single plants) was extremely low.

The trend was reversed in the 1980s. Hiring procedures were gradually liberalized, first by increasing the possibility of discretionary, individual hiring for the employers, and then by abolishing anonymous hiring altogether.[45] Various incentives to hire younger workers were introduced, through so-called job-training contracts (*contratti di formazione-lavoro*). These contracts (theoretically) provide for alternation of work and training activities for those aged fifteen to twenty-nine. Hiring is discretionary, and the duration of employment is limited to 24 months. Social security contributions are partially subsidized, and this reduces labor costs on average by 30 percent.[46] Subsequent legislation further increased the financial incentives available for these types of contracts by introducing the so-called entry-level wage for younger workers, lower than normal wages, creating a de facto two-tier wage system.

Part-time contracts were introduced in another attempt to enhance employment flexibility. About 1.3 million part-time contracts were signed between 1984 and 1991. Of these, 75 percent of the new hires and 83 percent of those shifting from full-time to part-time jobs were women.[47] Legislative attempts to promote "solidarity contracts" (involving reductions of wages and working hours for all workers of a company) as alternatives to the cassa integrazione met with limited success. In contrast, between 1984 and 1991, almost 2.5 million young workers were employed under the job-training contracts. Of these, about 50 percent were retained as full-time employees following the expiration of their initial contracts.[48] Much more questionable, however, was the quality of training provided in these jobs. Notwithstanding local successes, increased labor market flexibility failed to reduce the number of unemployed, which continued to rise from 7.4 percent of the workforce in 1980 to well above 12 percent in 1997. Moreover, the plague of high and persistent youth unemployment, particularly in the South, remained.

In sum, Italy's economic authorities reacted to the supply-side shocks of the late 1970s-early 1980s with a shift in macroeconomic policy, the privatization of public-sector companies, and various efforts to "flexibilize" the labor market. Essentially, by joining the EMS, Italy's government relinquished the autonomous exercise of control over major macroeconomic variables like exchange rates, interest rates, and money supply, and accepted the discipline of an international monetary regime. Although this discipline was never particularly stringent, since until the late 1980s the lira benefited from the larger oscillation band of 6 percent, it provoked an overall redefinition of economic policy. While the Italian government had sought to respond to the economic crisis which followed the first oil shock by avoiding harsh deflationary measures and boosting firms' profits through subsidization; instead, following the second oil shock, Italy adopted a more standard stabilization packet, involving more rigorous monetary and fiscal policies, privatization, and labor market deregulation.

During the 1980s, the Italian government sought repeatedly to reduce the degree of wage indexation guaranteed by the scala mobile, in an effort to bring inflation down (described later in this chapter). The results of these policies were mixed. Although inflation was gradually reduced, restrictive monetary policies provoked a constant appreciation of real interest rates during the 1980s, contributing to the depression of investments and employment.[49] Spurred by growing costs of debt servicing, public debt increased throughout the 1980s, so that by the early 1990s, it largely exceeded the country's GDP. The lira also experienced constant real appreciation throughout the 1980s, subject as it was to the combined effect of an inflation-fueling mechanism like the scala mobile, and semifixed nominal exchange rates. As a result of these developments, in the fall of 1992, the lira was targeted by speculative attacks which forced the Italian monetary authorities to first leave the EMS, and then substantially devalue their currency. These speculative attacks were, in turn, spurred by the diffuse perception among international speculators that the lira was much overvalued vis-à-vis other leading currencies like the U.S. dollar and the deutschemark and that a devaluation was imminent.

Although they did not suffice to restore macroeconomic stability, the new macroeconomic policies (most important for our concerns) decisively impaired the economic viability of the industrial relations system based on the institutional reforms of the 1970s. A mechanism of wage indexation like the scala mobile needed exchange rate flexibility to keep real exchange rates constant. Instead, Italy's real exchange rates appreciated throughout the 1980s, reducing the cost competitiveness of Italian goods on international markets and squeezing profit margins. As a result, Italian employers were forced to restructure their companies to regain competitiveness, and they did so in many cases through an attack on the unions' rigid control over the pace and content of work. We now turn to an examination of employers' strategies during this period.

The Employers: Union "Busting" or Labor Inclusion?

Italian employers had quite varied reactions to the various changes just described above. Differently from employers in countries like the United Kingdom and Sweden, Italy's organized employers made no consistent attempt at dismantling national, industry-based collective bargaining. They sought to exploit the changing balance of power with labor to reduce the power of unions at the local level, and thus, have a free hand in restructuring their companies. But even here, their attitudes were mixed. Some employers' federations affiliated with the *Confindustria* (e.g., the metalworking federation *Federmeccanica*), adopted an aggressive stance vis-à-vis the local unions. In the early 1980s, the director of Federmeccanica explicitly theorized about the end of trade unionism and the establishment of direct relations between companies and workers, modeled after the U.S. nonunion model of human resource management.[50] Other employers' federations, however, like the associations of chemical and textile companies (Federchimica and Federtessile), adopted a more participative approach aimed at involving local unions in negotiations over redundancy plans and workplace restructuring.[51] Public enterprises also sought to develop a more negotiated approach to industrial restructuring. In December 1984, a model of participatory industrial relations (the so-called *Protocollo IRI*) was formally adopted by IRI, Italy's major state holding company. Agreed to initially as a two-year experiment, but renewed and extended in February 1986, the *Protocollo IRI*, between Italy's largest state holding company and the three major union confederations, established new institutions aimed at enhancing union participation in firm restructuring efforts. It established a number of bilateral committees of "experts" at various levels (firm, territory, corporate) of the holding company. Composed of equal numbers of union and management representatives, they were empowered to discuss all issues concerning the investment, restructuring, and employment policies of IRI-affiliated firms. In this way, unions would be able to influence strategic decisions in the early stages of their formulation. The agreement also set up procedures to promote consensus. Arbitration and conciliation processes were created and a "cooling-off" period was required before either side took action. A number of manpower programs aimed at shedding redundancies, retraining workers, and enhancing internal mobility were also included in this agreement.[52]

Although the *Protocollo-IRI* formally affected only state-owned companies, some private companies adopted similar models of union-management cooperation. Conversely, certain state-owned companies sought to restore managerial discretion tout court. Thus, differences in the strategic choices pursued by employers cut across the private vs. public divide, and appeared to be shaped by the particular socioeconomic characteristics of the local contexts in which the actors were embedded.[53] For example, while in the early 1980s management at Fiat sought to marginalize unions within its plants, another of Italy's leading private firms, Pirelli (tires), concluded a process of negotiated restructuring and work transformation during these same years. Both companies were in deep financial crises when restructuring began, and both had to face strong and militant unions. The styles of restructuring were, however, very different in the two cases.[54] Likewise, although various

IRI-affiliated companies like SIP and Italtel (telecommunications) established quite articulated arrangements for union-participation in work reorganization efforts,[55] the management of Alitalia (Italy's state-owned airline company) adopted a more confrontational bargaining strategy to force the confederal unions representing its ground personnel to grant various concessions.[56] Interestingly enough, the model of participatory management envisaged by the Protocollo IRI was most coherently implemented by a private company, Zanussi (domestic appliances), which is controlled by the Swedish multinational Electrolux. Beginning in 1984, Zanussi implemented a model of labor relations which stands out, vis-à-vis similar experiments conducted in other large companies,[57] for its explicit recognition of the role played by the unions in assuring the independent expression of workers' "voice," and for its refusal to engage in nonunion forms of workers' representation.[58] This model was articulated at different geographic and hierarchical levels. At the national level, top management and the leaders of the national metalworkers' unions constituted a permanent committee (instituted by a 1990 accord) in which all major strategic guidelines (product strategies, new technologies, investments, alliances, etc.) were discussed. Collective bargaining at plant and divisional levels was shaped by the strategic guidelines set by this committee. At the grassroots level, various joint committees were to deal with issues which required detailed knowledge and local monitoring, like health and safety, new technologies, job classifications, equal opportunity, sexual harassment, training, organizational innovations, and contingent pay schemes. In 1994, a company-wide forum for dispute resolution, consisting equally of union and management representatives plus a neutral mediator, was established. The unions agreed to resort to strikes only when this conciliation process failed.

If at the beginning of the 1980s, the employers' strategies oscillated between managerial unilateralism and union-management cooperation, with time even companies like Fiat, which had adopted an arm's length approach vis-à-vis the unions, modified their attitude. Realizing that it was unable to purge its factories of union activists altogether, FIAT decided that some form (albeit weak) of union involvement in workplace management was preferable to outright confrontation in order to manage the introduction of innovative, flexible work systems, necessary to face the imperatives of the "new competition."[59] Thus, the evolution of Fiat's industrial relations during the 1980s and early 1990s can be considered as representative of a general strategic shift towards more consensual labor relations.

The Evolution of Employers' Strategy in Italy: A Case Study of Fiat Auto

In the late 1970s, Fiat, like most automobile producers in Western Europe and the United States, was experiencing very serious organizational and financial problems. In many ways, Fiat's troubles were related to the more general crisis of the auto industry. Yet, because of insufficient capital investments and extremely conflictual and rigid industrial relations practices throughout the 1970s, Fiat's productivity, profitability, and plant utilization rates were all lower than those of its major competitors.

As a result, the firm launched a restructuring process, including massive introduction of new process and product technologies, reorganization of its supplier and sales networks, and reassertion of managerial control over the shopfloor. As part of its reorganization plan, Fiat proposed to place 24,000 workers (out of about 139,000) in cassa integrazione during the fall of 1980. The local union rejected this reorganization plan and broke off relations with the firm. Claiming it was suffering from economic duress (which permits Italian firms to dismiss workers permanently and not merely lay them off temporarily), Fiat, in turn, declared its intention to dismiss 15,000 workers, beginning on October 6. Things heated up as the union blockaded the firm and Fiat sent out letters of dismissal. The ensuing strike lasted thirty-five days, but rank-and-file participation was low. Finally, on October 14, Fiat foremen and supervisors organized a successful demonstration calling for a return to work. Forty thousand people marched against the union, among them many blue-collar workers.[60] That very night an agreement completely embracing management's position was signed; it marked a major defeat from which the union never recovered.

With the union out of the way, Fiat embarked on what proved to be a successful reorganization of its production process. Profits rose, productivity improved, and market shares grew. However, the consequences of restructuring were disastrous for the unions. Immediately following the rupture in relations in 1980, the firm took a hard line with the labor movement. Within the factories this new policy translated into the recreation of traditional hierarchies and managerial control on the shopfloor, the discriminatory use of layoffs to rid the factories of union activists,[61] and the near halving of the active workforce. In the 1970s factory delegates in many ways controlled the flow of work on the shopfloor, but after 1980, foremen reasserted their traditional roles and ran things unilaterally. At most, they would merely inform shopfloor delegates of their prior decisions.[62]

In the following years, Fiat adopted a manufacturing strategy based on what has been called "computer-aided neo-taylorism," i.e., the integration of flexible automation technologies and Fordist work systems.[63] In 1985 the new plant Termoli 3, located in the South of Italy, began assembling the new Fire automobile engine. Product, plant, and work organization were designed jointly. The automation rate of the new plant was extremely high (85 percent), but in contrast to earlier experiments with flexible automation in various northern facilities – i.e., the Robotgate at the Rivalta plant or the LAM at the Mirafiori plant[64] the robots were placed sequentially and product variation was quite limited. Semiskilled, blue-collar labor, almost absent from the new plant, was replaced by indirect, maintenance labor. New categories of highly skilled workers capable of performing a variety of tasks – the so-called system conductors *(conduttori di sistema)* – were introduced in this new plant and were responsible for technological development in different areas of the production process.[65]

The principal long-term goal of this effort was to create an "unmanned factory" in which the problems of labor conflict and *anomie* would be completely absent. At first, it appeared as if the Termoli 3 plant was a big success. Its extremely rigid but very efficient production system allowed Fiat to cut the price of its best-selling car, the Uno, by 10 percent. Given the success of Termoli 3, Fiat engineers started to study how they could apply the lessons learned at Termoli to final assembly as well. With this plan in mind, in 1987 the Cassino assembly plant in central Italy was radically restructured.

The Cassino plant adopted highly sophisticated flexible manufacturing systems. However, the high number of different models being assembled at Cassino rendered coordination of the various production phases very difficult to manage.[66] Consequently, in December 1988 actual production levels stood at 760 cars per day, as opposed to the 1,800 cars per day that had originally been planned. In many parts of the assembly process, flexible machines remained idle and manual operations were reintroduced.[67] In 1989 automated operations constituted only 22 percent of the total production process performed at the Cassino plant, as opposed to the 50 percent originally planned.[68] Frequent jams in the automated systems of production occurred and could be resolved only through the flexible use of labor. However, since work organization was still modeled along Fordist lines, this flexibility was limited. In many cases, work teams and employees had to "breach the rules" and informally redefine their job assignments if they wanted to reach production goals.[69]

The debacle at Cassino convinced Fiat management that technological innovation alone could not guarantee production flexibility and product quality, and that these objectives were to be pursued primarily through organizational changes. Consequently, the new assembly plant of Melfi, also in the South of Italy, implements various organizational innovations modeled after the lean production model described by Womack, Jones, and Roos.[70] Work is organized into *Unita' Tecnologiche Elementari* (UTE) (minimal technological units), in which multifunctional teams operate. However, only technical workers enjoy real job enrichment and teamwork.[71] Hierarchy has been reduced and workers' skills have been given particular attention. Furthermore, all employees receive on-the-job training, albeit of very different durations: from two years for technical and supervisory staff to two weeks for manual workers. Finally, the unions have been relegitimated as workplace partners by management. They are involved in various joint committees and are informed regularly about various production plans and career development programs.

In sum, the evolution of industrial relations at Fiat illustrates how even those employers who had vehemently attacked the unions at the beginning of the 1980s, came to realize throughout the decade that they needed a form of union involvement to manage the new, flexible work systems introduced in their companies. Faced with industrial restructuring, internal chaos resulting from previous (failed) reform efforts, and more aggressive, if not outrightly hostile, strategies by both the employers and the government, how did the Italian unions respond? The next section traces the strategic evolution of the Italian union movement in the 1980s and early 1990s.

The Evolution of Union Strategy

Throughout the 1980s, the unintended consequences of the various institutional reforms of the previous decade combined with the dramatic changes in the Italian economy (both at the macro- and microeconomic levels) to augment the traditional fragmentation of Italian labor relations. In the early 1990s, however, things began to change as a result of three factors: 1) the demise of Italy's traditional party system and its effects on union autonomy; 2) the passage of major legislation in two critical areas – the regulation of strikes in essential public services, and the privatization of public sector employment, which strengthened the unions vis-à-vis rival organizations like the COBAS; and 3) the internal organizational reform of the unions themselves, which enhanced their ability to organize and represent different categories of workers. Although Italian labor relations continue to be characterized by internal dissent, nonetheless, it appears as if a slow, if at times inconsistent, transformation in the self-perception of the unions from agents of political and social dissent to parties in the process of economic change and governance, has occurred. This section illustrates this process of transformation by examining the most significant changes in the unions' various strategies.

Political Strategies: The End of "Transmission Belts"?

Italian unions have historically had close ties to political parties, often acting as their "transmission belts" or agents in the economic sphere.[72] In the early 1980s, the confederal unions tried to assume a position of relative autonomy vis-à-vis their long-term political allies. The issue of "union autonomy" from the party system was particularly strong within the CISL. In fact, the leadership of the CISL became convinced that the labor movement needed to contribute to a general reform of the country's institutions, especially existing collective bargaining arrangements, if Italy was to successfully pull itself out of the political-economic crisis. The CISL argued that the unions' previous bargaining strategy had exacerbated this crisis, and thus was particularly supportive of the government's attempt to relaunch neo-corporatist economic concertation. This effort also resonated with various elements of the CISL's ideological heritage, i.e., the union's long-rooted concern with economic growth, productivity, and profitability.[73] Moreover, drawing on the CISL's own self-conception as an independent "political subject"[74] (nourished especially after the Hot Autumn), the CISL's leadership considered the tripartite accords of 1983 and 1984 as qualitatively different from the previous experiments of 1977-79. Whereas in 1977-79 the unions' shift toward concertation had been spurred by a political shift, i.e., the inclusion of the Communist Party (PCI) in the governments of "national solidarity"; in 1983-84 the unions claimed to be dealing with government as "direct representatives" of the workers, completely circumventing any form of party mediation.[75]

In other words, for the CISL, the tripartite accords of the early 1980s were intended to produce more than just anti-inflationary policies. Instead, the union hoped that through tripartite negotiations over macroeconomic policy and institutionalized participation of the unions in company decisionmaking, it could construct a new, more concertative model of economic governance.[76] Through their control over wage determination, the unions would assure the progressive reduction of inflationary expectations; and through their control of the Fondo di Solidarieta' (solidarity fund),[77] the unions planned on directly contributing to new productive investments. As Pierre Carniti (general secretary of the CISL) articulated on a number of occasions, the CISL was aware that the unions' "political" role would be compromised if industrial restructuring were unilaterally decided and implemented by management.[78] Moreover, given that the political parties had proven incapable in the previous years to promote economic reform, the CISL believed that only a "social contract" between the unions and organized business could stimulate growth and pull Italy out of its recession.

Notwithstanding these ambitious goals, the tripartite agreements of the early 1980s focused almost entirely on reducing the cost of labor, particularly through reform of the scala mobile (wage indexation mechanism).[79] Due to Italy's high inflation rates, the scala mobile had gained massive weight in the determination of wages, accounting for over 60 percent of annual wage increases by the early 1980s.[80] This not only caused problems for management, but also for the unions whose control over wage determination had been severely reduced by indexation. The government, too, wanted a reform of this system since it ostensibly blocked all government measures aimed at fighting inflation.

Although bargaining over this agreement took place at separate tables, with labor leaders in one room and business representatives in another and government officials racing back and forth between them, all three actors signed the 22 January 1983 agreement. The agreement eliminated bracket creep, improved family allowances, established the Fondo di Solidarieta' to raise money for investment, reduced coverage provided by wage indexation by 15 percent, and banned plant-level bargaining for eighteen months.[81] Disagreements over certain clauses of the agreement subsequently broke out between labor and management, and the agreement was not automatically renewed the following year. As a result, the government presented its own proposal to fix wage indexation for 1984, regardless of the actual rate of inflation.[82] This attempt met with staunch opposition from the communist component of the CGIL. The government implemented this policy through an executive order and the unions split along partisan lines. The socialists in the CGIL, and the CISL and UIL all supported the government's position. The rest of the CGIL staunchly opposed it. Supported by the PCI, the communists within the CGIL mobilized workers against the new modification of the scala mobile.[83] In 1985, they also promoted a referendum aimed at abrogating the government decree. The results of the referendum, held on 9 June 1985, were favorable to the government and the moderate union forces that supported the 1984 accord.[84]

Thus, only twelve years after the birth of the Federazione *Unitaria*, labor unity once again dissolved in Italy. This not only eliminated the functional equivalent structures necessary for concertation in Italy,[85] but also dashed many of the dreams associated with the Hot Autumn. After this episode, tripartite collective agreements ceased for the rest of the 1980s.[86] The three union confederations continued to cooperate informally at the industry and company levels, although differences among them persisted and the old political cleavages reopened. In many cases, the unitary *Consigli di Fabbrica* were replaced by Rappresentanze *Sindacali Aziendali*, which were divided according to affiliation to different confederations.

In the aftermath of the recent corruption scandals known as *Tangentopoli*, however, many of Italy's traditional political parties collapsed, contributing considerably to reducing the political differences among the three main union confederations. Indeed, all confederal unions support the current left-of-center coalition government. This political rapprochement has on the one hand, favored the resumption of centralized collective bargaining and on the other, spurred efforts to reunite the three major confederations (CGIL, CISL, and UIL) into one single labor confederation. It is still too early to know where these efforts at rapprochement will lead but one thing is nonetheless clear: the demise of the traditional political parties may have finally given the unions the space they need to develop their own autonomous political strategies.

Legislative Strategies

Another significant change in the unions' strategies was reflected in their legislative efforts. In the early 1990s, the Italian unions encouraged the Italian government to pass two important laws regulating strikes in essential public services[87] and employment relations in the public sector, respectively. Both the 1990 law on strikes and the 1993 reform of the public sector sought to rationalize industrial relations in the service and public sectors, where the COBAS were imposing their role as bargaining agents through a systematic recourse to industrial conflict.[88] The COBAS used the so-called contractualization of public-employment relations, introduced into a law in 1983, to obtain very large wage increases for their own constituencies – increases much higher than productivity gains. These wage gains were, in tun, generalized to the rest of the economy, including the sectors exposed to international competition, by the economy-wide wage escalator, the scala mobile. Thus, leaving aside the deleterious effects these behaviors had for Italy's growing public deficit, collective bargaining in the public sector was contributing to both undermine Italy's international competitiveness (due to its inflationary consequences) and erode the credibility of the confederal unions as bargaining agents.

The explosion of industrial conflict in the public sector in the late 1980s[89] and the COBAS' continuous blockage of crucial social services such as railways, airlines, health care, and schools created a general consensus among Italy's key economic and political actors that legal regulation of the right to strike was required. The confederal unions had long opposed legal interventionism in the realm of industrial relations, arguing that it represented an unwarranted limitation of the unions' bargaining power. In order to guarantee the provision of minimal services in case of strikes, the CGIL, CISL, and UIL promoted the adoption of the so-called *codici di autoregolamentazione* (codes of self-regulation) in the latter half of the 1980s. However, since the COBAS refused to adopt these codes, or rather systematically violated them, the confederal unions eventually came around to support legal intervention. As a result, a law was approved in 1990 to curtail the unlimited exercise of the right to strike and guarantee the provision of certain "essential" services in case of strikes.

This law (Law 146/1990) regulated strikes in essential public services through a peculiar combination of legal and contractual tools.[90] In fact, it delegated to collective bargaining the definition of a list of basic services whose provision was to be assured even in case of strikes. The law also defined particular criteria that a union had to meet in order to gain access at the bargaining table. For example, only those unions that had already adopted a code for the self-regulation of strikes were admitted to the bargaining process. This clause de facto excluded most of the COBAS. Substantive restrictions concerning the length and timing of the strike were also included in the law. For example, strikes had to be announced at least ten days prior to their initiation. Moreover, in the case of illegal strikes workers could be forced back to work by prefects and ministers through executive orders (the so-called *precettazione*). The law also introduced a Commission of Experts which acted as mediator in the definition of the essential public services and was provided with a certain number of disciplinary and legal tools in case of violations.

So far, Law 146/1990 has proven instrumental in reducing the number of strikes in the service sector, while at the same time avoiding authoritative interventions.[91] In most cases, the bargaining parties have been able to reach agreements over the list of services to be guaranteed. Strikes of limited or intermittent duration have almost disappeared, while wild-cat strikes have become quite rare.[92] However, in some sectors like the railways, the COBAS have been able to exploit certain provisions of the new law to keep their bargaining power intact, perhaps even to enhance it. For example, since the law requires that strikes be publicly announced in advance, the *Comitato Macchinisti Uniti* (COMU) (the engine-drivers' version of the COBAS) has often proclaimed strikes only to call them off at the very last moment. As a result, the law has sometimes paradoxically provided the COBAS with a way of pursuing their objectives but at little or no cost.

Another attempt to restore order and predictability in industrial relations through legal regulation was represented by the reform of labor relations in the public sector, accomplished through Law 421 of 1992 and Legislative Decree 29 of 1993. This reform aimed at producing a major overhaul of human resource practices in the public sector. In particular, the main goal of the reform was to eliminate a web of clientelistic work practices in the public sector. For this purpose, the reform introduced techniques of human resource management generally adopted in the private sector, and increased the power and autonomy of the public managers vis-à-vis their bargaining counterparts.[93]

In the public sector, a tradition of particularistic and informal collective bargaining, involving the presence of various autonomous, professionally oriented unions,[94] predominated. In fact, for much of the postwar period, complacent politicians treated the public sector as a reservoir of party consensus, passing legislation which guaranteed special pension regimes, differentiated working conditions, status demarcations, and wage allowances to various professional groups within the civil service.[95] In 1983, a legislative reform introduced collective bargaining into the public sector. The reform sought to produce uniformity in wages and working conditions. However, like other previous attempts at reforming Italian industrial relations, it produced paradoxical results. Since the law of 1983 rigidly designated which issues were to be regulated through collective bargaining and which were to be left to legal regulation, a peculiar interpretation of the law prevailed, according to which union consensus was required on all issues for which legal regulation was not explicitly contemplated. Consequently, as an unintended consequence of the 1983 reform, a clientelistic version of codetermination emerged in which unionists and public officers agreed to mutually beneficial bargaining outcomes at the expense of the public good (and national treasury).

To restore efficiency and equity in public-sector employment relations, the reform of 1992-93 established that unilateral decisions by public managers could legally constitute a possible alternative to collective bargaining. This relaunched the role of the public managers by according them exclusive responsibility for the deployment of both human and physical resources, increased their remuneration (depending on performance), and augmented their capabilities through investments in training. Public managers were given the power to decide the organization of work in their offices, the articulation of working time schedules, and the introduction of flexible pay schemes. In other words, public managers were no longer legally required to reach an agreement with the trade unions on these issues, but needed only to inform, or alternatively consult, union representatives. Other innovations also sought to strengthen the bargaining power and autonomy of public officials vis-à-vis their political counterparts. To avoid political interference in collective bargaining, the reform assigned the task of negotiating collective agreements with the unions to an autonomous agency, called ARAN (*Agenzia per la Rappresentanza Negoziale*), composed of experts and therefore, at least in theory, isolated from political pressures. Reforms in public-sector bargaining were mirrored by major shifts in both the structure and strategy of private-sector bargaining.

The Evolution of Bargaining Strategy: From Fragmentation to Concertation

Historically, master agreements (CCNL's) negotiated by the national industry unions were predominant and structured the contracts of most, if not all, firms in the industry. As in the United States, leading firms were targeted by the unions for a particular year's bargaining round, and the national contract was usually little more than the diffusion of that company's agreement to the rest of the industry. These contracts were negotiated every three years and renewals were essentially automatic.[96] Negotiations by union locals at individual firms were mere addenda to these more standardized national contracts and usually took place within one year of the signing of the national agreements.

Fragmentation

During the 1980s this pattern broke down. Essentially, the national industry agreements were squeezed between confederal-level tripartite agreements and local- or firm-level bargaining.[97] Attempts by the peak-level confederations to engage in macroconcertative deals over the cost of labor, the scala mobile, fiscal reform, and the annual budget increasingly constrained national industry unions as they sought to negotiate their own contracts covering many of these same issues. At the same time, unwilling to be limited by overly broad industry contracts (which lump together within a single "category" extremely diverse economic realities – firms of different sizes and degrees of technological sophistication engaged in different lines of business, and employing alternative strategies),[98] firm- and territorial-level unions engaged in decentralized collective bargaining. These more microlevel contracts usually focused on firm restructuring efforts, the introduction of new technology, and shifts in the organization and timing of work. National industry unions, as a result, experienced substantial difficulties in developing, let alone implementing, master agreements in a number of industries.

The content of collective bargaining also began to shift away from the national contracts. A 1986 study on collective bargaining in Italy revealed that contrary to past practice, local union contracts were the most innovative and important agreements covering workers in industry. While national union agreements appeared to be quite generic, at most setting broad parameters on wages and working conditions, local unions were actually negotiating the most significant elements of the contract.[99] Thus, negotiations over the pace and timing of work, bonuses and profit sharing, new technologies and redundancies were increasingly negotiated at the firm and/or local levels. In the Italian textile industry, for example, the national contract established a thirty- six hour workweek, but local unions decided whether to concentrate the workweek in three or four long days or spread it out in the form of six shorter days, according to the needs and desires of the local workforce. In more agricultural areas, having shorter workdays permitted textile workers to also tend their fields. In more urban areas, fewer but longer days gave workers longer weekends or larger blocks of time to dedicate to a second job.

Even the sequencing of contract negotiations shifted in favor of local unions. Whereas before, national agreements were negotiated first and local contracts later – often with a prescribed lag period – during the 1980s many local unions negotiated their own contracts first with the national agreement emerging later as an aggregation and ratification of prior local deals.[100] Similar phenomena of decentralization could be observed in the implementation of laws regulating hiring and firing,[101] the use of redundancy funds (cassa integrazione),[102] and union relations with local governments[103] and business associations.[104]

Economic Crisis and the Relaunching of Concertation

After this phase of decentralized collective bargaining, the economic and financial crisis of the early 1990s focused the attention of both political and social actors on the need for a more radical restructuring of both bargaining arrangements and the scala mobile. Introduced initially in the national contracts of 1945 and 1946, the scala mobile was a cost-of-living adjustment escalator aimed at safeguarding workers' real wages against inflation. Price increases were periodically calculated in relation to an "average" working-class family's "shopping basket" of goods. An increase in the cost of the basket translated automatically into a proportional rise in workers' wage. In the early postwar years, the scala mobile was calculated as a lump sum amount equal for all workers. In 1951, however, the scala mobile was modified so that payments were more differentiated by age, gender, skill levels, and geographical locations.[105]

In 1975, in an attempt to moderate labor conflict, control inflation, and recast Italian industrial relations along more predictable lines, *Confindustria* and the major union confederations (CGIL, CISL, and UIL) negotiated an accord which enhanced benefits provided by the scala mobile, especially for lower paid semi-skilled workers. The main aspects of this accord were a 100 percent indexation and a secondary agreement guaranteeing 80 percent of workers' wages in the event of layoffs. The wage increases linked to the scala mobile consisted, like in the early postwar period, of equal sums for all employees (the so-called *punto unico di contingenza*). These measures would provide industrial workers in Italy with significant wage guarantees against both inflation and industrial restructuring. The *Confindustria* hoped that this accord would also shift the center of gravity of bargaining to the national level, and, in so doing, transfer power away from the militant industrial unions to the more moderate peak-level confederations.[106]

Yet this effort at controlling prices and moderating labor relations through indexation backfired in several ways. Due to Italy's double-digit inflation rates in the late 1970s and early 1980s, the scala mobile gained massive weight in the determination of wages[107] and became perhaps the major determinant of Italy's high inflation rates during the 1980s. This caused problems not only for employers, who particularly after Italy joined the European Monetary System in 1979 could no longer directly transfer greater labor costs into price increases, but also for the national unions, who lost control over wage determination through collective bargaining.

Thus, the early 1980s saw repeated attempts at reforming the scala mobile through centralized, tripartite agreements. In 1983, the three confederal unions agreed to a 15 percent reduction in the degree of coverage against inflation. In 1984, the government proposed to limit the amount of wage increases linked to the scala mobile, as a way of breaking inflationary expectations.[108] As we saw earlier, although the CISL, the UIL, and the socialists within the CGIL all supported the agreement, the communist majority of the CGIL opposed it.

Negotiations over the reform of the scala mobile began again in the late 1980s. Initially, the objective of both the *Confindustria* and the unions was not to reform the scala mobile but rather to reduce indirect costs (such as social security payments and taxes), which, when added to wages, rendered Italian workers among the most expensive in Europe. In January 1990, the unions and the *Confindustria* jointly tried convincing the government to reduce social security payments for employers and payroll taxes for salaried workers (i.e., the core of the unions' membership) but to no avail. Instead, in July 1990, the social partners signed an agreement to continue working together to reach a new accord over labor costs and the structure of collective bargaining by June 1991.

The 1991 negotiations were quite drawn out, and (not surprisingly) no accord was signed by June. But in December 1991, a new, partial agreement was finally signed by the unions and the *Confindustria* committing them to a comprehensive overhaul of the collective bargaining system by June 1992, and in the meantime, "superseding" the current system of wage indexation (i.e., the scala mobile). As Italy's macroeconomic situation deteriorated steadily over the course of 1992, they were pushed by the Amato government to sign a new agreement on 31 July 1992.

Seen as a revolutionary break with recent industrial relations practices, the 31 July 1992 "Protocol on Income Policy, the Struggle against Inflation, and the Cost of Labor" was not strictly speaking a collective agreement but rather a document in which the Italian government outlined its future economic policies. The "social partners" were called upon to underwrite this document and to conduct themselves within the parameters established by the document. The main features of the agreement included the abolition of the scala mobile; a one year moratorium on firm-level wage negotiations; a lump-sum (20,000 lire) wage increase to be paid in lieu of indexation; a freeze in industrial wages for the rest of 1992; and a freeze in government rates, administrative fees, and salaries.[109]

The July 1992 accord was a central element in the Italian government's radical reorientation of economic policy. The new policy sought simultaneously to lower inflation rates, reduce government expenditures, and improve the country's trade balance. In return for the unions' concessions, the government committed itself to three major reforms. The first reformed the pension system by raising the minimum retirement age (from sixty to sixty-five for men and from fifty-five to sixty for women) and eliminating certain benefits for public sector employees (e.g., the so-called baby pensions in which public-sector workers became eligible for retirement after only twenty years of service). The second "privatized" public-sector employment relations, as pointed out earlier. Finally and perhaps most important, was an important tax reform aimed at eliminating various inequalities and reducing tax evasion through the introduction of the "minimum tax" to be paid by all independent workers and small business owners.

The July 1992 accord provoked a major crisis within the Italian unions, especially within the CGIL. Sergio D'Antoni, secretary general of the CISL, and Bruno Trentin, secretary general of the CGIL, were both assaulted by protesters at open rallies, and Bruno Trentin was harshly criticized by a large share of the CGIL's leadership. Notwithstanding the CGIL's commitment to "codetermination" and the democratic governance of the economy following its twelfth National Congress in 1991,[110] a significant minority within the confederation, closely linked to the left-wing faction *Essere Sindacato*, opposed the 31 July 1992 accord. Because of this internal organizational turmoil, Trentin offered (but later retracted) his resignation. Trentin claimed that he was compelled to sign the agreement, both out of a sense of "responsibility" toward the nation, and because he did not want to see a repetition of the 1984 split among the unions fostered by an analogous austerity package.[111]

The following autumn witnessed numerous demonstrations against the accord. Various factory councils in the North even established a movement of the so-called *autoconvocati* to contest the July 1992 accord. Interestingly enough, prominent within these demonstrations were not only members of the militant metalworkers unions but also large numbers of chemical workers, often seen as more moderate union members. Moreover, several local business owners in the North defected from the agreement and signed firm-level contracts providing wage increases, preferring to pay higher wages to persistent industrial conflict.

Between July 1992 and July 1993 there was much debate between the *Confindustria* and the unions over the final terms of the agreement. The debate centered less on the demise of the scala mobile (which appeared to be certain) and more on the future structure of collective bargaining. According to the *Confindustria*, wage levels and salaries should be determined only through the national industry agreements (*Contratti Nazionali di Categoria*). The unions, however, wanted wage bargaining to take place at both the industry and company levels (or territorial level for small and medium-sized companies). After a series of delays, due in part to the replacement of the Amato government by a government of "technicians" headed by Ciampi, a new agreement over the structure of collective bargaining was reached on 3 July 1993. As with the July 1992 accord, this agreement contained a number of policy measures concerning vocational training, technological innovation, government fees, and various labor market policies. The parts of the 1993 accord explicitly devoted to industrial relations included the following provisions:

- The scala mobile would be abolished, but space would be left for some indexation (the equivalent of 30 percent if the national industry contract has expired for over three months;

and 50 percent if the national industry contract has expired for over six months).

- Wage guidelines and the rate of increases in nominal wages would be determined through periodic tripartite consultations (in May and September) and should be consistent with the government's macroeconomic predictions as stated in its yearly budget.
- The structure of national industry contracts would be modified so that the contracts resembled those in Germany: normative clauses (i.e., those clauses of the national contract that govern hiring and firing practices, job classifications, career trajectories, etc.) would be negotiated every four years, whereas more strictly economic (wage) clauses would be renewed every two years.
- Bargaining would take place at both the industry and company (or territorial, in the case of small companies) levels. This clause represented an important victory for the union movement, since the employers had pushed for a single locus of collective bargaining at the national level. The accord also specified that company bargaining could take place on issues not already regulated by the national contract. Moreover, wage increases deriving from company-level bargaining would be financed through productivity increases or performance improvements. To create incentives for flexible forms of remuneration, social security taxes paid by the employers would be partially subsidized, provided that contingent pay schemes were negotiated with the unions.
- Employees would pay a greater share of their benefit contributions, hence reducing indirect labor costs for employers.

Other aspects of the accord included increased labor market flexibility, with provisions for paying slightly lower wages to new entrants, and a restriction in the use of *cassa integrazione* Guadagni (the government-financed redundancy fund). With this accord, the unions gave up what was once seen as a major victory of the Hot Autumn era – extensive indexation and protection from inflation. Giving up the scala mobile also implied a reversal in the unions' egalitarian policies and a recognition of wage inequalities for differently skilled workers.[112] At the same time, by agreeing to participate in trilateral negotiations over wage increases, the unions were committing themselves to working with organized business and the government on containing wage growth and thus stimulating demand for Italian goods on world markets.

It is important to note that the 1992-93 accords were not merely a repetition of the 1983-84 tripartite agreements. First, the unions' commitment to wage moderation was not counterbalanced by favorable welfare legislation, as it was in the early 1980s. Second, the 1992-93 accords were accompanied by a major reform of public-sector employment relations, which means that wage moderation was extended to the public sector as well. Third, the collapse of the traditional party system eliminated possible partisan conflicts among the unions over these reforms. Finally, the July 1993 agreement included an organizational reform of the unions, aimed at revitalizing plant-level structures and eliminating conflict with the COBAS. Interestingly enough, the future destiny of Italy's new architecture of collective bargaining and incomes policy depends upon the success of this organizational reform. If the new plant-level structures, the *Rappresentanze Sindacali Unitarie* (RSU), are able to aggregate the interests and gain the loyalty of diverse kinds of workers, then the "nonoverlapping" and "functional specialization" clauses of the July 1993 accord will hold. Otherwise, if these new plant-level structures fail to gain legitimacy and the unions continue to suffer from a crisis of legitimacy, then the accord and its elaborate bargaining structure will collapse as a result of renewed labor conflict. Because of their importance, we now turn to a more detailed discussion of the unions' organizational reforms.

Organizational/Representational Strategies

The organizational structure of the Italian union movement reflects its tumultuous and uncoordinated development. Each confederation has both vertical (industry-based) and horizontal (territorial) structures. During the 1950s, when the union movement was fragmented, weak, and politically isolated, the horizontal structures, especially the so-called *Camere del Lavoro*, were predominant. With the increase in collective bargaining at the industry and firm levels during the 1960s, however, the national industrial unions became ascendant.[113] Following the Hot Autumn struggles and the federative pact in 1972, factory councils – elected by and composed of union and non-union workers alike – were established at the shop floor.[114] These became the official workplace organs of the three confederations, replacing the earlier *Commissioni Interne* (factory grievance committees). [115]

In the late 1970s, while the strategic shift toward concertation was being pursued, the Italian unions embarked on an organizational reform aimed at developing a clear, mutually agreeable division of labor among the various levels of the union hierarchy. This organizational reform (referred to as the *Riforma di Montesilvano*) was formally embraced by the *Federazione Unitaria* CGIL-CISL-UIL in 1979, but had already begun with the 1975 reform of the scala mobile which had severely curtailed the scope of decentralized wage bargaining.

The initial goals of the Montesilvano Reform were quite different from its results. The reform sought to decentralize union structures to better match recent changes in the administrative structure of the Italian state.[116] New zonal, departmental and regional confederal union structures were to replace the old provincial unions. At the company and plant levels, the reform envisaged the consolidation and institutionalization of the Factory Councils and their extension to the service sector, where they had not spontaneously emerged. Besides creating new structures for interindustry coordination, the reform also mandated the merging of several national industry unions, especially in the transportation and public sectors.[117]

Although the three confederations differed on specific aspects of the reform,[118] the project was essentially unitary. Through organizational decentralization and the encouragement of mass participation, the unions sought to strengthen their "political role" in Italian society. By merging together various smaller industrial unions, they also hoped to block the emergence of more particularistic demands within some of these smaller unions, which had previously hindered the development and the implementation of an united approach to social and political reform.[119]

Instead of territorial decentralization, however, the Montesilvano Reform resulted in a recentralization of the unions' structures. For example, the introduction of departmental union structures was, at best, incomplete.[120] Moreover, the "reform" actually weakened the national industry and provincial unions – two union structures which had become more powerful and autonomous during the late 1960s and 1970s – by restricting the bargaining power of the former and by reallocating the resources and responsibilities of the latter to the new regional and departmental structures. The confederations hoped that this more centralized structure would provide them with the organizational control and resources necessary to pursue their strategy of concertation.

This did not materialize either. Since various organizations within the union movement fought hard to protect their autonomy, the reform's result was to dilute rather than rationalize the unions' structures. For example, at a time of shrinking resources, the various unions significantly increased their staff (20 percent by the CGIL, 17 percent by the CISL).[121] Within the transportation, health care and education sectors, previously characterized by an array of smaller, more professionally oriented unions only loosely tied to the confederations, the reform was even more damaging. In these sectors, workers felt that the central confederations were imposing on them an inappropriate, industrial union model of organization – which failed to recognize their particular needs and interests.[122] Not surprisingly, it was within these same sectors that alternative labor organizations like the *Sindacati Autonomi* and the COBAS emerged a few years later.

In reality, this process of internal fragmentation of the Italian union movement occurred in two phases. During the first phase (1970s), in response to the unions' egalitarian bargaining strategy, a myriad of so-called *Sindacati Autonomi* (autonomous unions) appeared in the air transportation, banking, insurance, health care, and school sectors. In 1977, for example, the *Confederquadri* (representing lower management ranks) and the SNALS (representing secondary school teachers) were founded. These so-called autonomous unions succeeded by contesting the confederal unions' bargaining policy, especially its concern with various political and ideological goals. Instead, they proposed a more "bread and butter" focus, such as the reopening of wage differentials, the negotiation of merit pay, and new organizational structures through which skilled workers could express their "voice." A few years later, these unions adopted more stable organizational structures.[123] During the 1980s they established new confederations, such as the CISAL, the CISAS, the CONFAIL, and the CONFSAL in different sectors.

During the latter half of the 1980s, the more innovative and intransigent *Comitati di Base* (COBAS) (grassroots committees) appeared, often in the same sectors in which the autonomous unions were also present. In many cases, the COBAS were established by previous members of the CGIL, contributing further to the erosion of the confederal unions' representational monopoly.[124]

Protest against the representational strategies of the three major union confederations exploded in 1986-87, when all major contracts in the public sector were up for renewal. School teachers contested the collective agreement that the CGIL, CISL, UIL, and the professional union SNALS, had just negotiated. On 25 March 1987, 40,000 people demonstrated in Rome against both the confederal unions and the government. Most of them refused to provide end-of-year student reports.[125] During the summer of 1987, engine drivers contested the contract signed by the CGIL, CISL, UIL, and the autonomous union FISAFS, and organized a wave of wildcat strikes which paralyzed railway transportation. Participation in the strikes was as high as 78 percent in some cases.[126] Finally, in autumn 1987, ground personnel at Alitalia (Italy's major airline company) rejected the new contract and forced the company to reopen bargaining.[127] In all of these cases, the COBAS took the lead in organizing the protests.

These developments faced the confederal unions with growing disaffection from within and a weakening in their bargaining position vis-à-vis management, increasingly concerned that the established unions could not control their own rank and file. In an increasing number of sectors and among numerous professional groups, the confederal unions appeared to have lost their hegemony over union representation. In sum, twenty years after the Hot Autumn, egalitarianism which had once contributed to bring about organizational cohesion within the Italian labor movement, now appeared to be causing internal defections and fragmentation. Skilled workers in the public sector came to perceive the egalitarian wage policies pursued by the three major union confederations as a violation of basic equity norms (i.e. that remuneration should be in proportion to capacity and effort) and responded with a new wave of wildcat strikes, similar in many ways to those of the Hot Autumn but this time aimed at increasing (rather than reducing) wage differentials between different groups of workers.

Besides impairing the representation of skilled workers in the public and service sectors, the Montesilvano Reform had another unintended consequence: the decline of grassroots union structures in the industrial sectors. In the early 1980s, while the unions were pursuing a strategy focused on macroeconomic concertation, political exchange, and organizational centralization, grassroots representation structures sank into oblivion.[128] The consolidation and extension of the Factory Councils were never accomplished, although they constituted an important part of the Montesilvano Reform.[129] Nor were precise norms concerning the election and reelection of workers' representatives and the relations between employee councils and external unions ever established. As a result, the responses given by the Factory Councils to the wave of industrial restructuring of the early 1980s were increasingly particularistic, making the emergence of a unitary union strategy more difficult. Plant-level activists pursued different policies based on the degree of support which they enjoyed from the rank and file, based on the level of recognition accorded to them by management, and, ultimately, based on the particular sociopolitical features of local economies in which they were embedded.[130] As a result, industrial employment fell, net real wages and salaries stagnated, and union membership declined. Union membership, which had doubled between 1969 and 1980[131], fell from 49 percent to 39.3 percent between 1980 and 1990.[132]

Relaunching Internal Democracy

In the late 1980s, increased competition from rival organizations like the COBAS and the autonomous unions, and growing dissent from within, forced the traditional unions to reexamine several of their organizational practices. In the early 1990s, the CGIL proposed revision of the *Statuto dei Lavoratori* that would transform the Factory Councils into more democratic and vibrant organizations. It would replace the "presumed" representativeness of the major unions with "effective" representativeness established through regularly held elections. Any organization that collected the signatures of at least 3 percent of the employees in a given production unit was allowed to stand for election to the proposed new enterprise council. It would not only terminate the legal monopoly over firm-level representation which CGIL, CISL, and UIL enjoyed for over twenty years but would also ensure that elections to these worker councils occurred regularly.

But the proposal went nowhere. Instead, the tripartite agreement of July 1993 provided for the replacement of existing plant-level union structures, the so-called *Rappresentanze Sindacali Aziendali* (RSA), with unitary union structures, the *Rappresentanze Sindacali Unitarie* (RSU). Unlike in the past, elections for the new RSU could be contested by any organization capable of gaining at least 5 percent of the workforce.[133] However, only two-thirds of the representatives in these new firm-level structures are elected, whereas the remaining one-third is appointed directly by those unions which have signed the national industry contract. Interestingly enough, this clause of the July 1993 agreement was requested by the employers federation in order to establish an institutional link between bargaining agents at the national and plant levels.[134] In other words, the *Confindustria* wanted to avoid engaging in collective bargaining at the plant level with union organizations that were not bound by the provisions established in the national industry contracts.

The RSU are both organizational structures of the trade unions and representational structures of all workers. They are to be elected every two years. As opposed to previous workplace structures, they have been recognized by the three major union confederations as legitimate bargaining agents at the company and plant levels. They have also inherited the information and consultation rights previously exercised by union structures.

The confederal unions hoped this would revitalize their plant-level union structures, eliminate a major source of shopfloor conflict (recall that the COBAS and other competitive union organizations contested previous collective agreements because they were excluded from negotiations) and more importantly, relegitimize their role as representatives not only of sectional interests but of the labor movement as a whole. Yet the COBAS and other "autonomous" unions vehemently contested these new structures, particularly the "one-third" clause. They argued that this was just an astute repackaging of the "most representative" clause of the *Statuto dei Lavoratori*. For example, on the basis of the existing rules, if the three major confederal unions (CGIL, CISL, and UIL) won only 18 percent of all votes, they would still obtain the majority of seats in the new councils because 33 percent of the seats are automatically assigned to them.[135]

The results of the recent elections for the RSU have belied these cynical interpretations. Not only was participation in the elections remarkably high (around 75 percent of all workers), but the three major union confederations managed to obtain an overwhelming majority: about 90 percent of all votes in more than 4,000 elections. In fact, the COBAS have been forced by these results to reconsider their claim to represent specific categories of workers. For example, in the railroad transportation sector where they are strongest, they represent only 40 percent of all engine drivers, which is less than 6 percent of all workers in the overall transportation sector.[136] In short, recent RSU election results indicate that the "representativeness" of the CGIL, CISL, and UIL is being confirmed. The "one-third" clause thus appears more as a "majority premium" intended to consolidate an already clear and stable majority of votes rather than an attempt to cheat on democratic rules.

As stated earlier, the confederal unions' ability to relegitimize themselves as representatives of different categories of workers is key to the stability of Italy's new industrial relations system. The future destinies of the new plant-level representation structures and of the new collective bargaining arrangements, including income policies, appear to be strictly intertwined. Only if the major confederal unions are capable of aggregating the interests and gaining the loyalty of different categories of workers at the plant level, can they enforce their pledge to abstain from bargaining demands already covered by national industry contracts or from wage increases not immediately tied to productivity increases or company performance. Otherwise, the confederal unions will continue to suffer a crisis of representation, as they did throughout the 1980s, and the elaborate new architecture for collective bargaining and "political exchange" introduced in the early 1990s will collapse as was the case with an analogous reform effort of the 1960s – the so-called clausole di rinvio – which were swept away by the Hot Autumn wave of strikes.

Conclusion

During the 1970s, Italy tried to build a new industrial relations model as a way of coping with its internal, distributional problems. Following the Hot Autumn of 1969, growing union militancy and rising labor costs seriously impaired the socioeconomic stability of the country. Italy's reformers looked at other national systems as sources of inspiration on how to remake their country. In particular, they tried to adapt the northern European model of neo-corporatist policymaking. Thus, the *Statuto dei Lavoratori* of 1970s attributed special organizational privileges to the so-called most representative unions, i.e. the confederal unions CGIL, CISL, and UIL. The reforms of the scala mobile and the cassa integrazione of 1975 guaranteed protection of workers' wages against inflation and industrial restructuring, thus eliminating two major sources of labor conflict. Finally, the tripartite agreements of 1977-79 sought to coopt the confederal unions into a comprehensive system of political-economic concertation.

These various reform projects failed, however, to produce their anticipated results. For example, since the Statuto defined "most representative" as the ability to sign a provincial or national collective bargain, it provided strong incentives for competitive, nonconfederal unions to resort to industrial conflict in order to gain recognition as legitimate bargaining agents. Similarly, given the way the scala mobile was calculated, i.e. as a lump-sum payment equal for all categories of workers, it led to the flattening of wage differentials and the emergence of discontent among the most educated and skilled segments of the workforce.

In addition to the various internal contradictions contained within these early reform efforts, the simultaneous globalization and decentralization of the economy severely undermined the stability of institutional arrangements, which assumed that the scope of markets still largely coincided with the extent of the national territory. Italy's decision to join the EMS in 1979 reduced national policymakers' capacity, let alone discretion, to use important macroeconomic variables like exchange rates and money supply to govern economic relations. At the same time, the decentralization of production and industrial restructuring provided management with new, more powerful tools to challenge union power at the workplace level and thus challenge the political balance of power undergirding the institutional reforms of the 1970s.

Following the initial failure to remake Italian industrial relations along the lines of a coherent national model, Italy's social actors engaged in a series of experiments throughout the 1980s. Some of these efforts sought to revitalize previous reforms; others intervened on political economic spheres left untouched by the reforms of the previous decade. The tripartite agreements of 1983-84, for example, briefly restored economic concertation as a conjunctural measure against rising inflation and unemployment. The introduction of collective bargaining in the public sector in 1983 sought to equalize wage and working conditions across private and public sectors. Finally, in these same years new laws tried to partially deregulate the labor market, in the hope that this would increase employers' demand for labor.

Once again, the results of these ad hoc, sometimes internally inconsistent attempts to recast the Italian industrial relations system did not live up to expectations. Writing in the latter half of the 1980s, the industrial sociologist Gian Primo Cella observed that almost twenty years after the Hot Autumn Italy's labor relations were still suffering from informality and underinstitutionalization.[137] The confederal unions CGIL, CISL, and UIL were hit particularly hardly by the crisis of the 1980s. The appearance of new unions, the so-called *Sindacati Autonomi* and the COBAS, gave voice to the malcontent of highly skilled and white-collar workers against the egalitarian wage policies pursued by the confederal unions. The COBAS organized a series of frequent, intermittent strikes which virtually paralyzed sectors like air and rail transportation, schools, and health care. Even in the industrial sectors, the unions were in dire straits. They seemed incapable of elaborating a coherent response to the massive wave of industrial restructuring. While national collective bargaining stagnated, local unions responded to companies' reorganizations in very different ways, based on the particular socioeconomic features of the local economies in which they were embedded.[138] This rendered the development of a unitary union strategy even more difficult to achieve, but also facilitated the emergence of innovative experiments with union-management cooperation and negotiated restructuring both in large firms and industrial districts.[139]

In the early 1990s, Italy's economic situation worsened, partly due to the crisis of industrial relations. Faced with growing labor costs, increasing public debt and trade deficits, rising unemployment, and a resurgence of industrial conflict in the service sector, the Italian government, along with the confederal unions and the *Confindustria*, engaged in new institutional reforms. In 1990 a new law limited the right to strike in essential public services; in 1992 the scala mobile was abolished; and in 1993 the government accomplished a major overhaul of public-sector employment relations. None of these reforms was explicitly planned as part of a comprehensive institutional redefinition of Italian industrial relations. Each constituted, on the contrary, a pragmatic response to specific problems: the law on strikes curtailed the COBAS's capacity to proclaim sudden and highly destructive strikes; the abolition of the *scala mobile* eliminated the major source of Italy's persistently high inflation; and the "privatization" of public employment sought once again to equalize wages and working conditions across private and public sectors. However, notwithstanding their ad hoc introduction, these new institutions, and with them the July 1993 reform of collective bargaining arrangements, might prove to constitute the building blocks of a new, innovative and coherent "national model" of industrial relations – one which promises to reconcile the country's desperate need for macroeconomic stability with decentralization and local flexibility through the establishment of clear institutional links between national negotiations over pay increases and decentralized bargaining over issues like work reorganization, contingent pay schemes, and flexible working hours.

In sum, ten years after what can now be considered as the first phase of Italian neo-corporatism, Italy's social partners are trying again to institutionalize a variant of neo-corporatist concertation. In the meanwhile, however, many things have changed. The confederal unions have come to realize that their "representativeness" is by no means automatic, nor does the legal recognition provided by the *Statuto dei Lavoratori* suffice to guarantee it. Consequently, they have modified their organizational structures in order to relaunch internal democracy, particularly at the plant level. Furthermore, the disappearance in the early 1990s of most traditional parties, due to the wave of scandals known as mani pulite (clean hands) eliminated one of the major sources of division among CGIL, CISL, and UIL. Finally, and perhaps more importantly, the confederal unions have also considerably modified their self-perception. Perhaps the clearest example of this shift in the unions' identity from agents of social dissent to partners in processes of economic change came from the 1991 National Congress of the CGIL. In fact, in that congress the majority of the union delegates approved a new strategy involving the end of class struggle, the "demise" of the "centrality" of industrial workers' bargaining demands, the adoption of bargaining demands compatible with the firms' ability to pay, the pursuit of codetermination, and the dissolution of political factions within the union.[140]

It is ironic that at a time when the fortunes of neo-corporatism are declining due to its supposed lack of flexibility and responsiveness to the needs of a post-Fordist economy, when income policies are being abandoned even in their Scandinavian homeland, they are being revived in Italy – a country which was understood to have none of the institutional supports and legacies once deemed necessary for these kinds of arrangements to work. It is still too early to evaluate the stability and performance of Italy's new national system of industrial relations. The new industrial relations system has contributed to the revitalization of the Italian economy, permitting a radical reduction in the rate of inflation without a large increase in unemployment. This system has lived through various political and economic vicissitudes in the 1990s. It survived both the collapse of the traditional party system and the election of Berlusconi's center- right coalition. The new industrial relations system has also proven itself to be quiescent as well. The 1994 renewal of the pattern-setting metalworkers' contract was signed after five days of negotiations and no recourse to strikes. In 1995, participatory policymaking was extended to welfare reform as well. For the first time since 1968, the government and the three confederal unions negotiated a structural reform of the pension system which reduced state expenditures on pensions and thus, contributed to the reduction of Italy's budget deficit.[141] The 1996 renewal of the metalworkers' contract was slightly more conflictual than the 1994 negotiations, but in the end, it too conformed to the guidelines established by the national income policies. Similarly, various national contracts in the public sector – the source of much of Italy's labor conflict in recent years – also respected the wage limits established by the government and social partners. All of this can be interpreted as signs of resilience for Italy's new system of industrial relations and economic governance.

Clearly, the future of this system does not depend solely on the Italian unions' strategic choices. As demonstrated by the brief Berlusconi government's experience, concertation depends heavily on the governments acceptance of it as a method of policymaking. The center-left government of Romano Prodi continues to pledge its allegiance to this concertative approach, but nobody can exclude that in the future a new center-right government will come to power and adopt a completely different approach to policy-making. In addition, as the Swedish case shows clearly, organized employers have to be committed to this kind of centralized consultation as well.

Italian employers benefited tremendously from wage restraint in the early 1990s. The business sector's rate of return on capital grew from 13.8 percent in 1993 to 15.9 percent in 1995 and is still, as of this writing, higher than it has ever been in the 1970s and 1980s.[142] During the 1994 general elections (when Berlusconi triumphed), *Confindustria* advanced a formal request to both political coalitions that income policies continue in future years.[143] In more recent years, however, dissenting views within *Confindustria* – especially among the federation of metalworking employers – have arisen. These employers argue for a return to unfettered collective bargaining and the elimination of income policies. Clearly, we can not rule out the possibility that this position could become predominant within *Confindustria*, thus provoking a Swedish-like dismantling of incomes policies. Stranger things have been known to happen in Italy. However, at the moment, the Italian unions' resurgence appears quite strong.

Notes

1. All translations are those of the authors unless otherwise noted.
2. See Gian Primo Cella, "Criteria of Regulation in Italian Industrial Relations: A Case of Weak Institutions," in *State, Market and Social Regulation: New Perspectives on Italy*, Peter Lange and Marino Regini, eds. (New York: Cambridge University Press, 1989).
3. See Peter Lange, George Ross, and Maurizio Vannicelli, *Unions, Change, and Crisis.*
4. See Cella, "Criteria of Regulation."
5. See, Pietro Merli Brandini, "Italy: Creating a New Industrial Relations System from the Bottom," in *Worker Militancy and its Consequences, 1965-75*, Solomon Barkin, ed. (New York: Praeger, 1975); Alessandro Pizzorno, Emilio Reyneri, Marino Regini, and Ida Regalia, *Lotte operaie e sindacato: Il ciclo 1968-1972* (Bologna: Il Mulino, 1978); and Charles F. Sabel, *Work and Politics* (New York: Cambridge University Press, 1982).
6. Miriam A Golden, *Labor Divided: Austerity and Working Class Politics in Contemporary Italy* (Ithaca: Cornell University Press, 1988, 47).
7. Michele Salvati, *Economia e politica in Italia dal dopoguerra a oggi* (Milan: Garzanti Editore, 1986).
8. For more on this see Richard M. Locke, *Remaking the Italian Economy* (Ithaca: Cornell University Press, 5-10).
9. Golden, *Labor Divided*, 16.
10. The *Statuto dei Diritti dei Lavoratori*, Italy's first comprehensive labor code, combined elements of French and American labor law. This law, enacted in 1970, on the crest of the strike waves of the "Hot Autumn," had two major components. Like the American Wagner Act, the first part consisted of a series of articles guaranteeing the freedom of workers as citizens: freedom of thought and expression were protected, job security was ensured, the roles of security guards and supervisors were strictly limited, and various surveillance techniques were curtailed. The second part provided institutional guarantees for unions. Blacklists were prohibited, the right to join a union affirmed, and unions were authorized to constitute their own structures on the shop floor.
11. The main aspect of this accord was a 100 percent indexation of the scala mobile; see Stefano Patriarca, *La nuova scala mobile* (Rome: Ediesse, 1986) This reform was accompanied by another important agreement over the *cassa integrazione guadagni*

(CIG), which extended the duration of state-funded partial unemployment benefits and guaranteed 80 percent of workers' wages in the event of layoffs; see Tiziano Treu, "Italy," in *The International Encyclopedia of Labour Law and Industrial Relations*, 11th edition, Roger Blainpain, ed. (Deventer, The Netherlands: Kluwer, 1986, 80-1). The CIG was therefore transformed from a temporary protection of workers' incomes, aimed at facilitating industrial restructuring, into a substitute for dismissals; see Emilio Reyneri, "The Italian Labor Market: Between State Control and Social Regulation," in *State, Market and Social Regulation: New Perspectives on Italy*, Peter Lange and Marino Regini, eds. (New York: Cambridge University Press, 1989, 137).

12. Due to Italy's economic crisis in the second half of the 1970s, the three confederal unions began to rethink the dualistic strategy of pushing for wage increases and changes in work organization and major institutional reforms at the national level, which they had adopted after the Hot Autumn. As a result of this self-criticism, CGIL, CISL, and UIL embarked on a major reform of their strategy, involving a tradeoff between wage moderation and greater labor mobility in return for influence over industrial and labor market policies aimed at restoring economic growth and sustaining employment. By 1978 the *Federazione CGIL-CISL-UIL* officially adopted an austerity policy in the form of the EUR document; see Marino Regini, *I dilemmi del sindacato* (Bologna: Il Mulino, 1981).
13. Peter Swenson, *Fair Shares: Unions, Pay, and Politics in Sweden and West Germany* (Ithaca, NY: Cornell University Press, 1989).
14. For example, the *Statuto dei Diritti dei Lavoratori* sought to recast Italian labor relations along more procedural (and, it was hoped, less conflictual) lines. However, the Statuto limited workplace representation to the "most representative" unions and defined this in such a way that actually created a very strong incentive for nonconfederal worker organizations to provoke strikes and contest previously negotiated contracts; see Michael Terry, "Workplace Unions and Workplace Industrial Relations," *Industrial Relations Journal*. 24, no. 2, 1993: 138-50.
15. Renato Brunetta and Leonello Tronti, "Italy: The Social Consequences of Economic and Monetary Union," *Labour* (Fall 1995).
16. For a similar "historical compromise" between labor and capital, see Walter Korpi, *The Working Class in Welfare Capitalism: Work, Unions and Politics in Sweden* (London: Routledge and Kegan Paul, 1978).
17. Fabrizio Barca and Marco Magnani, *L'industria fra capitale e lavoro* (Bologna: Il Mulino, 1989).
18. Locke, *Remaking the Italian Economy*, chap 1.
19. On the crisis of Fordism, see Michael Piore and Charles Sabel, *The Second Industrial Divide* (New York: Basic Books, 1984).
20. Guido Rey, "Small Firms: Profile and Analysis, 1981-85," *in Small Firms and Industrial Districts in Italy*, Edward Goodman, Julia Bamford, and Peter Saynor, eds. (London: Routledge, 1989, 71).
21. Fabrizio Barca and Marco Magnani, "Industrial Development and Work Organization: From Restructuring to Capacity Expansion," in *Labour and Employment Policies in Italy Report* '89, Ministero del Lavoro e della Previdenza Sociale (Rome: Istituto Poligrafico e Zecca dello Stato, 1989, 67, table 1).
22. Marco Bellandi, "The Role of Small Firms in the Development of Italian Manufacturing Industry," in *Small Firms and Industrial Districts in Italy*, Edward Goodman, Julia Bamford, and Peter Saynor, eds. (London: Routledge, 1989, 49).
23. Rey, "Small Firms," 79; Barca and Magnani, *L'industria fra capitale e lavoro*, 171-89.

24. Barca and Magnani, *L'industria fra capitale e lavoro.*
25. Barca and Magnani, *L'industria fra capitale e lavoro*, 225-85; Luciano Consolati and Alberto Riva, "Crescita e riposizionamento della grande industria italiana negli anni '80 (1981-1986)," in *Concorrenza e concentrazione nell'industria italiana*, Pier Carlo Padoan, Andrea Pezzoli, and Francesco Silva, eds. (Bologna: Il Mulino: 1989).
26. For more on the transformations of the big Italian companies, see Marino Regini and Charles F Sabel, eds., *Strategie di riaggiustamento industriale* (Bologna: Il Mulino, 1989).
27. Gianfranco Viesti, "Size and Trends of Italian Direct Investment Abroad: A Quantitative Assessment," in *The Italian Multinationals*, Fabrizio Onida and Gianfranco Viesti, eds. (London: Croom Helm, 1988, 32, table 2.3).
28. The low degree of internationalization of Italian enterprises is due to long-standing structural characteristics of the Italian economy, particularly the predominance of small and medium-sized companies, and the country's overall specialization in traditional sectors like leather, textiles, clothing and footwear, wood and furniture, and ceramics, in which the comparative relevance of international location is limited. For more on these issues, see Fabrizio Onida, "Patterns of International Specialization and Technological Competitiveness in the Italian Manufacturing Industry," in *The Italian Multinationals*.
29. In some cases, international subsidiaries produced semiproducts or components that the parent company reimported back to Italy, giving rise to considerable intrafirm trade. Among these groups there were Olivetti, Fiat, and SGS Microelettronica. For more on these issues, see Gianfranco Viesti, "International Strategies of Italian Multinationals," in *The Italian Multinationals*, 79.
30. The same phenomenon of employment decline had already occurred in the first half of the 1970s. In that period, though, this loss of jobs had been more than compensated by a simultaneous reduction of per capita working hours. However, between 1981 and 1985 the reduction of 2.9 percent in total working hours was accompanied by an increase in per capita working hours of 0.6 percent (1.7 percent in 1984-85). See Barca and Magnani, *L'industria fra capitale e lavoro*, 35, for more on this.
31. Barca and Magnani, "Industrial Development and Work Organization," 72.
32. Barca and Magnani, *L'industria fra capitale e lavoro*, 35.
33. Barca and Magnani, *L'industria fra capitale e lavoro*, 37.
34. For more on economic adjustment in Great Britain, see Peter Hall, *Governing the Economy The Politics of State Intervention in Britain and France* (New York: Oxford University Press, 1986, chap. 5).
35. Franco Giavazzi, and Luigi Spaventa, "Italy: The Real Effects of Inflation and Disinflation," *Economic Policy*, no 91 (1989): 133-171. Reprinted in Ministero del Lavoro e della Previdenza Sociale, *Labour and Employment Policies in Italy. Report* 89 (Rome: Istituto Poligrafico e Zecca dello Stato, 45).
36. Giavazzi and Spaventa, "Italy: The Real Effects of Inflation and Disinflation," 53.
37. Giavazzi and Spaventa, "Italy: The Real Effects of Inflation and Disinflation," 46, 51-4.
38. Italy's primary deficit grew by 34 percent of GDP in 1981 alone (Giavazzi and Spaventa, "Italy: The Real Effects of Inflation and Disinflation," 58, table 9). However, in reconstructing the evolution of Italy's economic policies, Giavazzi and Spaventa argue that Italy's public debt does not depend solely on expansionary fiscal policies adopted in the late 1970s-early 1980s, but mainly on a structural increase in public expenditures accomplished in the years 1970-73, and never compensated for in the following years (see pp. 59-61).

39. For more on the so-called divorce between the Bank of Italy and the Italian Treasury, see Franco Cotula, "Financial Innovation and Monetary Control in Italy," *Banca Nazionale del Lavoro Quarterly Review* 37 (1984): 219-655; Tommaso Padoa Schioppa, "Reshaping Monetary Policy," in *Macroeconomics and Finance: Essays in Honor of Franco Modigliani*, Rudiger Dornbusch, Stanley Fischer, and John Bossons, eds. (Cambridge: MIT Press, 1987, 265-86); Gerald Epstein and Juliet Schor, "The Divorce of the Banca d'Italia and the Italian Treasury: A Case Study of Central Bank Independence," in *State, Market, and Social Regulation*, Peter Lange and Marino Regini, eds. (New York: Cambridge University Press, 1989, 147-66); and John Goodman, *Monetary Sovereignty: The Politics of Central Banking in Western Europe* (Ithaca: Cornell University Press, 1992: chap. 5).
40. These and the following figures were taken from Patrizio Bianchi, Sabino Cassese, and Vincent della Sala, "Privatization in Italy: Aims and Constraints," *West European Politics*, 11, no. 1 (January 1988): 87-100. For more on this process of privatization, see Patrizio Bianchi, "The Privatization of Industry: The Alfa Romeo Case," in *Italian Politics : A Review*, vol. 2, Raffaella Y. Nanetti, Robert Leonardi, and Piergiorgio Corbetta, eds. (London: Pinter Publishers, 1988: 109-25); and Giorgio Stefani, "Privatizing Italian State Holdings," *Rivista Internazionale di Scienze Economiche e Commerciali*, 35, nos. 10-11 (1988), 935-950.
41. For more on this, see Bianchi, Cassese, and della Sala," Privatization in Italy," 98.
42. These figures are taken from Bianchi, Cassese, and della Sala," Privatization in Italy," 88.
43. See Bianchi, "The Privatization of Industry" for a comparison of these two cases.
44. On the unions' labor market policies, see Reyneri, "The Italian Labor Market," 129-45
45. In 1991, Law 223 (Article 25) generalized the principle of discretionary hiring for all categories of workers.
46. Caterina Guarna, "The Extent and Nature of Labour Policy in Italy: 1984-88," in *Labour and Employment Policies in Italy Report* '88, Ministero del Lavoro e della Sicurezza Sociale (Rome Istituto Poligrafico e Zecca dello Stato, 1989, 224).
47. Caterina Guarna, "Labour Policy Measures in the 1990s," in *Labour and Employment Policies in Italy Report '90-91*, Ministero del Lavoro e della Sicurezza Sociale (Rome: Istituto Poligrafico e Zecca dello Stato, 1992, 233).
48. Guarna, "Labour Policy Measures in the 1990s," 227.
49. For more on the causes of Italian and European unemployment, see Franco Modigliani, "The European Unemployment Crisis: A Monetarist-Keynesian Approach and Its Implications," Goethe Universitaet, Frankfurt am Main, Working Paper (December 1994).
50. The *Federmeccanica* was founded in 1969 as a reaction to the so-called Pirelli reform (a proposed strategic and organizational reconfiguration of Confidustria aimed at favoring negotiations with labor, and constructing a new, more stable system of industrial relations) For more on the origins of Federmeccanica, see Ada Becchi Collida', "Le Associazioni Imprenditoriali," in *Relazioni Industriali: Manuale per l'analisi dell'esperienza italiana*, Gian Primo Cella and Tiziano Treu, eds. (Bologna: Il Mulino, 1989: 146-7). For more on different models of business representation in Italy, see Antonio M. Chiesi and Alberto Martinelli, "The Representation of Business Interests as a Mechanism of Social Regulation," in *State, Markets and Social Regulation*, 193-203.
51. See Locke, *Remaking the Italian Economy*, for more on these developments.
52. IRI's attempt to promote neo-corporatist-like arrangements within state-owned firms built on IRI's early legacy as an innovative employer and pacesetter in industrial relations but was highly influenced by central European experiences with co-management

as well; see Walter Kendall, "Labor Relations," in *The State as Entrepreneur*, Stuart Holland, ed. (London: Weidenfeld and Nicholson, 1972); Alberto Martinelli, "The Italian Experience: A Historical Perspective," in *State-Owned Enterprises in Western Economies*, Raymond Vernon and Yair Aharoni, eds. (New York: St. Martin's Press, 1981, 94).

53. Locke, *Remaking the Italian Economy.*
54. On restructuring at Fiat, see Richard Locke and Serafino Negrelli, "Il caso Fiat Auto," in *Strategie di riaggiustamento industriale* Marino Regini and Charles Sabel, eds. (Bologna: Il Mulino, 1989); on restructuring at Pirelli, see Serafino Negrelli, *La societa' dentro l'impresa* (Milan: Franco Angeli, 1991, chap. 4.).
55. See Negrelli, *La societa' dentro l'impresa*, chaps 5 and 7 on SIP and Italtel.
56. This took place in 1987 and proved disastrous for industrial relations at Alitalia. In fact, the confederal unions, which had initially agreed to certain concessions, were later bypassed by more militant grassroots structures (COBAS). On this episode, see Serafino Negrelli, "Costi e benefici delle relazioni di lavoro nel trasporto aereo," in *Nuove relazioni industriali per l'Italia in Europa*, Carlo dell'Aringa and Tiziano Treu, eds. (Bologna: Il Mulino, 1992).
57. On these other experiments, see Regini and Sabel, *Strategie di riaggiustamento industriale*; Negrelli, *La societa' dentro l'impresa.*
58. For more on the characteristics of union-management cooperation at Zanussi, see Maurizio Castro, "Orizzonti d'impresa nuova e itinerari di partecipazione: il caso della civitas zanussiana," manuscript, 1995
59. Michael Best, *The New Competition* (Cambridge: Harvard University Press, 1990)
60. Alberto Baldissera, "Alle origini della politica della disuguaglianza nell'Italia degli anni '80: La marcia dei quarantamila," *Quaderni di sociologia*, 31, no 1 (1984), 1-78.
61. Ada Becchi Collida' and Serafino Negrelli, *La transizione nell'industria e nelle relazioni industriali: L'auto e il caso Fiat* (Milan: Franco Angeli, 1986, 167).
62. For more on these developments, see Locke, *Remaking the Italian Economy*, chap 4.
63. Giuseppe Bonazzi, *Il tubo di cristallo Modello giapponese e fabbrica integrata* (Bologna: Il Mulino, 1993).
64. For more on these plants, see Locke and Negrelli, "Il caso Fiat Auto."
65. Bruno Cattero, "Inseguendo l'integrazione Il percorso verso la fabbrica integrata alla Fiat di Termoli," *Politiche del Lavoro*, 17 (1992), 185-208.
66. In particular, coordination of the "appointments" between chassis and various macro-components assembled off-line, for example, doors, proved problematic (Arnaldo Camuffo and Giuseppe Volpato, "Making Manufacturing Lean in the Italian Automobile Industry: The Trajectory of Fiat" Manuscript, Department of Business Economics and Management, University Ca' Foscari, Venice, 13 November 1993.
67. Andrea Paltrinieri, "Fiat: innovazione tecnologica ed emergenza dell'organizzazione reale nel montaggio della Tipo allo stabilimento di Cassino," in *Galassia Auto*, Oscar Marchisio, ed. (Milan: Franco Angeli, 1991).
68. In the second half of the 1980s, Termoli 3, too, began experiencing serious organizational problems. Consumers' demand had become both more sophisticated and diversified. Therefore the plant had to produce three different models of the *Fire* engine for a total of thirty-six versions. This created several problems, particularly in logistics. The production process was obstructed by a series of jams: misfunctioning of the automated inventory systems, low quality, and machine break-downs. Consequently, like at Cassino, at Termoli 3, too, daily production of engines was much lower than expected (Bonazzi, *Il tubo di cristallo*, 82).

69. Paltrinieri, "Fiat."
70. See James Womack, Daniel T. Jones, and Daniel Roos, *The Machine That Changed the World* (New York: Rawson Associates, 1990).
71. Camuffo and Volpato, "Making Manufacturing Lean."
72. Peter R Weitz, "Labor and Politics in a Divided Movement: The Italian Case," *Industrial and Labor Relations Review*, 28, no. 2 (January 1975), 226-42; Golden, *Labor Divided*.
73. Guido Baglioni, ed., *Analisi della CISL*, 2 vol. (Rome: Edizioni Lavoro, 1980).
74. On the ideological heritage of the CISL and on the role of "autonomy," see Tiziano Treu, "La CISL degli anni '50 e le ideologie giuridiche dominanti," in *Materiali per una storia della cultura giuridica*, Giovanni Tarello, ed. (Bologna: Il Mulino, 1973); and Guido Baglioni, *Il sindacato dell'autonomia* (Bari: De Donato, 1975).
75. That the Federazione Unitaria's "EUR-Policy" was to be considered primarily as the unions' response to a major political shift, i.e., the inclusion of the PCI in the governmental majority, was articulated by Luciano Lama, general secretary of the CGIL, in various occasions. See Luciano Lama, *Intervista sul sindacato* (Bari: Laterza, 1976); and Luciano Lama, *Il potere del sindacato* (Rome: Editori Riuniti, 1978, 16).
76. Pierre Carniti, *Remare controcorrente* (Rome: Edizioni Lavoro, 1985).
77. The Solidarity Fund resembled the proposal of risparmio contrattuale, advanced by the CISL in the 1950s. The fund would be financed by 0.5 percent of wage bills.
78. On the importance of a two-pronged union strategy, focused both on the enterprise and the political sphere, see Carniti, *Remare controcorrente*, 186.
79. Marino Regini, "Relazioni industriali e sistema politico: l'evoluzione recente e le prospettive degli anni '80," in *Il teorema sindacale Flessibilita' e competizione nelle relazioni industriali*, Mimmo Carrieri and Paolo Perulli, eds. (Bologna: Il Mulino, 1985).
80. Luigi Di Vezza, "Retribuzioni: andamento e struttura," in Le relazioni sindacali in Italia Rapporto 1985-86, CESOS (Rome: Edizioni Lavoro, 1987).
81. For more details of the agreement, see Golden, *Labor Divided*, 82-84.
82. The predetermination of the scala mobile was based on the assumption that reducing inflation would relaunch employment For a theoretical justification of this assumption, see Ezio Tarantelli, *Economia Politica del Lavoro* (Turin: UTET, 1986). However, between 1983 and 1984, employment decreased 5.1 percent. For more on the results achieved by income policies in 1983-84, see Stefano Patriarca, "Caratteristiche e risultati della politica dei redditi in Italia," in Carrieri and Perulli, eds., *Il teorema sindacale*, 66-69.
83. Golden, *Labor Divided.*
84. Peter Lange, "The End of an Era: The Wage Indexation Referendum of 1985," in *Italian Politics: A Review*, vol. 1, Robert Leonardi and Raffaella Y. Nanetti, eds. (London: Pinter, 1986).
85. Marino Regini, "The Conditions for Political Exchange: How Concertation Emerged and Collapsed in Italy and Great Britain," in *Order and Conflict in Contemporary Capitalism*, John H Goldthorpe, ed., Oxford: Clarendon Press, 1984.
86. On 18 December 1985, the three major confederal unions (CGIL, CISL, and UIL) and the government signed an accord to reform the scala mobile. The new wage escalator was divided in two parts: one (580,000 lire) was fully indexed, while the difference between total remuneration and this fixed part was indexed at 25 percent. This new mechanism had an important symbolic component: it recognized the principle that protection against inflation had to be differentiated across skill categories. For more on this reform, see Stefano Patriarca, *La nuova scala mobile* (Rome: Ediesse,

1986). With the implicit assent of the *Confindustria*, the new scala mobile was also extended to the private sector through a law (Law 38/1986) which limited its duration until 1989.

87. The law on strikes (Law 146/1990) rubber-stamped a preliminary draft elaborated by a union-sponsored commission of experts; see Tiziano Treu, "Strikes in Essential Services in Italy: An Extreme Case of Pluralistic Regulation," *Comparative Labour Law Journal*, 15, no 4 (summer 1994), 469.
88. On the characteristics of the strike in the tertiary sector, where users of services are damaged rather than the bargaining counterparts alone, see Aris Accornero, "La 'terziarizzazione' del conflitto e i suoi effetti," in *Il conflitto industriale in Italia*, Gian Primo Cella and Marino Regini, eds. (Bologna: Il Mulino, 1985).
89. See Lorenzo Bordogna and Gian Carlo Provasi, "La conflittualita'," in Cella and Treu, *Relazioni Industriali.*
90. For more on the content of the law, see Treu, "Strikes in Essential Services in Italy," 461-87
91. For example, the average number of workdays lost for strikes in the transportation sector in 1991-1992 was 80 percent lower than the 1987-90 average.
92. Treu, "Strikes in Essential Services in Italy," 482-83.
93. On the major features of this reform, see Tiziano Treu, "La contrattazione collettiva nel pubblico impiego: ambiti e struttura," *Giornale di diritto del lavoro e relazioni industriali*, no. 61 (1994), 1-52. See also Tiziano Treu, "Verso la riforma del pubblico impiego," *Aggiornamenti Sociali*, 9-10 (1993), 641-52.
94. Lino Codara, "Accorpamenti: una decisione difficile Il faticoso cammino dei nuovi inquadramenti categoriali," *Prospettiva Sindacale*, 63, no. 18 (March.1987).
95. Aris Accornero and Vincenzo Visco, La selva degli stipendi *Politica e sindacato nel settore pubblico* (Bologna: Il Mulino, 1978).
96. Often, new contracts were approved and signed before the expiration of the previous ones.
97. Guido Baglioni and Rinaldo Milani, *La contrattazione collettiva nelle aziende industriali in Italia* (Milan: Franco Angeli, 1990, 37-56).
98. In the metalworkers category, for example, firms as different as Fiat (autos), Olivetti (computers), Ansaldo (engineering), and Ilva (steel) are lumped together.
99. Raul Nacamulli, Giovanni Costa, and Luigi Manzolini, *La razionalita' contrattata* (Bologna: Il Mulino, 1986).
100. Daniela Guidotti, *Strategia generale e azione decentrata: I precontratti dei tessili in Lombardia nel 1983* (Milan: Franco Angeli, 1986).
101. Reyneri, "The Italian Labor Market."
102. Emilio Reyneri and Renata Semenza, "Strategie di adattamento dei lavoratori espulsi dalle grandi imprese," in *Collana Ricerche* (Milan: IRES Lombardia, 1986).
103. Ida Regalia, "Sindacati e governi periferici," Democrazia e Diritto, 5 (1985); Ida Regalia, "Centralization or Decentralization? An Analysis of Organizational Changes in the Italian Trade Union Movement," in *Technical Change, Rationalization, and Industrial Relations*, Otto Jacobi et al. (London: Croom Helm, 1986); Raffaella Y. Nanetti, *Growth and Territorial Policies: The Italian Model of Social Capitalism.* (London: Pinter, 1988).
104. Chiesi and Martinelli, "The Representation of Business Interests"; Mirella Baglioni, *Regions and Business Interests: The Italian Case*, Parma: Istituto di Scienze Economiche, Universita' degli Studi di Parma, 1989.
105. Roberto Lungarella, *La scala mobile* 1945-1981 (Padova: Marsilio Editori: 1981, 41-54).

106. Robert J Flanagan, David W. Soskice, and Lloyd Ulman, *Unionism, Economic Stabilization, and Income Policies: European Experience* (Washington, D.C.: Brookings Institution, 1983). The 1975 accord appeared to provide benefits for both sides. For the unions, it not only protected workers in their already established bastions (primarily large, well-organized plants in the North) but also extended this bargain to workers in smaller, less organized plants. Perhaps more importantly, given the way the scala mobile was calculated, it also provided the union confederations with a means to satisfy the egalitarian demands of their more militant industrial federations while at the same time containing rank-and-file mobilization. Major Italian firms gained as well. Since compensation for price increases would in any event be paid by large firms, because of strong unions within their plants, little was lost by imposing automatic compensation on smaller, potential competitors. Moreover, by removing disputes over price increases, this accord would eliminate a primary source of conflict within large plants, therefore reducing the power of the factory councils as well.
107. See Ida Regalia and Marino Regini "Between Voluntarism and Institutionalization: Industrial Relations and Human Resource Practices in Italy," in *Employment Relations in a Changing World Economy*, Richard Locke, Thomas Kochan, and Michael Piore, eds. (Cambridge: MIT University Press, 1995, 148, table 5.3).
108. See Tarantelli, *Economia Politica del Lavoro.*
109. For more on the 31 July 1992 accord, see Richard Locke, "Eppur si Tocca: The Abolition of the scala mobile," in *Politica in Italia*, vol. 9, Carol Mershon and Gianfranco Pasquino, eds. (Bologna: Il Mulino, 1994).
110. Carol A. Mershon, "The Crisis of the CGIL: Open Divisions in the Twelfth National Congress," in *Italian Politics: A Review*, vol. 7, Stephen Hellman and Gianfranco Pasquino, eds. (New York and London: Pinter, 1992).
111. For more on this episode, see Bruno Trentin, Il *coraggio dell'utopia* (Milan: Rizzoli, 1992: chap 9).
112. See Lucio Baccaro and Richard M. Locke, "The End of Solidarity? The Decline of Egalitarian Wage Policies in Italy and Sweden," *European Journal of Industrial Relations* (Fall 1998).
113. Ettore Santi, "L'evoluzione delle strutture di categoria: Il caso CISL," *Prospettiva sindacale*, 48 (1983).
114. Ida Regalia, "Rappresentanza operaia e sindacato: mutamento di un sistema di relazioni industriali," in Alessandro Pizzorno et al., *Lotte operaie e sindacato.*
115. For an interesting historical reconstruction of the Commissioni Interne, see Guido Baglioni, "L'istituto della Commissione Interna e la questione della rappresentanza dei lavoratori nei luoghi di lavoro," in *Annuario del Centro Studi CISL*, vol. 8 (Florence: Centro Studi CISL, 1969, 35-64).
116. On these changes, see Robert Putnam, *Making Democracy Work* (Princeton, NJ: Princeton University Press, 1992).
117. The CISL, for example, reduced the number of industry federations from thirty-seven to seventeen, while the CGIL also consolidated its thirty-nine industry federations into eighteen For an interesting analysis of the inconsistencies of the organizational reform, see Mario Napoli, "Osservazioni attorno ai rapporti fra relazioni collettive e modelli organizzativi del sindacato." *Prospettiva Sindacale*, 63, no. 18 (March 1987).
118. The most controversial issue was the role of the departments The CGIL wanted them to have only a coordination role between the regional and zonal level. The CISL, on the other hand, wanted them to inherit the same powers and responsibilities as the old provincial unions. For more on these differences, see Rinaldo Scheda, *Il sindacato che*

cambia. Intervista sulla riforma organizzativa a cura di Corrado Perna (Rome: ESI, 1979, in particular pp. 7-48 and 222-29). Interestingly enough, the CISL, which was born as a federation of industry unions, proposed the strengthening of the departmental level, to "consolidate solidarity links above and beyond the industry level." See again Napoli, "Osservazioni attorno ai rapporti tra relazioni collettive e modelli organizzativi del sindacato," 198.

119. On the excessive autonomy of some industry federations and its consequences on the reform strategy, see Pierre Carniti (secretary general of CISL in the early 1980s), *Il sindacato dell'autonomia* (Milan: Coines, 1977, especially pp 37-38).
120. The were essentially three reasons why the introduction of departmental structures was incomplete: i) lack of resources; ii) opposition by the provincial leadership; and iii) absence of analogous state and employers' structures In fact, the departments did not have clear counterparts, both in collective bargaining and at the institutional level. For more on these issues, see Alessandro Castegnaro, "La struttura orizzontale del sindacato," *Prospettiva Sindacale*, 63, no. 18 (March 1987).
121. Andrea Gandini, "La divisione del lavoro nel sindacato," *Prospettiva Sindacale*, 63, no. 18 (March 1987, 118).
122. In fact, in these sectors the merging of industry unions met with tremendous internal resistance. For more on the merging of industry unions, see Codara, "Accorpamenti: una decisione difficile."
123. Ritanna Armeni, *Gli extraconfederali* (Rome: Edizioni Lavoro, 1988).
124. Lorenzo Bordogna, *Pluralismo senza mercato* (Milan: Franco Angeli, 1994: chaps 2-4); Emanuele Lombardi, 1989, *Cobas: una spina nel fianco* (Rome: Sovera Multimedia, 1989).
125. Lorenzo Bordogna, "The Cobas: Fragmentation of Trade Union Representation and Conflict," in *Italian Politics: A Review*, vol. 2, Robert Leonardi and Piergiorgio Corbetta, eds. (London: Pinter, 1989).
126. Lorenzo Bordogna, "Il caso delle Ferrovie," in *Gli attori: I sindacati, le associazioni imprenditoriali, lo Stato*, Giuliano Urbani, ed. (Turin: Giappichelli, 1992).
127. Negrelli "Costi e benefici delle relazioni di lavoro nel trasporto aereo."
128. On the decline of the Consigli dei Delegati, see Ida Regalia, *Eletti e abbandonati Modelli e stili di rappresentanza in fabbrica* (Bologna: Il Mulino, 1984).
129. On the historical evolution of the Factory Councils, see Ida Regalia, "Works Councils in Italy," mimeograph: IRES Lombardia, 1992.
130. On these issues, see Salvatore Vento, "Le rappresentanze sindacali di base," *Prospettiva Sindacale*, 63, no. 18 (March 1987, in particular pp. 72-76), and Locke, *Remaking the Italian Economy.*
131. Between 1969 and 1980, the unionization rate grew from 29.4% to 49.0%.
132. Besides membership decline, two additional changes in union representation took place in the 1980s: 1) a process of substitution between active and retired workers. In fact, retired workers, which constituted 15.1 percent of the total confederal membership in 1980, grew to 38.4 percent in 1990. In 1989, retired workers represented 45.6 percent of the CGIL's total membership. And 2) a process of sectoral redistribution between industrial workers and service workers. While some industry federations like the metalworkers and the textile workers lost about 40 percent of their memberships, other federations in the service and public sectors maintained or even increased their membership slightly. For more on trends in unionization, see Corrado Squarzon, "La sindacalizzazione," in *Le relazioni sindacali in Italia.* Rapporto 1990-91. CESOS (Rome: Edizioni Lavoro, 1992, 83-93).

133. The *Rappresentanze Sindacali Unitarie* (RSU) were formally already introduced in March 1991 by an interorganizational accord among CGIL, CISL, and UIL. However, it was only in July 1993 that the *Confindustria* recognized their role. Consequently, before 1993 their implementation had been virtually nil; see Aris Accornero, "Introduzione. Le rappresentanze sindacali di base nei luoghi di lavoro," in Mimmo Carrieri, *L'incerta rappresentanza*" (Bologna: Il Mulino, 1995, 8).
134. Roberto Mania and Alberto Orioli, *L'accordo di San Tommaso I segreti, la storia, i protagonisti dell'intesa sul costo del lavoro* (Rome: Ediesse, 1993, 62).
135. Based on interviews with several leaders of the COBAS, Rome, March 1995.
136. Carrieri, *L'incerta rappresentanza*, 41-51.
137. Cella, "Criteria of Regulation."
138. Locke, *Remaking the Italian Economy*.
139. Locke, *Remaking the Italian Economy*; Regini and Sabel, *Strategie di riaggiustamento industriale*.
140. For more on the 1991 Congress of the CGIL, see Mershon, "The Crisis of the CGIL." For more on the recent strategic evolution of the CGIL see Trentin, *Il coraggio dell'utopia*, pp. 55-89 and 205-16.
141. Lucio Baccaro and Richard M. Locke. "Public Sector Reform and Union Participation: The Case of the Italian Pension Reform." MIT Sloan School of Management Working Paper, September 1996.
142. *OECD Economic Outlook, 1997* (Paris: OECD, 1997, annex table 25).
143. Marino Regini and Ida Regalia, "Italia anni '90: rinasce la concertazione?" Milan: IRES Lombardia Working Papers, 1996, 19.

Chapter 7

TIGHTROPE

Spanish Unions and Labor Market Segmentation

Lydia Fraile

Introduction

Spanish unions have faced a special set of constraints derived from the two transitions the country underwent over the last twenty years: democratization and economic liberalization linked to EU membership. Concern for protecting and consolidating democracy led unions to restrain wage growth and industrial conflict in a neo-corporatist experiment lasting from 1977 to 1986. But Spanish unions were unable to prevent economic adjustment from exacting high social costs. Unemployment has averaged over 20 percent in the last decade, even though the actual rate may be some two-three points lower when allowing for unaccounted submerged labor.[1] Moreover, the number of temporary workers rose rapidly after the launching of fixed-term labor contracts in 1984, to a staggering 35 percent of the work force in 1995. Both unemployment and temporary work are concentrated among women and especially young people, while the family serves as safety net.[2]

The unions' ability to cope with the challenges posed by the transformation of the Spanish political economy has been severely impaired by legacies of the past. First, political divisions promoted competition and subordination to allied parties. Neo-corporatist concertation was under-

---

Notes for this section begin on page 307.

laid, paradoxically, by fierce competition between the two main labor confederations, the socialist General Workers' Union (UGT) and the communist Workers' Commissions (CCOO), which allowed employers and the state to play one union against the other. Second, the unions' fledgling organizations and low penetration of small firms enabled employers to cut costs through productive decentralization and the unchecked use of informal and temporary labor. In other words, Spanish unions were too weak to foreclose the "low road" of adjustment based on short-term price competitiveness through lower costs and numerical flexibility of labor in response to fluctuations in demand. Third, labor laws inherited from Franco that made dismissals costly and subject to administrative and judicial controls proved to be a double-edged sword. Unions rallied behind these laws as employers demanded liberalization, which meant that job security was only attacked at the fringes, via individual layoffs and temporary contracts. This compromise allowed firms to downsize more easily and gave them more flexibility in deploying labor, while preserving the status of most employees. But it soon backfired, leading to rampant labor market segmentation. The gap between temporary and open-ended contracts in wages and dismissal costs gave firms an incentive to let temporary workers go once their contract time was up, inducing very high turnover rates and the substitution of precarious for permanent labor. For the unions, precarization meant shrinking memberships and a growing lack of credibility as protectors of worker interests in the context of ever expanding secondary labor markets. The intensity of the process arguably threatens unions' internal cohesion – that is, their ability to aggregate demands – and eventual survival.

Labor market segmentation constitutes, therefore, the central issue facing Spanish labor. The main argument presented in this chapter is that since 1988 (with the 14 December general strike marking the turning point), unions have made a series of strategic adaptations which place them in a better position to address this predicament. First and foremost, the two rival confederations CCOO and UGT overcame political divisions by "unity of action." They also abandoned the strategy of macroconcertation that had dominated the period of democratic transition, instead turning to mobilization and decentralized bargaining to increase their contractual power and membership. The confederations distanced themselves from allied parties, most dramatically, the UGT from the governing Socialists. They articulated broad social policy demands, in a direct political appeal that extended to those excluded from core employment (i.e., youth, the unemployed, pensioners). Finally, they geared political exchange and bargaining strategies to stem the tide of precarization.

A possible breakthrough may have been reached recently with the 1997 Interconfederal Accords for Employment Stability and over Collective Bargaining. In these accords, the social partners tried to build a better articulated bargaining system and to alter the perverse structure of incentives facing firms, by promoting a new type of permanent labor contract with lower dismissal costs while setting some curbs on temporary contracting. These responses have brought unions a measure of recovery. They have regained "voice" in the political arena and won modest increases in organizational and institutional resources, even though their future remains uncertain.

The Spanish unions' journey since 1988 evokes the image of a tightrope walker. Dependent on a shrinking core of labor market "insiders" and conscious of the abyss of deregulation beneath, they set out in search of a more viable basis. Politics has served as balancing pole, providing a language of solidarity beyond the often conflicting interests of the unemployed and temporary workers and those of permanent employees, as well as opportunities to compensate, through state action, their weak standing in workplaces. As we will see, UGT and CCOO have inched and stumbled their way toward a deal that accepts greater flexibility for insiders in exchange for greater employment stability and training prospects for a majority of workers. It is difficult to predict whether employers and the conservative government will stick to this deal or pursue further deregulation and unilateralism in EMU. Moreover, unions' capacity to deliver consensus could falter, especially if there are no tangible results in abating precarization. The tightrope walk is risky, but it may lead to union revitalization.

Spanish Unions Then and Now

Spanish unions had a lot of catching up to do. When they were legalized in 1977, the economic climate was not favorable to their consolidation. They have struggled to build resources long enjoyed by others, such as industry-wide bargaining and union structures, participation in social security, unemployment and training systems. Neo-corporatist concertation advanced some of these goals by producing a supportive legal framework, although within limits, since participation often involved consultative, non-decision-making roles. The demise of neo-corporatism in the late 1980s led unions to focus more on collective bargaining and organization and less on the state. "Unity of action" was also key to this shift, allowing more congruent bargaining stands and gradual convergence in organizational models. Paradoxically, the climate of political crisis surrounding the fall of the Socialists and the narrow conservative victory in 1996 led to a revival of peak-level concertation. The unions negotiated pension reform with the Aznar government and several major pacts with employers but not an incomes policy, and without returning to neo-corporatist macroregulation of the economy.

CCOO emerged as the largest union force at the end of the dictatorship. It was a loose movement with a plurality of Christian and leftist groups dominated by the communists, since the PCE had decided in the 1960s to infiltrate the state-controlled union apparatus and run candidates in workscouncil elections. It became, through strike action, a major actor in the transition pushing democratization forward. UGT had been – together with the anarchist National Labor Confederation (CNT) – a mass union organization at the time of the civil war, but its decision to boycott the official unions left it with virtually no presence in Franco's Spain. After 1977, however, UGT grew strongly, banking on traditional worker identities and the electoral ascendancy of the PSOE, with whom it had close ties. It also benefitted from support from the Suárez government, the German unions, and the employers' CEOE, all interested in breaking communist hegemony over the labor movement. By 1982 UGT had surpassed CCOO in workscouncil elections, although at the price of fierce interunion competition. The USO, a third confederation with a social-Christian orientation, which also played a role in the labor movement under Franco, retained only a very small presence after it split in 1979 to join UGT. There are also three regional unions: the nationalist ELA and LAB, which hold a majority in the Basque country, and a Galician union (CIG). Finally, a number of independent unions organize professionals, such as doctors, nurses, pilots, and train engineers, and play a significant role in the public sector.

Union membership today is low, at about 15 percent of wage earners.[3] Lack of consistent data for early years makes it difficult to track figures over time, but the main trends are clear: unionization was initially high, with over 50 percent of industrial workers in 1978, but declined sharply in 1979-81 and only began to pick up slowly after 1986.[4] The initial enthusiasm can be attributed to the highly politicized atmosphere of the democratic transition and the prominent opposition role played by the union movement, then at the crest of a strike wave equivalent in many ways to the Italian "Hot Autumn." But unionization was more a measure of the political following of unions than of a stable dues-paying membership, and it waned rapidly under the impact of unemployment. Scholars also point to the lack of selective incentives to benefit members over nonmembers, either in collective bargaining or in providing unemployment benefits or training.

Membership increases since the late 1980s have been concentrated in the service sector, particularly among public employees. This reflects the fact that public-sector employment grew significantly in the 1980s as Spain caught up with European welfare spending levels and constructed a regional tier of government. Both unions were able to expand to include service workers and women: 54.7 percent and 25 percent of total membership for UGT and 51.2 percent and 22 percent for CCOO.[5] UGT's presence is also somewhat higher among private-sector technicians, cadre, and private-sector unskilled workers. This is consistent with UGT's image as a more moderate, pact-prone union that is more palatable to private-sector employers. CCOO's militant image is more attractive to public-sector technicians, cadre, and blue-collar workers in the state-enterprise sector, high-unionization groups where competition from independent, corporative unions is stiff. Such differences in the occupational profile of the two main confederations are, however, relatively small.[6]

Several factors help compensate for low union density. Workplace elections are the primary source of unions' legitimation. Elections for works councils (in firms with more than fifty workers) and staff delegates (in firms with less than fifty and more than six workers) involve large numbers – 4.7 million workers in 1990. Their results are aggregated to determine which unions are empowered to conduct collective bargaining at higher levels and to grant "most representative union" status, which carries public funding and institutional privileges for unions winning at least 10 percent of the vote (or 15 percent within a certain region). UGT and CCOO have steadily increased their joint share of elected representatives to nearly 80 percent in the 1990 elections. It then went down seven points in 1995 due to decline of the UGT, shattered by the bankruptcy of its housing-cooperative venture. However, in smaller firms candidates often run on CCOO and UGT tickets when unions enlist them, even though they may not be union members and maintain only tenuous links to the union after their election. Next, Spanish unions have maintained a relatively high capacity to mobilize. The strike rate has been declining since the 1980s, but Spain still ranks at the top end of the EU strike league, including three large general strikes over the past decade. According to Labor Ministry data, a quarter of strikes were linked to collective bargaining in 1986-1995, 20 percent were caused by issues such as restructuring and redundancies, and 56 percent responded to broader issues. Strikes occur at similar levels in the service and industrial sectors.

Thirdly, Spain has broad collective bargaining coverage, largely due to extension of agreements through the *erga omnes* principle, plus a French-like tradition of state interventionism reflected in labor law and courts. Thus collective bargaining covered 7.6 million workers in 1995: 85 percent of all wage earners (most public-sector employees are excluded from collective bargaining). But whether firms actually comply with collective agreements or state regulations varies considerably according to firm size and to regional and sector differences in union presence. Despite the centralization promoted by neo-corporatist pacts, Spain's underlying bargaining structures remained highly dispersed, with multiple overlapping levels and shallow content. Only in recent years have collective agreements begun to move beyond wages and worktime to wider issues.

The Political Economy: Transition to Democracy to EMU

Democratization after Franco was the product of a series of transactions between reforming elites within the regime and opposition parties. The first democratic election was in 1977 with Suárez heading a minority center government. Spain was in the midst of economic crisis and also faced Basque terrorism and the risk of authoritarian involution. These difficulties nourished a politics of party compromise and social concertation to ensure smooth transition. Economically, this involved a gradual approach to adjustment out of fear that labor unrest might destabilize democracy. It also brought state restructuring to allow regional autonomy. This "politics of consensus" began with the Moncloa Pacts, extended throughout 1978, during the drafting of a new constitution, to the Worker's Statute of 1979. The PCE, which had embraced Euro-communism, played a key role in this, going beyond its relatively low electoral strength, endowed by its ability to demobilize society through ties to CCOO.

The oil crises and the opening of the economy severely impacted Spain's industrial base, which was largely concentrated in mature sectors facing overcapacity and NIC competition. An explosion of labor militancy during the late Franco years compounded external shocks to double unit labor costs in manufacturing from 1973 to 1977.[7] Political uncertainty added to these problems, discouraged investment, and postponed adjustment policies. Over half a million manufacturing jobs were lost in 1976-1990, plus another 1.3 million jobs lost in agriculture.[8] GDP per capita was nearly 78 percent of the EU average in 1975; it dropped eight points by the mid-1980s and then recovered gradually to 76 percent of the EU average in 1996.[9]

The transfer of power to González's Socialist party in 1982 marked the end of political transition. Close ties to labor and a comfortable majority allowed the Socialist government to more decisively pursue the policy of macroeconomic stabilization and structural reforms initiated under Suárez. Union support for these policies broke down after 1985, however, in the face of persistently high unemployment and a steep growth in temporary jobs. Maastricht led to further conflict with unions, as the Socialists imposed cuts in social spending and more flexible labor rules. The tasks of qualifying for EMU fell to Aznar's conservative government whose narrow electoral margin forced it to seek some consensus from unions as well as from Basque and Catalan nationalists.

State Policies

After the first democratic elections, governments proceeded to stabilize the economy through devaluation, monetary restraint, and a reduction of the growth rate of nominal wages to contain inflation. The 1977 Moncloa Pacts, signed by all parties in parliament, changed the basis for calculating wage increases from past to expected inflation, and set a single increase band across the economy. This centralized wage policy was continued until 1986. Moncloa also contained the broad lines of economic policy and the structural reforms to follow: fiscal reform, welfare state expansion, financial liberalization, labor market flexibility, and industrial restructuring.[10] Suárez succeeded in controlling inflation and raising revenues by modernizing the tax system (with a new tax on wealth and a progressive reform of the income tax, which made filing standard practice for the first time). But labor costs still grew too fast, due in part to increased payroll taxes. Unemployment also rose to 16.6 percent, and by 1982 the public deficit had reached 5.5 percent of GDP.

González's policies were tougher in preparation for EU membership. They included very high interest rates, financial liberalization, increased fiscal pressure, and curbs on deficit spending, including caps on public-sector wages and a restrictive pension reform in 1985. Although the PSOE's pre-electoral promise to create 800,000 jobs suggested a more expansionary position, the government soon abandoned its promise to concentrate on improving competitiveness. The Socialist government was also able to extract more concessions from labor. Social pacts in 1983-86 brought no real wage increases and launched temporary contracts in 1984 (part of the AES pact). There was also an industrial restructuring program leading to the dismissal of more than one quarter of those employed in the steel, shipbuilding, and textile industries, and promoting streamlining and privatization in state enterprises.[11] On the other hand, social protection policies expanded considerably and universal entitlement was introduced. Basic pensions were added to supplement the contributory system and a national health system replaced previous corporative schemes. Schooling was made compulsory until age sixteen and vocational education was expanded. Social spending grew from 9.9 percent of GDP in 1975 to 17.8 percent at the end of the 1980s.[12] However, unemployment climbed to 21.7 percent in 1985, and even though it declined during 1986-1990, its lowest point was only 16 percent in 1990. From 1985-93 the economy actually created jobs at a higher rate than the EU average, but this was outpaced by growth in the labor force, due primarily to the rapid incorporation of women.

Spain became a full member of the EU in 1986 and joined the ERM in 1989. Integration had two main effects: the balance of trade deteriorated, and there was a large inflow of foreign investment. The impact of financial assistance through EU structural funds was modest in contrast – net EU transfers amounted to 0.3 percent of GDP in 1990 and to around 1 percent of GDP since 1996.[13] Imports grew faster than exports (at an annual average rate of 15.2 percent in real terms vs. 3.9 percent for exports between 1986 and 1990), and the share of the domestic market held by Spanish manufactures declined.[14] Since 1993, the trade deficit has been contained (from 5.9 percent of GDP in 1990 to 2.5 percent in 1997) following devaluation and strong exports (which grew 13.3 percent in real terms in 1997), while tourism has helped balance the current account.[15] There was a sharp increase in net capital inflows, which reached 4 percent of GDP in 1990. The lion's share went to direct investment in the financial sector and industry (mostly buyouts or expansion of existing firms), and came from EU countries. Foreign multinationals came to control about 50 percent of industrial capacity by 1988, the practical totality of key sectors such as automobiles (including the first tier of suppliers) and chemicals.[16] Direct investment slowed down in the 1990s as Eastern Europe appeared as alternative location, but Spain remained a large net recipient of financial capital, amounting to 3.5 percent of GDP in 1996.[17] In 1997, this was partly offset by the growing expansion of Spanish firms abroad, mostly in Latin America. Economic integration helped modernize Spanish industry but made it more dependent on multinational corporations.[18] Technological dependency persists despite state efforts to promote research and development spending, which stood at 0.9 percent of GDP in 1992, as against 2.3 percent for the average of Germany, France, the U.K. and Italy.[19]

Governments sought wage restraint through concertation. Neo-corporatist pacts brought a sharp fall in industrial conflict and a real wage moderation process. Collective bargaining stayed within the parameters of the pacts, although actual earnings were somewhat higher due to wage drift.[20] Wage growth augmented after the breakdown of concertation: non-farm business-sector hourly wages grew by 2 percent per year in 1987-93, despite rising unemployment since 1991.[21] Most of the burden of inflation control fell now on monetary policy, which was tied to a policy of exchange-rate stability once Spain joined the ERM in 1989. But inflation took a long time to converge towards average EU levels, while high interest rates attracted a large inflow of foreign capital, resulting in an overvalued peseta and a loss of competitiveness.[22]

Preparing for EMU took place in the midst of a sharp recession, with unemployment rising to 22.7 percent and the public deficit to 6.2 percent in 1993. In 1991 Spain had fulfilled only one of the Maastricht criteria, that for public debt. Inflation had rebounded to 5.5 percent, largely driven by price increases in the nonexposed service sector, and interest rates were 12.4 percent. González's Convergence Plan focused on the reduction of the budget deficit and labor market reform. In 1994, changes in labor law removed restrictions on mobility, decentralized bargaining, expanded temporary contracting, and made dismissals easier. These changes were major steps in a protracted liberalization process, in which the state has responded to the unions' defense of job security safeguards by creating countervailing mechanisms in the form of individual layoffs and temporary contracts.[23]

Individual dismissals where termination occurs by agreement between worker and firm at the state mediation service, introduced in 1977, were expanded in 1994 to include groups of workers below certain thresholds. They carry a minimum severance pay of twenty days per year of seniority to a maximum of twelvemonths, the same as for collective dismissals. Employers prefer this approach, even if it tends to be more expensive, because it allows faster layoffs without the need for justification to the labor authority and consultation with the works council. In case of disagreement, the worker may challenge the decision before the labor courts. If the court rules the dismissal unjustified, severance pay goes up to forty five days per year of seniority to a maximum of forty two months, which is very high in comparative terms. The minimum cost of fair dismissals (12 months of salary after 20 years) is also higher than the EU average but lower than Italy's and more in line with other Southern countries.[24] Severance pay tends to be more generous in large firms where workers have more bargaining power (6.1 million pesetas, including early retirement, according to the Economy Ministry bargaining survey for 1993). At the other end, the Wage Guarantee Fund picks up 40 percent of the tab for small firms under twenty five workers.

Fixed-term contracts were launched in 1984, after timid steps in 1977 and 1981. They were aimed to maximize job creation and lower barriers to entry for youth. It was also expected that they would help resurface submerged labor. A menu of fourteen contracts was offered, including subsidized youth contracts and a blanket "employment promotion contract" of three years maximum and twelve days per year of seniority severance pay. This was most widely used until the 1990s, when shorter contracts "for determined work or service" and "for eventualities of production" took its place. In 1994, a new flexible part-time contract and a youth "apprenticeship" contract with weak training provisions, below-minimum wage pay, and no unemployment or sick-pay benefits were added.

Labor market policy has been part of the state's thrust to lower labor costs by promoting temporary contracts and offering subsidies for new hires that account for a very high share, in comparative terms, of active labor market policies[25]. Training programs have nonetheless expanded considerably since 1985, cofinanced by EU structural funds. Spain's lagging professional training system was overhauled in 1993 when a dual system alternating school and workplace training was introduced. Vocational training courses were targeted to the unemployed, while a further training system for active workers was set up through concertation. Other changes aimed at improving the match between skills and jobs and developing a national certification system, but implementation has been slow. There has been an effort to prioritize "active" policies over income maintenance programs, particularly since unemployment benefits were curtailed in 1992.

The ERM crisis in 1992-93 led to three devaluations of the peseta which underpinned recovery since 1994 through growing exports. The favorable economic context helped achieve Maastricht targets. Fiscal consolidation (largely through public-sector wage freezes and attrition, and a reduction of public investment) brought the budget deficit down to an estimated 3 percent of GDP in 1997. Inflation also decreased below 2 percent through much of 1997 due to several factors in addition to fiscal restrain including wage moderation and the effect of liberalization measures in certain sectors.[26] Finally, the prospect of joining EMU from the outset spurred a sharp reduction in interest rates, stimulating growth and employment creation.

Spanish Employers and the Attractions of the "Low Road"

The Spanish Confederation of Employer Organizations (CEOE) was established in 1977, drawing on preexisting organizations both within and parallel to the Franco-era vertical syndicates. Firm membership was 60 percent of total employment in 1977, rising to 95 percent by 1987.[27] The CEOE serves both the functions of employer and trade association, somewhat overlapping with the Chambers of Commerce and Industry. It includes the Spanish Confederation of Small- and Medium-Sized Firms (CEPYME). No independent organizations exist, as in Italy, for smaller firms, and the representativeness of provincial associations is often low.

In 1979, the CEOE adopted a strategy of social concertation, but opted for a "weak" form of neo-corporatism. It favored bilateral agreements between business and labor and resisted implementing tripartite agreements that involved broader social policy commitments by the state.[28] It developed a pattern of organization with weak internal mechanisms of coordination and control. Finally, it sought to promote interunion competition. With the ABI pact, the CEOE effectively pitted the UGT, which was at the time a minority union, against CCOO. The CEOE advocated a bilateral model of industrial relations, reducing state intervention, and undoing the rigidities inherited from the dictatorship, especially in regards to dismissals. An interesting perspective on this issue is provided by Fina, Meixide, and Toharia, who argue that the labor market under Franco was more flexible than has usually been assumed because of widespread temporary work and ample possibilities for disciplinary dismissals in the absence of union freedoms. As both these sources of flexibility eroded in the late Franco years, the demand for "free dismissals" emerged not only from the economic imperative of adjustment, but also as a political drive by employers to restore their shopfloor authority.[29] The CEOE has continued to champion the elimination of administrative controls over dismissals while pushing for greater flexibility, reduced payroll taxes, and a differentiated legal framework for small firms.

By the mid 1980s, the CEOE had lost interest in macro concertation and took an ambivalent stand toward collective bargaining. While it officially continued to favor the goal of rationalizing the bargaining structure through national-sector agreements, it showed an increasing preference for decentralized bargaining. On one key occasion, in the context of a harsh conflict with the Socialist government over the 1990 law on union monitoring of labor contracts, it even called into question the *erga omnes* principle. One indicator of bargaining decentralization is the increase in firm-level agreements since 1977, although the "leaning" of firms has caused the share of the workforce covered by company-level bargaining to remain stable. Many employers tackle new bargaining issues through informal firm-level accords and individual negotiation.

These collective employer strategies must be set against the background of two distinct phases in firm-level restructuring patterns. The first phase covered the recession from 1978 to 1985 and was characterized by cost cutting through downsizing and subcontracting to small firms, plus an expanding submerged economy. The combined impact of the oil crises and the opening of the economy was hard on Spanish firms, which also faced a wage explosion in the late 1970s, and the advent of free unions and a modern taxation system. This explains the externalization of production to small nonunionized firms and the use of informal labor. Manufacturing jobs declined 19.5 percent in 1975-83. Downsizing large firms received public subsidies while most smaller firms went through unregulated or "wild" restructuring, which, in sectors such as footwear, included false bankruptcies and the conversion of firms into commercial agents for submerged workshops and home workers.[30] Productive decentralization is reflected in the growth of small undertakings. The number of small firms (under fifty workers) increased from 95.1 percent in 1978 to 97.6 percent in 1985; their share of employment rose from 38.4 percent to 48.5 percent. The trend continued in the late 1980s. Small firms (under fifty workers) accounted for 98.1 percent of firms and 52.2 percent of total employment in 1989.[31] The second restructuring phase began with economic recovery in the late part of the 1980s. More offensive, it was characterized by an important investment in equipment and the introduction of new technologies, as well as by the use of temporary labor contracts.

These temporary contracts constitute the dominant restructuring strategy of small firms, where almost 50 percent of staff is temporary.[32] Loyalty is sought by recruitment through family and other "trust networks" (a practice that is also prevalent among large firms, who hire relatives of their employees). The insecurity of many workers in small firms and their proximity to the submerged economy has reinforced traditional paternalist and individualized employment relations.[33] Much flexibility exists in small firms, both external and in the deployment of labor through overtime, vacations, use of part-time work, and rotation between jobs, particularly among temporary workers. Sector agreements have little relevance and wages depend more on the competitive situation of the firm. On the other hand, precarization has disrupted the traditional process of skill formation and promotion in many small firms; there is a loss of craftsmanship[34] which formal training has not replaced, and which may constrain the firms' capacity to move into higher quality and value-added market segments.

The restructuring strategies of large firms have a more hybrid and experimental character, particularly regarding organizational changes and the management of labor.[35] Temporary work has been used more intensely by the service sector than by industry (although this situation has changed recently with the legalization of temp agencies). Large industrial firms continued to shed labor during the economic recovery, "investing" in early retirement and voluntary redundancy schemes to reduce their aging workforce. They began to hire young workers by the end of the 1980s, usually under temporary contracts. Precarization was just one part of the process, however. The professionalization and technical progress in firms linked to the internationalization of the economy has resulted in a strong growth in highly skilled jobs.[36] Large firms have pursued increased individualization of employment relations, which grow more intense as one moves higher in the company hierarchy. Individualization includes managerial staff formally excluded from collective bargaining (4 percent in 1990) plus individual and small-group negotiation over specific items (e.g., the workday, training, promotions, and wage complements). In contrast, firms have tended not to expand the prerogatives of works councils beyond legal minima and to give out information quite sparingly on issues such as technological innovation and new investments.[37]

Large firms tend to segment their workforce into differentiated internal labor markets for technicians and cadres, and for stable and contingent labor. Temporary workers often serve as flexibility buffers, covering peaks in production and undesirable work shifts. Not all firms use temporary contracts in the same way, however. Where technology investment has been more intense, hiring young workers with higher educational credentials (e.g., FP2 for production workers) may lead to career paths characterized by mobility and polyvalence, continuous training, and the professionalization of promotion criteria. The banking industry is a case of "human-resource management" (HRM) along these lines.[38] Temporary contracts have been used to recruit college graduates for entry-level positions, often under individual agreements that allow for flexible worktime and mobility outside the parameters of collective bargaining. Banks use temporary contracts as a screening mechanism, expanding the trial period to two-three years (the maximum duration of fixed-term contracts), after which about 50 percent become permanent. Training and mobility continue afterwards with wage incentives linked to individual performance and/or business targets. There is strong differentiation in HRM practices between "new" and "old" staff, particularly in regards to those employees not promoted to commercial technicians and cadre categories. The use of temp agencies to perform data entry and other unskilled tasks is one more dimension of segmentation in the banking industry.

Large firms have also decentralized internally, giving product units more autonomy and externalizing production and services (e.g., cleaning, maintenance, security). Data on out- and subcontracting from the Ministry of Economy showed a 15 percent increase in 1991. And 33.5 percent of large firms had introduced product or process innovations during 1991, 58. 6 percent of them with union agreement. The introduction of new technology and equipment is followed by changes in work organization, chiefly by worktime flexibility (e.g., additional shifts, work on weekends, vacations, and, more recently, annualization). In the 1990s multinationals, particularly those in the auto industry, have undertaken changes in work organization such as just-in-time (JIT), total quality management (TQM), quality circles, and work groups. None of the automakers applies "lean production" as a whole, but they have introduced some of its components incrementally[39]. The pace of implementation and difficulties differ from firm to firm. The main problem for U.S. automakers stems from their own corporate culture, still anchored in Taylorism; whereas European and Japanese automakers are hindered by older plants with older and less educated workforces. All automakers are adopting JIT techniques, with GM the most advanced. The new SEAT-VW plant in Martorell is also operating under JIT and has built, like GM, a suppliers' park in its proximity, even though more than half the parts come from Germany. Kan-ban has been introduced in most firms, together with the assumption of quality control functions by production workers. Autonomous work groups have operated in Renault since the mid 1980s; they also function in SEAT-Martorell and have been introduced at Ford and GM. Quality circles were adopted by almost all automakers in the 1980s and still operate in GM and Citroën, but had a short life elsewhere. Changes in work have incorporated quality control, small maintenance, machine programming, and retooling functions, as well as greater job rotation. However, these new functions coexist in most firms with the old occupational classifications and Taylorist incentive systems.

Generally speaking, flexibility has been more quantitative and external, than qualitative and internal. Despite union directives, overtime continues to be widespread. Investment in training – as a proxy for the kind of flexibility pursued by firms – has been low, involving 43 percent of workers in 1990 at a cost of 1 percent of the gross wage mass according to the Ministry of Economy large-firm bargaining survey. In contrast, redundancy payments equalled 1.84 percent of the gross wage mass for the same year. Training remains a critical issue given the large educational deficit among older generations of workers, a constraint on work reorganization inhibiting functional mobility and multiskilling. The young are far better educated, but their potential may well go to waste if precarization is not checked. Temporary contracts gave firms flexibility and contributed to lower labor costs, especially in personal services and low skilled industrial jobs.[40] But they also had perverse effects like very high turnover with detrimental consequences for skill formation and worker commitment. This tends to reinforce a "low road" option over moving toward the "high road," where firms compete more on the basis of quality and flexible specialization. Another perverse effect is segmentation between "insiders" and"outsiders" within firms. To the extent that temporary workers provide a "buffer" that insulates permanent workers from layoffs, this may lead the latter to bargain for higher wages.[41] Finally, there were indications in the early 1990s that the high prevalence of contingent work was beginning to have negative effects in the form of intensified employment loss during economic downturns, large unemployment insurance deficits (not to mention the long-term impact on social security), and an inhibiting effect on domestic consumption. It looked as if the Spanish economy was locking itself into a low skill, low employment equilibrium trap that might become less and less compatible with European levels of welfare protection.

Union Strategies

Unions' political strategies remain primary in Spain, informing other areas. This was true in the early years when union behavior was conditioned by political transition and the establishment of a new institutional framework. It continued after the unions abandoned neo-corporatist concertation and sought to exert greater weight in the market arena. This primacy of politics reflects the weakness of collective bargaining and the importance of state regulation in Spanish industrial relations. At the same time, unions have taken advantage of a political context that provided opportunities for political exchange at the national, and increasingly, the regional level.

There have been two distinct phases in the political strategies of UGT and CCOO. The first phase (1977-86) comprised the emergence and gradual unravelling of neo-corporatist concertation. The second phase (1988-1994) began with the general strike of 14 December 1988 when unions took a stand against the Socialist government's economic policy, thereby becoming the main source of opposition to the then hegemonic PSOE. It ended with another general strike on 27 January 1994, which showed unions on the defensive and unable to stop a reform of labor law that substantially flexibilized employment relations. This reform triggered a transition with some resurgence of concertation, highlighted by the 1997 peak-level accords on employment stability and bargaining reorganization.

The Rise and Fall of Macroconcertation

Neo-corporatist pacts were part of the broader political agreements of the democratic transition. Their cornerstone was a wage moderation policy that brought down inflation and industrial conflict at a time of high political uncertainty. The Moncloa Pacts were signed by the main political parties and endorsed by unions in 1977. They embodied Suárez's effort to build consensus over a program of economic stabilization and structural reforms that was carried further by González after 1982. The desired consensus involved policy compromises and compensations for labor restraint, including progressive tax reform, expansion of welfare spending, a labor market policy that preserved most restrictions on dismissals, and a program for restructuring mature industries. Preserving democracy was a prime cause of union participation, one that surfaced again in the National Employment Agreement (ANE), which followed shortly after a coup attempt in 1981.The Moncloa Pacts changed the basis for calculating wage increases from past to expected inflation and set a single economy-wide increase band. The same wage formula was followed by later pacts.

Concertation stumbled in 1979, partly because the unions believed that the state was not living up to promises. Electoral politics was also highly significant. CCOO was pushing for a broad three-year pact to include political parties, impyling extension of "consensus politics" and a continued key role for the PCE. The UGT, supporting PSOE prospects in a new election, favored a narrower tripartite pact. The government issued a wage norm by decree and industrial conflict soared when the unions sought to break it. At this moment the employers' CEOE made its strategic move, cutting a separate deal with UGT on the basic contours of the new framework for industrial relations to be developed by the 1980 Worker Statute (WS). UGT and CEOE signed the Interconfederal Basic Agreement (ABI) and the Interconfederal Frame Agreement (AMI), setting a wage norm for 1980-81. These accords introduced the concept of "representative" and "most representative" unions, and established minimum representation requirements for bargaining legitimation, stressing the need to rationalize the collective bargaining structure toward greater concentration and articulation. They also introduced union sections, using UGT's preferred form of workplace representation, which the statute superimposed on the existing works councils favored by CCOO.

UGT embraced concertation as a strategy for building up union organizational power through the adoption of a supportive legal framework and the extension of centralized bargaining. It took the position that economic crisis and growing unemployment required wage restraint and cooperation in firm restructuring[42]. By signing the ABI-AMI, UGT also gained political recognition from employers, who promoted it as a moderate alternative to CCOO. Through this, UGT sought to appeal to less militant workers and become the hegemonic force in the labor movement, following the social-democratic pattern. Concertation was thus part of fierce competition among unions, as UGT and CCOO strived to fill essentially the same occupational space in the aftermath of legalization. Paradoxically, CCOO's strength in the labor movement under Franco made it more difficult for it to adapt to the new situation.[43] Organizationally, it clung to the model of union as social movement once the conditions that had sustained it (i.e., clandestinity and the popular struggle for democracy) ceased to exist. CCOO's active support of Moncloa provoked strong internal dissent and the emergence of a large antipact minority, and this, together with the PCE's push for restraint, compromised its ability to develop a coherent strategy. At the same time, unionists encountered a more moderate mood among workers facing economic crisis and widespread strike failure. This helped persuade activists and leaders to support peak-level pacts even after they had lost enthusiasm for the strategy.[44] CCOO signed the next two – the ANE, in the aftermath of the 1981 coup attempt, and the Interconfederal Agreement (AI), the first under a Socialist administration. Another important item on the pacts' agenda was work-sharing policies: worktime reduction, early retirement, curbs on moonlighting and overtime.[45] These measures, to be carried through collective bargaining and/or state action – the Socialist government legislated the forty-hour week in 1983 – were unevenly implemented (e.g. overtime controls), and brought disappointing results in fighting unemployment.

Concertation began unravelling with the last pact, the Economic and Social Agreement (AES) of 1985-86. CCOO refused to sign because it launched temporary contracts and contained an ambiguous statement on adapting labor law to EU norms. Employers, who insisted that this clause promise to eliminate the administrative authorization required for collective dismissals, soon distanced themselves from the accord. Finally, UGT felt shortchanged by the Socialist government's failure to expand unemployment coverage as agreed, and by the enactment in 1985 of a social security reform that imposed cuts in pensions. Nicolás Redondo, UGT general secretary, voted against the law in Congress before resigning his seat in 1987. There were joint union demonstrations against the pension law, but UGT did not support CCOO's call for a general strike, which had a limited impact.

These conflicts reflected the changing calculations of actors. Political stability and a recovering economy made the government less interested in payoffs for union consensus that would add to the budget deficit. Wage restraint also became less critical for employers, who pushed instead for further deregulation and flexibility. The unions found themselves in a weak position, with very low membership, dependent on state funding, and, although present in large- and medium-sized firms, with low contractual power.[46] As the costs of exercizing restraint in terms of an internal crisis of representation began to outweigh the benefits, they came to reassess the value of concertation.[47] This was especially true for UGT, who alone bore the cost of legitimizing the industrial reconversion program which brought large-scale redundancies in core union constituencies and triggered militant conflicts in the steel and shipbuilding industries. Other signs of trouble came from the 1986 works council elections in which UGT lost to CCOO in large public-sector firms, and in 1987-88 when teachers and bank workers rejected settlements negotiated by UGT. The breakup of centralized wage negotiations in 1987, when UGT demanded a higher wage increment reflecting productivity increases, must thus be understood as an attempt to dispel the image of caving in too much to employer and government demands.

The 1988 General Strike and the Priority Union Proposal

The dramatic divorce between the Socialist government and UGT[48] in the late 1980s marked a major shift in union political strategies. In essence, UGT did not expect PSOE to continue the same restrictive macroeconomic policies once the economy recovered (annual GDP growth was above 4 percent in 1986-90). Moreover, the use of temporary contracts soon became alarming. Atypical work rose to 20 percent of the labor force by 1989, more than double the EU average. Given high unemployment (19 percent) and the concentration of union membership in declining industries, the rapid expansion of precarious work constituted a time bomb for the unions, threatening their organizational future. As the other actors placed less value on social pacts, the unions resorted to mobilization to alter the balance of forces.[49]

With the 1988 general strike, UGT and CCOO redefined their strategy. The first new axis was "unity of action" along with its prerequisite: autonomy from political parties. The second was a recourse to politics. Unions appealed to constituencies beyond their membership base (e.g., pensioners and temporary workers) with universal demands for welfare protection and employment stability. In their campaign for a "social turn" they denounced the high unemployment and precariousness that coexisted with economic recovery in the 1980s, while pointing to other indicators of inequality such as the declining share of wages in national income, the rising tax burden on wages in contrast to extensive fraud in other incomes, and the fact that Spain was next to the bottom of EC welfare spending, followed only by Portugal. The third axis was the abandonment of macroconcertation. The unions shifted their attention from the peak level to the shopfloor to increase recruitment and contractual power vis-a-vis employers and expand collective bargaining to issues of employment, training, and work organization. This was consistent with the decentralization of bargaining from the confederation to the industry level and with organizational steps to boost the sectoral federations. These principles were further developed into the Priority Union Proposal (PSP), a joint platform to guide negotiations in the aftermath of the strike which set the union agenda for the 1990s. The PSP articulated a package of demands around four themes: employment, welfare, income redistribution, and participatory rights. A fifth theme, industrial policy, was added later. Employment demands included worktime reduction toward the thirty five-hour week, union monitoring of hiring contracts, and a tightening of temporary contracts to restore the causal link between fixed-term contracts and the temporary nature of the job. Expanded training, including further training/retraining with social partner participation in the planning and management of training programs was also high on the list.

The strike was a big success, paralyzing the country. This was all the more impressive since it came after an adverse media campaign with government accusations that the unions were only defending the interests of permanent employees at the expense of youth and the unemployed; and were, therefore, a special interest. But the strike was followed by political stalemate, as the PSOE won again a majority in the 1989 elections. The government shelved the youth scheme that triggered the strike (a three-year plan to subsidize 800,000 temporary jobs for school leavers), and adjusted pensions and public-sector wages to compensate for the 1988 inflation forecast error, as demanded by strikers. Finally, unions and government reached limited agreements in 1990 on unemployment benefits, pensions (indexing and making the minimum family pension equal to the minimum wage), minimum wage, public-sector wages, bargaining rights of public employees, and education reform.[50] The agreements included a law requiring that a "basic copy" of all new labor contracts be signed by the works council and created tripartite provincial commissions for contract monitoring and fraud control. Negotiations with regional governments yielded additional results in housing and training, as well as the introduction of a "minimum social income."

On balance, in the 1990s the unions managed to regain some "voice" in the political arena, becoming recurrent interlocutors on issues of welfare and pensions, education, training, and regional development. To some extent they were able to aggregate the demands of permanent employees and those sectors of the population with the lowest incomes, reinforcing their own collective identity and legitimacy as class-wide representatives. The organizational decline trend of the 1980s was reversed, and membership grew to about 15 percent by 1994. UGT and CCOO were also able to move beyond their traditional workerist core to attract women and service workers, particularly in the public sector. They expanded their "audience" among workers, as measured by their joint share of workplace representatives which rose to almost 80 percent in the 1990 workscouncil elections. They also made strides in advancing PSP demands through state policy or collective bargaining.

Labor failed, however, to attain its more ambitious objectives of altering macroeconomic policy and reversing the tide of precarization. The 1990 law on union monitoring of labor contracts proved ineffective because of employer resistance and worker connivance in holding onto precarious jobs. Labeling it a "Sovietization" of industrial relations, the CEOE challenged its constitutionality and waged a tug-of-war with the unions over the content of the "basic copy" to be reviewed. Union data for 1992 shows a majority of contracts lacked works councils signatures, due to an alleged absence of elected worker representatives in the firm.[51] Monetary restraints were tightened after the strike, and although the government proposed to return to a wage policy as part of a competitiveness pact in 1991, the unions declined. Maastricht intensified conflict between labor and the state, and González's convergence plan led to two more general strikes. The first, in May 1992, protested drastic cuts in unemployment coverage triggered by the soaring number of claims by temporary workers laid off during the recession. The "*decretazo*" reduced the amount and length of benefits, raised the minimum required period of work from six months to one year, and tightened eligibility. The second general strike took place in January 1994, against labor law reform. It followed an attempt in 1993 to negotiate a pact featuring budget deficit reduction, labor market flexibility, and a three-year incomes policy. The CEOE refused to discuss the budget at the concertation table. Instead, it relied on Catalan nationalists to extract a tax break for business in parliament, which also imposed a freeze on public-sector wages and other cuts opposed by labor. CCOO and UGT then tried to tie wage restraint to a compromise on the labor market that failed to materialize.

The 1994 Labor Law Reform and Beyond

The 1994 labor law reform removed restrictions on mobility, decentralized bargaining, and expanded temporary contracting. It made dismissals easier, although it did not eliminate the administrative procedure for collective dismissals as demanded by employers. Dismissals were made easier by broadening causes to include economic, productive, technological, and organizational reasons; establishing thresholds below which all dismissals are treated as individual; and by reducing processing costs, including eliminating in-process wages. Temp agencies were legalized and temporary contracts were expanded with a new flexible part-time contract (free of payroll taxes under sixteen hours/week) and the "apprenticeship contract" for youth under twenty five. Unions labelled this the "junk contract" because of its weak training provisions and pay below the minimum wage.

A major thrust of the reform was to make the regulation of work conditions more flexible by reducing the role of the law and state labor authorities in favor of collective bargaining. Some twenty eight matters, such as the length of the workday or the trial period, for which the Worker's Statue previously mandated legal minimums, could now be bargained down by collective accords. Prior authorization for geographical transfers as well as for other "substantive modifications of work conditions" was eliminated. These decisions could now be undertaken unilaterally by the employer, after consulting the works council if they were collective, and could only be challenged *a posteriori* through judicial review. Additionally, the repeal of all remaining labor ordinances, which dictated professional classifications and functional mobility, was scheduled for the end of 1995 (later extended), giving the social partners a deadline for negotiating substitute sector agreements.

The 1994 general strike and its failure to stop labor law reform initiated a period of internal turmoil for unions. Although strike participation reached similar levels to 1988, the social climate and the unions' credibility as effective representatives of the interests of workers was not the same. The UGT's image was also tainted by the fracas of its housing venture. This led to difficult congressional processes marked by sharp division, which reflected in part attempts by PCE and PSOE to reassert their ascendancy over the unions.[52] The UGT conflict was largely a struggle over a successor to Nicolás Redondo. But in CCOO, there was an emotional debate over union strategy that pitted the current leadership against a critical faction headed by Agustín Moreno and historical leader Marcelino Camacho, who had stepped down as secretary general in 1988 but still held the honorific post of union president. The critics, who obtained one third of the vote, denounced the union's decision to "turn the page" after the reform and focus on its implementation through collective bargaining while resuming partial agreements with the government and the CEOE, rather than force a political crisis through continued mobilization. The implicit hope was that a new coalition between the troubled PSOE and IU, the umbrella group headed by the PCE, would emerge from the process. They also questioned the unions' position on EMU and pension reform, while proposing to fight for the legal enactment of the thirty-five hour week by the year 2000. The congresses resulted in fortified "unity of action," a choice for negotiation over confrontation, and thorough generational change, with the retirement of almost all the key leaders from the democratic transition period.

In 1996, UGT and CCOO launched a campaign on work sharing and employment stability aimed at bringing unemployment and atypical work to levels closer to the EU average. This led to the 1997 accords promoting employment stability and collective bargaining, which followed a revival of peak-level concertation with CEOE after 1994 on conflict resolution and replacing the labor ordinances. UGT and CCOO also negotiated pension reform with the conservative government in 1996, largely based on a previous interparty consensus (the Toledo Pact). The reform included gradual measures to improve the financial situation of the system and to make it more equitable. The most important items were: widening the pension base from the last eight years of contribution to the last fifteen and stretching contribution periods; unifying contribution ceilings to the level of the highest one as well as contributions by farmers and the self-employed; separating funding for basic pensions from the contributory system while creating a reserve fund; and setting some curbs on fraud and disability pensions. Equity measures incorporated into law the indexing of pensions to inflation, eased eligibility for old-age pensions and early retirement, raised the minimum pension for young widows, and broadened the age conditions for orphan pensions.[53] The CEOE did not sign the pension pact, since employers demanded lower payroll taxes. For Aznar, union consensus helped allay popular fears that the conservatives would dismantle the welfare state (Spanish bankers had campaigned in favor of a Chilean-like system of pension privatization). Ironically, this pact took place in a political juncture that resembled in some ways that of 1993: a minority government, which is hard pressed to meet EMU criteria, relying on conditional support from Catalan and Basque nationalists. But this time the unions were not asked to legitimize government's efforts to cut the budget and could more easily pursue areas of agreement with employers once major changes in labor law had already occurred.

New Political Arenas: Europe and the Regions

Spanish unions have been staunch supporters of European integration. They may have opposed the specific terms of Spanish integration, particularly the early entry into the EMS and the government's convergence plan, but they never questioned the desirability of integration itself. Similarly, the unions gave Maastricht a "critical yes" as an important, if timid, step to political and social union, yet criticized the predominance of monetary convergence criteria over more ambitious mechanisms of economic coordination and solidarity to achieve social cohesion. More recently, they have called for a renegotiation of the EMU process that would include convergence on employment, industrial and fiscal policies, as well as guarantees of welfare and labor rights. The challenge they see for labor is twofold: advancing the political construction of Europe and developing an effective Euro-unionism. UGT and ELA, the Basque nationalist union, were early members of the ETUC. The CCOO was allowed to join in 1990, after the end of the Cold War and the lifting of UGT's veto. CCOO's entrance was the result of, and helped consolidate, the strategy of "unity of action." Both UGT and CCOO are strong supporters of ETUC reform, believing that ETUC must become a confederation with bargaining authority and that the European Industrial Federations should become sectoral federations capable of negotiating European collective agreements. Indeed, they see themselves, together with other Southern bloc unions, as the most Europeanist of all.

The European arena is therefore valued by Spanish unions, even though their relative weakness makes them minor players. One reason for this Europeanism is the potential usefulness of EU regulations. Unions saw the 1989 framework directive as a way to improve health and safety standards in face of a high incidence of work accidents. However, negotiations to transpose the directive reached an impasse in 1992, when employers and the economy minister backed away from extending health and safety worker representatives to small- and medium-sized firms.[54] The EU directive thus contributed to raise standards, but not decisively.

Two other aspects of EU institutions have had significant impact. EU-promoted interunion seminars and project partnerships have been a source of training and networking, triggering a rather intense learning process at different levels of the organization.[55] Next, the EU structural funds have helped fuel regional concertation.

The regions are another new political arena, opened up in the 1980s with the construction of a "quasi-federal" state initiated by the 1978 Constitution. The more active regions presently have substantial autonomy and resources which are growing because of the pivotal role played by nationalist parties in supporting the minority governments of the PSOE (1993) and the PP (1996). This context has created opportunities for "political exchange" at the regional level where regional governments, unions, and employer associations have been negotiating bi- and tripartite pacts over a growing range of policies since the mid-1980s. Regional concertation has had two distinct patterns. In Socialist-governed regions such as Valencia and Andalusia, it was built upon the ties between regional party "barons" and UGT; it focused on state policies and evolved to incorporate CCOO and employers into tripartite negotiations over regional development programs. In contrast, in Catalonia and the Basque country, regional concertation was more an extension of collective bargaining, focusing on industrial relations issues with a primarily bilateral business/labor character. Since the 1988 general strike, unions have been critical in the diffusion of these practices across regions in three different waves. The first wave occurred in 1989-90 with the negotiation of the PSP in ten regions leading to union-regional government accords about employment policies, welfare, and public services. The second wave was in 1992-93 involving mostly tripartite "industrial pacts" in eleven regions following a decentralized mobilization campaign that sought to rally support for an active industrial policy through demonstrations, marches, local and regional general strikes. A third wave of tripartite "employment parts" has taken place in 1996-98 with a focus on labor maket policies, including incentives for employment stability and, in some cases, for work sharing through worktime reorganization.

Regional concertation has been controversial. Critics, particularly in the UGT, caution against the development of centrifugal forces that could undermine the establishment of national standards and bargaining, perhaps even questioning interregional solidarity. They point to the Basque and Catalan aspiration to create "autonomous frameworks of labor relations" and the danger of fragmentation. On the other hand, union officials agree that the regions constitute an increasingly important political arena for worker representation and union recognition. Through regional pacts, unions have expanded their institutional resources and revenues and gained a foothold in policymaking and/or delivery in areas such as training, employment, and industrial promotion. Sometimes, the regional arena has served as an alternative venue or a prelude to negotiation at the national level.[56]

But perhaps the most significant fact about regional concertation is its potential for creating institutional networks that increase information flows and facilitate coordination and cooperation by industrial actors at the local level.[57] In Catalonia, the Labor Council provided a relatively secluded arena for social dialogue (away from the spotlight and high stakes of national politics), where unions and employers proceeded to tackle issues with direct bearing on industrial restructuring, such as conflict resolution, training, and labormarket intermediation. In 1993, they drafted a bilateral statement of objectives entitled "Toward a New Industrial Model" that suggested the emergence of a common ground for negotiated flexibility, away from the "low road." The document was explicit about the long-term pitfalls of the unchecked growth of temporary contracts:

> "An enterprise model – both economic and social – has developed, characterized by deep asymmetries in labor relations, that results in a reduction of professionalism, in lower prospects for learning and retraining, and in workers' uncertainty about career expectations; a diverse set of consequences which together discourage motivation among people and organizations, therefore having serious repercussions on industrial competitiveness."[58]

Nevertheless, Catalan employers became strong advocates of temporary "apprenticeship" contracts and of cheaper/freer dismissals in the prelude to the 1994 labor law reform. This reveals the employers' fundamental ambivalence between building a partnership with unions to obtain flexibility and cooperation from permanent workers on the one hand, and pushing for new rules of the game that would underwrite unilateralism on the other. Collaboration with unions then appears as a default option to further deregulation. This assessment seems consistent with more recent developments in Catalonia that gained national projection. In 1995, the Catalan Labor Council embarked on a dialogue to implement the reform and correct its shortcomings in promoting employment stability. For labor the reform had failed to limit the rampant use of temporary contracts, whereas for business it did not go far enough in lowering the cost of dismissals. The employers advanced a key argument at this point: that it was the uncertainty over the cost of dismissal, linked to the possibility of judicial review, that kept them from hiring workers under open-ended contracts. They stressed that, even though the reform expanded the causes for economic dismissals, the labor courts still interpreted them in a restrictive way, declaring most unfair. The regional government then proposed a "stable contract," a long-term temporary contract with the cost of dismissal previously fixed by negotiation. The idea was rejected by unions as further precarization and because it implied a radical change in the regulation of dismissals, exonerating employers from showing due cause. The Catalans came to the verge of a compromise in 1996 that would have addressed the uncertainty question through collective bargaining, but employers failed to ratify the pact in the last minute. Still, several elements of this dialogue were recaptured in the 1997 national accords.

Bargaining Strategies

Union bargaining strategies passed through phases of centralized vs. decentralized approaches. Basic objectives have remained the same, however. The first has been to concentrate and rationalize the highly fragmented bargaining structure inherited from Franco through establishing national-sector agreements and articulation between bargaining at different levels. The second is to enrich the content of bargaining beyond its almost exclusive focus on wages. Union success in expanding bargaining coverage (from 2.8 million workers in 1977, to 7.6 million in 1995 or 85 percent of wage earners, excluding state employees) is in sharp contrast to the slow progress made until recently in advancing these goals.

National-sector agreements covered 29 percent of workers in 1996. Nearly 52 percent were covered by provincial-sector agreements, which often follow narrow branch definitions carried over from Franco's vertical unions. Company-level agreements covered 12 percent, while the remaining 7 percent were covered by regional and local agreements. Company-level agreements are confined to larger firms, while the majority of small- and medium-sized firms are governed by provincial agreements which are negotiated with the limited participation of affected workers and firms. Their enforcement is uneven, given regional differences in union organization and the lack of union activity in small workplaces.[59] With some exceptions, sector agreements regulated a narrow set of issues. Matters such as work organization, professional categories, promotions, pay structures, and disciplinary measures were covered by labor ordinances – branch-specific legislation inherited from Franco that national-sector agreements were supposed to replace according to the WS. Even at company level, where there is a richer bargaining experience, content is often limited. This fragmented bargaining structure persisted beneath the centralization of wage bargaining undertaken during macroconcertation. After its breakdown in 1987, the unions walked away from a centralized wage policy, allowing the sectoral federations greater autonomy. Since then, some mechanisms of coordination have continued to operate. Every year, the government announces an inflation forecast and recommends wage increases compatible with that target to the social partners. The CEOE and the union head offices then issue guidelines for their members. But unlike in Germany, the industry-level actors which bargain first do not do so after a lengthy process of mediation internal to the employers and union associations, and thus do not set a pattern for others.[60]

Union pluralism has been, in my view, a major obstacle to bargaining reorganization. Neo-corporatist concertation was accompanied by intense competition between UGT and CCOO, who sought at times to undercut each other at lower levels. CCOO tried to thwart peak-level agreements signed by UGT through company-level bargaining, while UGT countered CCOO's more militant stand by entering limited applicability agreements with employers which were binding only to union members and had an ambiguous legal status. These tactics divided workers at the workplace, enhanced the autonomy of works councils from unions, and consolidated a fragmented bargaining structure. Following Moncloa a few new national-sector agreements were introduced, but the trend soon halted. Metalworking provides perhaps the best example of how such divergences compromised long-term bargaining objectives. In 1987, UGT signed a limited applicability agreement with CONFEMETAL after the metal branches of both unions had been in open conflict over the implementation of the Socialist government's restructuring program for mature industries. The agreement, which replaced the 1970 metal labor ordinance, was challenged in the courts by CCOO and contested by several provincial employers' associations. The incident is now regarded by unionists in both organizations as a missed opportunity to develop a national contract.

After 1988, "unity of action" reduced competition and has promoted convergence on the articulation models upheld by both unions. UGT traditionally advocated centralized bargaining, whereas CCOO wanted national-sector agreements to set bargaining floors to be improved at lower levels. The positions taken by the last union congresses were substantially closer, with both unions leaving sectoral federations at liberty to set up the particular mode of articulation best suited to conditions in their industry. In a departure from past views, CCOO assigned responsibility for bargaining to union sections in firms, as opposed to works councils, stressing the need for company and provincial bargaining to be articulated in national-sector agreements. But unions met less willing partners when employers began to extol the merits of decentralized bargaining in the later 1980s.

Bargaining reorganization has gained momentum since 1994, with labor law reform and the scheduled repeal of the remaining 126 labor ordinances – estimated to apply to between a fourth and a third of firms, especially small- and medium-sized firms.[61] The government targeted this as a key competitiveness issue because the narrow job demarcations derived from the ordinances have been an obstacle to functional mobility, discouraging more extensive changes in work organization. In October 1994, CEOE, UGT, and CCOO signed a framework agreement for their replacement by national-sector agreements.This has been difficult due to the lack of encompassing employers' associations in many subsectors and to pressure from provincial agents to retain their bargaining role, as in metalworking. To some extent, these conflicts reflect different employer interests. Small firms, in particular, have a stake in retaining ad hoc flexibility arrangements with individual workers rather than being subjected to joint union regulation of shop-floor practices.[62] Strong inertia also exists on the worker side, as shown by the difficulties in implementing a new grading system in shipbuilding following the 1993 INI-Teneo accord.

The national agreement in chemicals in 1988 was the first to replace old occupational categories with five broad professional groups. Negotiations in the construction industry led to a national agreement for the construction sector in 1992. This was a major success for the unions, which took advantage of the "crunch" provided by the Olympics and World Expo events scheduled for that year. In addition to restructuring bargaining and replacing the ordinance, the agreement introduced innovative sector-wide mechanisms for the joint management of training and health and safety. However – and this illustrates the "stickiness" of the old occupational categories – the design of a new classification system was left to further negotiations. A framework agreement on professional classification was reached in metalworking in 1996, when the national banking contract also replaced the ordinance. Given the banks' sharp differentiation between "old" and "new" (college graduate) employees, the union made an effort to focus on training and promotion rights for all workers, including an education campaign to induce women and middle-aged workers to view training as a right. The majority CCOO banking union has particularly strived to identify and incorporate the diverse interests of the growing number of women and technicians in the sector. In an innovative move, it successfully brought an anti-discrimination lawsuit against the Catalan savings bank in 1998, based on the disproportionate share of women promoted to management positions. Other recent negotiations of professional classification systems include textiles and clothing, and state employees. The 1998 accord on a new civil service statute reformed the job classification, grading and promotion patterns that resulted in the past in very short career paths and inflation of management ranks; introduced mobility mechanisms, and opened the door to performance incentives. It also strengthened bargaining rights of public employees by making collective agreements directly binding (without cabinet approval), and introduced arbitration.

The 1994 labor law reform opened a window of opportunity for enriching the content of bargaining, repealing the ordinances and setting bargaining agents free to negotiate many terms of employment previously regulated by law, within certain limits. In this sense, the reform matches a long-term objective of unions, particularly since the strategic shift in 1988. As firm restructuring took a more offensive nature in the second half of the 1980s, issues of worktime flexibility (e.g., more work shifts to maximize operation times of new machinery), training, and functional mobility came to the fore. Research on several sectors in Catalonia found firm-level accords on single issues such as shifts, vacations, and pay rates to be common, but seldom did the accords cover broader questions such as job classifications, promotions, technological innovation and changes in the organization of work.[63] The autonomy of works councils made union control of these deals tenuous. Some practices, such as staffing new shifts with temporary workers, or allowing functional mobility on a voluntary basis, reinforced the gap between protected and precarious labor within firms. Moreover, the dominant strategy among employers has been to restrict works councils to their traditional bargaining competencies while channelling the new issues through individual or small-group negotiations.[64] The unions eventually realized that they had to dispute this to counter the creeping individualization of employment relations fed by segmentation. After 1988, UGT and CCOO drew unitary bargaining platforms with new bargaining priorities: employment and the control of temporary contracts, training, work organization, information rights, and health and safety. They sought to integrate a broader spectrum of demands to reflect the increasing diversity of interests among different groups of workers, emphasizing bargaining as an instrument against discrimination. This agenda was to be pursued primarily through decentralized bargaining; attention was redirected to the firm to increase recruitment and contractual power vis-a-vis employers.

Important strides have been made recently in expanding the bargaining agenda. The National Accord on Further Training, signed in 1992, assigned half the payroll training tax for active workers. The accord involves social partner participation at firm level (training plans need works council endorsement), regionally where unions and employer associations produce amalgamated plans for firms under two hundred workers, and at sector level where national-sector agreements – or, in their absence, sector-wide training accords – establish the format and guidelines of training plans to be submitted to sector paritary commissions for approval. The new system benefitted two million workers in 1996. According to Labor Ministry data, non-wage bargaining clauses have been increasing since 1994. In 1996, training clauses were included in 35 percent of collective agreements (covering 58 percent of workers); health and safety clauses were included in 74 percent of agreements (covering 54 percent of workers); and union activity clauses in 61 percent of agreements (covering 74 percent of workers). Most significant, from the unions' strategic vantage, is the inclusion of employment clauses in 44.5 percent of agreements (covering 61 percent of workers),[65] and overtime controls in 15 percent of agreements (covering 43 percent of workers). Clauses regulating temporary contracts were inserted in 16 percent of agreements (covering 34 percent of workers), while 6 percent of agreements (covering 8 percent of workers) included contract conversion clauses. Among the clauses regulating temporary contracts, controls on apprenticeship contracts were common (e.g., improving wages, excluding unskilled jobs). But so were clauses on contracts "for eventualities of production" that actually expanded their maximum length and time frame (e.g., nine out of twelve months), in an acknowledgement of the widespread irregular use of these contracts to cover nontemporary positions. The tacit union acceptance of these practices may be explained by the fear that restrictions would result in fewer jobs, while longer stays of temporary workers in the firm would make their conversion into permanent employees more likely.[66]

New hirings and the conversion of temporary contracts have been increasingly tied in company-level bargaining to concessions on entry-level pay, early retirement, seniority, and worktime flexibility. Seniority pay has emerged as an issue that unions are willing to trade off, reasoning that it is a disincentive for firms to keep workers.[67] Another issue is worktime flexibility, as more collective agreements include flexibility provisions to be negotiated at the plant level. The national agreements for chemicals and textiles were among the first sector agreements to introduce time banking (100 and 130 hours/year, respectively) in 1995. Flexible worktime deals have also been reached in the automobile industry.[68] The contours of a tradeoff between external and internal flexibility seem to be emerging wherein unions accept greater flexibility in the deployment of labor within the firm, in exchange for greater employment stability and training opportunities for a majority of workers.

The 1997 Interconfederal Accord for Employment Stability is a major step in this direction. It introduced a new permanent contract for new hires and temporary workers. Under the new contract, severance payments in the event of an unjustified dismissal were lowered (thirty three days per year of service with a twenty four month maximum, down from forty five days per year with a fourty two month maximum). In this way, the pact sought to address the employers' claim that uncertainty over the cost of dismissals – linked to the eventuality of judicial review – raised the average price paid for redundancies, and kept them from hiring workers under permanent contracts. To the same end, the pact tried to clarify when employers are justified in laying off workers (and pay twenty days per year of service with a twelve month maximum), in light of complaints that the labor courts still adhered to an overly restrictive interpretation of economic causes. The new rule, which applies to both old and new permanent contracts, allows dismissals in order to surmount difficulties related to the firm's competitive position or to changes in demand. In addition to lowering dismissal costs, the accord sought to promote permanent employment by shifting financial incentives and tightening the use of fixed-term contracts. The government thus granted in June 1997 a two-year payroll tax cut of 40-60 percent for the new open-ended contracts, depending on the target group (i.e., temporary workers, youth, those over forty five, the long-term unemployed). All existing financial incentives for temporary hirings were revoked (except for the handicapped). The apprenticeship contract was scrapped in favor of a training contract with certificate, the maximum length of contracts "for eventualities of production" was reduced,[69] and social protection for part-time contracts under twelve hours per week was restored. But the issue of curbes on temporary contracts was largely left open, subject to further negotiation. Collective bargaining is expected to regulate the conditions and types of jobs for which temporary contracts may be used, their duration limits, caps in relation to total staff, etc. Finally, the social partners convened to regulate temp agencies, to monitor the evolution of contracts "for determined work or service" and "for eventualitites of production" and possibly penalize their use with higher payroll taxes, and to open a dialogue on worktime reduction and redistribution.

Two other recent peak-level accords have sought to strenghthen collective bargaining institutions. The 1996 Accord for the Extra-Judicial

Solution of Conflicts established mechanisms for mandatory mediation and voluntary arbitration of collective conflicts, including conflicts over mobility, lay offs and other substantive modifications of work conditions, the negotiation of minimum services prior to strikes, or when an impasse is reached in contract negotiations. The 1997 Interconfederal Accords on Collective Bargaining and Coverage Gaps sought to articulate a more flexible and integrated bargaining system. The signatories (CEOE, UGT, and CCOO) committed their member associations to review and/or redesign the bargaining structure and boundaries of sectors, while the accord set some general guidelines on an optimal division of responsibilities between bargaining levels. In particular, national-sector agreements should regulate wage structure but may leave wage settlements for provincial and company-level bargaining. National-sector agreements should set the maximum worktime and its distribution, remitting to lower levels issues such as the possibility of irregular distribution, rest periods, vacations, special worktime arrangements, etc. Other subjects to be covered preferably by national-sector agreements include the regulation of temporary contracts; professional classification and the setting of procedures to adapt grading systems at the company level; and expanded information rights of works councils (e.g., prior to the introduction of new technologies, new work organization and restructuring processes, mergers, subcontracting, etc.).

This accord must be understood in the context of the 1994 labor law reform, which introduced a strong decentralization bias via two mechanisms. First, through company-level pacts that can "opt out" of sector wage settlements when they affect the stability of the firm (although sector agreements may regulate the conditions and process by which this is done). They can also modify working conditions for economic, technical, organizational, and production reasons. The second mechanism is a new concurrence rule (Art. 84 WS) that allows territorial and sector or subsector agreements to break the discipline of higher level agreements outside certain protected subjects. This controversial rule was a political concession to Basque nationalists, but ended up adopting a very broad decentralizing formula that allows the successive segregation of bargaining units along both territorial and functional lines.[70] Both the CEOE and CCOO-UGT criticized it for creating the risk of uncontrolled fragmentation. The 1997 accord on Coverage Gaps was also prompted by the reform. Its purpose was to fill the gaps left by the repeal of the labor ordinances in twenty two subsectors that still lacked a replacement sector agreement. Bargaining restructuring is still underway. In 1998, a framework deal was reached in metalworking that will hopefully pave the way towards a new national-sector agreement. Another important novelty is the 1997 national contract for temp agencies which provides for the gradual convergence of pay rates to those of the user firm's sector agreement by the year 2000.[71]

The issue of worktime reduction has become prominent in recent months, due in part to developments in France and Italy. Unions are demanding a generalized reduction to the thirty-five hour week which, together with overtime restrictions, they believe would increase the number of people employed. There are some differences of opinion between the two confederations on how to effect this change. UGT has called for legislation complimented by negotiations between unions and employers, while CCOO proposes to achieve worktime reduction through collective bargaining, backed by financial incentives for those firms creating jobs as a result of reducing and reorganizing worktime. The Basque and Catalan regional governments have introduced some incentives along these lines, but not the national government, and peak-level dialogue on this issue has not made much progress so far.

Organizational and Representation Strategies

Following the abandonment of peak-level wage bargaining in 1988, UGT and CCOO embarked on a policy of strengthening their sectoral federations. The 1990s have been marked by a significant convergence in union models of organization and the introduction of institutional changes (i.e., reform of works council elections) to reduce interunion competition.

Differences in union organizational models stemmed, in part, from the circumstances in which each confederation found itself in 1977. The UGT's centralized model flowed from the fact that it had to be built up quickly from the top and with its strategy of peak-level concertation. CCOO's decentralized model was a legacy of its days as a socio-political movement under Franco. UGT's referent were the German unions, whereas for CCOO it was the Italian CGIL. Although UGT aspired to build an organization based primarily on industry unions, the reality after legalization meant that territorial structures acquired greater weight in both confederations. The relative weakness and underdevelopment of sectoral structures were only addressed in the 1990s after changes in overall union and bargaining strategies brought them into focus. Both UGT and CCOO took steps to strengthen the sector federations through mergers and by granting them greater autonomy over collective bargaining, as well as primary responsibility for conducting bargaining at the provincial level. There was a parallel consolidation of territorial structures on a regional, rather than a provincial basis. Both CCOO (in 1991) and UGT (in 1994) changed the financial and political representation rule for sectoral vs. territorial structures from 50-50 to 60-40 percent.

This organizational convergence between UGT and CCOO has been accompanied by other measures that make their organizational cultures more similar. In 1991, CCOO began a process of computerization and financial centralization which meant that money would start to flow upwards, from local and regional unions, and reach the rest of the organization. CCOO also became more centralized politically by departing at its 1996 congress from its tradition of accommodating internal currents on the executive board. UGT, in turn, took a crucial step in internal democratization in 1994, adopting a "one delegate, one vote" rule for congress processes. If both unions now look more alike, the new rules for works council elections included in the 1994 reform also tend to reinforce "unity of action." The previous three-month electoral period ending in a high-profile proclamation of results was replaced by an open election calendar, while the four-year mandate of elected representatives was maintained. These changes, aimed at reducing interunion competition, were proposed to the government by UGT- CCOO in light of the negative experience of the 1990 ballot when intense competition over the small-firm sector led to a scramble for votes and mutual accusations of fraud.

Recruitment efforts have intensified since the late 1980s. The main policy thrust in both CCOO and UGT is for recruitment to become an integral part of union activity rather than a separate sphere to be pursued by more or less sporadic drives. But this is a difficult area to change given the state of the labor market and cultural obstacles. One legacy of Franco's compulsory official unions is that workers do not feel that they need to become members to benefit from union representation, or even to "belong" to a union (people may say "I am a CCOO person" meaning that they voted for CCOO in works council elections). This perception is, to some extent, shared by union militants, particularly in CCOO, with its lingering social movement tradition. Unions also lack selective incentives. Union freedom is defined in Spain to include the right not to join a union, therefore barring "closed-shop" clauses. The only quasi-compulsory element recognized by the 1985 Union Freedom Act is the possibility of charging "bargaining fees" to nonmembers who do not object. Both unions began to provide services (e.g., insurance, travel, housing cooperatives) to increase recruitment. Unfortunately, the UGT's large-scale housing project failed precipitously in 1993, making similar future endeavors unlikely. In any event, internal surveys show that workers would not join unions for services, and that the only really valued service is the legal counsel on labor matters traditionally provided by unions.

An important innovation has been the use of "extension teams" that regularly map and approach small firms for information, bargaining, electoral, and recruitment purposes. Both confederations are bent on expanding these practices which depend on parallel organizational policies to control and accumulate works council credit hours (e.g., assigning unionists in large firms to work in small firms in the area). Unions have also sought to diversify their representation strategies to meet the needs of different types of workers. Specific groups or secretariats exist for technicians and cadres, women, youth, immigrants, and the unemployed. Unions have been fairly successful in recruiting women, but still lag in incorporating gender in bargaining agendas and women in leadership positions. There was a debate on gender quotas at the 1991 CCOO congress, but these quotas were voted down in favor of an alternative recommendation – that organizations take steps to increase participation by women and achieve leadership representation rates in parity with membership.

Conclusion

Spanish unions faced a dire situation in the 1980s. Their initial broad base of supporters had failed to consolidate into a stable membership, which dropped to very low levels. There was fierce competition between the two main confederations, UGT and CCOO. Both unions encountered increasing political marginalization, which eventually led to a dramatic divorce between the socialist union and the governing Socialist party. Above all, they faced a devastated labor market. Despite strong economic growth during the second half of the 1980s, unemployment remained very high and there was an explosion in temporary work, which soon reached two-three times the EU level. Since the late 1980s, UGT and CCOO have responded with strategic adaptations bringing a measure of recovery in terms of regaining "voice" in the political arena and a modest, yet significant, increase in organizational and institutional resources.

What have been the main elements of the unions' strategic reorientation? The first and most important strategic change has been "unity of action." Pitting one union against the other had actually been part of social concertation since the 1979 ABI pact signed by CEOE and UGT. Intense union rivalry had a negative effect on collective bargaining and undermined efforts to construct a national architecture of industry-wide contracts, illustrated by the 1987 failed attempt in metalworking. By overcoming division, the confederations sought to combat a major source of weakness. "Unity of action" and its prerequisite autonomy from allied political parties has held up until the present. More ambitious, organic forms of unity do not seem to be in the cards, but "unity of action" has been reinforced by a reform of workscouncil election rules that reduces competition, and by growing convergence in union organizational models. Earlier debates over models of workplace representation (works councils vs. union sections) and bargaining (centralized vs. decentralized) have been superseded. Both confederations have taken parallel steps to strengthen their sectoral structures and initiated other changes, such as internal democratization in UGT (with the introduction of the "one delegate, one vote" rule) and financial centralization in CCOO; these work to make their organizational cultures converge.

The second strategic change, epitomized by the 1988 general strike, was to appeal politically to broad sectors of the population beyond labor's shrinking organized core. The unions thus mobilized traditional social-democratic values, confronting the Socialist government with widely supported demands for employment stability and welfare protection in the face of growing dualism. They won an increase in social spending, but only briefly, as recession and the Maastricht targets exerted tight constraints upon the budget after 1992.

Decentralization was the third strategic component. The confederations abandoned macroconcertation, decentralizing bargaining to the industry level and taking organizational steps to boost the sector federations. This reflected a new focus on the shopfloor and the desire to expand collective bargaining beyond its traditional narrow wage content. As firm restructuring entered a more dynamic phase in the late 1980s, the unions sensed that major changes in the workplace were occurring outside their control, and that they needed to work on this terrain to restore their credibility and counter the creeping individualization of employment relations bred by segmentation. Thus the unions began to approach negotiated flexibility as an alternative to employer unilateralism, predicated on the pervasive use of precarious labor. Attitudes on this issue were not homogeneous throughout the organizations, however, with some branches and locals in both unions taking more defensive positions than others. By forcing the unions' hand, the state-imposed 1994 reform may be viewed in this light as a spur against conservatism, strengthening those voices – such as the chemicals unions – more bent on accepting the economic need for greater flexibility and developing union criteria for the negotiation and tutelage of new rights.

The strategy paid off in certain ways. Union membership increased in the 1990s, even if only to a low 15 percent. Membership growth was concentrated in the tertiary sector, especially among public employees, and UGT and CCOO expanded beyond their traditional base to include service workers and women. They were less successful among professionals where they faced strong competition from independent occupational unions. For the first time, recruitment became more integrated into regular union activity, but it still remains the weakest strategic area. The unions expanded their institutional resources and revenues, gaining a foothold in policy-making and/or delivery in new areas such as training, employment policy, and regional development (partly linked to EU structural funds). These emerging institutional networks may, in turn, increase information flows and facilitate coordination and cooperation among industrial actors at the local level, as developments in Catalonia suggest. Political exchange was resumed at the national level, where the confederations became interlocutors on welfare issues such as pensions and the rural dole for the South. On the other hand, the limits of the strategy appear clear. The unions failed to alter the course of macroeconomic policy, which became locked into the EMU path. And they have not yet succeeded in abating precarization.

There is reason for hope, however. This optimism is rooted both in the appearance of new elements in collective bargaining and in the 1997 peak-level accords on employment stability and bargaining reorganization. Bargaining over nonwage issues has increased in recent years. There are indications that the 1994 reform effort to reduce the role of law in favor of collective bargaining is beginning to have an impact in expanding bargaining agendas. The recent growth of employment and contract regulation clauses is most promising from the unions' vantage point. Bargaining reorganization is underway, spurred by the repeal of the labor ordinances, leading to a number of new industry-wide contracts. The peak-level accord is an attempt to complete this process and devise new rules of specialization and articulation between different bargaining levels. The contours of a basic tradeoff between external and internal flexibility seem to be emerging in bargaining. Unions have been willing to accept greater flexibility in work conditions in exchange for greater stability and training prospects for a majority of workers. This is also the implicit philosophy of the accord on employment stability, which introduced a new permanent labor contract with lower dismissal costs as well as some controls over temporary contracts. Taken together, these pacts embody an opportunity to improve the performance of the Spanish economy by reducing the dysfunctionalities of the labor market, encouraging firms to move away from the "low road" and to invest in their workers' training and commitment.

The ball is now in the employers' court. As CEOE president, José María Cuevas declared to *El País* on 20 May 1997: "This is the moment of responsibility, of being clear about what to do with profits, which must be reinvested, to improve competitiveness and to give stability to workers."

Business support has not been unanimous. The CEOE knew, however, that in the case of disagreement, the conservative government would not touch the issue of dismissals but would instead come up with yet another type of temporary contract. It chose, in this context, to rely on union cooperation to reduce segmentation and ensure more flexibility among permanent employees. It is widely agreed that the persistence of current levels of precarization will have detrimental medium-term results for competitiveness, but employers face strong incentives to continue along the same path. Temporary contracts have provided a massive subsidy to Spanish firms, beyond the financial incentives that some of these contracts carried, the loss of which will be difficult to make up. They have supplied a buffer of some three million workers with almost no bargaining power, who can be flexibly deployed within, as well as out of, firms according to short-term fluctuations in demand, while the cost of unemployment spells is transferred to the national deficit. The "low road" may have a self-reinforcing quality, therefore. Cost-based strategies exert a perverse externality on the society, making it riskier for competing firms to make the long-term investments needed to upgrade skills and change their organizational practices.[72] The 1997 pacts may be interpreted, in this light, as a way to shift incentives and build stronger bargaining institutions that could help solve this collective action problem.

One year later, results in terms of reversing precarization are encouraging but far from dramatic. There have been nearly one million new permanent contracts from May 1997 to May 1998. Permanent hirings have nearly tripled to an average 2,600 contracts/day, up from 956 the previous year. About 59 percent of the new contracts were for youth under 30 years of age, and more than half involved the conversion of temporary contracts.[73] There is still a long way to go, however. Unemployment is currently down to 18.5 percent, yet way above the EU average, and one in three workers still holds a temporary contract. The government is actively considering penalizing certain types of temporary contracts with higher payroll taxes, but employers oppose this measure. The CEOE has also rejected a recent government accord with CCOO and UGT on part-time work, aimed to improve social security coverage and boost the incidence of good-quality part-time jobs. Currently, 8 percent of the workforce holds part-time jobs, half the EU average. Employers opposed the upper limit set for part-time contracts (77 percent of full time) as well as the rules governing complementary hours that reduced the flexibility – or as unions argued, the unlimited availability – of part-time workers. Finally, persistent friction between organizations suggests that unity cannot be taken for granted. The tightrope walk continues for Spanish unions.

Notes

1. "Spain Survey," *The Economist* 14 December 1996, 7. "A survey designed to measure unreported activity in 1985 in Spain concluded that 10-15 percent of employment was irregular (i.e., not properly registered with the social security system). But it also concluded that most of those jobs were held by people already employed, so that adjustment for the underground economy could decrease the unemployment rate by 3.5 percentage points at most," O. Blanchard and J. Jimeno, "Structural Unemployment: Spain versus Portugal," AEA *Papers and Proceedings,* vol. 85, no. 2 , 1995, 214. (All translations are those of the author).
2. The ratio of economically dependent youth doubled in the last decade from 32 percent to 64 percent, while 52 percent of 25-29 years old lived with their parents in 1995. *El País,* 1 October 1996.
3. CCOO estimate for 1994 in *El País* 21 November 1995. Survey data for 1991 set union membership at 14 percent. O. Taboadela, "Clases sociales y acción colectiva," *Revista Española de Investigaciones Sociológicas,* no. 63 (1993) 79.
4. V. Pérez-Díaz, "Los obreros españoles ante el sindicato y la acción colectiva," *Papeles de Economía Española,* no. 6 (1981); F. Miguélez and C. Prieto, eds., *Las relaciones laborales en España* (Madrid: Siglo XXI, 1991), 216.
5. Organization Secretariat UGT (1993), CCOO (1995).
6. O. Taboadela, "Clases sociales y acción colectiva," 84, 87.
7. A. Espina, *Empleo, democracia y relaciones industriales en España* (Madrid: Ministerio de Trabajo y Seguridad Social, 1990), 53.
8. C. Alonso and M. Castells, *España fin de siglo* (Madrid: Alianza Editorial, 1992), 295.
9. "Spain Survey"; EU average excludes Eastern Germany.
10. N. Bermeo and J. García-Durán, "Spain: Dual Transition Implemented by Two Parties" in *Voting for Reform: Democracy, Political Liberalization, and Economic Adjustment,* ed., S. Haggard and S.Webb (Oxford: Oxford University Press,1994), 94. On economic policies and social pacts during the transition see also V. Pérez-Díaz, "Neo-corporatist Experiments in a New and Precariously Stable State" in *Political Stability and Neo-corporatism,* ed., Ilja Scholten (London: Sage, 1987).
11. N. Bermeo and J. García-Durán, "Spain: Dual Transition ...", 110.
12. J. M. Maravall, "Politics and policy: economic reforms in Southern Europe" in *Economic Reforms in New Democracies,* ed., L.C. Bresser Pereira, J. M. Maravall and A. Przeworski (Cambridge and New York: Cambridge University Press, 1993), 111.
13. The increase since 1996 reflects the implementation of the Delors II package and the cohesion program (applying only to Greece, Ireland, Portugal and Spain). *OECD Economic Surveys: Spain* (Paris: OECD, 1998), 33.
14. C. Alonso and M. Castells, *España fin de siglo,* 84, 102.
15. *The Spanish Balance of Payments* (Madrid: Banco de España, 1997), 41-42.
16. G. Allard and J. Bolorinos, "Spain to 2000: A Question of Convergence," *The Economist Intelligence Unit,* Special Report M207 (1992), 33.
17. *OECD Economic Surveys: Spain* (Paris: OECD, 1988), 33-34. Foreign direct investment was 844 billion pesetas in 1997, compared to 1,411 billion pesetas at its 1990 peak.
18. The increasing loss of control over strategic decisions to foreign corporations was highlighted in the 1992-94 economic downturn, when firms such as SEAT-VW, Suzuki, Merzedes, Valeo or SKF consolidated Spanish operations. The press also called attention to cases such as Sanyo, Akzo, and Phillips who cancelled investment

plans or transferred their production to Eastern Europe. See "Las multinacionales se repliegan," *El País 5 March 1994.*

19. "The Economic and Financial Situation in Spain," *European Economy*, Reports and Studies 7 (1994), 9.
20. For an assessment of incomes policies in Spain see A. Espina, "Política de Rentas en España" and S. Ruesga, "La negociación colectiva" in F. Miguélez and C. Prieto, *Las relaciones laborales en España, 345,386.*
21. *OECD Economic Surveys: Spain* (Paris: OECD, 1996), 60.
22. Unit labor costs in manufacturing rose by 22.5 percent in 1989-92 against a 5.1 percent rise in industrial prices and a 5 percent currency appreciation, putting the exposed sector of the economy in difficult straits. A. Espina, *Hacia una estrategia española de competitividad* (Madrid: Fundación Argentaria, 1995), 23.
23. M. Martínez-Lucio and P. Blyton, "Constructing the Post-Fordist State? The Politics of Labor Market Flexibility in Spain," *West European Politics,* vol 18, no. 2 (1995).
24. The EU average for the statutory minimum is about half the Spanish level. *OECD Economic Surveys: Spain* (Paris: OECD, 1998), 68. A comparison with Portugal, which has roughly the same degree of employment protection than Spain, and dramatically lower unemployment (6.8 percent), challenges the popular view that excessive employment protection is the main cause of Spanish high unemployment. O. Blanchard and J. Jimeno, "Structural Unemployment: Spain versus Portugal," 215.
25. J. I. Palacio Morena, "La política de empleo," in *Las relaciones laborales en España,* 326.
26. "Country Profile: Spain,"*The Economist Intelligence Unit* (1998), 18.
27. R. Pardo and J. Fernández-Castro, "Las organizaciones empresariales y la configuración del sistema de relaciones industriales de la España democrática, 1977-1990," in *Las relaciones laborales en España,* 161.
28. M. Martínez-Lucio and P. Blyton, "Constructing the Post-Fordist State?," 356. See also M. Ludevid and R. Serlavós, "El Fomento del Trabajo Nacional," *Papeles de Economía Española,* no. 22 (1985), 131-133.
29. Erosion took place through changes in jurisprudence and pressure from the rising union movement. L. Fina, A. Meixide, and L. Toharia, "Reregulating the Labor Market amid an Economic and Political Crisis," in *The State and the Labor Market,* ed., S. Rosenberg (New York: Plenum Press, 1990), 118-120.
30. L. Benton, *Invisible factories: The informal sector and industrial development in Spain* (Albany: SUNY Press, 1990). On the relation between legal and submerged production see A. Recio, "The restructuring of the Catalan wool industry," *Labour and Society,* vol 14, no. 2 (1989).
31. J. J. Castillo, *Informatización, trabajo y empleo en las pequeñas empresas españolas* (Madrid: Ministerio de Trabajo y Seguridad Social, 1991), 44.
32. F. Miguélez, "Cultura y tipología de la empresa y del empresariado. El caso de Cataluña," in *Ejes territoriales de desarrollo: España en la Europa de los noventa,* ed., J. Velarde (Madrid: Colegio de Economistas, 1992), 473. The following analysis is also drawn from F. Miguélez and P. López, "El trabajo en la pequeña empresa española," *Papers,* Universidad de Barcelona, 1989.
33. J. Blanco and A. Otaegui, "Informe de síntesis del estudio de trabajadores de pequeñas y medianas empresas," CCOO, 1990, 8.
34. "Loss of craftsmanship" was a central theme in the discourses of focus groups for both small-firm workers and employers in F. Esteve et al., *Sindicatos, Economía y Sociedad: Un futuro para el Sindicalismo Español* (Madrid: Ministerio de Economía y Hacienda, 1993), 277, 281.

35. C. Prieto, "Las prácticas empresariales de gestión de la mano de trabajo," in *Las relaciones laborales en España*, 206; V. Pérez-Díaz and J. C. Rodríguez, "Inertial Choices: An Overview of Spanish Human Resources, Practices and Policies," in *Employment Relations in a Changing World Economy*, ed., R. Locke, T. Kochan and M. Piore (Cambridge: MIT Press, 1995), 181.
36. A. Recio, "La segmentación del mercado de trabajo en España," in *Las relaciones laborales en España*, 107.
37. P. Carrasquer, X. Coller and F. Miguélez, "Polítiques de regulació de la má d'obra a l'Europa dels noranta. El cas de Catalunya," Working Papers No. 1, Universitat Autònoma de Barcelona, Departament de Sociologia, 1993, 37.
38. See C. Castaño, *Tecnología, empleo y trabajo en España* (Madrid: Alianza Editorial, 1994), and C. Iglesias, "Los mercados de trabajo de la banca privada española," *INFOFEBA*, no. 7, 1996.
39. C. Castaño, *Tecnología, empleo y trabajo en España* and A. Gómez et al., "Cambio tecnológico y organización del trabajo en la industria del automóvil," Federación Minerometalúrgica de CCOO, 1994.
40. The same work performed by a temporary worker may cost between 8.5 and 16 percent less, after allowance is made for service bonuses and for special skills acquired in the company. J. Gonzalez-Calvet, "Labor Market, Competitiveness and the European Monetary Union. The Case of Spain," Paper presented at ETUCO, Brussels, December 1995, 14. Discrimination based on contract type is illegal, but firms play around this by assigning temporary workers to low occupational categories.
41. S. Bentolila and J. Dolado, "Spanish labour markets," *Economic Policy* 18 (1994).
42. J. M. Zufiaur, "El sindicalismo español en la transición y la crisis," *Papeles de Economía Española* 22 (1985). For interviews of both UGT and CCOO leaders covering this period see S. Aguilar and C. Zeller, *Els líders, la cultura sindical del nucli dirigent de les organitzacions* (Barcelona: Jaume Bofill Foundation, 1991).
43. J. Roca "La concertación social," in *Las relaciones laborales en España, 375.*
44. Robert Fishman, *Working Class Organization and the Return to Democracy in Spain* (Ithaca: Cornell University Press, 1990), 243.
45. For more details on the pacts' content see R. Hawkesworth and L. Fina, "Trade Unions and Industrial Relations in Spain: The Response to the Economic Crisis," in *Trade Unions and the Economic Crisis of the 1980s*, ed., W. Brierley (Aldershot, England: Gower Publishing Company, 1987).
46. J. Jordana, "Del 14D al sindicalismo de los años noventa," *Sociología del Trabajo* 8 (1989).
47. On the changing calculations of actors see especially F. Esteve et al., *Sindicatos, economía y sociedad*, 189-92.
48. An excellent analysis of this issue is R. Gillespie, "The Break-up of the 'Socialist Family': Party-Union Relations in Spain, 1982-89," *West European Politics*, vol. 13, no. 1 (1990). For the PSOE's perspective see L. Paramio "El socialismo y los sindicatos: ¿hacia el divorcio?," *Sistema* 82 (1988).
49. "The unions, in permanent institutional backslide, want to redefine the balance of forces – unfavorable to them – derived from the course of the transition and achieve a more favorable institutional position vis-a-vis the other two social actors, " S. Aguilar and J. Roca, *Sindicalisme i canvi social a Espanya 1976-1988. Epíleg: La vaga general del 14-D* (Barcelona: Jaume Bofill Foundation, 1991), 131.
50. A. Espina, *Empleo, democracia y relaciones industriales*, 279-283.

51. "Informe nº 2 sobre funcionamiento de las comisiones de seguimiento de la contratación," CCOO, 1993, 21.
52. "Sillas movedizas. Sectores del PSOE y del PCE quieren controlar a los sindicatos y volver a las relaciones de 1982," *El País* 5 March 1995.
53. *OECD Economic Surveys: Spain* (Paris: OECD, 1998), 70.
54. The Health at Work Act of 1995 limited these representatives to firms over 250 workers or in high-risk sectors, conferring prevention duties on the works council or staff delegates in other firms. But firms under six workers were exempted from the mandate to contract a prevention service and have a prevention delegate. The unions had proposed instead the creation of territorial prevention delegates for small firms financed out of insurance pool surpluses.
55. To cite some examples, construction unions and employers set up a training and social fund inspired on Nordic cases; UGT was working on a proposal for a job-coaching service based on a Dutch prototype; and the banking unions were enlisting help from German unions to create an accredited training institute. Firm-level participants in sectors such as auto, chemicals, and retail have learned from others (most often the Italians) in negotiating over flexibility, work organization, and training issues.
56. An interesting example is the introduction of a "minimum social income," which was first issued by the Basque government and extended, in a variety of forms, by regional pacts to the rest of the regions. Another example is conflict resolution, where regional mechanisms at work in the Basque country and Catalonia preceded the 1996 national accord.
57. This is the subject of research in progress for my dissertation at the Department of Political Science, MIT.
58. "Un nuevo modelo industrial. Situación y actuaciones en el ámbito de Cataluña," Fomento del Trabajo Nacional, CONC, UGT, 1993, 5.
59. "The 'poverty' of collective bargaining," *European Industrial Relations Review* 216 (1992), 20.
60. M. Regini, *Uncertain Boundaries. The Social and Political Construction of European Economies* (Cambridge and New York: Cambridge University Press, 1995), 134.
61. *OECD Economic Surveys: Spain* (Paris: OECD, 1992), 69.
62. "Replacing the labour ordinances," *European Industrial Relations Review* 234 (1993); "The development of labour flexibility," *European Industrial Relations Review* 252 (1995), 16.
63. A similar observation is made for the Basque country: "Only the consequences of immediate work organization changes on living and working conditions have been discussed in most cases," J. Larrea, "Labor Market Flexibility and Work Organization Initiatives in Spain," in *New Directions in Work Organization* (Paris: OECD, 1994), 143.
64. P. Carrasquer, X. Coller, and F. Miguélez, "Polítiques de regulació...", 16, 37.
65. This figure lumps together clauses on professional classification and mobility with those on employment maintenance, job creation, job creation through early retirement, temporary contracts, conversion of temporary contracts, etc. All 1996 data are provisional. *Estadística de convenios colectivos de trabajo 1995-1996 Avance* (Madrid:Ministerio de Trabajo y Asuntos Sociales, 1997).
66. M. García-Fernández, "Modalidades contractuales en la negociación colectiva," in *La aplicación de la reforma del Estatuto de los Trabajadores en la negociación colectiva* (Madrid: Ministerio de Trabajo y Seguridad Social, 1996), 34.

67. A case in point is the 1996 metal agreement for Barcelona, which suppressed seniority pay after 1999 (i.e. it will be frozen for current recipients and none will be given to new hirings).
68. An example is SEAT-VW's collective agreement for 1997-99: work on Saturdays (thirteen per year) is to accrue into a time bank, to be used in place of publicy-funded layoffs that the car industry employs routinely to accommodate short-lived fluctuations in production. In 1998, SEAT announced the conversion into permanent jobs of some 400 temporary workers, taken on two years ago at 85 percent of normal pay. These workers will now receive full pay.
69. The maximum duration was lowered to six months within a twelve month period, though collective agreements can raise it to three-quarters of an eighteen month period.
70. F. Valdés Dal-Ré, "Notas sobre la reforma del marco legal de la estructura de la negociación colectiva," Ponencia presentada a las VI Jornadas Catalanas de Derecho del Trabajo, Barcelona, November 1994.
71. The unions took advantage of the intense competition and concentration underway in the sector, to negotiate a wage floor with the employer associations representing the large companies, several of them multinationals, that control over 70 percent of the temp business.
72. R. Locke, T. Kochan and M. Piore, *Employment Relations in a Changing World Economy*, 374.
73. "Arenas reconoce que es necesario incrementar más la contratación fija", *El País* 20 May 1998.

Chapter 8

IN THE LINE OF FIRE

The Europeanization of Labor Representation

Andrew Martin and George Ross

Introduction

For trade unions, as for national states, the regulation of markets becomes more difficult as they are extended across national boundaries. Historically, as markets expanded unions had to enlarge their strategic domain to keep workers from being played off against each other, undermining wage and labor standards.[1] Never easy even within national boundaries, it is even more difficult to do so when markets transnationalize, particularly in Europe where transnationalization has been carried very far. Accelerated by the "1992" program, European integration will become even deeper when European Monetary Union (EMU) is implemented. Employers already operate throughout Europe, while national governments have given up important regulatory capacities to the Single Market and begun surrendering macroeconomic policy prerogatives to EMU.

European integration has thus given unions strong reasons to develop Europe-wide capacities. Moreover, its political framework is favorable: European Union (EU) institutions allow more political regulation than in other regional blocs or the global economy. Relatively greater intra-European similarity in institutional and development levels also

Notes for this section begin on page 359.

facilitates cross-border union action. The implications of integration for European unions have proven contradictory, however. While greater than elsewhere, transnational governance in Europe is limited by the EU's treaty/constitution in areas that most concern labor such as basic union rights – core issues like pay and the rights to organize and strike are explicitly excluded. Social policy more generally remains the prerogative of EU member states. Moreover, EMU institutionalizes restrictive monetary policies insulated from political accountability and raises formidable obstacles to reducing Europe's high unemployment. In most other respects, European institutions have not gained policy capacities that have been weakened at national level.

Because industrial relations and social policy are left in member states' hands, unions still have to act in national arenas. EU decision-making procedures have the same effect. While they uniquely combine transnational and intergovernmental processes, the intergovernmental Council of Ministers has the last word. Pressuring national governments is therefore a more promising way to influence Council decisions than working at the European level. Such disincentives to invest in European structures reinforce the chronic obstacles to transnational union action posed by institutional, cultural and language differences. Conflicts of interest, perceived and real, among national unions, often paralleling those of their governments within the EU, are further obstacles. So too is organizational inertia; unions are typically reactive, reproducing habitual behaviors until pressure from new challenges grows irresistible. Most important, despite labor's proclaimed "internationalism," European unions have been profoundly nationalized in the twentieth century.

Although European integration gives national unions reason to transnationalize, multiple factors accordingly induce them to "stay home." Yet, a thickening network of transnational union activities has recently been developing, largely within the framework of the European Trade Union Confederation (ETUC). Culminating a slow response to European integration, the ETUC was founded in 1973. For a decade thereafter it lobbied and issued statements with limited influence from a very small Brussels office (despite its large formal membership). But the new challenges of the later 1980s triggered changes in the ETUC's leadership, organization, and capabilities which gave ETUC increased visibility and importance. By the early 1990s it had become a limited but genuine participant in European policy formation, and its significance to its member confederations and sectoral organizations was growing. Awareness of the ETUC and the relevance of European action even began to filter down to national and local unions. A European trade union structure with some potential for becoming a European labor movement was thus emerging.

Why, despite all the obstacles, did this Europeanization of labor occur? The renewal of European integration itself provided much of the impetus. But an important part of the answer lies in initiatives taken by European political institutions, principally the Commission and Parliament. They provided new incentives to European unions to reconceptualize their strategic interests. The unions have consequently "Europeanized" more than could be expected in the recent decade, largely in response to what European-level policy-makers have offered them. But those policymakers had their own purposes, not always congruent with unions' interests. The first result of this was a particular form of European unionization which arguably failed to equip European unions to cope with the challenges posed by integration.

This chapter describes how support from European institutions combined with efforts of trade union leaders who were convinced of the need for transnational action to encourage and shape the Europeanization of labor representation. It begins by briefly reviewing European integration. Part II surveys the history of Euro-level unionization. Part III assesses the strategic consequences of the interaction between European integration and the ETUC, and the dilemmas posed by the construction of a – meager – European industrial relations system. The chapter concludes by proposing that a new era may be opening. This new era will present European-level unionism with new challenges and call for new thinking.

The Economic Approach to Integration

For the EU's founders and many of their successors, European integration was a geopolitical imperative, securing peace by binding Germany to its neighbors and uniting Europe in the face of the Soviet threat. They pursued their goals by a particular strategy of successive increments of economic integration, however. This "economic approach" was adopted because it seemed the only way to generate the necessary political support. But this approach meant that integration had to be consistent with the economic interests whose support was decisive, primarily European capital and national governments. This, plus the fact that social policy was an essential source of domestic political support which governments did not want to relinquish, meant that social policy, labor standards, and industrial relations institutions were largely excluded. The dominant thrust in building an integrated Europe became market building rather than market regulation – overcoming barriers imposed by national regulation without its relocation to the European level. The first phase of the process ran from the 1957 Rome Treaties until the early 1980s and involved the creation and consolidation of the "Common Market." The second began in 1985 with the program to complete the Single Market by 1992 and continues with the introduction of a single currency in 1999.

The Common Market Phase

The strategists of European integration came to believe that their purposes could best be achieved by concentrating on specific areas. After trial and error, they chose the trade/market area. The 1957 Rome EEC Treaty created a customs-free zone, common external tariff, and Common Agricultural Policy (CAP). The resulting "common market" was to be compatible with national models of economic development. Member states retained their industrial as well as macroeconomic policy autonomy. Social policy and industrial relations remained part of national sovereignty and politics.

The EU thus began as a narrowly trade-oriented venture with little authority in the areas which mattered to unions. Its originators hoped, however, that once Europeans had begun to cooperate, policy interdependence would promote "spillover," reinforced by deliberately built-in tension between the EU's original mandate and the institutions set up to implement it. The European Commission, through its monopoly of policy proposal, was specifically endowed with capacities to promote a broadening of the EU mandate. The early Commissions took this too seriously for member states, however. Just as the Commission began to flex its muscles in the mid-1960s, General de Gaulle's decisive intervention stopped spillover cold. The resulting "Luxembourg Compromise" made unanimity necessary to decide all controversial issues, even though the Rome Treaty anticipated flexibility in Council decision making, including majority voting.

In fact, the EU had reached a postwar boom equilibrium. European national economies thrived within a Keynesian-welfare state framework and entered the consumerist era. The EU's customs-free zone and common external tariff gave them the space to regulate themselves, strike viable domestic political deals, and trade with one another while being reasonably well insulated from the outside world, particularly the U.S. European governments desired little more. Clearly they did not need, nor want, transnational social policy and industrial relations. Trade unions themselves were largely indifferent to Europe, focused, as they were, on new Golden Age domestic environments where they were winning far more than ever.

The social provisions of the 1958 Rome Treaty were correspondingly limited, excluding employment and remuneration issues except for equal pay for men and women (Article 119).[2] It prescribed free mobility of labor, paralleling free movement of goods and capital; this led to rules governing workers' rights to move across EU territory, residence and equal treatment in hiring and firing, remuneration and other conditions for member state nationals working outside their own country.[3] National social security program differences aimed at securing competitive advantage were barred, leading to the first social legislation (in 1958) and Court of Justice litigation. The major "social" clause, Article 118, called for "improved working conditions and an improved standard of living for the workers" without establishing instruments for doing so beyond the "functioning of the common market." The Commission was empowered only to "cooperate" with member states. Broad matters of "social citizenship" remained the responsibility of individual states and the Common Market coexisted with as wide a variety of social policy and industrial relations regimes as it had members.

Integration was briefly revived in the 1970s by plans to "widen" the EU by including the British, Danish, Irish and Norwegians (who decided not to join), and "deepen" it with larger budgetary powers, new foreign policy coordination, and movement to EMU. Social matters were part of this revival. To build direct links to interest groups and encourage them to organize on a European basis, the Commission established a "Social Partners" office in 1972, giving European-level labor and business organizations privileged access to Commission deliberations on social and employment issues and participation in new sectoral Joint Committees. A 1974 Social Action Program embodied commitments by EU members to greater coordination of employment policies, more protection of migrant workers, more promotion of gender equality in work, and a common vocational training policy. It also proposed greater consultation on social protection policies, health and safety measures, pilot antipoverty schemes, and more management-labor involvement in EU decisions.[4]

The Social Action Program was partially implemented toward the "less favored" – migrant workers and their families, the handicapped, youth, and the poor. There were also directives on gender equality with respect to pay, working conditions, and social security, and on workers' rights in collective layoffs (plant closures), changes in firm ownership, and bankruptcies. This last provided that affected workers be informed and consulted, the first enunciation of a recurrent EU theme. Regional differences received heightened recognition through the creation of the European Regional Development Fund (ERDF) in 1975, although resistance to interstate transfers kept its resources small.[5] Most important was the workplace health and safety area. The tripartite Advisory Committee on Health and Safety at Work (ACSH), established in 1974, proposed much legislation, though most was subsequently watered down or blocked.[6] More legally binding health and safety regulation was nevertheless enacted during the next decade than in the preceding one.[7]

The burst of activity was shortlived. Growing pains from the expansion from six to nine member states after 1973 created chronic budgetary conflicts that paralyzed decision-making. National governments increasingly subverted adopted measures and very few new ones got through the Council.[8] In the social realm, proposals for workers' participation (the 1980 Vredeling Directive) as well as regulations on part-time and temporary work were stymied. By the later 1970s, the Social Action Program was a dead letter. Thus, the economic approach continued to marginalize European level labor market regulation, whether by social policy or trade unions. While proponents of such regulation held it a necessary concomitant of economic integration, they had limited ability to promote it.

Integration was basically stalled by worsening economic circumstances after the 1973 oil shock – high inflation which employment-destroying deflation could not root out. In response, EU member states retreated to particular national solutions, creating divergent economic policies and disparity among EU economies. Growth levels fell by half and intra-EU trade expansion stopped. In this context, development of the EU institutional system came to a standstill. The European action that did occur, intergovernmental rather than supranational, largely involved new coping mechanisms – the European Monetary System (EMS), a Franco-German effort to limit damage from the collapse of the Bretton Woods system, and the European Council – periodic summits of heads of state and governments to coordinate general policy lines in the newly difficult period.

"1992" and the Renewal of European Integration

Changing intergovernmental politics in the European policy arena made a resumption of integration possible in the mid-1980s. The French government's 1982-83 abandonment of its reform hopes in favor of austerity increased economic policy convergence, enabling the Franco-German "couple" to be reunited, and making a renewed search for European solutions more attractive and politically promising. This opened new space for the European Commission to play its accelerator role. A new Commission installed in January 1985, led by President Jacques Delors, brought political entrepreneurs to use this new space.[9] They concluded that completion of the internal market, at the EU's traditional trade/market core, was the most politically feasible way of re-energizing integration. The June 1985 White Paper listed 279 measures needed to establish "an area without internal frontiers in which the free movement of goods, persons, services and capital is assured by 1992." To ease their enactment, the Rome Treaty was revised, by the Single European Act (SEA, ratified in 1987) to prescribe decisions by a "qualified majority" (QMV) for most White Paper issues.[10] Henceforth member states might have to accept legislation they did not desire. Finally, the SEA enlarged EU "competences" – the legal basis for action – in research and development, the environment, foreign policy cooperation, and "economic and social cohesion" (regional policy), and made it easier to act in certain existing areas by extending QMV.[11]

"1992" ignited business and public enthusiasm. It also created somewhat greater scope for labor market regulation. While preserving unanimity rules over most social and labor measures, the SEA did allow QMV on health and safety issues, to keep national regulations from being used as barriers to competition. New openings were also provided for regional development policy, rapidly developed in the "reform of the structural funds" in 1988. Next, Commission promotion of "social dialogue" between capital and labor at the European level was encouraged. Finally, the European Parliament got new "cooperation" (amending) powers which proved significant when the Parliament's Social Democrat-Christian Democrat majority became a major proponent of enlarging EU's social policy role.

"Market building" nevertheless continued to take precedence. Only after the 1992 program was well underway, the EU budget reorganized, and EMU deliberations started did the Commission turn to labor "market correcting." The 1989 Community Charter of Basic Social Rights for Workers was its centerpiece. Drawing on policy legacies from the 1970s and early 1980s, it was first broached in 1987. Delors then advertised the idea to the 1988 Stockholm ETUC Congress, implying social rights that were enforceable as the ETUC urged.[12] Rather than laying down a set of enforceable rights, however, the Social Charter ended up as a "solemn commitment" on the part of member states – eleven, given British rejection – to a set of "fundamental social rights" for workers.

The Action Program which followed in November 1989 proposed legislation to implement the Charter. By January 1993, forty-seven different proposals would be submitted to the Council. Only some were for directives or regulations while others were for nonbinding "recommendations" or "opinions." Moreover, only proposals based on Article 118a,

100A, or Article 119 (equal treatment) had much chance of enactment. The rest brought little new (often updating existing instruments), involved health and safety matters, or were targeted on specific groups.

The results were modest, excepting the health and safety measures, which rapidly became a strong grid of transnational regulations.[13] Of the nine most juridically and politically contentious legislative proposals, three were meant to regulate "atypical" (part-time and temporary) employment, and only one passed the Council. A "working time" directive passed in watered-down form. Directives also passed on "pregnant women" (to prevent firing, stipulate minimum remuneration for maternity leave, and protect health and safety during pregnancy), employers' obligations to inform employees about their employment contract, and to provide advance notice of collective layoffs (plant closures). Most significant was a proposal for "European Works Councils" (EWCs) in transnational firms. But this, plus one applying the legal and collectively bargained rules of a member state to workers "posted" by employers to work there temporarily, and a proposal prescribing parental leave, were not dealt with until later.

The social policy activism launched by the Social Charter was aimed at mobilizing political resources for the Commission itself, to calm some of the fears which the Single Market aroused in the European labor movement and, in the process, to help the Commission acquire labor support for its strategies. Moreover, to the degree to which EU action failed to fulfill the promise of the Social Charter, the Commission might then count on indignant voices (including the Socialists and Christian Democrats in the European Parliament) to mobilize support for "Social Europe," contributing to future pressure for EU social policy.

In the wake of 1989 and end of the Cold War, the pace of integration intensified, marked by two new, and simultaneous, Intergovernmental Conferences in 1991 culminating in the Maastricht Treaty on European Union (TEU).[14] Once again, social policy was peripheral. Maastricht's main effect was to initiate movement to EMU. EMU will replace separate national currencies by a single currency managed by a European System of Central Banks (ESCB), comprised of a European Central Bank (ECB), where authority over monetary policy will be vested, and member state central banks. The primary objective assigned to the ECB is price stability. To assure this, the ECB is to be independent, formally even more than Germany's Bundesbank. Membership in EMU is contingent on similar independence of national central banks and satisfaction of "convergence criteria" – tough targets for lowering public deficits, debt, inflation levels, interest rates, and the stability requirements of the Exchange Rate Mechanism (ERM).[15] Continued compliance once EMU is established is assured by a "stability and growth pact" adopted at the December 1996 Dublin Summit. EMU thus committed Europe to a highly restrictive policy regime to prevent inflation whatever the cost in unemployment.

Maastricht also included a "Social Protocol" which modestly expanded the EU's social policy authority. It specified subjects on which eleven member states agreed that action could be taken through the normal EU legislative process without the participation of the British, who opted out. It extended QMV to "working conditions" and "information and consultation." Moreover, it made negotiated agreements possible as a binding substitute for legislation, a provision remarkable both because it made bargaining between European-level union and employer organizations a formal part of European social policy formation, and because it was itself the product of such bargaining. Action could also be taken on social security and the social protection of workers, protection of workers whose employment contract is terminated, and the "representation and collective defense of the interests of workers and employers," including co-determination. However, it requires a unanimous vote of the eleven (fourteen after 1995) to adopt legislation in these fields, while legislation concerning "pay or the rights to organize, strike, or impose lockouts" – i.e. the heart of "representation and collective defense" – is entirely excluded.

The first Social Protocol proposal, in 1993, after delayed ratification of Maastricht, was on the "information and consultation of workers" in multinational corporations. Failing a negotiated agreement, a 1994 directive mandated EWCs in all multinationals above a certain size with a European presence. A new try in 1995 on parental leave, led to the "first European bargain," in December, 1995 (subsequently made law by Council Decision). The Commission then reopened "atypical work," leading to agreement on parity for part-time workers in 1997. The "burden of proof" (a Social Charter proposal about workplace sexual harassment), European Company Law, including "information and consultation," the regulation of short-term contracts (part of the atypical work agenda), and the extension of information and consultation to all EU companies of more than fifty employees, were other issues being explored.[16]

The Commission's 1995-1997 Medium Term Social Action Program anticipated little new legislation. European institutions, member states, and social partners are to engage in "collective reflection" aimed at the "creation of jobs," the "top priority" of social policy, but for which "responsibility lies mainly with individual Member States."[17] Under the rubric of "subsidiarity," European institutions are now conceived as facilitating the pooling of experience and ideas, and encouraging decentralized action rather than setting binding common standards – the atypical work bargain being a good example. The one change, following from the British Labour Party's 1997 election victory, was the end of Britain's opt-out of the Social Protocol, incorporating its language into the treaty base for all further EU social policy.

The Tentative Europeanization of Trade Union Structure

The story of trade union Europeanization is one of complex interactions between European institutions seeking to stimulate Euro-level interest representation, unionists who perceived Europe as important, and the growing significance of European integration itself. From the beginning, the architects of European integration tried to promote transnational interest representation. Jean Monnet's functionalist strategy saw the development of Euro-level interest representation around the Commission and other EU institutions as a royal road toward policy "spillover" and full-fledged European political culture. European institutions and political entrepreneurs should accordingly devote some resources to enticing important interest groups to invest in Euro-level processes. In the case of unions, however, receptiveness depended on Europe being salient and on the existence of a critical mass of well-placed unionists who believed transnationalization was essential. In the first (Common Market) period, Europe was an adjunct to the national political economies where national union movements were central players. Little transnationalization was to be expected then, and little occurred. The situation changed decisively beginning in 1985.

The ETUC's Founding Years

Employers responded to integration more rapidly than labor, forming the Union of Industrial and Employers' Confederations of Europe (UNICE) a year after the Rome Treaty.[18] Although some trade unionists also saw a need for organization geared to the EU, ideological and organizational divisions delayed the establishment of the European Trade Union Confederation (ETUC) until 1973.[19] By then, with the customs union fully implemented, initial discussion of Economic and Monetary Union (EMU), prospective membership for the four EFTA states, and growing Europeanization of business, the case for a labor counterpart to UNICE was stronger than ever. Socialist and Christian confederations both set up

European regional organizations. The prospect of EFTA countries in the EU then stimulated a desire to integrate ICFTU (International Confederation of Free Trade Unions) unions from the two regions more closely. Differences arising from the conflicting principles of preexisting organizations were resolved sufficiently to make the founding of the ETUC possible.

The new ETUC included all EFTA unions, not just those within EU member states, and was open to Christian and communist unions, not just those within ICFTU. In addition, it gave limited representation to the European Industry Committees (renamed Federations (EIFs), as we will call them throughout, by the 1995 ETUC Congress) – regional sectoral organizations linked in some cases to the International Trade Secretariats (ITSs). From the outset, therefore, its membership included European sectoral organizations, not just national intersectoral confederations. The ETUC was thus launched on its way to becoming a broad, encompassing organization with a claim to sole representation of unions at the European level. Operationally, the ETUC was the Secretariat, running the organization with a very small staff (about twenty). Membership dues yielded just over a half million U.S. dollars, barely enough to pay for a Brussels office in the dingy downtown ICFTU building. The ETUC was resource poor, dependent on supplementary support from its affiliates and Commission funds. This undoubtedly reflected the national unions' limited expectations for it. The head of the largest union in Europe, IG-Metall, referred to the ETUC as "letter-box," for example, and never attended Executive Committee meetings.[20]

Between 1973 and the "1992" project, the ETUC was as preoccupied with implementing its organizational principles as with establishing itself in the European arena. There was an important initial phase of ideological enlargement when Christian unions were admitted in 1974 and the Italian communist-affiliated CGIL in 1976. Cold War tensions persisted, however, and further admission of communist-affiliated confederations was blocked by their national counterparts.[21] By 1983 the admission of unions from new members of the EU (plus some from outside it) had increased ETUC affiliates from a founding seventeen (covering 36 million members in sixteen countries), to thirty-four (about 41 million members in twenty countries). The number of participating EIFs had also risen from six to ten.

The ETUC's purpose was defined vaguely, to "represent and advance the social, economic, and cultural interests of the workers on the European level in general and toward European institutions in particular." The policy positions it took were not much more specific because, according to one observer, "claims had to be acceptable to a maximum number of members" without impinging "too much [on] issues of national controversy," while remaining "sufficiently relevant and mobilizing to legitimate the existence of a European union structure."[22] The Executive Committee (elected by the triennial Congress) could decide by two-thirds majorities (weighted by membership), but consensus became customary. Nothing at all could be decided without the agreement of the two largest confederations, the British TUC and German DGB, who themselves differed over European integration itself. The ETUC concentrated on broad issues on which it could pronounce, but not affect, such as employment, reduction of working time, training, and information and consultation in multinationals. It made a few efforts to mobilize its affiliates' members, a rare instance being a demonstration against unemployment by 80,000 unionists at the 1983 Stuttgart European Council. Beyond that, ETUC affiliates did not allow it any action role.

The ETUC's early attempts at exerting outward influence were confined to the Brussels arena, largely dissociated from the union members it nominally represented. This was encouraged by the Commission when it set up a "Social Partners" unit plus various sectoral tripartite bodies, the most important being the tripartite ACSH. The ETUC initially had high hopes for such proto-corporatist initiatives, but withdrew from most in 1978 after concluding that neither employers nor governments were interested in serious commitments. By then, however, energies for broader European integration had all but disappeared and Euro-pessimism set in.

The "1992" Period: European Institutions Pitch In Once More

The momentum that "1992" gave to integration led to new efforts by European institutions to promote Euro-unionism which, combined with heightened union awareness of the need for effective European-level action, began a revitalization of the ETUC. The SEA signaled increased receptivity to European problem solving by member states and business. Unions took this as a threat to national regimes of labor rights and standards, and began strident warnings about "social dumping." The prospect of a single transnational market also fed a new willingness among unions, increasingly on the defensive nationally, to look to transnational strategies. The SEA offered some new opportunities, albeit limited, for doing so and the Commission actively encouraged the unions to make the most of them.

Strengthening ETUC Resources: Delors's Social Dialogue Strategy

The Commission focused on promoting "social dialogue" between the European organizations of unions and employers. Delors succeeded in making it an explicit Community objective in the SEA's Article 118B, requiring the Commission to "develop the dialogue between management and labor at European level which could, if the two sides consider it desirable, lead to relations based on agreement." There were formidable obstacles, however, including an imbalance in the social partners' purposes and resources. Neither ETUC nor UNICE had mandates to negotiate binding agreements. For UNICE this was an asset, since one reason for its existence was to avert European-level regulation and bargaining.[23] ETUC wanted European-level regulation, whether through legislation or negotiation, but like UNICE, it was primarily an organization of national confederations. Because neither of its most powerful constituents, the DGB and the TUC, were empowered to negotiate, it was difficult to imagine ETUC itself officially bargaining. In resource terms, although UNICE was formally small in size and budget, employers' firm-level power and control of technical, legal, linguistic and financial knowledge provide a very large pool to be tapped as needed.

The initial "Val Duchesse" discussions with which Delors sought to initiate social dialogue in 1985 broke down quickly. Social dialogue was relaunched in 1989 in the glow of the Social Charter, but the organizations' contradictory purposes again made discussion frustrating.[24] This time, however, the Commission was eager to make it work better. Given evident differences in the social partners' stakes and resources, it decided upon an asymmetrical approach, seeking first to encourage ETUC and national union movements to become stronger European actors. Recognizing that resources from national unions alone were unlikely to suffice, it viewed EU resources as necessary, while also giving ETUC a new incentive to promote European-level discussions. A more effective ETUC might then cause UNICE to reconsider its nay-saying posture. Moreover, a stronger ETUC, partly dependent upon Commission resources, could also be an ally for the Commission in broader political matters. This new Commission strategy turned out to be important.

Delors launched it in a speech to the 1988 ETUC Congress in Stockholm previewing the Social Charter.[25] His address to the TUC's Bournemouth Conference later that year prodded a major, formerly anti-European, ETUC constituent to new European commitments. Delors also engaged important unionists privately. His staff and DG V (Employment and Social Affairs) systematically encouraged ETUC, not least by supplying money for ETUC's internal activities to the tune of several million ecu per year – underwriting ETUC meetings in Brussels and elsewhere (travel, translation) and funding for the European Trade Union Institute (ETUI), the ETUC research arm, and an organ called AFETT (set up in 1986) to train unionists about new technologies. In 1989 it added support to ETUC health and safety activity through the newly established Trade Union Technical Bureau (TUTB) and, in 1990 to another new unit, the European Trade Union College (ETUCO), set up to train unionists for European-level activity. The amounts were small in absolute terms, but they allowed ETUC to pay for new personnel and build a larger, more autonomous, headquarters organization. TUTB and ETUCO were important because they provided new capabilities. The Commission also nourished privileged networks of communication between itself and ETUC. Delors knew many of the ETUC's officials and gave time to cultivating them further, as did key personnel in his Commission staff and DGV, some of whom had come from the CFDT and CISL.

The interplay between European institutions and ETUC is epitomized by the creation of the TUTB. Accelerated even before the SEA, EU health and safety regulation was broadened by the new treaty to keep national diversity from maintaining barriers to trade. Moreover, the Single Market norm of mutual recognition, requiring each member state to allow entry of goods satisfying standards where they were produced, was unacceptable to high-standard states. The alternative, harmonization, was long and arduous because of the volume of standards and the need for unanimity. To circumvent this, the Internal Market Council adopted a "new approach" in 1985, whereby directives specified "essential requirements" goods had to meet, leaving it to European standardization bodies (initially CEN and CENELEC) to set technical standards for doing so. While making harmonization more efficient, however, this attenuated its legitimacy. CEN and CENELEC were private bodies, themselves composed of private national standardization bodies dominated by manufacturers.[26] Other interested parties, including workers, had no voice. That standards, European or national, were "voluntary" – binding only on the bodies' members without force of law – was no solution. Products conforming to standards were presumed to meet the EU requirements, obliging member states to allow their entry unless noncompliance could be proven. To unions this was unacceptable because the standards de facto determined workplace health and safety issues.

The ETUC had lobbied for European-level occupational health and safety action, and for tripartite arrangements giving unions a voice in it, since the later 1970s. The SEA and the "new approach" intensified these efforts. The ETUC pressed for union participation in formulating the 1989 "new approach" Machinery and Framework Directives, particularly because the specifications for implementing the far-reaching machinery directive were left up to the standardization bodies.[27] While unions had some rights but few resources for influencing national standardization, they had none whatever at international level.[28] The ETUC accordingly demanded rights for unions to influence European standardization through the ACSH and called upon the EU to finance a "technical tool" to assist the ACSH workers' group.[29] There was a debate within ETUC over whether that tool should itself be attached to the ACSH or be an independent body providing ETUC with its own technical expertise. The ETUC ultimately opted for the latter, supported by the Commission which was trying to Europeanize the "new approach" standardization process as well as expand the scope of European health and safety regulation.[30] The Parliament seized the initiative, establishing a line in the 1989 budget to give ETUC new technical capacity.[31]

Financial support from European institutions also strengthened sectoral-level trade union structures, the EIFs. There are now fifteen with various relationships to their international (ITS) counterparts. Some, like the metal, construction and wood, chemical, and now the public services union EIFs, are entirely independent while others, like that for commercial, clerical and technical unions, are regional bodies of the internationals.[32] As organizations of unions rather than of confederations, like ETUC, the EIFs are European-level bodies directly accountable to national unions, and hence potentially more acceptable instruments for cross-national joint action.[33] In the late 1980s, however, they were tiny operations with minimalist staffs, reflecting their member unions' small expectations. They served mainly to link national unions and the ETUC, enabling unions to bypass national confederations in lobbying the ETUC as well as the Commission, and as a mechanism for building cross-border networks of union officials and exposing them to European issues.

The Commission pushed social dialogue less actively at sectoral than peak level,[34] but, with the Parliament, it supported EIF efforts to organize worker representatives in multinational corporations (MNCs).[35] The EIFs initially got some EU money for such meetings pending adoption of a 1991 proposal for a directive on EWCs. When it became clear that the directive was stuck in Council, the Commission decided to fund EIF efforts to prepare EWCs proactively. Meetings quickly proliferated, financed by a new budget line (up to 17 million ecus per year) set up by the European Parliament in 1992.[36] The money came to more than four times EIF budgets at the time. The meetings typically produced permanent "trade union committees" to seek management agreement for the establishment of EWCs – in essence, the beginnings of European trade union structures at company level. Although most of the money covered meeting costs, it also enabled EIFs to hire additional staff, and added substantially to their meager resources, giving them a higher profile and legitimacy within ETUC, with their own member unions, and with workplace activists attending the meetings.

Various organizational components of the ETUC were thus added or strengthened with European institutions' support. But the ETUC itself could not be a useful ally for them or a forceful representative of national unions concerned about Europe without becoming a more effective organization. Though encouraged by European institutions, actual change could only come from within.

What Kind of ETUC? Organizational Reform and an Expanded Vision

Serious efforts to rethink ETUC did not begin until its 1988 Congress, where the confluence of impulses toward change from within ETUC and the Commission became evident. Jacques Delors's Stockholm speech epitomized the latter, ending with a plea for unions to join in defending the "European model of society":

> We need all our strength at the moment [of] the great peaceful revolution ... which will mean the disappearance ... of physical barriers between the twelve but will also result in a common home, Europe. In order to do this ... we need a powerful trade union movement which shares our overall vision and which will help us and thus prove we are moving forward.[37]

This resonated powerfully with delegates who urged that the ETUC be given "increased means to become a united and coherent force" for "a true social and contractual European policy," through "strengthened structures and increased membership, enhancing efficiency both in terms of finances and staff," and increased cooperation among an increased number of EIFs. This clearly implied greater delegation of authority to the ETUC.

The Congress authorized reform proposals to be prepared for the next Congress in 1991. Only the national confederations could achieve reform, and the German DGB, representing the most powerful European labor movement and dissatisfied with the ETUC's responses to the Single Market, became the prime mover.[38] The DGB found allies in Italian confederations who strongly desired a more supranational ETUC. Together they overcame the then Secretary General's resistance to set up a working group on ETUC organization in December 1989, chaired by Johan Stekelenburg, president of the Dutch Confederation of Labor (FNV). The "Stekelenburg Report," adopted in 1990, recommended that the ETUC "become a genuine confederation with appropriate competences and tasks," implying "the transfer of some competences from national to the European level" including " setting priorities but also executing them," to "coordinate collective actions, build up international trade union countervailing power and organize solidarity through actions promoting common objectives." The Report proposed changes in policy-making structure and enhanced power for the ETUC leadership. It also urged an increased role for the EIFs, making the ETUC, until then an organization of national confederations, one consisting of cross-national sectoral bodies as well.[39]

The 1991 Congress ratified these recommendations, prioritized European union action, and emphasized that the ETUC was the vehicle for it. The role envisioned for the ETUC included formulation and implementation of joint strategies in collective bargaining and representation of joint interests in the EU legislative arena. The Congress also approved changes to shake up the ponderous policy process, engage leaders of national member organizations more actively (rather than just sending international department bureaucrats to meetings), and facilitate consensus building in preparation for Executive Committee decisions.[40] At least as importantly, a new leadership was selected. In a deal brokered by the DGB, Emilio Gabaglio from the Italian CISL became the new General Secretary (over a Dutch candidate backed by the Nordic unions); Jean Lapeyre, the French master of the Delors Commission connection became a Deputy General Secretary; and a Finn was given a second Deputy position created to offset the Northern coalition's loss in the leadership contest as well as other issues. The other main organizational change turned the EIFs into member organizations more nearly equivalent to national confederations, moving the ETUC closer to a supranational organization.[41]

There was no consensus on this supranationalist vision of the ETUC, however. The Italians and Belgians pushed it vigorously, the Nordics and the TUC opposed abandoning established "intergovernmental" practices, while the DGB itself, so instrumental to the changes, could then not support supranationalization because of opposition from its member unions, notably IG Metall. Deciding which competences would be transferred "from national to the European level" was left to the Executive Committee, where the diverse structure and interests of national constituent bodies would retard change. The ETUC thus remained dependent for its authority on the member confederations. At the same time, financially strapped member organizations were in no position to enlarge ETUC resources, so that it was still a small organization with a six-member secretariat backed by a staff of thirty, still dependent on the additional funds from European institutions.

The 1991 Congress may have been a milestone, but the ETUC still had a long way to go. Quickly, however, its path took a new turn, again because of European institutions. The Maastricht Treaty and, in particular, the Social Protocol, inescapably forced the issue of the ETUC's negotiating authority back onto the internal agenda.

Turning the ETUC into a Bargainer: The Social Protocol

The interaction of European institutions and ETUC reformers had strengthened the trade union side of social dialogue, but not sufficiently to bring employers to the table for serious negotiations. UNICE would only bargain under constraint, and the Commission sought ways to provide it. The threat of EU legislation was one possibility. Beginning in later 1990 the Commission produced a small flood of Action Program legislation, in the process consulting regularly with the "social partners." Employers could expect that much would not pass, but some legislation would, and UNICE disliked what it could anticipate. From UNICE's standpoint, however well-designed EU legislation might be, it would be more constraining than no legislation or a bargained agreement. Worse still, there was always the chance that legislative precedent would further embolden the Commission and even lead to a broadened treaty.

The legislative threat strategy bore fruit in the Maastricht process. The Commission tabled an ingenious "negotiate or we will legislate" proposal early in the game. In addition to new clauses to expand the EU's social policy competences and scope for QMV, it proposed that the "social partners" be given a short period to negotiate an agreement on subjects on which the Commission intended to propose legislation. A negotiated agreement could then replace legislation with Council approval. The Commission reasoned that expanding its competences and QMV would persuade the social partners to perceive new interests in European-level negotiating. UNICE would see negotiating as a way of softening and "flexibilizing" what might otherwise be strong EU legislation, while the ETUC would see new paths to European-level collective bargaining open up.[42] This proposal, quickly buried in the spring of 1991, nonetheless ended up as the core of the Maastricht Social Protocol. On 31 October 1991, after assiduous Commission work, the "social partners" agreed to repropose the Commission's idea in their name. UNICE accepted in order to hedge its bets: if more social legislation came after Maastricht, it preferred bargaining because employers' bargaining strength would allow watering down. But this was a fall-back position. UNICE did not expect the 31 October proposals to pass, because the British vowed to block any such proposals. An unexpected turn of events at the very last minute, when the eleven decided to go ahead without Britain on the Social Protocol, exposed the risks UNICE had taken.

For the ETUC, the Social Protocol was a sudden breakthrough, beyond anything it could have reasonably expected, making it a participant not only in EU social policy formation but also in the theretofore exclusively intergovernmental arena of EU constitutional politics. But the Social Protocol's significance would depend on how it was used. In response to ETUC's call for the social partners to use it on their own initiative, UNICE said it would not even consider its use except at the Commission's initiative. After operationalizing the Social Protocol procedure early in 1993, the Commision chose to test it with the pending European Works Council Directive.

The "information and consultation of workers" proposal had a long EC/EU history, stretching back to the failed 1980 Vredeling Directive. The Action Program proposed a similar directive. Council inaction on it prompted the attempt under the Social Protocol.[43] Negotiations over EWCs offered prospects for success in achieving something of considerable symbolic value. By 1993 there was accumulated experience with works councils, the labor movement wanted them, and employers had learned that they were not very threatening. The social partners agreed to try, but it turned out that no agreement was possible, and the proposal returned to the legislative process. There it was put on a "fast track" to ensure enactment while Germany held the Council Presidency. The directive, passed in September 1994, is arguably the single most important piece of European legislation to date from a trade union perspective.[44]

The failure to get an EWC agreement left the Social Protocol's utility to be demonstrated. The Commission decided to try again in early 1995 with a proposal on parental leave, another issue with a long history.[45] This time the social partners reached an agreement, signing the "first European bargain" in December 1995. The Council then gave it legal force with a Directive in June 1996. The Directive gives all employees holding a job for at least one year a right to three months leave to take care of a child at birth, adoption, or any time up to the age of eight, plus a right to leave for "urgent family reasons" (to be specified by member states). The right is individual and nontransferable (to assure equal treatment of men and women).[46] Substantively the agreement made modest progress over what already existed in member states. This made the deal relatively easy, which was why it was proposed – for the important thing was to establish the political precedent of negotiated legislation under the Social Protocol.[47]

The Commission also started procedure on two directives on "atypical work" (types of jobs other than full-time and permanent). The first was on "flexible working time and worker security." It aimed at guaranteeing workers in "new formulae of work" the same rights and treatment as workers with full-time permanent jobs. The Commission presented the issue as a tradeoff, granting to employers more flexible work and to unions the need to "organize" and regulate such work. The basic principle was "nondiscrimination" between full-and part-time or other atypical work. ETUC and UNICE agreed to negotiations concluded in spring 1997 with the second "European collective bargain."[48]

The atypical work agreement was an important step because it concerned a more controversial high stakes matter than parental leave. The question was narrowed down to part-time work, leaving aside other forms of atypical work. The "principle of nondiscrimination" was then recognized for those employment conditions where the EU had legal responsibilities. The Council was asked to produce a Recommendation to member states about applying it in areas of "social protection" where the EU had no competences. The framework accord met UNICE's desires by avoiding new binding regulation and providing for decentralized implementation by national politicians and collective bargaining. The results would thus depend on unions' ability to make employers cooperate on the part-time work issues. The deal may give national unions incentives to organize part-time workers and, hence, to strengthen themselves in new, heavily feminized, sectors of the workforce. Unions, by signing, recognized the legitimacy of employers' quest for flexibility in employment patterns, however, and the agreement made it possible for national-level "social partners" to lower national barriers to part-time employment.[49]

The Social Protocol and the "negotiated legislation" which developed from it was an extraordinary culmination of the process begun so inauspiciously at the social dialogue meetings in 1985. The social dialogue structure provided the Commission with a forum in which to launch its "negotiate or we will legislate" initiative. But before doing so, it had already enlisted the ETUC in what amounted to a coalition to push a refractory UNICE into accepting a role as bargainer. This was a sharp reminder that while issues concerning the relationships between trade union structure and strategy can be debated within unions, they are determined quite as much by the state and other market actors. For the Social Protocol, the Commission's initiatives were decisive in opening an opportunity for ETUC to become a negotiating body – an opportunity which the newly installed ETUC leadership was eager to exploit.

The Commission has done nothing comparable to overcome employer resistance at the sectoral level. Their resistance is facilitated because most European sectoral business organizations are industry rather than employer associations. This fact is typically invoked to justify refusal to enter social dialogue, holding that it is UNICE's job to discuss social matters. UNICE tries to reinforce this virtual monopoly of representation by confining social dialogue to European-level intersectoral organizations. This division of labor between UNICE and sectoral organizations may simply reflect opposition to any European collective bargaining and an absence of strong countervailing pressures. If needed, the organizations' mandates could either be adapted or separate European-level employer organizations set up.[50] But even where they exist they are not necessarily willing social partners; the Western European Metal Trade Employers Organization (WEM) refuses even to meet informally with the EMF.[51]

Social dialogue has been established with Commission support in a few sectors, typically with special EU programs. Thus, restructuring plans for economically vulnerable sectors like textiles and clothing, shipbuilding or automobiles, where the Single Market created large transition problems, often obligated negotiated distribution of EU training and R&D funds. Sectoral discussion has also occurred on health and safety regulation in construction and retail distribution, where employers did not regard UNICE as representating their interests. Applying the Working Time Directive also necessitated negotiations in sectors where ordinary working schedules did not fit the Directive's general guidelines.[52] However, business participants have usually followed UNICE's line opposing anything like negotiations, while employers accounting for about half of Europe's jobs, including the core engineering sector, have not entered even minimal social dialogue. The existence of separate European-level sectoral business organizations nevertheless opens up possibilities of defection from UNICE's position.

EIFs have aimed at drawing employers into discussions over issues with potential for precedent-setting agreements.[53] These typically arise when employers expect more success at influencing Commission action by approaching it (or other bodies) jointly with unions, especially if they have insufficient access on their own, directly or via their governments. This excludes large multinational companies which can make their voices heard directly or through sectoral organizations they dominate. Getting money from the ESF and ERDF (regional development funds) is another inducement. EIFs have been particularly successful on health and safety issues, where incentives to engage in social dialogue are particularly strong for firms which cannot or do not want to avoid stringent national health and safety standards. Here, morever, the legitimacy of union claims to a European-level voice is widely conceded.

Still, the effectiveness with which EIFs can pursue this strategy depends heavily on Commission actions. Incentives at the Commission's disposal for sectoral negotiations may be greater than at the intersectoral level because they are not confined to proposals for legislation (a credible threat only if prospects for Council adoption are good). Yet, the EIFs argue that the Commission, notably DG V, has not used such incentives consistently. More serious is other DGs' denial of any responsibility for social dialogue on the pretext that social matters are DG V's responsibility. DG V has little voice in other DGs' measures, however, and cannot require them to take their social implications into account, so there is no forum where that must be done. Unions thus participate on "social" matters relegated to a relatively weak directorate. All interested social actors are not deprived of a voice by this, only employees. Employers, typically consulted as "industry," can articulate positions freely without having to address social implications or employee arguments. This amounts to an institutionalized insulation of EU economic and industrial policy from consideration of social consequences, reflecting the marginalization of social issues in the whole integration process. DG V conceded as much and sought to extend responsibility for taking social implications into account to other DGs in the course of a recent review of sectoral social dialogue, though without much prospect for success.[54]

Support from European institutions to EIFs has been concentrated on transborder representation in multinational companies.[55] EWCs are significantly extending the structure of European unionism down to company level. Over 1200 companies are affected by the directive.[56] If all these set up EWCs with thirty members (the maximum under the directive unless otherwise agreed), and if unions are involved, 36,000 workplace activists could be drawn into transnational union work, constructing transnational linkages among union bases within companies. The ETUC itself is generating the intellectual and financial resources to help train EWC members (through ETUCO and TUTB), and EIFs are developing the capacity to support them.

The European trade union bodies at intersectoral, sectoral, and company levels described so far are the main components of the transnational structure resulting from the interplay of European institutions and trade unionists. That interplay has spawned additional cross-border union linkages but they can only be mentioned briefly. In regions where there are local cross-border labor markets, the ETUC has set up Interregional Trade Union Committees (ITUCs). There were twenty-eight ITUCs by the end of 1995, but significant activity in only a few, mostly concerning problems of cross-border workers due to differences in national labor law and social security, and also economic development with EU regional funds.[57] Of greater long-term significance is the ETUC's integration of unions in the Central and East European countries (CEECs) of the former Soviet bloc. This began with a framework for contacts, the ETUC Forum for Cooperation and Integration, and observer status for CEEC unions at the 1991 Congress. Since then, nine confederations from six CEECs have been admitted to full membership, and four additional confederations became observers. As in the past, the ETUC embraces unions from countries beyond current EU boundaries, particularly those likely to enter the EU in the future, which are effectively part of the European economy. From the ETUC's standpoint, the "development of autonomous industrial relations at the level of the 'European model' in Eastern Europe" is vital to the common interests of workers throughout Europe.[58]

ETUC member organizations and affiliates have also set up European-level union bodies and activities outside the ETUC. Several confederations – e.g., the TUC, the Nordics, and the Italians – have separate Brussels offices. The ETUC sees them as complementary when they act as conduits for information and, as in the TUC's case, as liaisons between the ETUC and European Members of Parliament in the trade union group. But the ETUC sees them as competitive when they attempt independent lobbying. Thus it tried to discourage the DGB from setting up its own office. Some individual unions have also set up Brussels offices – e.g., Britain's General and Municipal Workers Union (GMWU), reflecting its leadership's Euro-activism, and the German postal workers union, dissatisfied with its international sectoral organization's neglect of Europe. There are also bilateral contacts between individual unions, notably between GMWU and IG Chemie, whose formal agreements might be viewed as first steps toward a pan-European union.

Of potentially greater importance are current efforts by national unions and confederations to develop cross-border coordination of wage bargaining. Most such efforts have been within the D-Mark zone, most notably by IG Metall and its counterparts in neighboring countries. At the initiative of its North-Rhine Westphalia region, wage-bargaining official from it and its counterpart unions in Belgium, Luxembourg, and the Netherlands sat in on each others' steel industry negotiations in 1997. IG Metall is extending this practice to its other regions. Through the EMF, it is urging its counterpart unions in other countries, and European unions generally, to agree on a common norm for wage increases based productivity growth plus the ECB's target rate of inflation.[59] A September 1998 meeting of confederations and a wide range of sectoral unions from Germany and the Benelux countries in Doorn, Netherlands, urged that such a norm be implemented so as to avert "bidding down," and agreed on a procedure for informing and consulting each other about wage demands on a continuing basis. While the unions involved were confined to part of the D-Mark zone, their effort was presented as a step toward "European cooperation on collective bargaining."[60] The logic of this incipient coordination within the D-Mark zone could indeed be extended beyond it once it is replaced by the Euro zone. Built up piecemeal by national confederations and/or sectoral unions to head off what IG Metall refers to as "ruinous wage competition," such coordination might be the most likely route to a Europeanization of collective bargaining. The EIFs could play a role, as could the ETUC (which welcomed the Doorn meeting), though without itself engaging in any collective bargaining. Nevertheless, the process is still at an embryonic stage, and the conflicting interests of the diverse national unions structures remain formidable obstacles.[61]

A Summing Up: The Emergent Structure of a European Labor Movement

There has been significant Europeanization of labor representation. The changes the 1991 ETUC Congress made, combined with new linkages to national constituencies (TUTB and ETUCO), and EIF formation of trade union committees in multinational companies, advanced construction of a three-tier structure through which the ambitious federalist vision of the ETUC could potentially be realized. No longer a "head without a body," the ETUC reached downward to draw national and local union officials into transnational activities. This has been largely a top-down process, however, driven by the interplay of actors in European institutions and ETUC with common stakes in a European union structure, more than by national and local unionists convinced of the need for European-level action. As one observer suggested, it has been a story of "structure before action."[62]

The forward-looking trade unionists who saw the need for European-level action could probably not have built this structure without the European institutions' support. This has produced a bias in the structure, however. Most development has been at the top, or intersectoral, level, where ETUC's leadership operates. It has also been significant at the MNC level, where EWCs are being formed. The least develpopment has been at the intermediate, or sectoral level. EIFs, except insofar as they have organized EWCs, have yet to make important breakthroughs. Recent developments reinforce this bias. At its 1995 Congress the ETUC itself identified the top and bottom tiers as the most important, citing the

Social Protocol and the EWC directive as the "two outstanding events ... in the social field" since 1991. At the intersectoral level, the ETUC's Social Protocol negotiating role has been consolidated. After much internal controversy, procedures allowing it to conduct such negotiations have been established and implemented successfully. The ETUC's organizational resources have also been strengthened. The TUTB has grown, gained legitimacy and extended its outreach. Trade union education services have been rationalized by the integration of AFFETT with ETUCO, while ETUCO's offerings have expanded considerably. The ETUC Women's Committee is more active, and played a role in the parental leave negotiations. The European Trade Union Institute, ETUC's oldest arm, has an energetic new leadership launching new activities, including conferences, publications, and a quarterly journal *(Transfer)*, attaining a higher profile and more influence. In general, different units of ETUC are better integrated and new synergy is palpable. At the MNC level, trade union committees have proliferated and are reaching a growing number of EWC agreements. One byproduct, as important as the agreements themselves, is the multiplication, however unevenly, of cross-border networks of company-level union activists that would otherwise not have existed.

Less has happened at the sectoral level. Employer resistance is virtually complete while Commission efforts thus far to overcome it have been meager. EIFs have thus had difficulty avoiding narrowly concentrating their activity on EWCs.[63] ETUC support for sectoral level negotiations has itself been ambiguous. The ETUC describes them as an important part of the European system it seeks and recently echoed EIFs' complaints about inadequate Commission support. Yet it has not backed EIFs in some situations where sectoral agreements might have been possible. Still, the EIFs have grown in status and resources aside from their EWC role. Renaming them as federations, on Italian initiative at the 1995 Congress, was a symbolic gesture. More significantly, the per capita dues paid to some have recently risen to three to four times those to ETUC, indicating increasing member union commitment and a decreasing dependence on European institutions. The EIFs have intensified cooperation among themselves, developing collective identity through regular joint meetings and joint organization of EWCs. Thus, European trade union structure at the sectoral level has been strengthened by growing support by the EIFs' member unions and their own assertiveness rather than the ETUC-Commission interaction. Still, they remain small and unevenly effective.

This raises basic issues about what the present European trade union structure can actually do. If the EIFs, the only trans-border union bodies directly linked to individual national unions, have to be the "main union parties in European-level bargaining" if there is to be such bargaining, then their resources and authority have to be increased. But that can only be done by their members, and they will not do so until they are more convinced of its necessity than they apparently are, notwithstanding their growing support for EIFs. The bias in the emergent European trade union structure therefore reflects the persistent reluctance of national unions to adopt European strategies. If they feel increasingly compelled to do so – by the threats and opportunities posed by EWCs, for example, and EMU – the debate within the ETUC over the role and distribution of authority among its various components will intensify. We turn now to that debate and the strategic dilemmas that underlie it.

Strategic Dilemmas

The ETUC has consistently articulated an expansive vision of its role. In the words of a 1995 Congress statement:

> The emergence of new economic and political power systems at European level calls for the establishment of countervailing force by the unions. This necessitates common objectives and common negotiating strategies, mechanisms for European trade union action to back up these objectives in the event of dispute, and real cross-border coordination. Building up trade union counter-pressure in Europe is thus essential in order to ensure that European construction pursues the objective of sustainable and lasting development, capable of creating jobs for all men and women, as well as social progress and solidarity. As a unitarian and pluralist organisation and the representative of the labour movement in all its breadth and diversity, the ETUC sees itself as the instrument which will serve that purpose.[64]

Thus, the ETUC aspired to become the negotiator of binding agreements with employers at the peak of a multitiered European industrial relations system as well as a player in European-level policy formation.

The Bargaining Arena

The Commission strategies, member state negotiations, and organizational maneuvers culminating in the Social Protocol propelled the ETUC toward its goal of bargainer by a distinctive route. National unions had almost always acquired power and position by mobilizing their members in the labor market and political arena. The ETUC, which had not really constructed its new position from its own resources, was in a very different situation. What could it do? Where would it get its bargaining power? What would its constituents, all more deeply rooted in dense sociopolitical settings than the ETUC, allow it to do? What resources would they provide for that purpose? How would the ETUC's new bargaining role be decided?

The Social Protocol and European Collective Bargaining

The most enthusiastic Europeanizing trade unionists hoped social dialogue would develop into European-level collective bargaining. As a "genuine confederation with appropriate competences and tasks," the ETUC would negotiate binding "framework agreements" with its intersectoral employer counterparts to be implemented at national and local levels. It would also coordinate European-level sectoral bargaining strategies and those of its national affiliates. In this light, the 31 October Agreement and the Social Protocol were major breakthroughs. But ETUC's members did not universally share this vision. The distribution of bargaining authority among different levels was a contested issue in national labor movements. The ETUC's two largest member confederations, DGB and TUC, themselves had no bargaining roles, and some others, like Sweden's LO, were losing significant bargaining roles they earlier had. The Social Protocol forced this issue to the top of the ETUC's agenda, precipitating a long internal controversy.[65]

Beginning with a June 1992 conference, the ETUC leadership staked out an ambitious claim to a bargaining role. German and Nordic participants, reacting against the Secretariat's rather autonomous conduct of the 31 October negotiations, opposed the claim.[66] The Germans argued instead for a "bottom-up" approach. Negotiating presupposed bargaining power, so that national unions had be strengthened before national collective bargaining could be coordinated and an "independent European trade union counterforce" developed, which would have to be at the sectoral level. The ETUC might facilitate such coordination but could itself only bargain at intersectoral level in the future. Finally, collective bargaining had to be distinguished from "negotiated legislation" under the Social Protocol. Skeptical even about this, the DGB was willing to allow ETUC to proceed under case-by-case mandates. The Nordics, rejecting negotiated European labor market regulation altogether, insisted upon ordinary legislation, while most Latin participants and the TUC supported negotiations by the ETUC. This division corresponded roughly to strong and weak national unions, with weak unions looking to European regulation to compensate for their lack of power.[67] These opposing positions were debated over successive Executive Committee meetings, culminating in a March 1993 compromise. This affirmed

ETUC's negotiating role but confined it to intersectoral negotiations under the Social Protocol, only when given specific mandates, and subject to strict and continuous control by the national unions through national confederation and EIF representatives on ETUC governing bodies. The EIF's accountability to member unions was similarly emphasized, as was the Germans' point that "collective bargaining at the transnational and European levels" depended on "relative bargaining power," which required a strengthening of national unions.[68]

The basic points were incorporated into a new Article 13 of the ETUC's constitution by the 1995 Congress, which left the Executive Committee to "establish the internal rules of procedure" for intersectoral negotiations. This was eventually done, but not until controversy dragged on another year. In this phase the Secretariat's efforts to establish authority over sectoral negotiations were supported by most of the confederations and resisted by the EIFs. The Secretariat exhibited ambivalence about such negotiations. It repeatedly attributed importance to them as a potential means of overcoming UNICE's reluctance to negotiate and its resistance to legislation.[69] Yet, the Secretariat sought a tight rein on the EIFs' attempts to reach sectoral deals, even discouraging them when rare opportunities occurred. Thus, when the EFBWW believed it could get an agreement on posted workers with the European construction employers equivalent to a proposed directive then blocked in the Council, the attempt was barred.[70] The Secretariat also sought formal authority over sectoral negotiations by amending the ETUC Constitution to require EIFs to notify the Executive Committee in advance of negotiations. The EIFs strenuously opposed this, and the 1995 Congress adopted compromise language requiring post facto reporting instead.[71]

In another instance, Euro-Commerce, the retail and wholesale trade-sector employers association, argued that UNICE did not represent its interests since it was not a member, so it was not bound by the intersectoral parental leave deal, or any other agreement negotiated by UNICE. This was unacceptable to EURO-FIET (the sector EIF), as to the ETUC. But in response to its affiliates' concerns, it got Euro-Commerce to agree on a separate draft agreement identical with the intersectoral arrangement. ETUC's Secretariat prevailed on EURO-FIET to hold off, however, evidently wanting to avoid supporting Euro-Commerce's claim that UNICE was not representative. ETUC had an interest in upholding the universal applicability of agreements struck with UNICE. To do otherwise might open the door to claims by union organizations outside the ETUC that it was not representative either, and that they, like Euro-Commerce, could negotiate agreements under the Social Protocol.[72]

While the commerce matter became moot when the Council made the parental leave agreement legally binding in June 1996, the broader issue of ETUC's sectoral role remained.[73] Efforts by the Secretariat to assert authority over the EIFs it had failed to get into the Constitution were welcomed by most confederations but adamantly resisted by the EIFs.[74] To avoid a damaging split, rules meeting most of the EIFs' objections were adopted at the October Executive.

In the end, the Secretariat had to settle for less than it sought. It did get clear confirmation of its role as bargainer, but only in the very special context of "negotiated legislation" under the Social Protocol. This was already established in practice in the negotiations over EWCs and parental leave, during which close contact between the General Secretary and affiliates was maintained. The part-time work deal was concluded under the newly adopted rules, including approval by a qualified majority of the Executive over some opposition.

The ETUC's bargaining role was thus institutionalized, and its leadership in forging common positions was accepted. Getting there intensified national affiliates' involvement in European activity. Social Protocol negotiations, by demonstrating that significant matters could be at stake, compelled national union leaders with real power – responsible for collective bargaining at the national level – to become personally engaged, even if only to avert perceived threats. On the other hand, the ETUC did not come much closer to its vision of a European industrial relations system. The potential for moving toward it through Social Protocol negotiations is severely limited as long as employers negotiate only under the shadow of law, which can only be cast over the narrow range of subjects within the limits of the EU's legislative authority. Even then everything depends upon the initiative of the Commission, unlikely to propose much new legislation in the foreseeable future.

Sectoral Bargaining: A Strategic Alternative?

If the prospects for turning intersectoral social dialogue under the Social Protocol into European-level collective bargaining are slim, are they any better for sectoral social dialogue? The obstacles, as we saw, have been formidable. Employer resistance is but the largest. The Commission's failure to this point to do much to overcome such resistance is another, though it now promises more support at the sectoral level. ETUC ambivalence also stands in the way, though it could concede the sharp distinction between negotiated legislation and collective bargaining and back the EIFs' efforts more consistently. However, even a renewed ETUC-Commission coalition would have little leverage over employers unwilling to enter into sectoral social dialogue, not to speak of collective bargaining.

The classic incentive bringing employers to the bargaining table is the capacity of unions to disrupt and regulate production by mobilizing their members to strike and by securing their compliance with agreements. Only the national unions have such capacity, however diminished and uneven it may be. To the extent that they retain or can restore it, they could do much to build European cross-border bargaining if they became convinced of such bargaining's importance, but only insofar as they retained strategic control. Since only the EIFs are directly controlled by the unions, the EIFs are the only part of the existing European trade union structure through which unions might be willing to organize cross-border coordination of bargaining and, if this induces employers to engage in cross-border coordination, perhaps even to conduct it. To be sure, unions might instead try coordinating cross-border bargaining selectively on their own, as IG Metall is doing, but the EIFs provide a readily available vehicle. If the EIFs' authority and capabilities were thereby increased, so too would be their weight in the ETUC, probably shifting its emphasis from intersectoral to sectoral bargaining and perhaps reconfiguring its internal structure, along with its conception of its role in an emerging European collective bargaining system. But the EIFs could only move toward collective bargaining if their member unions authorized them to do so and backed them by bringing their bargaining power to bear, constructing "an independent trade union counterforce" at sectoral level "from the ground up," as urged by the German unions.

National unions still seem unconvinced of the need for such a counterforce, however. They have conferred increasing authority and resources on the EIFs, but very cautiously. The process seems to have gone furthest in the EFBWW, the EIF closest to becoming a European trade union. But its member unions are divided over making it a tool for cross-border concertation of bargaining demands and supporting actions to induce employers to negotiate at European level on working conditions, such as health and safety which are so crucial in the sector (not to speak of wages).[75] Member unions of the other EIFs seem even less convinced. Yet nothing short of that would enable the ETUC and the EIFs to escape dependence on Commission initiatives to get employers to negotiate binding agreements at the European level.

What would convince unions to use EIFs in cross-border collective bargaining strategies? One possibility is the threats and opportunities presented by EWCs. Another is the pressures produced by EMU.

European Works Councils: Euro-Bargaining or Micro-Corporatism?

Having pressed for a works council directive for nearly a quarter century, the ETUC could justifiably hail the 1994 directive as "a major breakthrough." UNICE, having resisted equally long, warned that unions would use EWCs "as a major step toward ... pan-European structures and collective bargaining."[76] But other scenarios are possible, depending on employer and union strategies, including "transnational 'microcorporatism' at the MNC level" detached from any collective bargaining structures above the company level, national or European.[77]

The directive left employers a lot of leeway. Nothing in it prevents them from bypassing unions in the establishment or operation of EWCs, integrating them into unilateral mechanisms for "direct communication" or "employee participation."[78] Some have tried excluding unions, though fewer have than unions anticipated.[79] Doing so is difficult if at least some subsidiaries are unionized. Moreover, most national transposition laws assign selection to statutory works council-like bodies (present everywhere except in Britain and Ireland) whose members are typically elected on union slates.[80] Even in the unlikely case of union involvement in all EWCs, however, they would provide cross-border mechanisms for not much more than 10 percent of the European labor force.[81] Whatever the extent of unions' involvement, their ability to use EWCs for serious negotiations can be minimized. Managements can resist anything more than the minimum requirements of one meeting a year, to simply "inform and consult," with consultation defined as a mere "exchange of views." In most existing agreements, "managements ... have successfully demarcated information and consultation from collective bargaining," as they are by law in countries like France and Germany whose works councils were models for EWCs.[82] In less than a handful do the agreements provide for consultation more meaningful, at least on paper, than an "exchange of views" after the fact.[83] And in only one case, Danone, has an EWC gone beyond consultation to negotiation.[84] Company and employer organization spokespersons have left no doubt that if "European-level company bargaining is not going to happen unless managements want it to," it will indeed not happen.[85]

To be sure, a dynamic leading to European-level company bargaining could develop. EWC meetings facilitate cross-border communication among employee members (especially in prior meetings without management present), which would be much harder if companies were not obliged to cover the costs of travel, translation, information gathering, and released time for delegates. Such communication, supported by cross-border networks that probably would not otherwise exist, permits information beyond what management provides to be exchanged, enabling unions to verify local management claims, compare situations, and formulate demands – for upgrading at lagging sites or improvements where precedents for others could be set, leading toward a kind of pattern bargaining across the company. Beyond that, information could be fed back into national and local collective bargaining, calling bluffs, bolstering demands, and putting new issues on the agenda.[86] EWCs could thus facilitate new cross-border strategic coordination among unions.

Central MNC management could combat such whipsawing by harmonizing contested conditions unilaterally and requiring subsidiaries to resist precedent-setting changes.[87] From such management coordination across subsidiaries, unions might in turn conclude that to make gains "they have to negotiate at European level and so the pressure for a bargaining dimension at European company level will intensify." Because the "integration of production across borders" increases unions' bargaining power by enhancing their ability to disrupt production, the pressure could be difficult to resist.[88] But companies' vulnerability can be minimized inosfar as components or stages of production can be kept outside unions' strategic domain.[89] Moreover, central management could undermine coordination among subsidiary workforces by making them compete for new investments. Accurate information through EWCs can make such "investment bargaining" more, rather than less, effective if it bolsters the credibility of threats to relocate investment and jobs.[90]

Instead of resisting, however, MNC managements could "embrace ... collective bargaining with 'their' EWCs," turning it to their own ends even if unions do not have the bargaining power to force them into it. "Framework agreements" with EWCs could even accelerate "the spread of best-practice methods, ... with positive effects for both sides: better cost and productivity performance in the various subsidiaries as well as an improvement of working conditions through the entire Euro-company." Where such "mutual gains" are possible, cross-border "productivity coalitions" could thus be forged through EWCs. The EWCs' competences and infrastructures might consequently be expanded to the point where they become the means for company-specific Europe-wide regulation of industrial relations, strengthening "the company's European 'corporate identity' in the process."[91] Unions, rather than employers, would then have reason to be wary of turning EWCs into collective bargaining bodies.[92]

To the extent that EWCs foster cross-border identification with MNCs, their employees might readily support the decentralization of collective bargaining to the subsidiary level at the expense of multi-employer bargaining by national unions, reinforcing "common trends toward more decentralized company-specific forms of regulation" in national industrial relations systems, further undermining national unions' "ability to create national solidarity." In its place there could develop a transnational 'neo-syndicalism,'" bifurcating the European labor force into a "new 'labor aristocracy' ... consisting of a relatively privileged core workforce in the Euro-companies and a growing peripheral workforce in widely deregulated labor markets."[93] In this scenario, EWCs become the basis not for European collective bargaining but for a transnational micro-corporatism that erodes national regulation of employment relations.

It might only be possible for national unions to avert this danger by joining forces to reestablish regulation on a European basis, building structures for transnational labor representation at the cross-company level to link representatives in different EWCs with one another as well as with those in other companies, and to decide common norms for company-level practices and strategies for enforcing them. The EIFs, again, are the only available instruments for doing so. They have links to EWCs by virtue of their role in establishing them, and continue to provide them with assistance. But they are still a long way from being instruments for regulating employment relations on a cross-border, cross-company basis. That could require authorizing the EIFs to negotiate binding cross-border multi-employer agreements, or at least coordinate cross-border negotiations with individual employers by member unions in different countries, and supporting such negotiations with cross-border industrial action.[94]

Few member unions are ready to cross that threshold from national to transnational bargaining strategy. The threat of transnational micro-corporatism could convince them that the risks of not "pooling their sovereignty" in European structures are greater than those of doing so. But this threat is still a distant one. If, in its absence, unions will not be driven by EWCs to pursue cross-border bargaining strategies through the EIFs or any alternative structures, is there anything else that would drive them to it? A more imminent development that might do so, some suggest, is EMU. But this momentous step in European integration also has ambiguous implications for union strategies.

EMU: The Euro-Bargaining Imperative?

Establishing a single currency will profoundly alter the economic context of collective bargaining. Changes in exchange rates will no longer be available to offset the adverse employment effects of "asymmetric shocks" and other processes impairing the relative "competitiveness" of regions previously separated by national currencies.[95] Such effects can be limited where "automatic stabilizers" or funds deliberately provided to adversely affected regions make offsetting changes in the regional distribution of taxes and transfers. However, such fiscal federalism is precluded by an EU budget equivalent to little more than 1 percent of Community GDP.[96] With little intra-EU labor mobility as well, adjustment will be concentrated almost entirely on labor costs, including the "social wage."[97] If a deterioration in relative (unit) costs cannot be reversed by productivity improvements, unions in affected areas will be pressed to accept nominal wage reductions or low increases as well as cuts in nonwage costs, eroding bargained or statutory social benefits. This may happen even without asymmetric shocks, insofar as employers (and governments) seek price advantages, no longer attainable by currency depreciation, through wage and benefit cuts instead. Given variations in unions' capacity to resist, regions with stronger unions could lose competitiveness to regions with weaker unions, increasing pressure on the stronger unions to accept cuts.[98] Unions in all regions could thereby be drawn into a deflationary vicious circle of labor cost dumping, or competitive "internal depreciations," which could cumulatively lower aggregate EU income, demand, and employment.

Consequently, some argue, EMU makes "the development of a related [i.e. European] structure for collective bargaining ... necessary and unavoidable," forcing national unions over the threshold to Europeanized collective bargaining strategies.[99] Others counter that while EMU makes such Europeanization necessary, it also makes it impossible.[100] As a German economist put it, "an optimal currency area is one that is larger, possibly many times larger, than the area for which an effective wage cartel can be established."[101] No matter how centralized they are, national or sectoral trade unions that are able to dampen wage competition within labor markets separated by national currencies would become regional unions in competition with one another in a single European labor market. Common ground would be difficult to find precisely insofar as such competition became the only available mechanism to protect jobs. Creating a currency area too large for "an effective wage cartel" would thus produce a decentralized European wage bargaining structure with some strong unions but no coordination.[102]

These dangers are vastly amplified by the restrictive macroeconomic policy regime built into EMU. With unemployment at Great Depression levels and governments locked by Maastricht and its sequels into policies likely to worsen it, unions are under enormous pressure to save jobs wherever they can, straining solidarities not just nationally or sectorally but even within individual companies. Under these circumstances, the prospects for constructing common cross-border cross-company collective bargaining strategies, not to speak of mobilizing the bargaining power to implement them effectively, seem extremely slim (even if IG Metall and other unions have begun talking about doing it on a limited scale). Instead of providing the impetus for a Europeanization of union strategy that could avert the threat of micro-corporatism that EWCs may pose, EMU, as designed, may accordingly reinforce that threat. The unions' response to that threat as well as the one posed by EMU may well be to try to shore up national collective bargaining structures rather than intensify the development of European-level structures. Such a "re-nationalization" of bargaining is most strongly evidenced by the numerous "social pacts" recently negotiated or attempted, suggesting a tendency toward "competitive corporatism."[103]

The Political Arena

EMU shows most clearly that possibilities for the European trade union counterpressure envisioned by the ETUC ultimately rest on the political trajectory of European integration. The ETUC's most fundamental strategic challenge is how to change that trajectory. Whether ETUC and its member unions can meet that challenge depends on the influence they can exert in the political arenas shaping Europe.

The ETUC has always held political integration to be essential to assure that the "European model of society" survives in an economically integrated Europe, as its response to Maastricht illustrates. Given that "the economic and monetary integration of the European economies is happening anyway," it said, "what is required is the empowering of democratically-accountable institutions so as to regain at the European level those powers to manage our economies which have increasingly been lost at the national level."[104] ETUC has also shared with EU's leaders the faith that political integration could be achieved through successive installments of economic integration. In one ETUC official's words, "... just as internal market integration led inevitably on to economic and monetary integration, and that on to greater political integration, ... so we were convinced that all this would have to lead on to Social Union. And indeed we did get the social protocol."[105] But the gaps between the ETUC's "spillover" hopes and the course of integration since the mid-1980s have underlined the dilemmas of relying on the "economic approach." Far from being automatic consequences of economic integration, political and social union have depended on decisions made in arenas where the ETUC and its members have had little influence.

Social Policy: The Narrow Entry

The ETUC consistently criticized the failure to accompany creation of a European market with social regulation at the European level. While welcoming the 1985 White Paper's promises of growth and employment from a single market, for example, it opposed its "one-sided approach," which posed "serious dangers for workers" by failing to take into account "social realities and necessities." Subsequently, the ETUC called repeatedly for measures to assure that integration promoted upward convergence of social and labor standards rather than a race to the bottom.[106] These views were elaborated in ETUC's 1988 "European Social Programme" and, encouraged by Delors's speech at its 1988 Congress, and also in its proposal for a "Community Charter of Fundamental Social Rights." To avert social dumping, the ETUC argued, rights had to be guaranteed at the European level through the "two channels" of legislation and negotiation. "Basic social legislation" was needed to establish the general principle of "fundamental social rights," defined as "… the classical basic rights" of workers to organize, bargain collectively and strike, and to social protection, health and safety at the workplace, and equal treatment regardless of gender. They would also include "completely new standards such as the right to information or participation in the introduction and application of new technologies," cross-border "representation structures for European multinational companies," a "framework for European industrial relations," and rights to training, recognition of credentials, and educational as well as parental leave. These rights should be enforceable in the courts, with "the right to appeal to the European Court of Justice," just as are the rights of those engaged in cross-border trade and investment.[107] The Commission would then have to propose legislation to assure the specific rights. Anticipating the Social Protocol, the ETUC called for the negotiation of agreements between European-level social partners to generate additional legislation as well as to secure compliance at all levels.[108]

The ETUC's quest produced mixed results, as our survey of EU social policy showed. The Social Charter was a "solemn commitment" rather than an enforceable set of rights. Since Action Program legislation was confined within the boundaries of EU legislative authority set by the treaty, there was none assuring collective bargaining and social protection rights, while Maastricht explicitly excluded collective bargaining. The ETUC got better results on workplace health and safety, to which the SEA had extended QMV. Here the ETUC had good access to the key policy arena and was able to exert some influence, but mainly as part of a coalition with other actors in European institutions who also had a stake in enhancing ETUC's effectiveness in this arena.[109] There was also sufficient support among governments, particularly those with higher standards, for preventing regime competition in health and safety.[110]

The ETUC did make a breakthrough in the 31 October Agreement, quickly incorporated in the Maastricht Social Protocol. Penetrating the theretofore exclusively intergovernmental arena of EU treaty-making, the ETUC succeeded in becoming a participant in policy formation, if only in the narrowly circumscribed area of EU social policy competence. In turn, this made possible the EWC directive, the parental leave and atypical work agreements. The ETUC achieved these modest successes, once again, as part of coalitions, often led by Delors and deftly managed by his lieutenants, for policies which had substantial member state support.

The political constellations favorable to social policy advances of this kind largely disappeared in the post-Delors period.[111] In this new context, the EMU macroeconomic policy regime has squeezed social policy between unemployment and the convergence/stability pact criteria. By confining demand management exclusively to price stability, EMU relegates policies against unemployment to supply-side "structural reforms" that supposedly increase the employment intensity of growth by increasing the labor market's "flexibility" – reducing the "reservation wage" by decreasing social benefit replacement rates; lowering labor costs, especially of the less skilled; increasing inequality; and reducing employment security through lower legal hurdles to and costs of layoffs.[112] EU social policy has been assimilated to this supply-side conception of "employment policy."[113] The ETUC's social policy task has thus been redefined as resisting such "negative flexibilization" and pressing for "positive flexibilization," which is negotiated rather than imposed unilaterally.[114] The ETUC also points out that supply-side reforms can do little to bring unemployment down without the demand stimulus that EMU rules out. Yet the political decisions shaping EMU are made in a policy arena where the ETUC, together with labor within the member states, has little voice.

Macroeconomic Policy: The Closed Door

All along, the ETUC has supported the idea of EMU while criticizing its implementation, increasingly as EMU's costs in unemployment have grown. Apprehensive about the design for EMU being drafted in 1988-89, the ETUC urged the Delors Committee to view the "objectives of economic cooperation" as "growth, full employment and regional balance, and not just monetary stability." It should "concern itself as much with how to create the economic and social cohesion essential for the introduction and continuation of the EMU, as with the more technical details," and recognize that "the complete liberalization of capital movements must be accompanied by much stronger coordination of macroeconomic policies."[115] The Delors Committee fell far short of this.

When EMU emerged from Maastricht, ETUC similarly criticized it as "unbalanced," setting up a monetary, but not an economic, union, whose objectives are confined to price stability, omitting "growth, employment and regional balance." The only European institution with effective power over the European economy that Maastricht creates, the ECB, cannot be compelled to take objectives other than price stability into account. Member states' capacity to pursue these other objectives is severely constrained by the convergence criteria while no offsetting capacity for doing so is established at the European level. There is no expansion of fiscal federalism to cushion recessions or other shocks beyond the existing, and modest, structural funds. There is no provision for the harmonization of taxation, opening the way to "tax dumping" and the ultimate evisceration of taxation (especially on capital income) and consequent aggravation of fiscal pressure on the public sector and social protection. Finally, while there is provision for "surveillance" of compliance with the convergence criteria, there is none for the coordination of macroeconomic policies that monetary union needs to pursue growth and employment.[116]

The ETUC thus judged EMU's design to be fundamentally flawed. It has nevertheless continued to back EMU. In keeping with the economic approach to integration, the ETUC has argued that EMU is needed politically to keep integration going. In this light, an independent ECB is a political price worth paying to keep Germany on board. Economically, a common monetary policy is also needed to avoid competitive devaluations and constraints by international financial markets. The Bundesbank had already imposed such a policy; it is better that it be under European control. EMU is thus a necessary, if not sufficient, component of coordinated macroeconomic management of the European economy.

Accordingly, ETUC's position has been not to reject EMU but to remedy its flaws. It called for EMU to start on schedule in 1999 to avert instability and underpin the confidence needed for investment and recovery. To realize EMU's potential contribution to recovery, however, governments had to abandon their "mechanical" application of the convergence criteria, especially for budget deficits, and adapt them to the changed economic conditions of the mid-1990s. EMU was designed at a moment of optimism, the ETUC pointed out, whereas the late 1980s recovery proved shortlived, undercut in part by Bundesbank restrictivenes after deficit increases to finance German unification. Recovery from the resulting recession was hobbled by the rigid application of the convergence criteria, which was legally unnecessary as well as economically perverse. Restrictive fiscal policy in the context of excessively restrictive monetary policy was counterproductive, making it so much harder for countries to meet the deficits criteria as to threaten EMU's introduction on schedule. The "sequence has to be recovery and employment that reduces deficits, not the reverse."[117] The way to get that was to decouple EMU's introduction from the schedule for meeting the deficit criteria. A new approach to convergence was needed that would tie pre- and post-EMU steps together rather than insisting on meeting the criteria in advance. In addition to changing the transition process in this way, the ETUC reiterated its call to redress the fundamental imbalance between price stability and other goals built into EMU. Thus, in the context of the 1996-1997 Intergovernmental Conference to revise the treaty and since, the ETUC agitated to make employment and growth explicit objectives of economic union, establish institutions to achieve such objectives, and provide a role for the social partners.[118]

In the political context which prevailed, however, the ETUC's criticisms and proposals had no discernible effect on EMU's design and the process of transition to it. The ETUC's member organizations have largely shared ETUC's rationale for EMU, officially supporting it with varying degrees of enthusiasm while having little impact on its restrictive bias.[119] EMU was shaped in political arenas where labor was not present. Central bankers and finance ministers dominated all key venues – the Delors Committee, the EMS Monetary Committee, and ECOFIN (the Council of Economics and Finance Ministers). Along with the European Council, they have operated behind closed doors, insulated from direct political pressures.[120] In social policy the ETUC broke into closed arenas as part of coalitions in which it joined with the Commission and some member state governments. In the "high politics" of monetary union, however, there has until now been no political coalition in which the ETUC could join to deflect the course of integration via EMU from the path it has criticized so consistently. Acknowledging as much, it noted that governments have ignored its warnings that "cutting expenditure during a recession risks both intensifying deficit problems ... and plunging Europe into a beggar-thy-neighbour, deflationary spiral," and that the policies which associate EMU "with unemployment could be disastrous for the whole project."[121]

An attempt to forge a coalition in support of a higher priority for employment was one of the last projects of Jacques Delors's tenure. The vehicle for this was the 1993 White Paper on Growth, Competitiveness and Employment, which was launched in such a way as to circumvent opposition in ECOFIN. The Economics and Finance Ministers nevertheless won the game, preventing any reorientation of macroecomic policy and blocking the fiscal stimuli Delors had proposed. Employment was made an explicit objective at the 1994 Essen European Council, but pursuing it was defined as a supply-side matter. The Employment Pact proposed by the weak Santer Commission in 1996 did not deviate significantly from this supply-side approach. French success in adding growth to stability in the title of the agreement reached at the 1996 Dublin Summit was a cosmetic change. The 1997 French and British elections seemed to open up prospects of more significant change, but the employment policy clauses inserted in the Amsterdam Treaty and the Luxembourg Employment Summit in November 1997 left employment in its supply-side ghetto.[122]

In this political context, the ETUC was confined to taking positions on decisions it had little prospect of influencing. It tried to forge alliances in support of these positions, seeking alliance partners wherever available. This includes the social dialogue mechanism, through which it has tried to get UNICE to join in lobbying for expansionary policy. UNICE has agreed only to statements with token references to stimulating demand that do not challenge the prevailing supply-side approach.[123] Within the European institutions, potential parters in an expansionary coalition cannot add much political weight. In the European Parliament, the socialist group pushed the Swedish Social Democrats' "Larsson plan" and, together with the Christian democrats, passed a verson of the simliar "Coates plan" but with no effect. DG V, of which Larsson became Director-General and with which ETUC has had long contact, has stressed employment, but it is obliged to elaborate the supply-side approach by a Commission division of labor which assigns macroeconomic policy to DG II. That directorate is thus in a better position to have some influence, and the ETUC has been developing its contacts with it. These have so far helped get the European Monetary Institute (EMI, the ECB's predecessor) and now the ECB to agree to discuss monetary policy with the "social partners" – i.e., an extension of social dialogue. This, and the introduction of an employment chapter, including consultation of social partners, into the treaty, are seen by the ETUC as promising steps toward obtaining a role in economic policy like that in social policy.[124] But in its public positions at least, DG II seems no more ready than UNICE to challenge the ECB's monopoly of demand management and the relegation of employment to the supply-side. The possibilities for any Commission actors to do so are indeed limited by the intergovernmental politics that fundamentally determine the direction of integration.

Hence, any prospects for an expansionary coalition continue to rest on what happens in member state politics. At the time of writing, those prospects seem to have been improved much more by the outcome of the 1998 German election and change of government in Italy than by the British and French elections of 1997. The presence of center-left governments in large as well as smaller member states may have finally created a new political context in which an expansionary coalition of which the ETUC can be a part is now possible. How far such a coalition could counterbalance the power of central bankers institutionally entrenched in the ESCB remains to be seen.

However EMU unfolds in the new political context, the position of critical support for EMU by the ETUC and its constituents has so far put them in an excruciating bind. It ties them to the particular version of the economic approach to political integration that has been pursued despite its social costs and rising popular disenchantment, including among union members.[125] It is difficult for the ETUC and its constituents to express this disenchantment without seeming to abandon support for European integration as long as its fate is linked to EMU. How much longer can the ETUC and its member organizations go on supporting EMU in its present form, however critically? And if they withdrew their support, what would the consequences be? Could this derail EMU? And integration as well? Or would it make little difference, testifying to the European labor movement's political weakness? Commitment to the economic approach to integration as it has evolved thus confronts the European labor movement with a daunting strategic dilemma. Contrary to the functionalist hopes the ETUC has shared with many of Europe's builders, social and political union does not automatically follow from economic integration. Explicit political choices intervene. So far, the ETUC and its affiliates have had limited impact on those choices.

Conclusion

We began with a puzzle. European integration has created transnational markets in a setting of national industrial relations systems. As market building progressed, it would have seemed logical, a priori, for national unions to follow their market adversaries toward transnationalization. Without this they would face new and serious dangers. There were obstacles, however. Unions were deeply rooted in their national societies. Their resources and ideas about using them were national. Returns from the national use of these resources, if dwindling, still seemed greater than any foreseeable returns from trans-nationalization, which risked diluting national union power. Differences between national economic structures, union organizational patterns, industrial relations systems, and "cultures" (including languages) provided further reasons for unions to "stay home." The structure of European integration itself was an obstacle. The "economic approach" to integration leaned heavily toward transnational liberalization and deregulation – "market building" – while discouraging relocation of regulatory activities and social policy to the European level. Given the intergovernmental character of EU decision-making, pressure on national governments was the best way to try to influence Europe.

Yet there has been considerably more union transnationalization, largely through the ETUC's development, than these obstacles would lead us to expect. Much of the explanation, we suggested, lay in the ways in which particular European institutions – especially the Commission – tried to induce unions to invest more energy and attention at the European level. Exogenously provided incentives reinforced the efforts of those in European unions who themselves advocated further Europeanization of union strategies. The confluence of these incentives and Europeanizing union actors' efforts, in the larger context of post-1985 integration, was enough to produce a significant degree of union Europeanization.

The puzzle was solved, but the pattern of union Europeanization which resulted was ambiguous. The ETUC was strengthened and changed in response to market integration and the growing role of European legislation in regulating it – some of which, in workplace health and safety, for example, is very important. The interaction led to the Maastricht Social Protocol and its enticing promise of European-level collective bargaining. The products have been relatively slim, however. The parental leave agreement was an important precedent for intersectoral bargaining at the European level, but it was inconsequential in substance. Moreover, apart from accords on atypical work, that precedent seems unlikely to be followed in any important new areas. The EWC directive, the greatest advance to date, could, in the best of circumstances, promote the development of genuinely transnational unionism. Alternatively, it could foster a transnational micro-corporatism that would further weaken national unions.

The ETUC did not get quite what it perhaps expected, therefore. The Maastricht Social Protocol only spawned sporadic "negotiated legislation" dependent on Commission initiatives. If this was symbolically important, it was not real collective bargaining and was unlikely to become so. Moreover, by the mid-1990s the Commission's political position had deterioriated so much that few new initiatives were likely in any foreseeable future. More disturbing was the very weak development of European collective bargaining at the sectoral and company levels, where initiatives by European institutions had not helped much. The ambiguous potential of European Works Councils may hinge more on building new trade union strategic capacity between the company and intersectoral levels than on help from the EU. Building such capacity is up to the unions themselves. The surprising union Europeanization that has occurred thus seems seriously flawed: the structure is weakest where it needs to be strongest if there is to be real European collective bargaining.

The ETUC has had some success in the European political arena rather than in the market. Even in the political arena, however, ETUC influence has been confined to a narrowly circumsribed area of social policy/labor market regulation. The ETUC has been essentially excluded from more fundamental matters of economic governance. This is most obvious in relation to EMU, the most advanced point reached in the post-1985 renewal of integration. EMU will have far more impact on social policy/labor market regulation than the limited range of decisions to which ETUC has gained access. EMU will establish a form of European economic governance, but from the ETUC's point of view, it will clearly be the wrong kind geared to the wrong goals. The ETUC tried to get the right kind, but without success.

Organizations, movements and industrial relations systems are shaped by the interactions between different strategic actors at specific historic junctures. Particular interactions between national European union movements, "Europeanizing" elements in and emanating from them, and European institutions played central roles in shaping the ETUC's structure, goals, and strategies. The most significant byproduct of these interactions may have been the ETUC's commitment to a general vision of European integration held by the Commission and other key institutional players.

Identifying the tradeoffs built into this commitment has been central to our argument. The ETUC, prior to the "1992" period, was a small and weak Brussels lobby. Those in charge may have "gone native" in the rarified atmosphere of Euro-discourse, but it mattered little because the ETUC was not very important. Changes after the mid-1980s made the ETUC more important, however, and it began to desire and claim broader roles. In the process it developed a deeper commitment to the particular trajectories of European integration being promoted by the Commission and other key Brussels actors, and to what one might label the "European ideal."

The trajectory of – primarily economic – integration which the ETUC embraced turned out very different from what enthusiasts had foreseen in the heady years from 1985 to 1990. Then there were high hopes for spillover from market liberalization into European-level market regulation in social policy. The years after Maastricht clarified the dynamics of events. The 1980s had led to massive market liberalization without much spillover. Preparations for EMU guaranteed that there would be little in the future. The ETUC may thus have bet on the wrong horse. Perhaps it had not been sufficiently alert to the dangers involved or had overestimated its own capacity to limit these dangers. In any case, the surprising degree of union Europeanization that has occurred has not produced the results union Europeanizers expected from it. ETUC strategy was evidently premised on an idealistic vision of Europe which reality ultimately betrayed.

European integration has been promoted, from Monnet through Delors, by an ideology whose core notion is that building Europe is a supreme good in itself, worth promoting through thick and thin. Behind this lies a mixture of propositions about the virtues of undercutting nationalism and national identities, the positive economic and social contributions of a unified market space, and the need to defend the special nature of European culture and society. The usual repertory of specific groups seeking their own goals is somewhere in the background, since EU Europe has been designed to produce positive change for central economic interests. Ideological commitments function to persuade a broad spectrum of actors that the final goal is for the common good. The European ideal is no exception.

Being "European" is being virtuous in an otherwise menacing setting, analogous to being a socialist, conservative, or devotee of a particular religious creed in other contexts. There are "Europeans" all over Europe, to be sure, but Brussels is their capital. And the critical mass of Europeans live in those European institutions, primarily the Commission, whose mission includes producing and sustaining this European credo. Commissioners, high level Eurocrats, and Euro-parliamentarians are not only technicians and skilled administrators; they are also, and simultaneously, militants. Groups that become unduly dependent upon contact with and the resources of these militants and their institutions are almost certain to be tempted toward "conversion experiences" to the European ideal.

ETUC insiders, committed but critical "Europeans" to begin with, must have understood in the later 1980s that accepting the resources offered by the Commission was one way to generate the prominence and strength which they needed to promote their urgent messages about the importance of transnational organization and action. They could then rely for additional support for their goals on their more "European" contacts in different national movements. In return for those resources, however, the ETUC was drawn into a coalition to advance the initiatives of those supplying them, particularly the Delors Commissions. In this exchange there was an implicit promise that the Commissions' particular European strategies would lead to a real expansion in European social regulation and the foundation of a European industrial relations system. The Commission was unable to produce anywhere near as much as it had promised, however. The result was that European trade unionism found itself being restructured along lines that were only partly its doing and not always clearly to its advantage. In exchange it had to commit itself, albeit often critically, to the deeper trajectories of European integration traced from the Single Market through Maastricht. This made most sense in the Social Charter period when it seemed that the dam against European-level social policy was about to give way in compensation for the liberalization in the Single Market Program. This did not happen, however, and committing to Maastricht was an even larger leap of faith.

As designed, EMU is arguably inimical to the interests of European workers and unions. Yet all good Europeans – and the ETUC has to be seen as such – had to line up behind EMU. EMU is costing jobs, making it virtually impossible for governments to confront the consequences of these job losses, and it is quite likely that the future will bring more of the same. EMU also deepens the EU's "democratic deficit." It removes policy capacities from member states and gives them to unelected and constitutionally independent central bankers. Yet if EMU fails there will be substantial monetary dislocations in the immediate future and a huge setback for European integration in the longer term. ETUC, with many other actors, has been put in a position of being damned if it does support EMU and damned if it does not.

The coming of EMU on January 1, 1999, with 11 original members, brought the beginnings of an important change in the ETUC's strategic environment, however. By then, member states had begun to speak of national "pacts" in which unions and employers would collaborate, in one form or another, to secure national competitiveness in anticipation of the changes EMU would bring. This process, if it deepens, could "renationalize" union concerns. At its core, national unions, in their various weakened states, are called upon to make sacrifices in the interests of greater flexibility and efficiency. These sacrifices will likely include wage moderation and consent to labor market and welfare state reforms. What unions can ask in exchange is less clear, but there is space for creative response in the form of new commitments to serious training programs, for example, of progressive rather than dismantling reforms of social protection programs, and safeguards against the "savage" dismantling of labor law and contractual protection which "flexibility" might otherwise bring.

These changes could close off opportunities for the ETUC to continue the intersectoral bargaining and lobbying strategies it has pursued since the later 1980s. Other things equal, they could also undercut many of the arguments that ETUC has built up over recent years for its own significance. They could create new opportunities as well, however. "Pactism" and renationalization pose dangerous problems to national unions. Narrow national agreements to make economies leaner and meaner for EMU could lead to a race toward the bottom. Individually, national unions might then face a collective action trap from which they could escape only if an external actor exists to enable them to act jointly. It is precisely this essential "public good" that the ETUC is in a position to provide. The function of coordinating its national constituents' strategies which it had envisioned but was denied on traditional wage bargaining would thus become indispensable to them in the new context of negotiating terms of national adjustment to EMU.

In performing this role, the ETUC could also enter into new coalitions with European institutions. New initiatives from the Commission and Parliament reflect a search for ways to foster "upward" emulation among national responses to the constraints and opportunities of EMU. The 1997 Amsterdam Treaty's employment clauses were quickly translated into the proposal of the Luxemburg Summit for annual "national action pacts" for employment (the first in spring 1998). This exercise, if carried out effectively, could make national trajectories toward employment creation more vigorous and transparent, making clear as well when any given member state seems set on pursuing a "beggar thy neighbor" course. These national pacts will eventually be articulated with national economic policy programs which the Commission is also fostering. ETUC could become an important player politically in the instances where the national pacts are commissioned and then considered. It could also play a very significant role in coordinating – and thereby "Europeanizing" – national union responses to the demands which pact writing will pose for wage restraint, bargaining for greater flexibility, and social protection reforms. And although the Commission's employment initiatives mainly involve labor market supply-side innovations (training and "life-long learning") rather than demand-side macroeconomic initiatives, there is no reason why ETUC could not push for both. Thus it could exercise its position in the process to maximize the positive possibilities of supply-side proposals while also arguing for greater demand-side action from the ECB and member states. Europe's rapidly changing political context, marked by shifts toward renewed social democratic governmental strength promoted by national concerns about employment, might make this approach more productive than it was in the earlier 1990s.

How could a transnational industrial relations system develop in Europe? The question is unanswerable. National industrial relations systems took a much longer time to take shape than the brief period we have surveyed. If the development of such national systems is a precedent, though we have no reason to think that it is, then we must be careful to avoid premature conclusions. It may turn out that the trajectories begun so tentatively by ETUC and its constituents lead to something resembling a real European-level industrial relations system with capacities to protect and sustain workers' interests in the new global economy, even if this seems wildly optimistic now. A pessimistic outlook may be more realistic, however. What we can say is that, to this point, the development of ETUC as a "movement" has not really followed the historic lines of most national labor movements where long decades of debate, mobilization, and struggle made unions strong and confident enough to oblige states and employers to concede their legitimacy. The ETUC has so far developed largely by borrowing resources from European institutions to gain legitimacy with its own national constituents and by using the openings provided by these European institutions to try to elicit changes in employer behaviors. ETUC, in other words, has developed from the top rather than as a mass organization built from below out of a broader social movement. EMU and the changes that it will engender offers new opportunities and new threats. Perhaps ETUC will be able to build upon these to become a different kind of transnational unionism in the next millennium.

Notes

1. L. Ulman,"Multinational Unionism: Incentives, Barriers, and Alternatives," *Industrial Relations* 14, No. 1 (February 1975); and, with M. Reder, "Unionism and Unification," in *Labor and an Integrated Europe*, ed. L. Ulman, B. Eichengreen, and W. T. Dickens (Washington, D.C.: Brookings, 1993); and F. Traxler, "European Trade Union Policy and Collective Bargaining – Mechanisms and Levels of Labour Market Regulation in Comparison," *Transfer* 2, No. 2 (June 1996).
2. D. Collins, *The European Communities: The Social Policy of the First Phase* (London: Martin Robinson, 1975); and E. Vogel-Polsky and J. Vogel, *L'Europe sociale 1993: Illusion, alibi ou réalité?* (Brussels: Presses de ULB, 1991). Article 119 took on importance only after the European Court of Justice (ECJ) 1976 decision in Defrenne vs. Sabena.
3. R. Blanpain and C. Engels, *European Labour Law* (Deventer: Kluwer, 1993).
4. *Bulletin of the European Community* 10, 1974.
5. H. Wallace, "The Establishment of the European Regional Development Fund: Common Policy or Pork Barrel?" in *Policy Making in the European Community*, ed. H. Wallace, W. Wallace, and C. Webb (London: Wiley, 1977).
6. The ACSH consists of two representatives each of government, trade unions, and employer organizations, respectively, nominated by each member state and appointed by the Council. Although the ETUC is not a member, it coordinates the trade union group. Each group adopts its own positions prior to plenary meetings chaired by the Commissioner in charge of DG V.
7. *Promoting Health and Safety in the European Community* (Brussels: European Trade Union Technical Bureau for Health and Safety, 1991); *Europe Social*, 2/90.
8. P. Teague, *The European Community: The Social Dimension* (London: Kogan Page, 1989).
9. G. Ross, *Jacques Delors and European Integration* (Cambridge, U.K.: Polity Press, 1995).
10. Under "qualified majority," fifty-four of the seventy-six possible votes – distributed among the twelve according to size – were needed to pass a measure. This eliminated vetoes by any single member state while preventing the big four from carrying issues against the smaller states' wishes and enabling two large and one small state to block proposals.
11. A. Moravcsik, "Negotiating the Single European Act: National Interests and Conventional Statecraft in the European Community," *International Organization* 45 (Winter 1991); and D. R. Cameron, "The 1992 Initiative: Causes and Consequences," in *Euro-Politics: Institutions and Policymaking in the "New" European Community*, ed. A. M. Sbragia (Washington, D.C.: Brookings Institution, 1992).
12. J. Delors, *Le Nouveau concert Européen* (Paris: Odile Jacob, 1992).
13. *Social Europe* 1/90: 52-76; and Philippe Pochet, *Programme social: Le Bilan*, Working Paper 5 (Brussels: Observatoire Social Européen, 1993).
14. P. Pochet, ed., *Synoptic Analysis of the Treaties before and after Maastricht* (Brussels: European Social Observatory, n.d.).
15. B. Eichengreen, "European Monetary Unification," *Journal of Economic Literature* 31 (September 1993); and K. Dyson, *Elusive Union: The Process of Economic and Monetary Union in Europe* (London: Longman, 1994).
16. G. Falkner, "The Maastricht Protocol on Social Policy: Theory and Practice," *Journal of European Social Policy* 6, no.1 (1996).
17. Commission of the European Communities, *Medium Term Social Action Program 1995-1997*, Communication, Brussels, 1995, 2-3.

18. E. Arcq, "L'UNICE et la politiques sociale communitaire," in *Quelle union sociale Europeene?* ed. M. Telò (Bruxelles: Editions de l'Université de Bruxelles, 1994); J. E. Døolvik, *Redrawing Boundaries of Solidarity: ETUC and the Europeanisation of Trade Unions in the 1990s,* (Oslo: ARENA and FAFO, 1997), chap. 7.
19. For ETUC's history, we draw on Dølvik, *Redrawing Boundaries of Solidarity*, chap. 6, and C. Gobin, *L'Europe Syndicale* (Bruxelles: Presses de L'ULB, 1998).
20. Peter Seideneck, ETUC, interview by authors, June, 1994.
21. The Spanish Workers' Commissions were only admitted in the late 1980s, the Portuguese Intersyndical in the mid-1990s, while the French CGT remained outside as of 1998.
22. J. Goetschy, "The Construction of European Unionism: A Sociological View on ETUC," in *The Challenges to Trade Unions in Europe: Innovation and Adaptation,* ed. P. Leisinck et al. (Cheltenham: Edward Elgar, 1995); J. Visser and B. Ebbinghaus, "Making the Most of Diversity? European Integration and the Transnational Organization of Labour," in *Organized Interests and the European Community,* ed. J. Greenwood et al. (London, 1992).
23. For the UNICE Secretary General's view, see Z. Tyszkiewicz "European Social Policy – Striking the Right Balance," *European Affairs* (Winter 1989).
24. J. Goetschy, "Le Dialogue Social Européen de Val Duchesse," in *Travail et Emploi* 1/91;
25. Delors, *Le Nouveau concert Européen,* 80.
26. CEN and CENELEC refer to Comité Européen de Normalisation and Comité Européen de Normalisation Electrotechnique. F. Verbbon, S. Andriessen, and J. H. Kwantes, "Trade Union Involvement in the Process of Harmonization and Standardization in the European Community, " in *The Trade Union Contribution to European Standardization,* ed. J. Delahaut (Brussels: European Trade Union Technical Bureau for Health and Safety, 1992).
27. A. Martin and G. Ross, *Lessons from the Social Dimension*, Report to the U.S. Department of Labor (September 1994), 27-28.
28. *The Trade Union Contribution*, ed. J. Delahaut, 159-161.
29. Ibid., 161-62.
30. C Brekelmans, DG III, interview by A. Martin, 1993; Martin and Ross, *Lessons from the Social Dimension,* 34-36.
31. M. Sapir, TUTB, interviews by A. Martin and G. Ross, 1993, 1994. Such discretionary budgetary issues are among the few which Parliament can decide. This instance reflected the Danish labor movement's influence and the strength of the Socialist-Christian Democratic coalition.
32. *European Industrial Relations Review* (EIRR) 211 and 212 (August and September 1991); B. Christensen, *The European Industry Committees and Social Dialogue* (Brussels: ETUI, 1993).
33. The EIFs could become the "bodies which might one day be the main union parties in European-level bargaining." EIRR 211 (August 1991), 25.
34. *Social Europe* 2/95.
35. The metal EIF (EMF) pioneered these efforts, securing EWC agreements with French and German MNCs beginning in 1985, long before EU support.
36. Budget line B3-4004. *Official Journal of the European Communities* 902 (31 December 1994). EIF budget estimates are in Christensen, *The European Industry Committees.*
37. Delors, *Le Nouveau concert Europeen*, 71-80.
38. For German unions, a stronger ETUC in which they had a powerful voice could guard against European-level decisions that threatened their solid system of sectoral corporatism.

39. All the developments making ETUC's reform essential were related to European integration except for the transformation in the East catalyzed by the fall of the Berlin Wall. Stekelenburg Report, "For a More Effective ETUC," ETUC, Brussels, 1990.
40. A Steering Committee was established, composed of the President, General and two Deputy Secretaries, and fifteen members chosen by and from the Executive Committee, to meet eight times a year to frame issues to be decided by the Executive Committee. The President and General Secretary became full voting members of the Executive Committee, meeting quarterly. All member organizations would continue to be represented in the Committee, which would remain the authoritative policy-making body between Congresses.
41. Reflecting its controversial character, this change was limited. The EIFs got voting rights on the Executive Committee except on constitutional and financial issues (because the EIFs did not pay dues, since their affiliates paid dues to the national confederations), and they were allotted three seats, rotated among them, on the new Steering Committee. The Congress report also called for "positive action" to remedy the extreme underrepresentation of women within the organization and fuller integration of women's issues into the ETUC's agenda, in part by giving the ETUC Women Committee additional delegates to the Congress, three voting seats on the Executive Committee, and expanding the Secretariat by adding a woman. Finally, the report proposed a European Trade Union Forum " to institutionalize links with the re-emergent unions in central and eastern Europe" and formally recognized Interregional Trade Union Councils.
42. Ross, *Jacques Delors*, chaps. 3 and 6.
43. R. Blanpain et al., *The Vredeling Proposal: Information and Consultation of Employees in Multinational Enterprises* (Deventer: Kluwer, 1983). On the directive, see *Le Comité d' entreprise Européen*, ed. G. Deregnaucourt, Working Paper of the Observatoire Social Européen (Brussels, 1991); P. Marginson, A. Buitendam, C. Deutschmann, and P. Perulli, "The Emergence of the Euro-Company: Toward a European Industrial Relations?" *Industrial Relations Journal* 24, no. 3 (September 1993); M. Hall, "Behind the European Works Councils Directive: The European Commission's Legislative Strategy," *British Journal of Industrial Relations* 30, no. 4 (December 1992).
44. An EWC or other "procedure for informing and consulting employees" must be established in all "Community-scale undertakings" or groups with at least 1,000 employees within the member states (excluding Britain) and at least 150 in each of two member states, if requested by a minimum of 100 of its employees in two or more states. Companies must then convene and negotiate with a "special negotiating committee" (SNB) of employees about whether to establish an EWC or alternative procedure and, if so, the form it should take. If companies do not do so within six months, do negotiate but fail to reach an agreement by the end of three years, or if the SNB and management agree to do so, an EWC is set up in conformity with a set of "subsidiary requirements" in the directive's Annex.
45. *Social Europe* 3/91.
46. It also protects the right's users against discrimination, entitling them to the same or equivalent job and acquired rights, while permitting some variation in compliance under special circumstances. Income during leave is left to member states and social partners. Commission of the European Communities, Proposal for a Council Directive on the framework agreement on parental leave concluded by UNICE, CEEP, and the ETUC, Brussels, 31 January 1996, COM(96) 26 final.

47. It added the right in only three countries while adding to gender equity in more countries by making the right individual and distinguishing parental from maternity leave. ETUC, "Parental Leave – Results of the Negotiations," Brussels, 9 November 1995.
48. Commission of the European Communities, Proposal for a Council Directive concerning the framework agreement on part-time work concluded by UNICE, CEEP, and the ETUC, Brussels, 23 July 1997, COM(97) 392 final.
49. Some, including the DGB and the construction EIF, voted against the agreement, arguing that ETUC settled for too little just to get any agreement, and that the proposed directive would have achieved more. Others argued that an agreement was important to help get the Social Protocol negotiations provision into the treaty at the Intergovernmental Conference to revise the treaty, and that the centrality of the agreement's subject made it an important precedent. The General Secretary complained that more could have been accomplished if affiliates had backed the ETUC by putting pressure on their employer counterparts. Communications from Joachim Kreimer-deFries, DGB, 23 May 1997, Jon Erik Dølvik, 16 June 1997 and Jan Cremers, EFBWW, 24 June 1997.
50. While the German chemical industry employers opposed the European industry association's participation in social dialogue to preserve the industry/employer associations distinction, they did not oppose dealing with the ECFGW and accordingly proposed creating a European-level employer association. Franco Bisegna, EFCGW general secretary, interview by authors, July 1995.
51. Correspondence between Bert Thierron, EMF General Secretary, and Doris Oberhoff, WEM General Gecretary, 7 April and 11 May 1993.
52. European Commission, D (95) V/D1 DB/db, Communication Concerning the Sectoral Social Dialogue (Draft) (Brussels, 26 September 1995), 8, 17.
53. As EURO-FIET's director put it, "If you want an agreement, start on a subject where you're likely to get an agreement, even if it's not the key issue." Bernadette Tesch-Ségol, interview by authors, July 1995.
54. Allan Larsson, "Comments to the Draft of the Communication on the Social Dialogue," 2 January 1996. European Commission, Communication concerning the development of the social dialogue at the Community level, COM (96) 448 prov., Brussels, 18 September 1996, 7.
55. Over 490 preliminary meetings occurred, usually at union request, in 290 multinationals between 1991 and the summer of 1994. The EMF alone held 155 meetings in over 100 different companies, culminating in agreements in eighteen companies. Once the directive was adopted, many companies which had refused to set up works councils rushed to make voluntary agreements before September 1996 when the directive, with its specific requirements, went into effect. The EC/EU funds were renewed annually even after the EWC directive was enacted.
56. *Multinationals Database: Inventory of Companies Affected by the EWC Directive* (Brussels: ETUI, 1998), 5. The actual number is somewhat higher.
57. J.-C. Prince, "Les Conseils syndicaux interrégionaux en Europe," ETUI, DWP 95.03.1; and S. Dürmeier, "The Increasing Importance of the Interregional Trade Union Councils," in *European Trade Union Yearbook 1995*, ed. E. Gabaglio and R. Hoffmann (Brussels: ETUI, 1996).
58. *Forum Facts* 1, 1 (September 1994); P. Seideneck, "Trade union integration in Europe – Remarks on the ETUC's Policy in Eastern Europe," in *European Trade Union Yearbook 1995*; and "Rapprochement Based on Common Interests Between the ETUC and the Trade Unions in Central and Eastern Europe," *Transfer* 1, no. 3 (July 1995).

59. T. Schulten, "Tarifpolitik unter den Bedingungen der Europäischen Währungsunionen – Überlegungen zum Aufbau eines Tarifpolitischen Mehr-Ebenen-Systems am Beispiel der westeuropäischen Metallindustrie." *WSI Mitteilungen* (Juli 1998), 482-493.
60. The meeting was the second of its kind, resulting from an initiative by the Belgian confederations in 1996. J. Kreimer-de Fries, Communication, 14 October 1998.
61. There are also a few small European level confederations outside the ETUC with little real significance.
62. L. Turner, "The Europeanization of Labor: Structure before Action," *European Journal of Industrial Relations* 2, no. 3 (November 1996).
63. At one end of the scale, with no MNCs, the agricultural workers EIF, EFA, devotes its main energies to the long-established social dialogue in its sector. At the other, confronted by WEM's absolute refusal to meet under any circumstances, the EMF has concentrated on negotiating EWCs.
64. ETUC, "Jobs and Solidarity at the Heart of Europe," Eighth Statutory Congress, Brussels, May 1995, 27, 29.
65. The following account is based primarily on interviews and correspondence with participants in the deliberations. This material was gathered by the authors and by Jon Erik Dølvik, who generously shared his information with them. See his *Redrawing Boundaries of Solidarity?* chap. 9.
66. The ETUC negotiators kept a small ad hoc group of Executive Committee members, including the DGB, informed, but IG Metall was apparently taken by surprise.
67. The TUC's position paralleled its new reliance on Europe for legal protection unattainable at home, although individual TUC affiliates were more skeptical of what European bargaining could achieve. There were other differences between confederations and individual unions, but they cut different ways. The Nordic confederations opposed sectoral Euro-bargaining, which threatened their strong (but weakening) national positions relative to their member unions, while the DGB supported it in line with its own affiliates' views.
68. "European Collective Bargaining – ETUC Strategy," adopted by the Executive Committee, March 4, 1993.
69. "Note de Debat," ETUC Secretariat, 13 November 1995.
70. Divisions within the Executive, for diverse reasons, were a factor. Wolfgang Weipert, EFBWW board member and international secretary of its German affiliate, and Peter Cassells, General Secretary of the Irish TUC, interviews by A. Martin, May 1995; and Report on the Seventh EFBWW General Assembly, Blankenberge, 20-21 November 1995, 35.
71. ETUC Constitution, Article 13.
72. The fact that EURO-FIET continued to be a regional office of the ITS based in Geneva, rather than a free-standing body like most EIFs, left EURO-FIET more isolated than it otherwise might have been.
73. Once the parental leave agreement was turned into European law, Euro-Commerce could acknowledge its applicability to the commerce sector without conceding any obligation to comply with an agreement negotiated by UNICE or setting the precedent of bargaining with EURO-FIET.
74. ETUC Secretariat, "Explanatory Note on the Role of the Sectoral Social Dialogue," Brussels, 9 July 1996. For the Nordic confederations' position, see Nordens Fackliga Samorganisation, "Arbetsmarknadsdialogen I EU," Stockholm, 22 August 1996. The EIFs' position is set out in letters from the EMF, EFBWW, and EURO-FIET, 4 June, 9

September, and 23 September, 1996, respectively, and was supported by the DGB, which never had the authority the Nordics wanted to protect.

75. The EFBWW's dues will almost triple during the 1990s. It got a standing mandate to negotiate agreements on EWCs, a committee to pool collective bargaining information has been set up, and a form of European membership has been established. Documents for Seventh EFBWW General Assembly, Blankenberge, 20-21 November 1995. Wolfgang Weipert, interview by A. Martin, May 1995, and Jan Cremers, interview by A. Martin, December 1995 and interview by Stephen Silvia, January 1997.
76. ETUC's view is from "Jobs and Solidarity," 1995 Congress, 29; UNICE's is from the *Financial Times*, 6 May 1994, cited in T. Hayes, "Trade Unions and European Works Councils," Conference on European Works Councils – The Pragmatic Approach, London, 22 September 1995, 5.
77. T. Schulten, "European Works Councils: Prospects for a New System of European Industrial Relations," *European Journal of Industrial Relations* 2, no. 3 (November 1996), 320.
78. M. Gold, *Direct Communications in European Multinationals: A Case Study Approach* (Dublin: European Foundation for the Improvement of Living and Working Conditions, 1994).
79. M. Carley, S. Geissler, and H. Krieger, "European Works Councils in Focus" (Dublin: European Foundation for the Improvement of Living and Working Conditions, 1996), 4; M. Higgins, "Case Study: Germany Bayer PLC," European Works Councils – The Pragmatic Approach, 10-11. BP Oil Europe, Honda, and Pepsi have avoided union involvement. GM and DEC are two others that tried but may have given up. On DEC, see M. Blank, S. Geissler, and R. Jaeger, *Euro-betriebsräte: Grundlagen – Praxisbeispiele – Mustervereinbarungen* (Köln: Bund-Verlag, 1996), 87-101.
80. ETUC, "Transposition of the EWC Directive," Working Paper No. 25, Brussels, 30 September 1996, 3-4.
81. 1994 estimate of employees represented in EWCs from *SAFtidningen Näringsliv* 20, 14 June 1996, 12. Corresponding labor force data from European Commission, *Employment in Europe 1995* (Luxembourg: Office for Official Publications of the European Communities, 1995), 187.
82. M. Hall, M. Carley, M. Gold, P. Marginson, and K. Sisson, *European Works Councils: Planning for the Directive* (London: Eclipse Group Ltd and Industrial Relations Research Unit, 1995), 44. Even if agreements do not provide for advance consultation or anything more, EWCs obviously can go beyond them. Thus, the management of Bouygues, one of Europe's largest construction firms, is interested in developing general, company-wide health and safety standards jointly with EWC employee representatives and the EFBWW.
83. In VW, the Council or its executive committee has a right to comment on major planned changes and get a reply from management before the decision is made. Thomson has similar arrangements.
84. Several "joint texts" were agreed on, most notably on "trade union rights," described as the "first steps to a 'European collective bargaining system.'" Hall et al., *European Works Councils*, 21, 38.
85. Hall et al., *European Works Councils*, 44; Peter Reid, General Secretary, Engineering Employers Federation (EEF), at ETUC/ETUI Conference on "European Works Councils and the Europeanization of Industrial Relations," Brussels, 2-4 October 1996; Bill Shardlow, Group Personnel Director, Coats Viyella PLC, "Case Study: U.K. – Coats Viyella PLC," in Conference on Trade Unions and European Works Councils, 4.

86. Hayes, "Trade Unions and European Works Councils;" EIF officials involved in negotiating EWCs, interviews by authors, 1994-96.
87. Schulten, "European Works Councils," 309, 319; Hayes, "Trade Unions and European Works Councils," 4, 5. Such strategic interaction between central managements and coordinated union bargaining is viewed as a kind of "arm's length" or "virtual" transnational bargaining without direct negotiations. P. Marginson, and K. Sisson, "The Structure of Transnational Capital in Europe: The Emerging Euro-Company and Its Implications for Industrial Relations," in *New Frontiers in European Industrial Relations*, ed. R. Hyman and A. Ferner, (Oxford: Blackwell, 1994), 45. See also the same authors' "European Collective Bargaining: A Virtual Prospect?" ETUI, DWP 96.09.1
88. Hayes, "Trade Unions and European Works Councils," 5.
89. Schulten, "European Works Councils," 305.
90. F. Mueller, "National Stakeholders in the Global Contest for Corporate Investment," *European Journal of Industrial Relations* 2, no. 3 (November 1996), 364. P. Marginson, P. Armstrong, P. Edwards and J. Purcell, "Facing the Multinational Challenge," in *The Challenges to Trade Unions in Europe*, ed. P. Leisinck et al., 198.
91. Schulten, "European Works Councils," 303, 319.
92. An EIF general secretary said that when companies are willing to negotiate about flexibility, then "we are the ones with reservations," as long as such negotiations are not linked to and coordinated with sectoral and intersectoral frameworks. Jan Cremers, at ETUC/ETUI Conference on "European Works Councils and the Europeanization of Industrial Relations," Brussels, 2-4 October 1996.
93. Schulten, "European Works Councils," 320.
94. Bargaining can be coordinated throughout a market even if it is done in separate segments or units within the market, provided that unions (or employers) can coordinate bargaining through prior agreement on common bargaining positions or pattern bargaining. Given the improbability if not impossibility of even sectoral collective bargaining in Europe, company-level collective bargaining might nevertheless be coordinated at the sectoral level. F. Traxler, "European Trade Union Policy and Collective Bargaining," 295.
95. B. Eichengreen,"European Monetary Unification," *Journal of Economic Literature* 71 (September 1993).
96. The 1977 McDougall Report recommended a budget of 5 to 7 percent of community GDP, and the ETUC has been urging an initial increase to at least 3 percent. P. Pochet and L. Turloot, "Une construction inachevée," in *Union économique et monétaire et négociations collectives*, ed. O. Jacobi and P. Pochet (Brussels: Observatoire Social Européen, 1996), 24. While central governments in the U.S. and Canada account for at least half of general government expenditures, the EU budget accounts for only 2 percent of such expenditures in the Community. K. Busch, "Le danger de dumping social et salarial," in *Union économique et monétaire et négociations collectives*, ed. Jacobi and Pochet, 39.
97. L. Tsoukalis, *The New European Economy*, 2d ed. (Oxford: Oxord University Press, 1993), 173-74, 337.
98. Busch, "Le danger de dumping social et salarial," 38.
99. B. Keller, "Toward a European System of Collective Bargaining?" in *German Industrial Relations under the Impact of Structural Change, Unification and European Integration*, ed. R. Hoffmann, O. Jacobi, and B. Keller (Düsseldorf: Hans-Böckler-Stiftung, 1995), 124.

100. B. Mahnkopf and E. Altvater, "Transmission Belts of Transnational Competition? Trade Unions and Collective Bargaining in the Context of European Integration," *European Journal of Industrial Relations* 1, no. 1 (March 1995), 102.
101. O. Sievert, "Geld, das man nicht selbst herstellen kann," *Frankfurter Allgemeine Zeitung* 225 (26 September 1992), quoted in K. Busch, *Europäische Integration und Tarifpolitik: Lohnpolitische Konsquenzen der Wirtschafts- und Wärhingsunion.* (Köln: Bund-Verlag GmbH, 1994), 99.
102. This would be the macroeconomically most unfavorable position on the Calmfors-Driffill U-curve. L. Calmfors and J. Driffill, "Bargaining Structure, Corporatism and Macroeconomic Performance," *Economic Policy* 3 (1988).
103. 106 M. Rhodes, "Globalisation, Labour Markets and Welfare States: A Future of 'Competitive Corporatism'?" EUI Working Papers, RSC No. 97/36; G. Fajertag and P. Pochet, eds, *Social Pacts in Europe* (Brussels: European Trade Union Institute and Observatoire Social Européen, 1997); A. Martin, "EMU and Wage Bargaining: The Americanization of the European Labor Market?" ETUI/OSE Working Paper, forthcoming. See also chapters on Italy, Germany, and Spain in this volume.
104. Declaration on the Treaty on European Union. ETUC Executive Committee, 5-6 March 1992, 3.
105. P. Coldrick, "EMU Revisted," Hans Böckler Stiftung/Observatoire Social Européen Seminar, 8 December 1995, 1.
106. "Creating the European Social Dimension in the Internal Market: European Social Programme," adopted by the Executive Committee, February 1988, Preamble.
107. Ibid., 2, 7.
108. "European Social Programme," and "Community Charter of Fundamental Social Rights," adopted by the Executive Committee, December 1988.
109. There is little research on how much influence ETUC had in this field, but it achieved much of what it sought in the important 1989 Framework Directive. L. Vogel, *Prevention at the Workplace* (Brussels: European Trade Union Technical Bureau for Health and Safety, 1994), 72-76.
110. Enactment may also have been eased by an awareness of slippage between legislation and its enforcement, minimizing the threat to lower-standard states. Ibid., 39-61. See also Council resolution on the transposition of Community social legislation, Official Journal C 168, 4 July 1995.
111. It remains to be seen whether the shift toward left-center governments in a majority of EU member states will make the political conditions more favorable again.
112. The manifesto for this view is the *OECD Jobs Study*.
113. European Commission, "European Social Policy: A Way Forward for the Union," COM(94) 333, Brussels, 27 July 1994; and Communication from the Commission and proposal for a Council Decision on the Commission's activities of analysis, research, cooperation, and action in the field of employment (Essen) COM(95) 250 final, Brussels, 13 June 1995.
114. ETUC, "Jobs and Solidarity at the Heart of Europe," 18; ETUC "Employment Manifesto," 4-5, Brussels, February 1996.
115. Executive Committee Resolution, December 1988, summarized in "Delors Committee Report on Economic and Monetary Union," draft resolution, 23 May 1989.
116. Coldrick, "EMU Revisited": and E. Gabaglio, "Economic and Monetary Union," speech, 23 February 1996. See also D. Foden, "EMU, Employment and Social Cohesion," *Transfer* 2, no. 2 (June 1996) and "From Essen to Madrid: Growth and Employ-

ment," in *European Trade Union Yearbook 1995*, ed. E. Gabaglio and R. Hoffmann (Brussels: ETUI, 1996).

117. ETUC, "Statement on Economic and Monetary Union," draft, 3 October 1996, 5.
118. "EMU: The Final Preparations," ETUC Memorandum, October 1996. The ETUC calls upon the Intergovernmental Conference to revise the treaty by including a new employment chapter, establishing an Employment Committee "with the same standing as the existing Monetary Committee," and requiring both committees to consult the social partners. See also P. Coldrick, "Employment and the IGC," in *The Future of the European Union*, ed. European Trade Union Trade Union Institute (Brussels: ETUI, 1996).
119. The TUC's support stems from its reliance on Europe for what it cannot attain in Britain. "European Common Currency," TUC Report, 29 January 1996. The DGB shares the German stake in depriving other countries of devaluation as competitive tool. See "Zur Europäischen Wirtschafts- und Währungsunion (EWWU)," DGB Informationen zur Wirtschafts- und Strukturpolitik 11/1995. The Spanish confederations' commitment to Europe also underlies its support for EMU, as does the Italian confederations more critical support. The French confederations have been divided on the question. The Nordics generally are the most skeptical. Peter Coldrick, interview by A. Martin, September 1996.
120. The ESCB was designed behind closed doors by committees of central bankers, finance ministers, and heads of government. D. Cameron, "Transnational Relations and the Development of European Economic and Monetary Union," in *Bringing Transnational Relations Back In: Non-State Actors, Domestic Structures and International Institutions*, ed. Thomas Risse-Kappen, (Cambridge, U.K: Cambridge University Press, 1995).
121. ETUC, "Statement on Economic and Monetary Union," draft, p. 3.
122. J. Goetschy and P. Pochet, "The Treaty of Amsterdam: A New Approach to Employment and Social Affairs?" *Transfer* 3, (November 1997); and *European Report* 2271, November 26, 1997.
123. *Social Europe* 2/95.
124. P. Coldrick, ETUC Confederal Secretary responsible for economic policy, communications to the authors, 20 February and 25 July 1997. See also his, "The ETUC's Role in the EU's New Economic and Monetary Architecture," *Transfer* 4, no. 1 (Spring 1998).
125. "ETUC supports EMU, but – and this is becoming a big but – a growing number of our members don't." P. Coldrick, "The European Employment Pact and EMU," speech, Rome, 16 May 1996.

Chapter 9

THROUGH A GLASS DARKLY

George Ross and Andrew Martin

European unions are under siege. Political leaders have accelerated European economic integration to create "globalization on one continent," rapidly lowering boundaries between national economies. Firms have sought greater flexibility, often by decentralizing bargaining and redefining the issues to be bargained. Macroeconomic policy commitments have shifted from full employment to price stability. Market neoliberalism has taken over the ideological outlooks and policy orientations of political forces. These processes challenge the basic premises of European unionism. Unions have lost clout in the all-important market arena. Traditional unionist identities no longer work well. Resource supplies from politics and the state are dwindling. Unions' organizational capacities are stretched thin.

How have these changes presented themselves to specific union movements? How have these unions understood them? What new approaches, if any, have they developed? How much has their strategic vision shifted to the European level? Where has all this left European unions? We anticipated variety in the answers to these questions. Changes have been refracted by variations in unions' organization, industrial relations systems, relationships to politics, and differences in national economic development patterns. Even if unions have had to confront similar challenges, therefore, these challenges came in specific national

---

Notes for this section begin on page 398.

contexts, at different points in time and with differing degrees of severity. Let us begin with a brief review of our cases in this light.

Compared to others, German and Swedish unions look well off. Swedish neo-corporatism and social democracy were long advertised as the solution to democratizing capitalism and extending social citizenship. Crisis did not hit the Swedes until the end of the 1980s, and the brief period since is hardly enough to know what the consequences will be for the Swedish model. The Swedes have maintained their very high level of membership but lost the national level of neo-corporatism. Swedish unions now face unprecedented unemployment, the beginnings of welfare state erosion (which, should it become more serious, could nourish serious gender divisions inside the union movement), and declining Social Democratic political reliability. German sectoral corporatism, constructed around the congruent interests of large firms and large unions, is under much new strain, but has largely held thus far, even through unification. High unemployment, labor-shedding, off-shore investing and strong pressure on the "social wage" have accentuated "insider-outsider" problems and could threaten earlier conquests, however. For both countries the issue is not whether recent troubles are minor perturbations, but how large they will turn out to be. In Sweden the eventual reconfiguration of union positions after neo-corporatism is far from clear. Will employers force even greater decentralization? Will governments become much less friendly? Will public/private sector, male/female, and large/small firm divisions inside the union movement overcome Swedish unions' ability to promote coherence and solidarity? Will high unemployment and tight public finances eventually damage the welfare state beyond repair. In Germany, the sectoral corporatism upon which the system rests has an unpredictable future. What if employers defect? What if unemployment continues to rise? What if welfare state retrenchment occurs?

Italian unions faced a major onslaught in the 1980s, costing them 25 percent of their membership. By the early 1990s the onslaught had been blunted. The unions were able to beat back the threat of autonomous action by COBAS in the public sector, for example. More recently, they have overcome chronic organizational pluralism. All this has helped union proposals gain a hearing in a context of continuing crisis. More important has been the willingness of the unions to trade off concessions, particularly in social welfare provisions, for new "neo-corporatist" positions. In the best of circumstances this could lead to a recasting of Italian industrial relations and solidify a new union role. Much of the impetus behind this has come from greater willingness on the part of the formerly pro-communist CGIL to assume the burdens of Italian integration into the EU single market and EMU. New Italian neo-corporatism is on a precarious footing, however. The political situation remains volatile. Reforming governments of the left could easily give way to coalitions of a harder right. Moreover, the bill to unions for greater European integration in terms of welfare state reform and higher unemployment could soon come due.

British unions have been harder hit. In the postwar years, British industrial relations "voluntarism" and decentralization were predicated upon a foundation of judicial precedents and the eventuality of pro-union Labour governments. Thatcherism in the 1980s sought a fundamental transformation of the labor market, dismantled much of its legal foundation, and kept the Labour Party out of power for nearly two decades. Austerity, monetarism, restructuring, and privatizations produced significant deindustrialization and deunionization. Employers followed the Tory lead toward "union busting." During this period, links between unions and the Labour Party were also transformed. Union relationships to "New Labour" remove any doubt that unions have been demoted from the center of Labour politics and relegated to a broader population of ordinary interest groups. British unions have been obliged to rethink from the ground up.

By the 1990s French unions had lost much of their already small membership and most of their political hopes. Yet they still clung to France's *étatiste* framework. In one expert's words, "the resources placed at unions' disposition by state administrators and large firms have allowed unions to ignore economic and social changes and avoid undue preoccupation with members and workers."[1] In this context the continuation of ruinous competitive union pluralism, despite the end of the Cold War, has reinforced paralysis and blocked strategic and organizational change. The French system after 1945 was built around unions threatening state and employer elites (often very similar people) with difficult-to-control, costly social unrest. Over time this odd system created a strong web of labor market regulation and institutionalized union power in firms (in works councils and other such legally established organisms), which provided indirect support for weak union apparatuses while also encapsulating them. The mutual bluffing between unions and the state upon which the system is based is contingent upon state elites loath to confront the infrastructure of the system itself. So far this willingness has persisted, but it may weaken.

Spanish unions have an exceptional history. With other democratic forces in Spain, they committed themselves to democratization after the Franco dictatorship. Building a new union movement while helping to consolidate a new political order brought more tasks than weak and divided unions could accomplish, particularly since Francoism left a protected, backward economy and archaic, authoritarian labor market regulation. Governments, including those of the Socialists after 1982, sought rapid Spanish integration into the EU, dismantling of the Francoist model and market liberalization. Attempts to include unions in these changes through "pactism" initially accentuated Spanish competitive union pluralism. In the later 1980s pactism collapsed, however, and the unions have since turned to organization building and strategizing to become a viable movement. Spain has an inordinately high official rate of unemployment which, even if discounted for statistical artifices and illegal work, makes this difficult. Deregulating and reorganizing Francoist labor markets has been fraught with pitfalls. While the EU has bolstered political stability and encouraged governments to build a new social protection system, it has also brought elite neo-liberalism.

EU-level unionism, which might have seemed a logical response to European integration, has made limited progress. The ETUC has been strengthened and its mandates expanded over the last decade. Moreover, "social dialogue," encouraged by the Maastricht Social Protocol has brought some "negotiated legislation" at the European intersectoral level. There have been other innovations as well, such as the institutionalization of European Works Councils.[2] To conclude that what has occurred amounts to the beginning of a Eurolevel industrial relations system is overoptimistic, however. At no point in any foreseeable future will EU level unionism and EU-level negotiating resemble those at national level. National industrial relations systems will remain central in Europe's future. The Eurolevel will supplement their workings, rather than incorporating them.

Challenges, Arenas, and Resources

Market Changes

The ravages of rising unemployment have been amply reviewed. As high unemployment loosens labor markets it reduces unions' ability to produce job security. Unions' mobilizing capacities and their ability to promote strikes and demonstrations are sapped. Even though wages may be sticky in areas where unions hold their strength, in general, unemployment makes it easier for employers to keep wages down and gain concessions. Unemployment also diminishes unions' importance to governments because union cooperation in controlling wage levels and inflation declines in importance. These

Table 9.1 Changes in the Level of Collective Bargaining

Country	Pre-1980s	Changes
France	*High Centralization* - Periodic national framework bargains on important general issues. - National sectoral basic wage determination, local variation. - National legal regulation of dimensions of work contract (hours, working conditions) and, indirectly, wages, largely through public sector-national minimum wage (SMIC) - Works Committees play local role	*Significant Decentralization … But …* - Primarily because of legislated reforms, the Auroux Laws encouraged new bargaining and made company level negotiations compulsory, leading to an increase in firm-level bargaining in context of firm-level union weakness. - Declining strikes, except explosions like 1995. - Employers seek new bargaining on flexibility, working time, individualization of labor contract. - Firm level bargaining does not significantly raise pay levels. - Declining importance of national sectoral bargains. - Privatization of former "model" public sector firms.
Germany	*Sectoral Corporatism* - No national bargaining: sectoral employer associations bargain regionally with single sectoral unions. Few companies unaffiliated with employers' associations.	*Little Decentralizing Change* - Unions defeat challenge in 1980s from works councils. - Working hours reduction prominent in bargaining. - Some employer defections, particularly in East, threat of defection increasing in mid-1990s. - Intermittent conflict.
Italy	*Centralization Becoming Multi-Level* - Effective firm level bargaining developed in 1960s, articulated with national and national sectoral levels. Hot Autumn leads to greater decentralization within sectors and firms.	*"Rebalancing" – Decentralization Plus Recentralization* - National sectoral level breaks down in earlier 1980s, employers do not press advantage. - RSUs (unitary trade union representations) in place in important workplaces. - Union defeat of public-sector fragmentation (COBAS). - State, unions, and employers try to recentralize to better articulate company, regional, national system in 1990s, leading to "neo-corporatism" on incomes policies (1993 accord), pensions (1995 accord).

Table 9.1 continued

Spain	*Fragmented Multi-Level Bargaining by Francoist Unions* - Multiple overlapping levels: small firms covered by sectoral/provincial agreements, company-level bargaining and union presence in larger firms. - Work somewhat regulated by laws. - Centralization through neo-corporatist pactism 1977-1986.	*Searching for New System* - Breakdown of peak-level bargaining in mid-1980s, unions try to construct national sectoral-level organizations and bargaining. - Employers more interested in decentralization, company-level bargaining on new issues, creeping individualization. - 1994 labor reform loosens legal regulations and promotes decentralization. - 1997 accord on bargaining reorganization: unions and employers seek better bargaining articulation among levels.
Sweden	*Multi-Tiered, Peak-Level Neo-corporatism* - Bargaining over wages between employers' organization and blue-collar unions, hegemonic over sectoral bargaining. - Strong union presence at all levels. - Separate organization of blue collar, lower and upper white collar workers. - Decentralized bargaining to fill in national deals.	*Decentralization by Dismantling National Level* - Employers try to break down sectoral level but with limited success; workplace and sectoral-level union presence persists. - Employers try to bargain locally on new issues, play off "collared" confederations against each other, and strive for agreements covering all workers within a firm to strengthen enterprise unionism.
U.K.	*Decentralization-Voluntarism* - Weak national concertation sometimes, but no national bargaining. Sectoral agreements existed. - In addition, substantial plant-level local bargaining. - Important challenge by shop steward/rank-and-file action.	*Governmental and Employer Attacks, Led by Government* - Termination of national concertation. - Decline in multi-employer sectoral bargaining. - Government pushes performance-tied pay in public sector; privatizes and marketizes. - End of minimum wage. - When employers bargain at all, often on non-wage issues. - De-recognition and union busting at company level leading to unilateral individualization of employment relationships.
European-level	*No Euro-level bargaining*	*Possibilities for European-Level Bargaining in Maastricht Social Protocol (British opt-out ended in 1997)*, only where allowed by treaties and on Commission propositions. - EWCs a factor for change, give unions new openings in MNCs but tempt formation of enterprise unions.

processes are cumulative. Declining mobilizing capacities and political clout promote further market and political weakening. Generating identity and organizational resources and supporters becomes much more difficult. With unemployment, changed macroeconomic policies, and new employer strategies it stood to reason that bargaining would be decentralized and bargaining agendas changed. Where both have occurred it is the prior national situation which has counted most, as Table 9.1 summarizes.

There has been significant decentralization in three cases. In Britain and France it occurred from political initiatives – Thatcherism in Britain and the Auroux Laws in France. The attack on national levels of Swedish neo-corporatism, in contrast, came from the engineering employers' association. In Italy, after decentralization in the 1970s, new threats in the 1980s were blocked. Italy now has an articulated system among all levels which points toward limited neo-corporatism (and recentralization) quite closely connected now to Italy's entry into EMU. In Spain, where the economy has been moving from autarky toward European integration and from protected rust belt industrialism toward new sectors, Spanish unions have had to struggle to build a modern union movement on sectoral level.[3] In Germany, sectoral-pattern bargaining has been under increasing strain but remains in effect.

There has also been a widespread employer drive for "flexibility." In most places employers would like deregulation of labor markets, including changed worktime rules, fewer constraints in hiring and firing, loosened job classification systems, and changed labor contracts to allow individualization. There is a desire for increased numerical flexibility as well, often contributing to further differentiation between a core full-time work force and peripheral groups without strong links to firms and unions. Many employers also seek to break down traditional job distinctions through multiskilling, teamwork, and the devolution of responsibility for production. Both approaches promote workforce fragmentation between "insiders" and "outsiders," often overlapping gender and age distinctions, which supplements the large insider-outsider difference already created by unemployment. Specific practices vary greatly, however, as Table 9.2 shows.

Union resource losses from unemployment and flexibilization have been great. The numerical decline of core union membership evident in France, the U.K. and Spain, and to a lesser extent in Germany and Italy, has serious implications. The dwindling group of insiders is usually composed of aging males while young and female outsiders are often in more precarious employment. Statistics for youth and female unemployment reflect important generational differences in labor market structures but also shows how acute these issues can be, particularly for youth (26.2 per-

Table 9.3 Government Composition and Major Policy Changes

Country	Composition of Governments	Policy Shifts
France	- Left President 1981-95, Right 1995-present. - Left Governments 1981-86; 1988-93, 1997-present. - Right Governments 1986-88, 1993-97	- Restructuring after 1983: austerity, de-indexation of wages, turn to Europe. - Franc fort monetarism, compress public sector. - Tolerance of high levels of unemployment. - Squeeze to meet EMU criteria.
Germany	- Christian Democrats-Liberals after 1982. - Social Democrats-Greens-present.	- Consistent price stability by Bundesbank. - Reunification (1 to 1 currency exchange). - Efforts to revamp welfare state 1996.
Italy	- Socialist-Christian Democrats until early 1990s, "New Right" after 1993, Left-Center 1996-present.	- Austerity and monetarism after joining EMS in 1979. - Attempts to undermine reforms of 1970s, (scala mobile). - Movement toward EMU after Maastricht produces cutbacks
Spain	- Socialists 1982-1996. Right 1996-present.	- Europeanization, liberalization and restructuring. - Monetarism, tolerance of very high levels of unemployment. - Cutbacks for EMU convergence since 1992.
Sweden	- Socialists and "Bourgeois" governments alternate.	- Socialist competitive devaluation in 1982 buys time. - Socialists liberalize capital flows and monetary policy, later 1980s, unable to halt dismantling of centralized bargaining - 1990s, rise in unemployment, squeeze on welfare state.
U.K.	- Thatcherism 1979-1997. - New Labour 1997-present.	- neo-liberalization → onslaught on unions. - New Labour refuses to roll back Thatcherism.
European level	- Delors Commission 1985-94, - Santer Commission 1995-1999. - Member States largely Socialist-Christian Democrat.	- "Market building" predominates over "state building"

Deteriorating relationships between unions and erstwhile party-political friends have been remarkable. Table 9.4 shows that unions can no longer rely upon "party allies" for influence over government policy. Old-style social democracy may be breathing its last in Sweden. Old-style communism is dead. New style, "third way," social democracy is much less union friendly.

Table 9.4 Unions and Their Party Allies: Losing Friends?

Country	Union Ties 1980	Mid-1990s
France	- Politicized competitive "idea unionism"; CGT tied to PCF; FO, CFDT vaguely PS.	- Socialists, never tied to unions, turn to liberal economic management. Socialist discourse drops "class" and opts for Europe to modernize France. - Communists decline precipitously, carrying CGT along.
Germany	- In sectoral corporatism parties less significant.	- SPD implausible political allies until 1998, except on *Land* level. - Christian Democrats reluctant to confront unions.
Italy	Competitive unionism; CGIL tied to PCI; CISL, UIL independent.	- Socialists of little use to unions, disappear in scandals. - Communists become social democrats, urge CGIL moderation, Rifondazione Communista maintains hold on left of CIGL. - Collapse of party system in 1990s. Left-center government from 1996 dedicated to EMU and austerity. - Unions move toward "syndicalist" union autonomy.
Spain	- Competitive pluralist, organizationally immature movement; UGT supports Socialists until 1988, then unity in action with CCOO.	- Socialists, from 1982, agents of liberalization, restructuring and Europeanization, (but make genuine efforts to build welfare state). - *ouvriérisme* replaced by modernization discourse. - Communists, although weakened by splits, hold influence on Left of CCOO.
Sweden	Powerful movement needs governmental cooperation.	- Socialists turn to price stability and public spending cutbacks. - Increasing tensions between unions and Social Democrats.
U.K.	Organic connections with Labour Party.	- Labour fails electorally throughout period 1979-1997. - New Labour attenuates connections with unions, produces legislation on recognition, 1998.
European level	Socialists Favor European integration.	- Socialist governments (France, Spain, Italy and Sweden) look to Europe to work domestic economic restructuring.

The final political factor has been European integration. One does not need hyperbolic concepts of "globalization" in Western Europe, because the EU's member states decided a *fuite en avant* of internationalization by political decision when they relaunched European integration in the mid-1980s. The effects have been different across countries. Britain has attracted a great deal of foreign direct investment which, in the wake of Thatcherism, is helping to change British manufacturing and industrial relations. The EU's "South" competes with Britain for FDI, creating similar issues to those of the U.K., even though now FDI shifts toward Central and Eastern Europe are more important. Outward foreign investment from Sweden, Germany, France, and even Italy, toward other EU market areas and the international market has increased substantially. These changes tend to put European unions into competition over jobs and make "social dumping" a more distinct possibility. The difficulties experienced by Europe in creating new jobs, the restructuring and labor-shedding effects of the Single Market, and the depressing effect of preparation for EMU accentuate these processes.

Recent European integration has internationalized firm strategies and stimulated a surge of cross-border firm reorganization, mergers and acquisitions, and strategic alliances. The opening of borders subjects all firms to increased competition. The nature of this integration – more "market building" than regulatory – has done little to compensate unions for lost national capacities.[6] Unions thus face growing disjunction between familiar national arenas and a "Europe" where they are weak and under-organized. Greater transnational union cooperation might seem to be an answer and, indeed, some has developed. A number of factors militate against it, however. The interests of national union movements within the EU may be in conflict, particularly since the Single Market and EMU bear economic threats to national economies. Next, and most important, unions are profoundly rooted in national systems of political and economic exchange. Habit leads them to prefer the devils they know rather than venturing into an unknown international arena. The nature of European institutions reinforces this. The Council of Ministers and the European Council are conclaves of national leaders best influenced through national political channels. The mandate of European institutions in the social policy area is quite limited, so that even if unions were more transnationalized they would have difficulty obtaining much.

Unions as Strategic Actors in Crisis

Our introduction depicted European unions as social movement organizations and strategic actors. In general, virtually all dimensions of unions' strategic positions have been affected negatively in recent times. Unions suffer from a decline in resources available from wage-earners. This, in turn, has weakened their capacities for exchange with employers. Unions have also lost much of their capacity to influence governments and politics.

Table 9.5 Challenges and Responses in Bargaining with Employers

Country	Challenges to Bargaining Approaches	Adaptations of Bargaining Strategies
France	- Tradition of sectoral, sometimes national framework bargaining. - Unions lose in private sector. - Unemployment. - Auroux Laws oblige decentralization. - Employers want greater flexibility, less demanding sectoral framework deals.	- *Failure of "Oppositionalism"* but unions without alternative. - More bargaining (without partners?) in new areas (more flexible hours). - Decentralized cacophony.
Germany	- Tradition of sectoral pattern bargaining, with possibilities for discussing training, technological change, and flexibility. - Tradition relatively unchallenged. - Unemployment.	- *Continuity Amid Strain* - Unification imposes traditional pattern bargaining on East. - Some "dialogical" mobilization of base (process bargaining). - More scope for local bargaining.
Italy	- Post-Hot Autumn decentralized bargaining under stress in 1980s from employer offensive (Fiat), end of scala mobile, COBAS in public sector. - Union divisions reemerge. - Unemployment.	- *Change, Uncertain Outcome* - Return of union unity at top. - Improved articulation between levels - Range of "flexibility" issues, demands for training. - Move away from egalitarianism. - Win legal blocks on COBAS. - Protocol on incomes policy, 1993 leads to tripartite efforts to reconstruct industrial relations systems. - From 1995, "pactism" on EMU.
Spain	- Organizational underdevelopment and division in context of democratization. - Neo-corporatist "pactism" breaks in mid 1980s. - Regionalism, weakness in public sector. - Vast resort to temporary contracts by employers. - Mass unemployment.	- *Changing Outlooks, Practices to Follow?* - Unity of action UGT-CCOO. - Attempts to build national organizations and bargaining. - Slow reaction to shopfloor change, new stress on training, flexibility issues in 1990s. - Bipartite efforts to increase articulation between bargaining levels and reduce temporary work rates.
Sweden	- Traditional neo-corporatism; solidaristic wage bargaining, active labor market policies attacked by employers. - End of full employment. - Europe and threats to public sector.	- *Challenge to Swedish Model* - Loss of national level bargaining. - National unions resist efforts to decentralize to firm level, but allow greater local variation. Coming of greater wage dispersion and inequality. - LO seeks new bargaining coalitions across sectors; unsuccessfully seeks cooperation "across collars" on incomes policy. - "Solidaristic Wages for Solidaristic Work" implies bargaining at subnational level over redistribution of profits for training. - "Wagearner feminism" to encompass gender issues.

Table 9.5 continued

U.K.	- Traditional decentralization, some sectoral, little national bargaining. - Loss of national leverage, sectoral dealing,. - Local employer hostility. - Privatization, subcontracting in public sector.	- *Experimentation Without Success* - More cooperative relations with employers. - New issues – flexibility, hours, etc. - Efforts to recruit women, youth, minorities. - "credit card" unionism. - As yet no compensation for political/legal losses.
European level	- No European-level bargaining. - Unemployment. - EMU.	- *Limited Progress* - Negotiated legislation under Maastricht Social Protocol. - Potential of EWCs. - Development of ETUC as organization of organizations, but without own resources. Partial dependence upon EU resources.

How, and how well, have union movements reacted strategically? Unions cannot avoid responding to common challenges in the market. Most have tried to diversify approaches to bargaining, moving away from, or supplementing, national or sectoral pattern bargaining toward more complex articulation among local, sectoral, national, and transnational levels. Often this has taken the form of "framework" deals at higher levels which leave considerable space for local differentiation. Unions have had to decentralize activities to follow employers toward firm-level bargaining, for example. They have also moved toward greater firm-level "partnership," becoming less conflictual, emphasizing dual representation with unions and works councils operating more symbiotically (roughly the German model), and opening more to firm-level bargaining about flexibility. In shifting they have tried to generate new payoffs for members in the realm of training, employment security, and work time reduction, in addition to wages. Table 9.5 shows considerable differences between unions in this general area, however.

Most unions have thought seriously about recruiting new support. Since the new world of potential supporters is composed of service-sector, white-collar, and atypical workers, often women, recruiting calls for new approaches. Some unions have tried hard, like the British, with limited results. Others, either because the problem is less pressing or because of their traditions, have been less energetic. The Germans, with a strong "male breadwinner" tradition, have stressed "qualitative" rather than quantitative recruitment efforts – a conservative approach to protect the boundaries around insiders. French unions have had great difficulty figuring out how to recruit at all, only partly out of ineptitude. The strong French legal framework, strengthened by the Auroux Laws, buffers them from spending scarce resources on new recruiting while French workers may calculate that since union benefits accrue without union membership it is not worth the trouble to join unions. The Swedish movement, which organizes everybody in sight, faces a less urgent problem. Its problems are more internal – tension between men and women *inside* its ranks, for example, particularly given labor market segmentation and the strong feminization of Swedish social services. "Wage-earner feminism" is a promising approach, but tensions between it and blue-collar industrial unionism may become more acute as the squeeze on public services intensifies. Many unions have also shifted toward "service" provision, offering legal services, credit cards and the like. The British have gone furthest toward seeing members as "customers."

Recruitment and outreach matters are connected with union efforts to reconstruct and rejuvenate their organizations, as Table 9.6 summarizes.

***Table* 9.6** Union Efforts at Organizational Reconfiguration

Country	Organizational Challenges	Responses
France	- Declining support. - Competitive pluralism. - Effects of Auroux Laws and long-term austerity.	- Internal conflict at Confederal level as Confederations reposition competitive positions, renewal of acute union pluralism. - Declining CGT retreats from overpoliticization to foreground sectoral federations while FO enhances militancy. - CFDT stakes out moderate, cooperative position. - FEN (teachers' federation) splits into warring parts. - Little mobilization except when provoked by government.
Germany	- Declining influence of DGB, financial crises, ineffectiveness of smaller unions. - unification.	- "Recreate West in East." - Mega-merger plans (IG Chemie, IGMetall), "Cooperative" alternatives proposed by smaller unions, DGB weakened.
Italy	- Competitive pluralism. - Employer attacks. - Crisis of state and parties.	- Truce in competitive pluralism. - Efforts in new neo-corporatist directions. - Root out COBAS - Quasi-syndicalist roles in political crises.
Spain	- Competitive pluralism. - Building organizationally after Francoism. - Low membership concentrated in declining industries.	- Overcome competitive pluralism in later 1980s. - Mergers, strengthening of sectoral federations. - Converging organizational models UGT-CCOO, new balance unions and works councils. - Organization in expanding public sector. - Mobilize around broad policy issues, partial resumption of peak-level dealing in 1990s.

Table 9.6 continued

Sweden	- Loss of neo-corporatism threat to Confederations. - Employer offensive. - Divisions LO-TCO. - Squeeze on welfare state.	- Experiments with mergers. - Cross-collar cooperation (LO-TCO).
U.K.	- De-industrialization. - Loss of political links. - Dismantling of public sector. - Employer attacks. - Weak TUC.	- Uncertainty. - Mergers – growth of general unionism, single unions. - Enhanced interunion cooperation. - TUC latches onto Europe.
European level	- Renewed European market-building.	- ETUC and sectoral industry committees strengthened. - EWCs will promote more Euro-union activity and action. - Problem of ETUC as lobbyist vs. bargainer unresolved.

Most cases show some innovation, if to different degrees and in different ways. The Swedish unions, with their long-standing organizational learning culture, continue to produce new ideas. The Spanish and Italian movements have been successful in muting the centrifugal forces of plural unionism. The Italians have beaten back autonomous particularistic unionism in the public sector. The Italians and Spanish have also tried to reconstruct linkages between local, sectoral, regional, and national levels. British unions have merged smaller organizations to concentrate resources more effectively; and they are sometimes prodded by employers seeking single-union representation at firm level (when employers were not determined to do without unions altogether). The French have also had to innovate, despite themselves, because of the changes in their legal surroundings. But change in France has mainly been toward intensified fragmentation. The Germans have made fewer changes, since the German context of sectoral corporatism still works, even though there have been persistent discussions about mega-mergers and cooperation among smaller unions.

The public sector poses particular problems to everyone. It is an important part of unions' support base, compensating for the slow erosion of industrial work, albeit in ways which have sometimes heightened conflict between different parts of the union movement. Public-sector growth largely stopped in the 1980s, however, when public finances deteriorated, the vogue for privatization and deregulation peaked, and the quest for price stability kicked in. The absolute danger is greatest in France because unions there barely exist outside the public sector. Deregulation and privatization, which began to pick up speed by the mid-1990s, could strike at the heart of unions' power bases, but so far they have been limited by the dangers they present to political elites – the 1995 strikes were a good indicator that even weak unions could mobilize.[7] Public sector mobilizations cut in several directions, however, because often they look to the general public like the purest forms of corporatist self-protection The French and Italians, and to a lesser extent the Spanish, have also faced financial squeezes and work reorganization as governments use the public sector as a tool for incomes policy and budget relief. The relative inability of French and Italian unions to protect public sector workers in the 1980s stimulated autonomous "category" mobilizations – COBAS and their French equivalents – in vital public-service areas like the railroads, where mobilizations quickly lead to chaos. In both cases mainstream unions attempted to marginalize these autonomous movements, but in neither case would it be safe to declare the problems resolved.[8]

Welfare state changes and cutbacks, the inevitability of new privatizations prodded by EU liberalization of telecoms, energy, and transportation plus cutbacks in military spending will be great challenges over the next period. At stake in France and Italy is the defense of the very notion of "public service" itself, which neither has been able to do so far except in particularistic terms. In the Swedish situation the issue will be how unions confront the effects of rolling cutbacks in social services. The feminization of the labor force in these areas may deepen gender divisions. British unions have faced subcontracting, privatization, cutbacks, and "managed competition" inside remaining public-sector areas, with negative consequences. Only the Germans have thus far avoided public sector problems, perhaps because so much German public employment is covered by civil service status. There are, however, large issues of overstaffing which will have to be confronted eventually.

European integration has presented a strategic conundrum to national unions. "Staying national" has real costs. Employers and capital can range freely over the international and EU arenas at the expense of unions' national resources. But "going European" may also be a risky misallocation of resources. The learning curve of union internationalization has thus barely begun, as Table 9.7 shows.

Unions have moved, tentatively, toward Europeanization when such moves have served their national purposes. While this is perfectly understandable, it has limited union investment in European-level activities. The ETUC, partly in consequence, has had to seek its resources from European institutions as much as from national constituents. This has made it more

Table 9.7 Unions and Transnational Unionism

Country	Attitude to Transnationalization	Consequences for Transnational Action
France	- Divided: CFDT a key European actor; FO more distant; for CGT, until recently, Europe = capitalist plot.	- CFDT uses ETUC/EU for domestic purposes, others emulate; Interested in EWCs.
Germany	- DGB and major unions are players in ETUC and Industry Committees. - European unionism should not threaten German pattern bargaining and industrial relations.	- Advance and retreat of German unions a critical factor for ETUC. - Germans wary of ETUC getting close to real negotiating role. - Interested in EWCs. - Major source of ETUC resources.
Italy	- Confederations strongly pro-European. - CGIL uses Europeanism to generate domestic legitimacy.	- Discreet but important actors, occasionally key partners of Germans.
Spain	- Strongly pro-European but weak.	- Stakes in structural funds.
Sweden	- Recent EU membership hence inexperience. - European trade unionism should protect Swedish specificities.	- Secondary actors thus far. - Pushed for employment criteria in EMU. - Act to protect Swedish labor standards.
U.K.	- Strongly anti-European until later 1980s, then TUC discovers political utility of Europe against Thatcherism. - More pro-Europe than Labour Party.	- Important actors in ETUC - Strong for signing Maastricht Social Protocol.
European level	- ETUC weak lobbyist until later 1980s.	- ETUC attempts to use enhanced integration to strengthen its lobbying position and move into bargaining area. - European Works' Councils a question mark – may strengthen the position of European Industry Committees and national unions, or undermine both.

bound to the European Commission's broad goals than it otherwise might have been, and from time to time it has placed it in difficulty with parts of the rank-and-file. In time, however, and particularly as EMU leads to a complete loss of national macroeconomic policy sovereignty, unions are certain to give more attention to Europe. The question is how.

Union Responses, Union Futures

All of the union movements that we have considered have lost ground in the market/bargaining arena. All face unemployment. Most have lost supporters. Many have seen their legal frameworks challenged. Still others have lost their earlier coherence. Almost all have been obliged to reconfigure workplace bargaining agendas and "flexibilize" earlier conquests. These losses undercut union efforts to "convert" market/bargaining resources into other types. One new choice imposed upon virtually all unions, therefore, is to attract new support, or at the very least, to reconfigure appeals to continuing bases. Unions that have attempted new outreach, recruitment, and organizational changes have not necessarily succeeded, however. Trying out new approaches when employers have the upper hand is difficult. Outreach and recruitment programs also engage complicated issues of union identity. Attenuating traditional union identities, let alone changing them radically, is risky. What kind of solidarity can come from a "soft" portrait of unions as quasi-service agencies, particularly when it is clear that payoffs from unionization have diminished?

It is no surprise that European unions' political positions have weakened: their political influence has always depended upon their market positions and their ability to present a persuasive face to the society at large. The changes in union relationships with the state and politics have been greater than one might have expected, however. European unions have participated in alliances with political parties and been a constituent of "the left" for most of their existences. What made the Golden Age golden was the ability of these "lefts" to shift national agendas, in particular to advance the goals of unionism. This once successful formula no longer works. Friendly governments and political parties are no longer willing and able to deliver what unions once could expect from them. Beyond this, European unions are now less effective at pressuring governments and parties.

Measuring Up to Challenge?

Have European unions taken full measure of this situation? Table 9.8 summarizes our findings.

Why have some unions been more adaptive than others? Unions are usually reactive: their mission is to defend their supporters. In part this is because they include powerful organizational stakeholders with interests in limiting change. Moreover, since coherence depends significantly upon continuous identities unions carry ideas embodied in their

Table 9.8 Union Strategic Responses

Country	Market Challenges	Political Challenges	Strategic Responses	Success?
France	*Severe* - Deindustrialization, high unemployment, employer aggressiveness. - Public sector squeeze. - EMU constraints. - Effects of labor law reforms.	*Severe* - Unionism faces: collapse of political hopes, - Socialist/elite partial neo-liberalization; communist marginalization.	*Confused* - Responses structured by competitive pluralism. - Hope for "new May 1968." - National organizations = general staffs without soldiers. - *Etatisme* as life raft.	- Competitive unionism creates fragmented responses - No strength in private sector; public sector threatened.
Germany	*Relatively Mild* - Corporatism holds; economy relatively strong. - Unemployment, union membership shrinkage. - Downsizing, outward investment underway.	*Relatively Mild* - Political relays less important. - Threats to social protection. - Unification mastered, at large cost.	*Conservative* - Preserve traditional practices. - Insider/outsider issues largely overlooked. - DGB less central.	Holding the line. Larger challenges in future?
Italy	*Severe* - High unemployment; threats to public sector; stress on flexibility. - Very high youth unemployment. - EMU constraints.	*Severe* - Collapse of Italian state, Socialist Party.	*Somewhat Proactive* - Adaptation to political collapse in later 1980s, overcome pluralism. - Redo organization. - Attempt to articulate new neo-corporatism.	Precarious adaptation, contingent upon future uncertainties.
Spain	*Severe* - Underorganized unions face restructuring, high unemployment, Europe at same time. - Insider/outsider problems severe. - Very high youth unemployment. - Extensive atypical work. - EMU constraints.	*Severe* - Socialists instrument of restructuring, Europeanization and liberalization, divorce with Socialist union. - Communists split and marginalized. - Complexity of regional differences.	*Tentative* - Unions overcome pluralism in later 1980s. - Develop ideas about new organizational structures. - Regain some political voice and make peak-level deals to enhance bargaining and reduce labor market dualism.	Spanish unions obliged to catch up on all fronts simultaneously. Will Spain modernize or specialize in "social dumping?"
Sweden	*Relatively Mild* - Collapse of national neo-corporatism; new employer aggressiveness, high unemployment. - Threats to public sector and welfare state. - EU effects unknown.	*New Difficulties* - Socialists face public finance problems, distance themselves from unions. - Fragmentation of left of political spectrum. - Bourgeois parties presently in background.	*Attempts at Proactivity* - High strategic debate. - Concrete efforts to reconfigure collective bargaining. - Crisis too recent to predict results.	Crisis will deepen. How rooted is Swedish social democratic culture?

Table 9.8 continued

U.K.	*Severe* - Deindustrialization – dismantling of public sector. - Employer union-busting. - Dismantling of earlier legal frameworks.	*Severe* - Labour Party flight from unions: Few promises on union rights and prerogatives (excepting Recognition).	*Attempts at Proactivity* - Recruitment and organization, response to new management techniques. - Europe as new source of regulation. - New rights-based legal framework?	What will New Labour Do? How will Europe impinge?
European level	*Severe* - Single Market and EMU rapidly moving targets. - European-level unionism as Brussels lobby. - Crisis leading to national *sauve qui peut.*	*Perplexing* - Europe marketizes pertinent matters, but treaties bar transfer of regulation to European-level. - Interests of certain EU institutions coincide with labor.	Attempts at Proactivity - ETUC expands beyond simple lobbying. - EWCs + negotiated legislation.	Modest building blocks toward some sort of European-level industrial relations system – Will they matter?

organizations which may constrain a more flexible response. As "membership," "mass" organizations, rather than "command" organizations like firms, they must win support before changing. This said, there is a rough-and-ready correlation between European unions willing to contemplate strategic changes and the severity of the challenges they face. Unions under less severe pressures will be less likely to change. This observation is complicated, however, by differences in timing which European union movements have experienced in confronting new European conditions. It would be unreasonable to expect radical change from the Swedish and German movements because their difficulties are more recent. It does not follow, however, that in time they will emerge better placed. Other movements, in contrast, have been in deep crisis for nearly two decades.

What then explains the variability in the adaptiveness of union movements under the greatest pressure? First, union movements with strong legacies of competitive pluralism, like those in France, Italy, and Spain, bear an additional burden. Particular unions may respond to challenges to hurt competitors rather than to advance the larger labor movement. Much depends upon the motivations behind competitive pluralism. There will always be a "game" to it, as one union attempts to build its influence relative to others. But if the system is built over bitter political rivalries, as it has been in Latin Europe, its propensity to change may well depend upon the willingness of external political actors to allow it. In France a rigid Communist Party continued to subordinate the CGT to its political strategies well into the 1990s, with signs of change only in the most recent period. In Italy the Communist Party already began in the 1960s to give greater autonomy to the unions it influenced, and processes of "social democratization" which led to the PDS have accentuated this over the past decade – opening up prospects for broader union cooperation. In Spain competitive pluralism began to fade in the later 1980s once the UGT was alienated by the policies of the Socialist government. The indicators which our research has provided are summarized in Table 9.9.

Table 9.9 Factors Determining Union Strategic Responses

Country	Pressure to Change	Propensity to Adapt	Causes
France	Great	Low	Strong incentives to adapt, but blocked by pluralism. - Organizational stakes in statist framework nourish hopes that the "system will hold."
Germany	Low	Low	Low incentives to adapt; continuing effectiveness of sectoral corporatist pattern bargaining. - German economy remains relatively strong. - Growing insider-outsider issues not yet impacting seriously. - Recent willingness to bargain on restructuring with employers.
Italy	Great	Relatively high	Strong incentives to adapt. - Legacies (post-Hot Autumn decentralization), ability to attenuate pluralism, successful recomposition at national level. - Long experience with weak state establishes openness to "pan-syndicalist" approaches.
Spain	Very Great	Medium	Strong incentives to adapt, but - underdeveloped organizations and bargaining system as legacies of Franco. - Competitive politicized unionism. - Dual labor market creates difficult insider-outside problems for unions.
Sweden	Medium	Medium	Medium incentives to adapt because of late arrival of crisis. - Legacies of past: ability to adapt flexibly in pre-crisis years vs. dislocation with end of national-level tripartite dealing and medium term threats to welfare state.
U.K.	Very Great	Medium	Strong incentives to adapt – Desperation promotes experimentation. - Legacy of decentralization helps. - Loss of legal framework and political allies crippling.
European level	Great	Medium	Greater Europeanization limited by national priorities, weakness of European-level organization, propensity of Euro-level unionists to buy into goals of European leaders (i.e. EMU).

Challenges to unions have been least severe where the unions have "social partners" – primarily employers, but also governments and central banks – with reasons to nourish a viable union movement. In Germany, for example, employers' associations have interests in keeping the German "model" intact. In Italy, when employers decided that they needed unions to modernize Italian industrial relations and the broader Italian economy, Italian unions were able to overcome some of their differences. Swedish peak-level neo-corporatism rested on a confluence of interests between employers and unions backed by a social democratic political hegemony. This has been partly shattered by an employer attack forcing bargaining down to the sectoral level, but some employers want more decentralization. In general, when such confluence of interests occurred in the postwar years it was to facilitate control of inflation. The decline of postwar forms is largely due to the abandonment of full employment and the reliance on unemployment to curb inflation. Can they be replaced?

There has been much discussion about interest confluence around cooperation for flexible restructuring (i.e., the pursuit of best practices and higher productivity). There was some of this in the pre-1990s Swedish situation, for example, and it has been important in Germany. In Sweden, as older patterns of neo-corporatist wage bargaining erode, the unions' ability to forge deals about flexible restructuring may be the key to their future. In Italian unions, consolidating new cooperation will require sustained commitments on all sides, in particular, on party and union political initiatives. Recent events in Spain, in particular the 1997 agreement to attenuate regulations on full-time employment, are also promising. New flexibility bargaining can be disconcerting for unions, however. Much depends on the give-and-take and the period is one in which unions will have to give more than they take. Moreover, the forms of such bargaining and the levels where they occur are critical variables. Flexibility bargaining at the European level in multinational corporations, perhaps nourished by European Works Councils, could disrupt the coherence of national industrial relations systems, for example. Transnational sectoral bargaining, likely to occur mainly in sectors where unions remain strong, could have the same effect. Decentralized flexibility bargaining within national systems is already under way in many places, and most specialists would agree that so far it has undercut the coherence of existing arrangements.

Where little actual or prospective interest confluence between "social partners" existed, unions were more dependent on favorable political conditions. In the Golden Age, British unions were only rarely able to help employers and instead relied on a favorable legal environment, Labour governments, and the threat of them, plus Conservative willingness to avoid challenging unions. These conditions were destroyed by Thatcherism. For British unions the effects have been catastrophic, despite union experiments in the market arena. French unions had long sustained themselves through reliance upon a statist legal framework and hopes for changes from the political left. Since 1981 and Mitterrand's externalization of reform through European integration, the relative indifference of the Socialists to union issues and the decline of French communism have been serious blows. The statist legal and procedural framework persists, however, but destructive union pluralism casts a huge shadow over the future of French unionism. Spanish unions, who devoted themselves to democratization, were stymied by the Socialists and European integration, and fell behind in building a modern union and industrial relations system. They have reoriented their strategy, with modest successes in winning new support and muting competitive unionism. The trend is vulnerable, however, because of labor market segmentation and strong temptations for employers to take the "low road."

The Millennium of All the Dangers

In the twentieth century, European unions set out to expand democratic citizenship to the economy and workplace. This quest had notable derivatives, in particular the massive assistance that unions and workers provided in constructing the postwar "European model of society." It led unions to adapt their strategies to the virtuous circle of growth and change which then occurred. Unions attempted, in national ways, to organize massively in manufacturing and the public sector to oblige employers to recognize them and provide high wages and job security for workers. In turn, employers received predictable workers, rules in the workplace, and a disciplined acceptance of technological change. Unions also sought social reform and favorable economic policies from political parties and the state. Parties, in return, acquired support from unions, and states enhanced their roles. The package worked when corporations, with their large profits, objected but mildly to higher wages and taxes.

Why did European unions thrive more during this golden moment than ever before? Circumstances were favorable for them to use their capacities in multiple arenas to maximize their opportunities. Their primary resource base was the labor market. But their influence spread, particularly in the political arena, because they had power and bore identities which resonated in their societies. Their visions of a better society, of the nature of equality, of "social citizenship," and of the need to negotiate vital distributive questions were widely shared. This was not completely good luck. It was also partly the product of strategy.

The Golden Age is history. European unions now live in an era of high unemployment, public austerity, transnationalization, liberal zeal for free trade, deregulation (including labor markets), and individualism. Many of their central tenets and expectations are under dark clouds. But why is this a turning point, rather than yet another of the bad moments that unions have known over the years? The answer is that changes since the 1980s have diminished European union resources across the board, and they will be extremely difficult to reconstitute. Finding renewed market/bargaining resources is a *sine qua non,* but in none of our cases has there been great success. Next, unions, like other large collective actors, are "meaning creators." *Ouvriérisme,* a proxy for the self-identifying notions which labor movements developed over decades, no longer conveys what is needed, even if it connects with a past which is difficult to forget.[9] Workers now come in a great variety of types – male, female, full-time, part-time, temporary, stably employed, precarious, multiskilled, unskilled, etc. "Meaning" and "identity" challenges, as difficult to confront as market problems, make European unions more vulnerable to employer contentions that they are a major source of the "rigidities" holding European economies behind. No matter what they do, unions now face the incessant denunciation that they are self-seeking "special interests." The success of such union-diminishing agitprop also reflects the collapse of unions' political resources. Former party allies cold shoulder unions and ignore their policy hopes. In general, there has been a shift to rhetoric facilitating "globalization" and Europeanization which strongly privileges the goals of employers.

Ideologically, European unions now face proposals to reduce citizenship to that of the liberal individual as a political and economic actor. In Eric Hobsbawm's words, this involves "theological faith in an economy in which resources were allocated *entirely* by the totally unrestricted market, under conditions of unlimited competition, a state of affairs believed to produce not only the maximum of goods and services, but also the maximum of happiness and the only kind of society deserving the name of 'freedom'."[10] This neo-liberal perspective has little place either for collective social actors (excepting capital) or for social decisions made through political mechanisms. European unions have always been large collective social actors, and they have insisted that social decision-making through political mechanisms is the essence of democracy. However weakened and confused, they still stand as the staunchest defenders against the marketization of social and political life and the largest single "associational" groups in their societies. But a turning point is at hand. European unionism has to reinvent itself. To survive and thrive, it must become something different. "Shoulds" are easy to pronounce, however. "How tos" are more difficult.[11]

In our chapters on individual nations we found that unions had little direct engagement in European integration, despite the serious threats it poses to them. The absence of such engagement was also a basic theme in our European-level chapter. Why, as the EU moves to EMU and the Euro, is this the case? It would be tempting, but facile, to conclude that unions are blinded by national habits from perceiving "reality." But there are substantial cultural, organizational, and juridical differences between national unions. Finally, the structures of the European political system, where ultimate power lays in the Council of Ministers and the European Council, points unions toward national arenas for influencing Europe.

There may be a much deeper explanation connected to the history of European integration itself, however. What may be most important about European integration is *when* it happened. The literature on globalization reminds us that there was substantial international trade liberalization in the later nineteenth century under the aegis of the British. From the First World War onward, however, Europe and North America both moved away from economic openness toward national self-containment, a shift consecrated by American policy during the Great Depression and the rise of fascism on the European continent. This new economic nationalism also correlated with the coming of Fordist production and of "corporatist" tendencies in interest representation. What is most important, and perhaps most overlooked, is that this "long wave" of nationally centered development continued for decades after 1945, with one very important change – the democratization of Western European societies – within which corporatist tendencies of interest representation continued. The Golden Age ought, in this light, to be seen as the culminating point of a period which lasted for nearly three-quarters of the twentieth century. The importance of this long term perspective cannot be underestimated. During much of the current century virtually all of the processes which mattered to European citizens were deeply nationalized. European integration, when it first came in the Golden Age, added value to newly democratized European national models of development, allowing their nationalization to deepen even more. As Charles de Gaulle announced peremptorily in the 1960s, what emerged was a "Europe of nations" in which these nations were strongly bounded systems which integrated citizens in national economic, political and cultural exchanges.

This particular kind of Europe was bound to be seriously threatened by new transnational processes of economic liberalization. One purpose of the EU was to promote European market liberalization and integration. The thrust of American policy was similar on an even broader scale. Liberalization and market integration were likely to undermine the relative self-sufficiency of the "nations" of Europe, and as this happened, national systems of exchange would lose capacities to respond to the needs of citizens. Events in the later 1970s precipitated European elites further and faster through the Single Market program and, ultimately, EMU. Multilateral moves like the Uruguay Round worked in similar directions.

The habits and patterns of economic, social, and political exchange constructed over the very long twentieth-century period of relative national self-sufficiency are deeply rooted. Such things change very slowly, whatever challenges come from their environments. This is not primarily because of culture or national identity. Deeply rooted national systems create systems of powerful incentives to which actors must respond to survive. National systems of exchange are still very much alive, therefore. European unions, along with other Europeans, thus still live within their boundaries.

Federalism was the dream of EU elites, but, unlike market liberalization, it was not seriously inscribed in EU treaties. The "functionalist" hope of EU founders and leaders was that market changes would lead to political "spillover" and, ultimately, to a genuine European state. This hope has not been realized. The EU was instead set on a liberalizing course of "selective integration," of creating transnational markets with quite limited prospects for fuller political and social union. The Single Market and EMU were the final large projects of this course of selective integration, and they are now in place. For the time being, there is unlikely to be much more transnationalization of politics and social policy. The "Europe of nations," albeit with considerably weakened nations, still exists, however. It stands to reason that it will remain the site for most responses to change in the next period, including union responses. Europe's nations now have to adjust as best they can, in the absence of any real Euro-polity, to the market liberalization which they have collectively created.

This is not likely to be a smooth process. For unions, however, the future will be structured by tensions between EU nations and European integration, and the most important location for their strategic action will be national. The combined pressures of the Single Market and EMU will be felt strongly in the immediate future. These pressures will lead governments and other actors to propose broad national "pacts" for distributing the burdens of restructuring. Interest in how to proceed lies behind the recent flurry of interest in the Dutch "polder model" of recurrent neo-corporatist social pacts, for example. The pacts will be about aligning wage and productivity growth, but they will also range more broadly into matters of national labor market policy (work sharing, in particular), to promote "best practice" flexibility and to restrain and reconstruct the "social wage."[12]

The emergence of new neo-corporatism in Italy, originally around quite specific issues, has blossomed into something like a pact for shaping up Italian society to face EMU. Klaus Zwickel of Germany's IG Metall first suggested a "pact for employment" in 1996 when the Kohl government suggested massive cuts in social protection.[13] The proposal for an "alliance for jobs" subsequently became a central plank in SPD leader Gerhard Schröder's 1998 election campaign and his government's policy. Swedish unions, historically prolific with pact-like schemes, may not yet face enough pressure from Europe (Sweden has opted out of EMU for the time being), but a pactist approach is not inconceivable, even if employers are reluctant. The French have moved in a similar direction recently as well, albeit in typically statist ways. Following its surprise election in 1997 the Jospin government, confronted by EMU convergence deadlines, proposed negotiated work sharing on a 35-hour week, new active labor market measures for young people, and redistributive tax reforms to confront welfare state financial difficulties. The Spanish unions, burned earlier by unsuccessful pacts, are more concerned now with laying the organizational foundations for an open future. But there are already pactist trends at the regional level (Catalonia, for example) and issue-specific deals at the national level. The British are outliers. Parts of the British movement would like nothing more than new interest confluence with employers and the state, but, in the main, governmental and employer attitudes make this unlikely.[14] There has already been a pactist turn at the European level. The employment policy clauses of the Amsterdam Treaty (1997) and the impetus to negotiated harmonization of EU employment policies beginning at the Luxembourg Summit in the fall 1997 have pushed all EU member states to put together national employment pacts around specific priorities (creating "new cultures" of entrepreneurship, employability, adaptability, and equal opportunities).[15] Thus if national pactism may pose an important strategic challenge to the European-level ETUC, its European counterpart may give it a new function as well, that of coordinating national union efforts.

The actual forms of pacts will be fundamental. In many national situations employers are vocally opposed to new deals with unions.[16] The thesis that European labor markets are too overregulated and welfare states too constraining and expensive is now dominant among European elites.[17] EMU may override even this, however. It will place the burdens of adjusting to changing circumstances on national employers, labor markets (wage levels), and social protection systems. Member states will find themselves in a situation where they will have to anticipate and negotiate burden-sharing arrangements or risk disruptive domestic conflict. The critical issues for unions will be the tradeoff terms they are able to obtain – or obliged to accept. Given the decentralization of employer strategic perspectives away from national bargaining levels, often the national sectoral level as well, the new deals are bound to be different from those of the Golden Age. Where unions have sufficiently strong national and national sectoral organizations to engage employers in serious discussion, as in Sweden and Germany, the best deals are likely to be struck. In other cases one may well see firms moving toward different forms of "micro-corporatism," whether at the firm or workshop level nationally or at the transnational firm level in the EU. This could help parts of union movements to survive, but national unions could lose even more coherence than they already have. In the worst-case scenario such decentralized micro-corporatism will encourage new whipsawing and races to the bottom.

New concertation may well present European unions with openings to assert their importance as representatives of working people, however, even if they have not yet resolved the multiple issues of whom they represent and for what. They are weaker, but they have something to offer which others need, namely concessions to smooth the transition to EMU and promote competitiveness. The new situation will not be "win-win" for most unions, rather "lose perhaps to win later." They have to figure out what they are willing to lose, what they want in exchange and how to get it. That this is a perilous enterprise goes without saying. Unions are likely to demand some form of longer-term security of employment for individuals – over their lifetimes, something which is likely to be winnable only in terms of more effective active labor market policies (training, in particular to deal with new technologies, plus serious efforts at job placement). They must demand the preservation of the essence of the "European model of society," but in innovative ways. They need to find ways to structure new decentralization and flexibility so that it does not destroy their own capacities and turn their supporters' lives into nightmares.

Those movements which remain strong enough to oblige their national "social partners" to deal seriously will do better at this. Others will have considerably more difficulty. The Germans will be the most important, since any concertation which they undertake will be both a model and a precedent for others. Moreover, the Germans are also in a position to initiate the sectoral cross-border concertation which may be critical to bringing different national movements closer. The Swedes will be less pertinent until they move toward EMU, but this is only a matter of time; how they handle this movement will also be significant. The Italians are already in concertation, but in Italy the necessary trust and union unity have more often than not been lacking in the past. The Spanish will be called, in their turn. The French will proceed, in the only way they know how, through statism, even though this is a much less satisfactory mode of generating unity of purpose than genuine negotiation. The British will be far behind, tempting employers to unilateralism rather than concertation. There are many Euro-dangers which will need to be controlled, and there is much international coordination to be done. Thus there is a new European-level strategy waiting to be found as well.

It is virtually inconceivable that European unions, however astute, will be able to generate the resources from a globalizing, neo-liberal capitalist order that they found in the Golden Age. European unions will have to accept more modest positions in their societies and in Europe more broadly. Historically, unions have never seen themselves exclusively as the servants of their members and supporters, but as providers of broader citizenship in general. They succeeded remarkably well at this in the first three-quarters of the twentieth century, especially in the Golden Age. The new capitalism threatens this historic quest, but unions could remain important players nonetheless if they act effectively to limit present neo-liberal trends, in itself a world-historical mission. The immediate future should give them new, if difficult, opportunities.

Notes

1. Dominique Labbé, *Syndicats et Syndiques en France Depuis 1945* (Paris: L'Harmattan, 1996), 109.
2. As we noted in Chapter 8, however, once EWCs are established they may lend themselves to micro-corporatism.
3. This brief description does not quite capture the Spanish case. The ending of pactism in 1988 looks like decentralization. However, the centralization of the pact period was illusory because of weak links between national-level bargainers and firm-level wage setting. The more recent focus on sectoral and regional deals involves some centralization insofar as it achieves unions' goal of gaining some actual control over local wage setting, though with few accomplishments thus far. See Philippe Pochet and Antonio Gonzalez, "L'Espagne: un conflit de modèle," in *Pactes Sociaux Européens*, ed. Philippe Pochet (Brussels: Editions Vie Ouvrière, 1995).
4. European Commission, *Employment in Europe 1997* (Brussels: DGV, 1998), 117 ff. tables.
5. OECD, *Employment Outlook*, July 1996 (Paris: OECD, 1996), 8, table 1.6; 72-73, table 3.2. Women are particularly penalized in Germany and the U.K.
6. See Wolfgang Streeck "From Market Making to State Building? Reflections on the Political Economy of European Social Policy," in *European Social Policy: Between Fragmentation and Integration*, ed. Stephan Leibfried and Paul Pierson, (Washington, D.C.: Brookings Institution, 1995).
7. In France, of course, much of what was nationalized after 1981 has been privatized, but what remains is substantial.
8. In Italy this led to cooperation among all unions and government to legislate limits on mobilization in certain public-sector areas. In France, as was seen in the December 1995 strikes, it led to official unions taking the lead in such mobilizations.
9. Moreover, *ouvriérisme* was never free of troublesome bias even when it was persuasive, since it subordinated those who did not fit the male blue-collar mold – with women's issues forming the paradigm case.
10. Eric Hobsbawm, *The Age of Extremes* (New York: Pantheon, 1994), 563.
11. One huge new dilemma is evident. To generate the political resources that unions need to function successfully in the market, they will have to become more effective political actors using their own resources. This is a large proposition and it is not clear what it might entail. Unions cannot replace parties, obviously. But should they try interest group politics? Or Gompersism – rewarding friends and punishing enemies on a non-partisan basis? The puzzle is gigantic and answers are likely to be complicated, varied, and slow in coming.
12. For useful analyses, see Jelle Visser and Anton Hemerijck, *'A Dutch Miracle:' Job Growth, Welfare Reform and Corporatism in the Netherlands* (Amsterdam: Amsterdam University Press, 1997).
13. IG Chemie has just made a major departure from insistence on wage floor uniformity in a new contract allowing for negotiated downward deviations.
14. The decentralization of British industrial relations leaves a lot of scope for variety, including situations where there is "confluence," local "productivity coalitions," or "micro-corporatism." True, this leaves national unions attempting to pursue cross-enterprise strategies in a quandary, but it is different from a situation of outright employer union busting.
15. See European Commission – DG V Employment and Social Affairs, *Forum: Special Jobs Summit* (Brussels: 1998)

16. Italian employers seem at least more open than others, but for how long? British employers may be more divided, particularly since the 1997 elections, than they seemed under the Conservatives, if only because of Britain's changing relationships to Europe – but how divided are they on dealing with unions? French employers are divided as well. They fear the chaos that growing absence of union control over workers can generate. Spanish employers, eager to shed left-over Francoist labor market regulations from the Franco era, have recently made some progress. But their goal is to do so while preventing further unionization. UNICE, the European level employers Confederation, is eloquent in opposing any regulation of the European labor market.
17. The OECD *Jobs Study* (OECD: Paris, 1994) is the bible of this position.

INDEX

C

D

F

G

H

I

N

O

P

R

S

T

U

V

W

Z